*f***P**

Strategy Is Destiny

HOW

STRATEGY-MAKING

SHAPES A

COMPANY'S

FUTURE

Robert A. Burgelman

The Free Press
New York   London   Toronto   Sydney

THE FREE PRESS
A Division of Simon & Schuster, Inc.
1230 Avenue of the Americas
New York, NY 10020

Copyright © 2002 by Robert A. Burgelman
All rights reserved,
including the right of reproduction
in whole or in part in any form.

THE FREE PRESS and colophon are trademarks
of Simon & Schuster, Inc.

For information regarding special discounts for bulk purchases,
please contact Simon & Schuster Special Sales:
1-800-456-6798 or business@simonandschuster.com

Designed by Leslie Phillips
Manufactured in the United States of America

10   9

Library of Congress Cataloging-in-Publication Data
Burgelman, Robert A.
  Strategy is destiny: how strategy-making shapes
a company's future / Robert A. Burgelman.
      p.   cm.
Includes bibliographical references and index.
ISBN 0-684-85554-2 (alk. paper)
  1. Intel Corporation—Management.   2. Semiconductor
industry—United States—Management—Case studies.
3. Computer industry—United States—Management—
Case studies.   4. Technological innovations—Management—
Case studies.   5. New products—Management—Case studies.
6. Organizational change—Case studies.   7. Strategic planning—
Case studies.   I. Title.
HD9696.S44 I562 2002
—dc21   2001040825
ISBN-13: 978-0-684-85554-7
ISBN-10:   0-684-85554-2

For Stefan and Oliver,
explorers of different realms

I say unto you: one must still have chaos in oneself to be able to give birth to a dancing star.

NIETZSCHE, Thus Spoke Zarathustra

CONTENTS

EPOCH III
INTEL THE INTERNET BUILDING BLOCK COMPANY

CONCLUSION
IMPLICATIONS FOR STRATEGIC LEADERSHIP

ACKNOWLEDGMENTS

Professors in academic business schools sometimes face a frustrating tension. Exciting teaching requires up-to-date material about the most advanced developments in business. It requires constant tracking of business news. The search is broad and almost by necessity somewhat shallow. Exciting research, on the other hand, requires staying with the same subject for an extended period of time in order to delve into it and ask the nonobvious questions that open the door to gaining new insight that makes a clear and distinct contribution to knowledge. Research must be deep and by necessity somewhat narrow. Seldom does the opportunity arise to resolve this tension in a totally satisfying way. This book is the result of such an opportunity.

In August 1988, I had the privilege of meeting with Andy Grove, then CEO of Intel Corporation. I had twice given a seminar at Intel, but I had not met Andy Grove before. While I very much enjoyed meeting him, I did not anticipate that more than twelve years later I would be acknowledging the good fortune that resulted from his visit. Andy was kind enough to write a foreword for this book with some of his reflections on how our working relationship at the Stanford Business School evolved and how he experienced it. It is how I experienced it as well. Andy and I collaborated on writing and teaching a dozen or so research cases tracking Intel's strategy-making over time. Andy's teaching of these cases in our MBA elective course produced additional data about major events that had just happened or were still going on at Intel. Being allowed to use this data to write several articles for academic journals, including one co-authored with Andy, while teaching about a company that *Time* magazine in 1997 called the "essential firm of the digital age," happily resolved the tension between research and teaching described above. I am grateful for it.

Gathering the data for the case material that serves as the basis for this book required the collaboration of Intel's top management and many dozens of senior and middle managers as well. There are too many to list all of them here. Many are mentioned by name in the chapters that follow. Some former Intel executives contributed data as well. They all retained a remarkable degree of respect for the company they had left for various reasons. I thank all of them.

Gordon Moore graciously agreed to be interviewed in early 1989 and ten years later again. Gordon's insightful comments and predictions in 1989 provided a background against which the actual unfolding of Intel's evolution during the next ten years could be tracked. His reflections in 1999 provide a new background against which the current Epoch in Intel's evolution can be tracked in the future. Special thanks is due to Dennis Carter, the architect of the Intel Inside campaign, who during 1998–99 co-authored a case entitled "Intel Corporation: The Evolution of an Adaptive Organization." Dennis not only helped with access, he also generously contributed his own views to help interpret some of the data and served as a reality check. Special thanks is also due to Frank Gill, a former Intel executive vice president, who left the company in 1998 but was willing in early 2000 to share his views on some of the issues Intel faced during the 1990s in trying to develop new businesses. Frank's candid recollections helped deepen the analysis of new business development at Intel during Andy Grove's tenure as CEO. Finally, I am grateful to Craig Barrett for inviting me to teach seminars on internal corporate venturing and strategic change to Intel's top 400 executives during 1997–98 in the "Growing the Business" course. Intel's Business Practices Network staff was helpful in putting together this course. Carol Tisson, in particular, provided access to internal survey and interview data that helped me prepare for these classes. These classes provided an extraordinary opportunity to check the face validity of the conceptual frameworks used in this book. They generated examples, additional information and alternative views that further clarified and sometimes changed what I thought I already knew.

Gathering the data and writing the cases during the longitudinal research involved several research associates over the years. Without their help this book could not have been written. George Cogan (Stanford MBA '89), Bruce Graham (Stanford MBA '91), Dan Steere (Stanford MBA '93), Ray Bamford (Stanford MBA '96), Ken Fine (Stanford MBA '97), Osamu Suzuki (Stanford MBA '98),

Chris Thomas (Stanford MBA '00), and Philip Meza (Wharton MBA '96) made important contributions to the research. Cogan and Graham, in particular, provided expertise in semiconductor technology early on in the research that helped me develop important parts of the arguments presented in chapters 2 through 5. Bamford co-authored the 1999 case with Dennis Carter and myself providing an historical overview of Intel mentioned above.

Stanford Business School has provided most of the support of the twelve-year-long research effort. The 1987–88 BP America Faculty Fellowship and the 1996–97 GSB Trust Faculty Fellowship have provided extra financial support. An international quarter supported by the school and spent as a Visiting Scholar at INSEAD in spring 1998 provided the time and space to get the writing of the book under way. The continuous availability of top quality research assistance was crucial in sustaining the longitudinal research effort. Sylvia Lorton, Diane Conlinn and Kerry Breuer provided excellent administrative support. Linda Bethel crafted most of the figures. Mary Petrusewicz edited the manuscript and provided many suggestions for improving its clarity. Thanks to former Dean Mike Spence and current Dean Bob Joss, as well as the colleagues that have served as associate dean for research and course development over the years, for the school's sustained support. Finally, thanks to the Harvard Business School for inviting me to spend academic year 1991–92 as a Marvin Bower Fellow. This allowed me to reflect full time on what I had learned from the field research at Intel during 1988–91, which helped build the foundation for the book.

Ideas are shaped through interaction with others. First and foremost, my teaching with Andy Grove during the last twelve years has been a source of tremendous intellectual stimulation. I have learned more from him than I probably realize. My colleagues in the Strategy Group at Stanford have been a great stimulus as well. In particular, Garth Saloner's efforts to formally examine parts of the logic embodied in the evolutionary framework of strategy-making presented in this book have increased both my understanding and confidence in its validity.[1] Bill Barnett's integration of organizational ecology and strategy at the population level raised several important questions about variation and selection for organizational adaptation,[2] which helped shape my thinking. Through their queries and comments, many other colleagues have helped sharpen my ideas. They include Chris Argyris, Joe Bower, the late Ned Bowman, Clayton Christensen, Yves Doz, Pankaj Ghemawat, Ranjay Gulati, David Garvin, Rebecca Henderson, Bruce Kogut, Dan Levinthal, Jeff Pfeffer, Dick Rosenbloom, Mal Salter, Kaye Schoonhoven, Andrea Shepard, Bob Simons, Jitendra Singh, Alva Taylor, Mike Tushman, Andy Van de Ven, Eric von Hippel, Sam Wood, Steve Wheelwright, Jeffrey Williams, and David

Yoffie. John Freeman, Don Hambrick, Arie Lewin, Dan Schendel, and David Vogel in their capacity as journal editors have also been helpful by managing review processes that have helped clarify and tighten the ideas presented here.

Several thousand executives from hundreds of different companies have reacted constructively to the ideas presented in this book in the many executive education programs that I have taught during the 1990s. I have valued their questions and feedback and their sharing of personal experiences. They provided reassurance that the issues and problems dealt with in the research were real and worth pursuing.

As on an earlier occasion, Bob Wallace, senior editor at The Free Press, has been extremely patient and helpful with editorial guidance. The book is immeasurably better because of his patience and suggestions.

Last but not least, writing this book was in large measure possible because of home front support. During the last three years, many weekends and countless evenings were spent writing—a solitary and consuming activity. My wife Rita has granted me the time and space to pursue my intellectual odyssey. I am grateful to her for that, and equally so for not allowing me to forget the other important things in life.

Portola Valley, California
May 2001

FOREWORD
Reflections of Andy Grove

It was twelve years ago that I walked into Robert Burgelman's office at Stanford University Graduate School of Business. I had never met him before, but I'd heard of him. He specialized in studying strategic change and why some organizations were better at adapting to it than others. My purpose in visiting him was to establish some sort of a relationship with Stanford's business school. It seemed wrong that Intel did not have a relationship with the preeminent school in Silicon Valley.

It turned out that Robert had been interested in the semiconductor industry for a while and had even constructed a hypothetical case study taking place at a fictitious semiconductor company to illustrate the nature of the industry to his students. This approach seemed a waste of time to me. I suggested that he write a real case study about a real strategic event that took place at a real company, and invited him to examine how two years or so earlier we at Intel had dropped out of the business that we were born to pursue, semiconductor memories, and metamorphosed into a microprocessor company. He was interested and, a short time later, came to visit us with a student in tow. That is how our collaboration started.

Our collaboration took two forms. Robert came to Intel to write case studies on how our management solved strategic conundrums, and I went to Stanford to teach these cases and others in his class on strategic management, first as a guest lecturer and then as a coteacher. We have jointly taught the class in strategic management for some ten years now. While the course has grown to encompass many different participants in the information technology industry and has evolved along with the industry, the anchor case has never changed. It remains that original case on Intel's strategic transformation in the mid-1980s.

During his frequent visits to Intel, Robert often acted as though he had died and gone to heaven. After all, how many professors of strategic management get to sit through a company's actual strategic planning process, taking notes as the members of the management team grope their way through strategic dilemmas, arguing and occasionally yelling at each other, even as the issues they dispute so passionately can be framed in a totally dispassionate, academic fashion?

Meanwhile, I found it equally exciting and gratifying to teach cases about Intel to a group of smart students. No two classes have ever unfolded the same way. The events of the case do not change, but the implications and insights continually shift when viewed by each new crop of students and reflected in a mirror of an ever-changing industry landscape.

And change this landscape did, in a dramatic fashion. When our collaboration started in the late 1980s, Intel had just begun to concentrate on microprocessors. The personal computer industry had started to exert pressure on the traditional vertically integrated computer industry, forcing this structure into a horizontal arrangement in which industrywide standards of hardware and software prevailed. This industry transformation gained momentum year after year, through the actions of Intel, Microsoft, Novell, IBM, Dell, and many others, all of whose actions were analyzed through case studies in our class.

No sooner was this fundamental change completed than a new wave of change threatened to restructure the landscape again. The Internet at first affected only those companies that were formed to exploit it, but it soon grew in strength and importance, making an impact on the strategic direction of every member of the computer industry, Intel included.

This book starts and ends by documenting these two transformations and their impact on Intel. Of course, real-life industry transformations don't occur in neat packages, but in fits and starts of strategic action and reaction. Robert, through his continued presence at and involvement with Intel, was able to observe and record these stutter steps of strategic change, some far-reaching, some even infamous, none insignificant in their implications and effects on the company's way of doing business:

- Whether it was worth staying in EPROMs even if we had to abandon our original memory business.
- How a competing microprocessor architecture that emerged almost as a subterfuge led to the business equivalent of civil war inside the company.

- Why Intel decided to enter into systems design and manufacturing and the re-action of our customers to such a potential encroachment on their territory.
- The launch of the Pentium processor in the face of a major competitive chal-lenge from IBM, Apple, and Motorola.
- How the successful evolution of the Intel Inside brand backfired in the case of the Pentium flaw crisis and how the results shook Intel to its core.
- Intel's attempts to create a new market in videoconferencing and extend an old one by bringing personal computers into the living room.
- Intel's handling of the potential phenomenon of network computers and the real phenomenon of low-cost personal computers.
- Lastly, how Intel dealt with the Internet as a threat and an opportunity, accel-erating efforts in the networking space and re-architecting the core micro-processor business in response.

While all of these cases were studied and analyzed by Robert and used as illustrations for his theoretical frameworks, these frameworks in return gave Intel management a visual alphabet, a vocabulary to describe each strategic situation.

In actual practice, the academic phrasing was soon supplanted by our own jar-gon. Many of the names we gave to Robert's frameworks became common corpo-rate shorthand. For example, Robert has studied for years the interaction between the forces of spontaneous change emerging in organizations and corporate strategy imposed by management from above on the one hand, and the push-and-pull be-tween the existing capabilities of the company and the capabilities it needs to pur-sue a new strategy on the other. We dubbed all this *the rubber band phenomenon,* and the term is now part of Intel's standard strategic management vocabulary. Sim-ilarly, Robert has long been interested in the ways in which firms balance efforts to protect and extend their existing business while at the same time undertaking ef-forts to move into a new market. In Robert's graphic, blue ink represented Intel's microprocessor business and green ink its new initiatives, leading us to brand this the *blue versus green dilemma.*

The extent to which these idiosyncratic phrases have spread throughout the Intel management is an indication of Robert's influence on Intel's strategic think-ing. When Craig Barrett succeeded me as CEO at Intel, he organized a training ses-sion for all of Intel's senior and middle management. The purpose was to prepare them for the changes in our strategic priorities that he thought would be necessary to adapt successfully to an Internet-driven environment. Robert's concepts were an important part of this, and his blue-versus-green metaphor became the rallying cry of the session. Through this process, we became more conscious of what we do and, we hope, do it somewhat better.

But the issues faced by Intel are not unique to Intel. Every corporation en-counters changes in industry structure, causing it to undergo substantive transfor-mations from time to time. During these transformations, its *rubber bands* get stretched. Its traditional *blue* business soaks up all the resources that are necessary to fund the *green* initiatives that are crucial to adjusting to and thriving in a new market.

Not every corporation has been fortunate enough to have a distinguished management strategy professor study it for over a decade. But I truly believe that the lessons of this book will be as useful to the universe outside of Intel as they have been inside it.

ANDREW S. GROVE
June 19, 2000

PREFACE

The emergence of the Internet and the dawn of the new century provide fertile breeding grounds for prophecies about the factors that will shape the future of the corporation. Some have identified commoditization, cost cutting, innovation, deflation, and human capital as key factors.[1] Leaving the discussion of the prospects of deflation and its potential consequences to the macroeconomists, it seems fair to say that competition and technological advances have made most manufactured things cheaper throughout the twentieth century. Cutting costs has always been a smart way of sharpening a company's competitiveness. Innovation has always been a major—if not certain—route to securing high profits for some time. Human capital has always been important for getting ahead of competitors. Turning atoms into bits (digitization) and network effects preceded the Internet.

What then has really changed? Perhaps the defining characteristic of the so-called New Economy is that the Internet has turbocharged the importance of all these factors and has led to the increased importance of speed, interdependency and concomitant ambiguity. If this is correct, then the importance of *strategy* is likely to grow: not simply as a set of analytical tools but as an approach to apprehending evolving reality and acting upon it.

How strategy shapes a company's future is the central question addressed in this book. It is a defining question for the field of strategic management because it focuses attention on the dynamic interplay of companies and their environments. It is a provocative question because it addresses head-on the views of some well-regarded organizational researchers that strategy may not matter much, while maintaining healthy skepticism in the face of management gurus' exuberant incantations about firms' unlimited capacity to adapt. It is a difficult question because it requires specificity concerning how strategy is formed over time in complex organizations, and how strategy can be unequivocally linked to performance outcomes. It is a timely question because it helps assess the validity of new prophecies about the impending transformation of companies as we know them, which are predictably arising at the dawn of the new century.

How strategy shapes a company's future inevitably touches on the perpetual tension between continuity and change. That strategy is the means for reconciling this tension in some workable fashion throughout a company's evolution is the major thesis of this book. Providing compelling insight in how strategy actually helps creatively resolve the tension required a research site offering unusual access over a long period of time. Intel Corporation provided that research site.

Written with the purposes of academic business school research in mind, this book speaks to the community of strategy and organization scholars as well as the current and future leaders of established companies who are or will be facing the strategic leadership challenges highlighted in this book. In view of this, the chapters that follow offer positive description and analysis of strategy-making followed by normative prescription and synthesis. One premise underlying these efforts is that a sound normative approach should be based on deep positive understanding of the fundamental phenomena. A second premise is that both scholars and business leaders benefit from familiarizing themselves with the positive and normative aspects of strategy-making. Scholars are on firmer ground when they propose prescriptions based on sound positive description and analysis. Business leaders can be more confident in using these prescriptions if they understand the descriptive and analytical foundation on which they are based.

This book is the culmination of almost twenty years of effort to integrate strategy-making with evolutionary organization theory. It reports findings from longitudinal field-based research of Intel Corporation conducted continuously in real time over more than twelve years. The research method is described in detail in Appendix I at the end of this book. While keeping in mind the limitations inherent in this research method, the findings are uniquely informative. Few other studies have matched the temporal and behavioral scope of the research reported here in documenting the role of strategy-making as adaptive organizational capability. In this book, the findings, the evolutionary research lens, and the conceptual tools combine to offer many potentially useful contributions to cumulative knowledge development.

READER'S GUIDE

The book is organized in terms of the major epochs of Intel's evolution from its founding until today. The first part of each of chapters 2–11 tells the unfolding story of Intel's evolution. The second part of these chapters (called Discussion and Implications or just Implications) each time revisits the story and interprets it in terms of the conceptual frameworks discussed in chapter 1.

The book can be read in two different ways:

Readers who are interested primarily in the Intel story may want to start with chapter 2. They can return later to chapter 1, which provides the theory guiding the research. They can read the first part of each of chapters 2–11 and revisit the Implications parts later.

Readers who like to think through the conceptual frameworks before getting to the story may want to start with chapter 1. If they want to see how the conceptual frameworks help generate specific insights into the evolving story, they should read the Implications part of each chapter before moving on.

Chapter 12 concludes the book by offering general recommendations based on conceptual frameworks used to interpret Intel's evolution which apply to all established companies. Readers who like to jump directly to the conclusions will find brief references to relevant parts of the Intel story in the notes to chapter 12.

Introduction:

An Evolutionary Perspective on Strategy-Making

Intel is the most important company in the history of the microcosm.

GEORGE GILDER, *Microcosm,* 1989

1   STRATEGY IS DESTINY

Caveat

A famous painting by Belgian surrealist René Magritte shows a huge briar pipe covering almost the entire canvas. Perplexing the viewer is the neatly painted text underneath the image: This is not a pipe. Beyond the facetious truth that this is a painting not a pipe, the incongruence makes some viewers look more carefully at the image: If not a pipe then what is it? It also gets some viewers to think harder about the meaning of "pipe." A mental search for the essence.[1] In some ways, this book is similar to Magritte's painting. Intel Corporation is writ all over its pages, but: This is not Intel. No single account could capture Intel's multifaceted reality. The longitudinal study of Intel's evolution, however, illuminates the essence of strategy-making as adaptive organizational capability.

Strategy

Strategy is destiny is the theme of this book. Destiny is an archaic idea of a fixed and inevitable future. Strategy, in contrast, is a modern idea, of an open-ended future to be determined by it.[2] In reality the two ideas exist in perpetual tension. Successful and unsuccessful strategies shape a company's destiny. But if strategy shapes destiny, destiny has ways of asserting itself and constraining strategy. New sources of strategy create the possibility of future destiny, and help the company evolve. Strategy as the means to gaining and maintaining control of a company's present and future destiny is the common thread running through the study of Intel's evolution.[3]

Strategy in the narrow sense involves planning the use of resources and the deployment of capabilities to achieve objectives and prevail in competition. In the broader sense, strategy also concerns the rational determination of a company's vital interests, the purposes that are essential to its continued survival as an institution and define it in relation to other organizations, and its objectives. Strategy is therefore concerned with the external and internal forces that have the potential to materially affect the company's destiny.[4]

Strategy has a strong thinking component. Strategic thinking is forward-looking and concerned with exploring multiple scenarios, alternatives, and options. It is externally focused and tries to anticipate states of nature and the behavior of the relevant actors in a situation. Incisive strategic thinking at its best requires considerable intellectual effort. But senior executives sometimes view strategy with skepticism, because great strategies are just that—great strategies. From the perspective of key players, strategy becomes real when significant resources are committed, when strategy is turned into action.[5] Strategic action is *consequential;* it involves resource commitments that cannot easily be undone and moves the company in a direction that is not easily reversible. This view provides a criterion for distinguishing between tactics and strategy: Actions are tactical if their outcome does not significantly affect subsequent degrees of freedom to act.

Strategy-Making

Strategy in large, established companies like Intel takes the form of *strategy-making,* a complex process involving the thinking and action of key actors throughout the company.[6] This implies that strategy-making processes can be usefully characterized in two dimensions. The first dimension concerns the degree of concentration of strategic decision-making. At one extreme strategic decision-making is highly concentrated in top management. At the other extreme it is widely distributed throughout the organization. The second dimension concerns the degree of simultaneity in strategic action to implement strategic decisions. At one extreme all organizational units act simultaneously. At the other extreme, organizational units all act in some sequence. These two dimensions give rise to four strategy-making processes.

Rational actor model. Many view the rational actor model as the ideal. A comprehensively rational leader is responsible for strategic decision-making and is able to get all the participants in the organization to simultaneously take action to implement his decisions.[7] In this model, there is strong alignment between strategy and action. This model is probably most effective to respond to environmental dynamics that can be reasonably well anticipated and influenced.

Bureaucratic model. The rational actor model turns into the bureaucratic model if participants take action sequentially.[8] In slow-moving environments this model may have advantages because it allows each part of the organization to optimize its operations in light of the overall strategy. In rapidly changing environments, however, this model will cause sluggish implementation of the overall strategy.

Internal ecology model. Distributed strategic decision-making and simultaneous strategic action define the internal ecology model.[9] Strategy-making is shaped by strategic initiatives of differentially positioned participants, who all act simultaneously to try to commit the organization. This is a highly dynamic view of strategy-making in which coherence depends on the characteristics of the internal selection processes operating on the strategic initiatives. It may be most effective in highly uncertain, opportunity-rich environments.

Garbage can model. The internal ecology model turns into the garbage can model if the simultaneity of strategic action becomes sequential.[10] In that case, organizational participants' strategic actions depend on the sequence in which problems, solutions, and decision opportunities arise. The coherence of strategy-making in this model depends to a great extent on chance.

Organizational and strategic management researchers have long highlighted the difficulties leaders encounter in aligning organizational action in the pursuit of deliberate strategic intent. The cumulative evidence suggests relatively modest prospects for the rational actor model to apply. Studying the rare cases in which leaders achieve this improbable state of affairs may, however, produce insight that is useful for augmenting knowledge about strategy-making and strategic leadership. Viewing strategy-making in terms of the internal ecology model, on the other hand, is somewhat novel for strategy researchers, who find it difficult to see its potential normative implications.

Both the internal ecology and rational actor models informed the study of Intel's evolution. Strategy-making during Intel's first epoch resembled the internal ecology model, as multiple new business opportunities emerged from the company's competencies in the new semiconductor technologies and competed for its resources, transforming the company. During the second epoch, Intel's strategy-making resembled the rational actor model. This was a rare case in which a company leader successfully set strategic intent and created a process for its relentless and successful pursuit. At the start of its third epoch, Intel was struggling to combine the discipline of the rational actor model with the strategic renewal capacity of the internal ecology model.

Strategic Interaction

Complex organizations such as Intel usually face other complex organizations in the external environment. The study of strategic interaction involving such organizations is somewhat different from the study of strategic interaction in well-structured situations.[11] Well-structured situations have clearly defined, if sometimes probabilistic, payoffs associated with particular combinations of the players' strategic moves that are drawn from a predetermined set of options. Such strategic interaction situations lend themselves well to the quantitative methods of decision theory and game theory. In complex organizations, however, the strategic interaction situations are usually not well structured, the strategies of different actors in the organization may not be well aligned, payoffs in competitive interaction are not always given, and strategic action is not limited to a predetermined set of options. The study of strategic interaction involving complex organizations is therefore likely to be relatively untidy, raising questions that supersede those addressed in more structured approaches.

STRATEGY-MAKING AND EVOLUTIONARY ORGANIZATION THEORY

Evolutionary Perspective

How strategy comes about and how strategy-making helps companies to gain and maintain control of their destiny are fundamental questions for scholars interested in the study of complex business organizations and for reflective practitioners interested in improving their company's chances of success. To begin answering these questions, it is useful to dissect strategy-making into its key parts and their interrelationships, and to identify the forces that determine how it functions. To do so, this book adopts the perspective of evolutionary organization theory.[12] Evolutionary organization theory uses four generic processes—variation, selection, retention, and competition—to explain how organizations emerge and evolve.[13] Dissecting strategy-making in terms of these key processes serves two purposes: First, it facilitates integrating strategy-making as adaptive organizational capability into evolutionary organization theory. Second, it illuminates facets of strategy-making that other theoretical perspectives do not contemplate.[14]

Internal Ecology of Strategy-Making

Each company is an ecology within which strategic initiatives emerge in patterned ways. Top management drives most initiatives but leaders throughout the organization also drive initiatives. These initiatives compete for limited organizational resources to increase their relative importance.[15] *Variation* comes about as individuals (or small groups) seek expression of their special skills and career advancement through different strategic initiatives. These initiatives draw on existing and/or new competencies and routines and take shape if they are able to draw the company's resources to their development. *Selection* works through administrative and cultural mechanisms that regulate the allocation of resources and attention to different strategic initiatives. *Retention* concerns the initiatives that survive in the external environment and grow to become important within the company. It also takes the form of organizational-level learning about the factors that account for the company's success. *Internal competition* arises from different strategic initiatives struggling to obtain resources necessary to grow and increase in importance in the company. Internal competition between strategic initiatives can be more or less tightly linked to the *external competition* that these initiatives encounter.

Evolutionary Research Lens: Three Conceptual Frameworks

At the pure theoretical level, the processes of variation, selection, retention, and competition are general, abstract, and nonexperiential. At the level of pure practice, on the other hand, common language describing strategy-making is particular, concrete, and experiential. Business leaders do not use the terminology of pure theory to think and talk about strategy-making and find it difficult to relate to the abstract mathematical and statistical models ideally constructed by such theory. Scholars, on the other hand, find it difficult to gain deeper insight when limited to common language and like to do more than produce a coherent and complete narrative of strategy-making practice. Conceptual frameworks help bridge the gap between pure theory and pure practice.[16] They are specific, substantive, and suggestive. The boxes-and-arrows charts used to represent them (such as figure 1.1 in this chapter) can be more readily understood and related to by both business leaders and scholars. The three approaches are summarized on the following page.

This book uses three conceptual frameworks as tools for studying the role of strategy-making in Intel's evolution. These three different but related tools form

Evolutionary Organization Theory	Conceptual Frameworks	Strategy-Making Practice
• General	• Specific	• Particular
• Abstract	• Substantive	• Concrete
• Nonexperiential	• Suggestive	• Experiential
• Mathematical and statistical models	• Boxes-and-arrows charts	• Narratives

the evolutionary research lens and give it strong "zooming" capability. The zooming capability is useful to examine variation, selection, retention, and competition processes at different levels of analysis and to study the interplay between the different levels. The evolutionary research lens is shown in figure 1.1.

Think of the evolutionary research lens in terms of video recording. Tool I shows the big panoramic scenes, which contain everything, but it does not focus on the details. Tool II zooms in on key parts of the scenes, showing how actors move in relation to each other. Tool III zooms in further on the specific actions of the protagonists and on details of the environment that shape action.

TOOL I: DYNAMIC FORCES DRIVING COMPANY EVOLUTION

Tool I in figure 1.1 focuses on the big picture. It helps examine strategy-making at the industry-company interface level of analysis, and the coevolution of industry-level and company-level forces.[17]

Basis of Competitive Advantage in the Industry

Most industries contain several viable positions that companies can occupy. External forces determine the basis of competition in each of these positions. Consistent with the tenets of traditional industry structural analysis, these forces encompass customers, competitors, suppliers, new entrants, and substitution. In high-technology industries, however, additional forces also play an important role and merit separate and distinct consideration. Nonmarket forces, such as government regulation, are also potentially important.

Distinctive Competencies

Distinctive competencies concern the differentiated skills, complementary assets and routines that a company possesses to meet the basis of competitive advantage

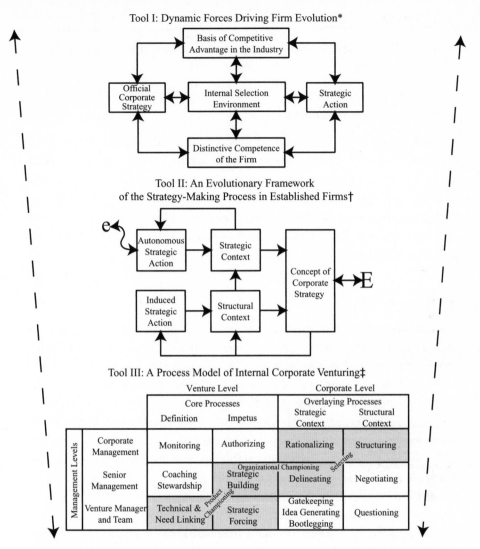

Tool I: Dynamic Forces Driving Firm Evolution*

Tool II: An Evolutionary Framework
of the Strategy-Making Process in Established Firms†

Tool III: A Process Model of Internal Corporate Venturing‡

		Venture Level		Corporate Level	
		Core Processes		Overlaying Processes	
		Definition	Impetus	Strategic Context	Structural Context
Management Levels	Corporate Management	Monitoring	Authorizing	Rationalizing	Structuring
	Senior Management	Coaching Stewardship	Strategic Building	Delineating	Negotiating
	Venture Manager and Team	Technical & Need Linking	Strategic Forcing	Gatekeeping Idea Generating Bootlegging	Questioning

Figure 1.1. An Evolutionary Lens on Strategy-Making. (SOURCES: *Adapted from R. A. Burgelman, "Fading Memories: A Process Theory of Strategic Business Exit," *Administrative Science Quarterly* 39 (1994), p. 31. †Adapted from R. A. Burgelman, "A Model of the Interaction of Strategic Behavior, Corporate Context, and the Concept of Strategy," *Academy of Management Review* 8 (1983), p. 65. ‡Adapted from R. A. Burgelman, "A Process Model of Internal Corporate Venturing in the Diversified Major Firm," *Administrative Science Quarterly* 28 (1983), p. 230.)

in the industry. They form the basis of the capabilities that a company can deploy. Distinctive competencies are intrinsic to a company's identity and character. For instance, they very much determine the generic corporate strategy—differentiation or cost leadership—that a company will pursue. Taken seriously, they are not easy to change. Deep competencies, on the other hand, are also likely to be a wellspring of new opportunities.

Official Corporate Strategy

Official corporate strategy concerns top management's statements about the company's intended strategy. These remarks reflect top management's beliefs about the basis of the company's past and future success. Key beliefs concern product-market domain, the relative importance of different distinctive competencies for competitive advantage, core values that help determine what the company will and will not do, and financial and other objectives. These are the most important drivers of a company's strategy.

Strategic Action

Strategic action is what the company actually does—the consequential actions that it engages in. Strategic action, position, and competencies mutually support each other.[18] Strategic action without position has limited ability to be exercised and without distinctive competencies is powerless. Position without strategic action is unlikely to fully exploit advantage and without distinctive competencies is precarious, because most positional advantages erode and eventually vanish. Distinctive competencies without strategic action are aimless and without position cannot be fully leveraged. Through strategic action that links position and distinctive competencies in novel ways, a company can attempt to proactively change the basis of competitive advantage in the external selection environment. Often, of course, strategic action must react to the changing external selection environment. Strategic action in large companies is usually distributed over different levels of management and different, specialized groups.

Internal Selection Environment

In principle, there needs to be alignment between the basis of competition and distinctive competencies and between official strategy and strategic action, but in dynamic environments this alignment is likely to come under severe pressure. The internal selection environment plays a crucial role in helping the company find new ways to reestablish alignment between the dynamic forces.

As Andy Grove pointed out in the foreword, Tool I became known at Intel as the rubber band framework. Tool I was particularly helpful in explaining why Intel was defeated in its original core business and why the company eventually exited from several semiconductor memory businesses (see chapters 3 and 4). It was also helpful in explaining Intel's enormous success in the microprocessor business (chapter 8) and the challenges to its continued success that arose in the late 1990s (chapter 10).

TOOL II: EVOLUTIONARY FRAMEWORK OF THE STRATEGY-MAKING PROCESS

Tool II in figure 1.1 zooms in on the strategy-making process at the company-level of analysis. Tool II gives substance to the variation, selection, retention, and competition processes by conceptualizing strategy-making in terms of induced and autonomous processes. Induced and autonomous strategic action correspond to variation; the structural and strategic contexts correspond to internal selection; and the concept of corporate strategy corresponds to internal retention. Competition involves the internal struggle of different businesses for corporate resources and the external struggle for survival in the competitive environment.

Induced Strategy Process

The induced strategy process (the lower loop in Tool II) resembles the traditional top-driven view of strategic management, but is different in five important ways.

Concept of corporate strategy. The concept of strategy—the official corporate strategy—is the theory that top management has about the basis for its past and future successes. It provides a shared frame of reference for managers at operational and middle levels in the company, and expresses top management's strategic intent.[19] It reflects organizational learning about the company's distinctive competencies (what it is good at), product-market domain (where it can win), core values (what it stands for), and objectives (what it strives to achieve).

Induced strategic action. Not surprisingly, top management wants to create a strategy process to direct the strategic actions of operational and middle-level managers. Induced strategic action involves initiatives on the part of operational and middle-level managers that fit with the concept of corporate strategy and leverage the organizational learning that it embodies. Induced strategic action is oriented toward gaining and maintaining leadership in the company's core businesses. Examples of induced strategic action are efforts to increase market penetration, new product development, new market development, and strategic capital investment projects for the existing businesses.

Structural context. When a company is small, the link between strategic action and the concept of corporate strategy is readily maintained, simply because there are few key players and they all know each other well. As a company grows larger this is no longer so. Strategy-making becomes increasingly distributed over differentiated groups (functional, product, geographical) and multiple levels of management, all of which take strategic action simultaneously. This provides an important source of internal variation, as individuals who possess data, ideas, motivation, and resources all strive to undertake specialized initiatives. But it also implies that unless a company is able to establish mechanisms to maintain a level of coherence, the corporate strategy will eventually be unrealized. Structural context comprises the administrative and cultural mechanisms that top management can use to maintain the link been strategic action and the existing corporate strategy. Structural context encompasses organizational structure, planning and control systems, resource allocation rules, measurement and reward systems, among other administrative arrangements, as well as cultural aspects such as recruitment and socialization processes and more or less explicit principles of behavior. Structural context is a key part of the internal selection environment that operates on strategic action.

Familiar external environment. The induced-strategy process takes place in the company's familiar external environment (**E** in Tool II in figure 1.1). Ideally, through this process top management can proactively influence the external environment to the company's advantage. This is reflected by the causal arrow going from process to environment. More frequently perhaps, that causal arrow goes from the environment to process forcing companies to respond to strategic change. Top management's role is to be alert to opportunities and threats that arise from environmental change, and to adjust the induced strategy process accordingly.

Creating alignment. The induced strategy process aims to align strategy and action. Through this process, a company's strategic actions are joined over time, distinct patterns of company-level strategy are realized, the organization's character is maintained, and the company successfully reproduces itself over time in its familiar environment. In a sense, the induced strategy process is a company's genotype—its genetic inheritance and makeup. This has important implications, because a strong induced strategy process is also likely to manifest strong strategic inertia. Resistance to change is a very old idea in organization theory. The induced strategy process provides a tool for elucidating further the rational roots of resistance to corporate change.

Autonomous Strategy Process

The autonomous strategy process (the upper loop in Tool II) is less well understood.

Autonomous strategic action. Autonomous strategic action involves initiatives of individuals or small groups that are outside the scope of the corporate strategy at the time that they come about. Autonomous strategic action is significantly different from induced strategic action in the technology employed, customer functions served, and/or customer groups targeted. Autonomous strategic initiatives typically involve new combinations of competencies that are not currently recognized as distinctive or centrally important to the firm. They often come about because a company's competencies are fungible and lead to new businesses that are different from the company's core business. Autonomous strategic initiatives may be complements or substitutes from the perspective of the core business. So-called disruptive technologies, for instance, often spring up as autonomous initiatives in established companies.[20] While autonomous strategic action often emerges fortuitously and is difficult to predict, it is not random because it is rooted in and constrained by the company's set of distinctive competencies at any given time.

Emerging external environments. If genotype is a metaphor for a company's induced strategy process, mutation is one for its autonomous strategy process. Like most mutations, most autonomous initiatives do not survive because they cannot continue to obtain resources. But like some mutations, some autonomous initiatives are important for the company's continued evolution. This is so because the autonomous-strategy process typically takes place in unfamiliar, emerging environments (e in Tool II in figure 1.1). Many of these emerging environments never grow to become important, but some do and may extend (complements) or even replace (substitutes) the company's familiar environment (**E** in Tool II).

Strategic context. At the time it comes about, the relation of autonomous strategic action to the firm's current strategy remains indeterminate: top management is not sure about its strategic importance and whether the company has the competencies to successfully pursue it. To resolve the indeterminacy, the strategic context for the autonomous initiative must become defined. Strategic context determination serves to evaluate and select autonomous strategic actions outside the regular structural context, usually through the interactions of various types of champions and top management. In contrast to the structural context, strategic context determination processes select initiatives for which the official strategy becomes fully articulated after the fact. Strategic context is thus also part of the internal selection environment.

Strategic context determination provides top management with the opportunity to evaluate the adaptive potential of autonomous strategic initiatives in an informed way. From an evolutionary point of view, only after it has become reasonably certain that an autonomous initiative is viable can top management legitimately amend corporate strategy. Such amendment, in turn, integrates the autonomous activities with the induced strategic process. The willingness of managers at operational and middle levels to engage in autonomous strategic action is influenced by their assessment of the probability that the strategic context determination process can be activated and successfully completed. Strategic contexts can also dissolve as autonomous strategic action leads new business opportunities to directly compete with existing ones for limited resources. This internal competition may lead to new businesses replacing existing ones, causing strategic business exits through abandonment or divestment.

Creating linkage. A key function of the strategic context is to link new business opportunities to the corporate strategy, thereby amending it. Lacking these created linkages, new business opportunities may be able to linger on for some time in the shadow of the core business but they will become resource starved and forgo the opportunity to demonstrate their full potential.

Simultaneity of Induced and Autonomous Processes

The induced strategy process is variation reducing. The autonomous strategy process is variation increasing. Strategic intent (induced strategy) and internal entrepreneurship (autonomous strategy), by themselves, are not sufficient for continued adaptation. Strategy-making as adaptive organizational capability involves keeping both processes in play simultaneously at all times, even though one process or the other may be more prominent at different times in a company's evolution.

Rationality of the Internal Ecology of Strategy-Making

A company rationally tolerates autonomous strategic initiatives because such initiatives explore and potentially extend the boundaries of the company's competencies and opportunities. They generate learning about variations in markets and technologies. Autonomous strategic action engages new environmental niches in which competition or institutional pressures are as yet less strong. Through such initiatives a company can also enter new niches opened up by others that might eventually pose a threat to the current strategy, for instance when they involve disruptive technologies. Through the autonomous strategy process, myopically purposeful initiatives by individuals may help the company find out what its strategic intent could be. On the other hand, autonomous initiatives can potentially have a dissipating effect on the company's resources and distinctive competencies. Resources can be spread thin if too many autonomous initiatives are supported, perhaps at the expense of the mainstream businesses. Distinctive competencies can also be diluted or lost if an autonomous initiative is not internally supported and important talent decides to leave the firm—with or without the help of venture capital. Most dangerously, autonomous strategic initiatives may undermine the existing competitive position of a company without providing an equally secure new position.

As Andy Grove pointed out in the foreword, Tool II became known at Intel as the blue (induced-strategy) and green (autonomous-strategy) framework. Tool II was particularly helpful in explaining Intel's transformation from memory company to microprocessor company (chapter 5) and in showing how Andy Grove created strong alignment between strategy and action during his tenure as CEO (chapter 6). It also helped explain the process of strategic inertia associated with Intel's success in the microprocessor business (chapter 9). Finally, Tool II provided a useful framework for identifying the strategic leadership challenges facing Intel in the late 1990s (chapter 11).

Related Evolutionary Ideas

Emergent and deliberate strategy. Induced and deliberate strategies are similar, but the induced strategy process provides more detail on what is involved in getting the organization to actually implement corporate strategy.[21] The link with autonomous strategic initiatives, on the other hand, is more complicated. Autonomous initiatives involved in generating and developing a new business opportunity usually involve deliberate actions taken by leaders below top management. The deliberate actions taken by these leaders help develop new competencies and help create a new strategic position that may open up a new business opportunity for the corporation. Thus, a strategy that emerges at a high level of the corporation often has its roots in deliberate actions by leaders at lower levels in the corporation.

Exploration and exploitation. The autonomous strategy process dissects exploration into autonomous strategic initiatives and the process of strategic context determination.[22] The latter serves to select viable autonomous initiatives and link them to the corporate strategy thereby amending it. The autonomous strategy process thus goes beyond exploration. It is also concerned with turning the results of exploration into new exploitation opportunities.

Ambidextrous organizations. Ambidextrous organizations are designed to handle both incremental and revolutionary change.[23] The idea is closely related to the framework of induced and autonomous strategy processes. Yet there are two important differences: First, induced and autonomous initiatives do not necessarily map onto incremental and radical technological change. Change in the induced strategy process, while incremental, can be very large. For instance, developing a new microprocessor is incremental for Intel but involves hundreds of millions of dollars in development costs and billions in manufacturing investments. In the induced strategy process, incremental simply means change that is well understood—doing more of what the company knows how to do well. Change through the autonomous process, on the other hand, can be radical but is initially usually rather small. However, it always involves doing things that are not familiar to the company—doing what it is not sure it can do well. Second, change through the autonomous strategy process usually comes about fortuitously and unexpectedly. Initially senior and top management have no clear understanding of its strategic importance for the company and how it relates to the company's distinctive competencies. Resolving this indeterminacy is the most difficult challenge facing autonomous strategic initiatives. This highlights the importance of the strategic context determination process.

Strategy-making and self-organization. The theory of self-organization and of organizations as chaotic systems is a useful perspective in organization theory and strategic management.[24] Self-organizing systems discover answers to their problems through experimentation. Because prediction is difficult in dynamic environments, the organization develops a catalog of responses and stimulates learning through experimentation. Similarly, ideas of deterministic chaos concern organizations that experience counteracting forces that produce nonlinear dynamics. Some forces push the organization toward stability and order; other forces push the system toward instability and disorder. Strategy-making as adaptive organizational capability balances variation-reduction (induced) and variation-increasing (autonomous) processes at any given time and over time.

Punctuated equilibrium. The punctuated equilibrium view of company evolution posits that organizations evolve through long periods of incremental change punctuated by discontinuous, frame-breaking change.[25] While there are many examples of sudden radical changes, punctuated equilibrium views beg the question of where these sudden radical changes come from. Truly exogenous shocks such as large meteorites hitting the earth and destroying existing ecosystems are always a possibility but fortunately a remote one. Many radical changes—technological or otherwise—are the cumulative result of continuous small changes over a long period of time. Sometimes these changes originate in the company's autonomous strategy process and sometimes outside of the company altogether. Often they happen inside and outside simultaneously. Companies always want to spot such changes sooner rather than later. The introduction of intracompany variation, selection, retention, and competition processes to study strategy-making provides a tool for identifying the underlying—more continuous and finer grained—strategic leadership activities that eventually, through sheer accumulation, cause lumpy radical strategic change.

TOOL III: PROCESS MODEL OF INTERNAL CORPORATE VENTURING

Zooming in still closer to the process, Tool III is useful to examine, at the intracompany level of analysis, the fine-grained strategic leadership activities involved in the autonomous-strategy process.

The Basic Structure of the Process Model

The process model of internal corporate venturing, shown in figure 1.1, is a matrix-like framework that documents the simultaneous as well as sequential strategic leadership activities of different levels of management (the rows in the matrix) in the different levels of strategy-making (the columns).[26] The model considers three generic levels of management: (1) venture team, (2) middle/senior management, and (3) corporate management. The model also considers two generic levels of strategy-making: (1) corporate-level strategy-making and (2) business-level strategy-making. Corporate-level strategy-making encompasses the determination of the structural and strategic contexts (overlaying processes). Business-level strategy-making encompasses definition and impetus (core processes). The process model documents the set of strategic leadership activities involved in linking the business-level strategy-making and the corporate-level strategy-making. The model is descriptive, not prescriptive. It serves as a diagnostic tool to better understand key problems that are encountered as well as generated by the organization's strategic leaders who are involved in entering a new business.

Major Forces Simultaneously at Work in the Process Model

There are two major opposing forces simultaneously at work in the process model. One force derives from the *structural context* part of the process. Creating the structural context is top management's responsibility; so the first force is to a large extent a top-down force. A second force derives from the *definition* part of the process. Definition revolves around initiatives driven by strategic leadership activities of operational and middle-level managers. The definition of new business entry usually, although not necessarily, originates at levels below top management. So, the second force is to a large extent a bottom-up force. Forces associated with *impetus* and *strategic context* integrate the top-down and bottom-up forces. Impetus is gained if operational-level champions are able to draw resources to their initiative and establish a beachhead in the market with their product or service. The strategic context for the new business initiative can be determined by middle/senior-level champions who convince top management to incorporate the new business into the corporate strategy and to put the full support of the company behind it. An important contribution of the process model is to clearly show that the bottoms-up and top-down forces are opposing forces, and that they are in play simultaneously. The process model provides a tool for representing the simultaneity.

Tool III was particularly helpful to examine the strategic leadership activities involved in the development of Intel's chipset venture (chapter 7) and ProShare, Hood River, and networking ventures (chapter 9).

IMPLICATIONS

The tools of the evolutionary research lens helped answer specific research questions. Tool I helped explain why the basis of competition in Intel's core business and its distinctive competencies diverged over time and why the company's strategic actions diverged from its stated strategy. It also helped explain how Intel overcame these divergences and managed to adapt. Tool II helped explain how Intel's induced- and autonomous-strategy processes took shape over time and why strategy could lead to inertia. It also helped explain how autonomous initiatives were selected and retained in Intel's corporate strategy. Tool III helped explain how the activities of leaders situated in different positions in the organization combined in the autonomous process and where and why the process was likely to break down. This book addresses these and related questions, shedding additional light on how Intel attempted to control its destiny in an extremely dynamic environment. The analysis informs two important subjects of evolutionary organization theory— organizational ecology and organizational learning—as well as the practice of strategic leadership.

Organizational Ecology

The radical view. Organizational ecology emerged as a new theoretical approach in the mid-1970s.[27] The key argument of the original formulation of the theory went as follows. Organizational change must be understood at the level of entire populations of similar organizations and as the result of replacement and selection rather than of adaptation. For instance, suppose one measured the average characteristics of companies in the semiconductor industry in 1960 and did so again in 1999. And suppose one found significant differences in average company characteristics. Organizational ecology would explain these changes in terms of incumbent companies exiting the industry (usually because of failure) and new companies (with different characteristics) entering the industry. Incumbent companies failed in the face of environmental change because organizational inertia prevents them from adapting. In short, organizational inertia causes companies to be selected against. The rates of founding and disbanding drive organizational change.

The revised view. During the 1980s, the organizational ecology argument was subtly modified because the original formulation begged the question of why companies would be inert in the first place.[28] The revised theory posited that companies need to develop routines and procedures that make their behavior reliable, predictable, and accountable to key constituencies, such as customers, suppliers, employees, and industry analysts. These attributes allow companies to overcome the liabilities of being new, give them legitimacy, and lead them to be selected by the environment over firms that are not reliable, predictable, and accountable. But these very attributes make it difficult for companies to change in major ways after they have been selected. Hence, the new argument was that environmental selection leads to organizational inertia. There is strong empirical evidence in support of this theory of organizational inertia. The study of Intel's exit from its original core business (chapters 2–5) adds to that evidence.

Newer views. New organizational ecology research continues to draw attention to important challenges that strategy-making faces. One such challenge concerns multibusiness companies, which often face pressures—inertial and/or political—to shield some of their businesses from the severity of competitive pressures that stand-alone businesses encounter.[29] Multibusiness companies may thus be weakened overall unless their internal selection environment matches the competitive intensity of the external selection environment.

Another challenge involves a potential tradeoff between competitive advantage based on position and competitive advantage based on distinctive competencies.[30] Companies that rely on positional advantage shield themselves from competitive pressures and do not need to develop strong distinctive competencies to succeed. But this makes them vulnerable to new competitors using novel strategies to attack their position. On the other hand, companies that rely on distinctive competencies to compete with similar others may be able to hone these competencies and become best in class. But such distinctive competencies become highly specialized and make the companies vulnerable to new competitors deploying different competencies.

Still another challenge faced especially by companies in opportunity-rich technological environments, even those with a well-functioning autonomous-strategy process, is that they will not be able to match the variation generated in their environment. Eventually, some variations may threaten the incumbent companies. As an example, witness the enormous variation spawned by the Internet in recent years, which no single established company could possibly match. To reduce this threat, established companies may have to complement the internal variation generated by their autonomous-strategy process with other approaches, such as corporate venture capital.[31]

An integrative view. This book integrates strategy-making and organizational ecology. The argument runs as follows. Almost all companies start small and are subject to liabilities of newness (they are unknown, untested, lacking legitimacy, and so on). The major force faced by small, new companies is environmental selection. Most do not survive external selection pressures. Organizational ecology provides a useful theoretical framework within which the evolutionary dynamics of small companies can be more clearly understood. Some companies, however, do survive and become large and established. Although large, established companies continue to remain subject to the selection force of the external environment—and many succumb to it in the long run—these companies have gained the opportunity to substitute internal for external selection. Analogous to external selection, internal selection is concerned with a company's entering new businesses and exiting from failing ones over time.

Chapters 2 through 5 of this book examine how internal selection combined with external selection to transform Intel from a memory company into a microprocessor company. They document the role of internal selection in strategy-making as adaptive organizational capability. They show that Intel faced the challenges identified by the newer ecological views, but also offer tools to help top management meet these challenges.

Organizational Learning

Indeterminacy. Adopting an evolutionary perspective implies that outcomes are viewed as indeterminate and can be explained only after the fact. As one evolutionary scholar put it, "We can say that some outcome has occurred because of some prior sequence of events, even though we could *not* have foreseen, prior to the fact, that particular sequence unfolding."[32] This seems almost the exact antipode of the traditional view of strategy, which is to determine in advance the ensemble of strategic actions that will achieve desired outcomes. There is no conflict, however, with the perspective adopted in this book, which views strategy-making in established companies as a dynamic organizational learning process.

Learning in the induced process. The induced-strategy process, which is concerned primarily with exploiting existing business opportunities, deliberately drives strategic action in a more or less foreseeable pattern toward desired outcomes. Induced strategic action commits a company to a course of action that is difficult to reverse. Thorough preparation prior to deciding on such a course of action is important. Equally important is the work that comes afterward, because top management is keen to understand why strategic actions produce the results that the company obtains. Such understanding provides a basis for taking further strategic actions. Sometimes this work involves abandoning a course of action, for instance, exiting from a losing business.

Learning in the autonomous process. The autonomous-strategy process, which is concerned with exploring new business opportunities, involves somewhat more complex organizational learning. Here, strategic action at higher levels in the management hierarchy benefits from interpretation of the outcomes of strategic action at lower levels. The effectiveness of the process depends on correct interpretation of results at each level. The learning at a lower level becomes the stepping-stone for more-encompassing strategic action at the next managerial level.[33]

The study of Intel's evolution illuminates strategy-making as organizational learning. Chapters 6–9 in particular show how Intel learned specific lessons from the defeat in its original semiconductor memory business which helped it develop its strategy for capitalizing on new opportunities in the microprocessor business. These chapters also document the tension between learning in the induced strategy process, with the concomitant benefits of a narrow business strategy[34] focused on exploiting opportunities in the microprocessor business, and learning in the autonomous strategy process, which could potentially broaden the strategy and open up new business opportunities.[35] Although this tension remained somewhat latent during Andy Grove's extremely successful tenure as CEO, chapters 10–11 show that it became highly manifest during the early days of Craig Barrett's tenure as CEO, as Intel was seeking new growth opportunities beyond microprocessors.

Strategic Leadership

The study of the role of strategy-making in Intel's evolution suggests that strategy-making as a multilevel process must continue to match the dynamics of the environment. This implies a first strategic leadership imperative: Leaders who want to maintain control of their company's destiny must embrace strategy and learn to think strategically while in action. They must learn to "engage, then see."[36] They must also remain alert to the fact that their experience has decisively shaped their outlook by the time they reach top position[37] and take steps to make sure that it does not become a trap.

The video-recording analogy was used earlier to suggest that the three tools of the evolutionary research lens could be used to zoom in on the strategy-making process, illuminating its workings in increasing detail and taking some of the mystery out of it. Each of the three tools helps identify key attributes of strategy-making as adaptive organizational capability. Tool I suggests that the divergence of forces that drive a company's evolution will create strategic dissonance in the organization.[38] Capitalizing on strategic dissonance is a second strategic leadership imperative. Tool II suggests that the induced and autonomous strategy processes are both important for organizational adaptation. Maintaining the effectiveness of both processes is a third strategic leadership imperative. Finally, Tool III suggests that the combined activities of differentially positioned leaders in the autonomous process determine whether and how fast the company can manage strategic change. Managing the cycle time of strategic change is the fourth strategic leadership imperative. Chapter 12 discusses these four strategic leadership imperatives, which promise to help top management guide their company toward its current destiny while preserving the capability to secure its future destiny.

CONCLUSION

Strategy shapes destiny, but strategy in turn is shaped by destiny. Strategy helps leaders understand and act upon the internal and external forces that affect the company's destiny over time. Strategy in large established companies takes the form of *strategy-making* because it involves the consequential actions of leaders throughout the organization.

The variation, selection, retention, and competition processes of evolutionary organization theory provide a useful perspective for analyzing strategy-making. Examining these processes at the intraorganizational level offers the opportunity to integrate strategy-making with evolutionary organization theory. It also highlights facets of strategy-making as adaptive organizational capability that escape other perspectives. In particular, it emphasizes the importance of identifying the entire set of planned and unplanned variations—successful and unsuccessful ones. Such alertness, in turn, helps identify implicit or hidden selection mechanisms, as well as unanticipated consequences of conscious efforts to change selection mechanisms in force at some point in time.

Variation, selection, retention, and competition are general, abstract, and non-experiential generic processes. The research lens used to study the role of strategy-making in Intel Corporation's evolution comprises three conceptual frameworks that are somewhat more specific, substantive, and suggestive of phenomena associated with strategy-making in companies. These three conceptual frameworks serve as tools to analyze variation, selection, retention, and competition processes at different levels of analysis and the interplay between these levels. The three tools together provide the evolutionary lens with a strong zooming capability. This offers the opportunity to move back and forth between studying detailed strategic leadership activities at the intracompany level of analysis, the role of induced and autonomous strategy processes at the company level of analysis, and the interplay between company-level and industry-level dynamic forces.

Epoch I:

Intel the Memory Company

We are really the revolutionaries in the world today—not the kids with the long hair and beards who were wrecking the schools a few years ago.

Intel founder and CEO
GORDON MOORE, *Fortune*, 1973

2   GENESIS AND TRANSFORMATION

> A common thread in all of Intel's success has been technology. Technology has tied it all together across the Epochs.
>
> GORDON MOORE, Chairman Emeritus, 1999

Intel Corporation has been among the most important high-technology companies in history. According to *Time* in December 1997, "the microchip has become—like the steam engine, electricity, and the assembly line—an advance that propels a new economy . . . Intel is the essential firm of the digital age."

Three Epochs

Intel's history can be divided into three epochs: "Intel the Memory Company," which lasted from 1968 until about 1985; "Intel the Microprocessor Company," which lasted from about 1985 until 1998; and "Intel the Internet Building Block Company," which was beginning to unfold in 1998. The three epochs correspond, to a large extent, to the tenure of the company's top leaders. Gordon Moore was Intel's CEO during most of Epoch I. Andy Grove ran the company during Epoch II. And Craig Barrett was leading the transformation to Epoch III.[1] Appendix II provides financial highlights of Intel's evolution.

In 2001, Intel was still one of the largest and most successful high-technology companies in the world. Looking back, the story is one of a remarkably adaptive organization. This is all the more so because at several points in its history, Intel's prospects looked far less promising than the results obtained today would lead one to believe. In the early to mid-1980s, in particular, Intel went through great upheaval and a transformation that led it to exit from the core business upon which it had been founded. At several other moments in its more recent history there were doubts that Intel would be able to continue hitting the ball out of the ballpark, as it almost invariably did during the 1990s.

GENESIS

Robert Noyce and Gordon Moore founded Intel—a contraction of Integrated Electronics—in 1968. Intel was the first successful company to specialize in designing and manufacturing large-scale integrated circuit memory products. Nearly a decade earlier, Noyce had shared credit for inventing the integrated circuit.[2] Moore, one of the leading physical chemists of his generation, was among the first to see the potential of Metal Oxide Semiconductor (MOS) process technology for mass-producing memory devices at low cost.[3] Noyce and Moore had developed a track record as leading entrepreneurs of the new electronic age by founding Fairchild Semiconductor, a Silicon Valley-based high-technology subsidiary of the Fairchild Camera and Instrument Corporation headquartered in Syosset, New York, in 1959. As director of R&D at Fairchild, Moore knew of the silicon gate MOS technology, which had been invented by a young semiconductor scientist in his department but had not yet been deployed in a large-scale manufacturing environment. Fairchild's corporate management however, was not ready to support new products based on the new technology. Also, Noyce had been bypassed for the CEO position at Fairchild Camera and Instrument and had become disenchanted with managing a large, complex organization. He was ready to move on, and he convinced Moore to join him in founding Intel to pursue the future they envisaged. At the time, bipolar technology was the standard semiconductor process technology, but the new MOS process technology was emerging.[4] In an interview in 1989 Gordon Moore said, "We started out with deciding to develop technology for semiconductor memory. We did not want to choose between bipolar and MOS process technology, so we tried both."

After Noyce and Moore left, most other senior Fairchild Semiconductor executives also departed. Fairchild headquarters replaced them with a team of executives recruited from Motorola's Semiconductor Division in Phoenix, Arizona. But it didn't work. Andy Grove, who had been Moore's assistant director of research at Fairchild, also left to join Intel completing what the company's historians have called the triumvirate. Grove reportedly joined Intel, in part, because he felt that the departure of Fairchild's middle management sealed the fate of that company.[5] Grove became director of operations and took responsibility for building the organization.

Planned Products: SRAM and DRAM

Intel's first product, introduced in 1969, was a bipolar static random access memory (SRAM) chip with 64 bits of storage capacity, which found some small initial markets.[6] Intel's strategic intent, however, was to replace mainframe computers' standard magnetic core memory.[7] Magnetic core memory was a complex product in which rings of magnetic metal were woven together with interlocking strands of copper. Magnetic core memory was well entrenched. Replacing it required the 10 × improvement in cost reduction that has been put forth as the rule of thumb for judging a new technology's chance of replacing technology existing.[8] Intel's SRAM offered the necessary 10 × reduction in cost per bit. Intel's sales took off and provided a foundation for betting on the new MOS technology for its next product.

Intel established itself as a leader in semiconductor memories by pioneering the metal-oxide-semiconductor (MOS) process technology for manufacturing microchips. MOS transistors consumed much less power than bipolar transistors and promised increased circuit density while reducing manufacturing steps. They posed, however, severe manufacturing problems because they were very sensitive to trace impurities in processing. Director of Operations Andy Grove was in charge of engineering and manufacturing; he and his team were able to solve the technical problems and to get manufacturing yields above the 10 percent minimum threshold for success. Intel was able to begin selling its MOS SRAM chips as shift registers (a common type of sequential access memory) for mainframe computers.

In 1970, capitalizing on its MOS breakthrough, Intel introduced the world's first dynamic random access memory (DRAM)[9]—the 1 Kilobit 1103.[10] While the SRAM required six MOS transistors per memory cell, the DRAM required only three transistors. With fewer elements in each memory cell, the 1103 contained more storage capacity in the same silicon area. DRAM came to replace magnetic core memory as standard technology for computers to store instructions and data as they executed programs. By 1972, the 1103 was the world's largest selling semiconductor and accounted for more than 90 percent of Intel's $23.4 million in revenue. DRAM remained Intel's core business throughout the 1970s. DRAM was initially a very attractive business, in part because Intel was somewhat fortunate to remain sole source supplier for some time. In 1999, reflecting on Intel's successful early days as a startup, Gordon Moore explained:

> Luck plays an important role. There were two big events that I would consider very fortunate. First, with respect to DRAM, it was standard procedure in the semiconductor industry that no customer would design in your product without a second source. The nominal reason was that

the customer wanted to have a guaranteed supply. The unstated reason was to have price competition. Especially as a small company, we had to second source our memory.

For our first DRAM, the 1103, we second sourced our technology to [a Canadian organization]. We transferred the process and the product, and set it up for them. We absolutely copied our own set up. They used to say that they ran Intel's process better than Intel did, and they were probably right. The initial process was run on 2-inch wafers.[11] We decided to change to 3-inch wafers because the economics were better. They tried to do this too—but beyond the time where we had to give them help—so they were on their own. They screwed up their 3-inch wafers and couldn't deliver production volumes. Our products were designed in, so when the production volumes came in we were the only ones shipping. That was luck! And this was a very profitable part of our story.

Moore's comments imply of course that Intel's luck was not quite independent of the company's deep distinctive competencies in silicon technology, which allowed it to get ahead of the original licensee and have served it well throughout its history.

Unplanned Products: EPROM and Microprocessor

Based on its deep competencies in silicon technology, Intel was a wellspring of technical variations that created new business opportunities in its early days. Besides SRAM and DRAM, Intel also invented the erasable programmable read-only memory (EPROM)[12] and the microprocessor,[13] which were unplanned product variations. Dov Frohman, an Intel scientist, invented EPROM and turned a previously intractable technical problem into a new product for Intel. EPROM products were the second source of Intel's "luck in the early days" that Gordon Moore referred to. According to Moore:

> The second big thing was that we misguessed the role that EPROM would play. EPROM was more expensive than masked ROM, and we thought it would only be used for prototyping. We expected all the volume would still be in masked ROM, so we kept the prices high for EPROM. It turned out that EPROM was the engineers' security blanket. The engineers would always want to keep tweaking their code, so people didn't design it out. So the quantities got to be pretty high, but not as high as DRAM. We ended up hiding this as well as we could. EPROM was our most profitable product line through 1985.

Microprocessors also came about somewhat fortuitously when a Japanese calculator company offered Intel a contract to develop a chipset for a desktop calculator it planned to introduce. Ted Hoff, an Intel scientist, together with Federico Faggin, who had invented the silicon gate MOS technology at Fairchild and had joined Intel, were able to reduce the envisaged set of fifteen chips to four, including one that was a "computer on a chip." Intel, however, did not immediately view microprocessors as an important new business opportunity.

Organization and Culture

Developing, manufacturing, and bringing to market Intel's innovative 1103 DRAM product required a very structured and disciplined management approach. Referring to the technical and organizational challenges involved in getting Intel's DRAM to work, one observer quoted Andy Grove in the late 1980s:

> Making the 1103 concept work at the technology level, at the device level, and at the systems level and successfully introducing it into high volume manufacturing required, if I may flirt with immodesty for a moment, a fair measure of orchestrated brilliance. Everybody from technologists to designers to reliability experts had to work to the same schedule toward a different aspect of the same goal, interfacing simultaneously at all levels. . . . This is a fairly obvious example of why structure and discipline are so necessary in our operations.[14]

The core values supporting these management challenges were shaped by the behavior of the founders, who had a strong appreciation of the importance of technical depth and excellence. They insisted on discipline in thinking and action, they focused on results and output, and they wanted to create an egalitarian meritocracy in which knowledge power was not subjugated by position power. A symbol of discipline as one of Intel's core values was the "late list," instituted by Andy Grove in 1971. All employees, including the CEO, had to sign a list when they arrived at work later than 8:05 A.M.The late list was in force until 1988. From its founding, Intel also had a strong profit and shareholder-value orientation and the finance group held a prominent position within the company.

TRANSFORMATION

By 1984, changes in the external selection environment and cumulative setbacks in Intel's internal selection environment created a major crisis for Intel's DRAM business. Intel found it difficult to respond effectively to the external changes and by late 1984 its market segment share in DRAM was less than 3 percent. Not only had Intel fallen far behind in the DRAM market segment but internally Intel's exit from the DRAM business was already well under way as DRAM accounted only for about 5 percent of Intel's revenue in 1984. In November 1984, Intel's top management decided not to invest in manufacturing capacity for the 1Megabit DRAM generation. It had become clear to top management that the company's future lay in the microprocessor business. Intel's DRAM business exit and transformation encompassed six partly overlapping stages that bracketed key events.

Stage 1: Development of DRAM and Initial Success

Intel's technical competence in DRAM. Competence in MOS process technology made it possible for Intel to succeed with DRAM where other memory start-ups such as Advanced Memory Systems had previously failed. Intel became the first successful mover in DRAM because its technologists (under the direction of Andy Grove and Les Vadasz) were able to get manufacturing processing yields above the threshold for viability in the market against magnetic core memory. To speed the adoption of DRAM, Intel started the Memory Systems Operation (MSO), which assembled 1103 chips along with the required peripheral controller circuitry for OEM (original equipment manufacturer) sales into the computer maker market.[15] Soon MSO was responsible for about 30 percent of Intel's business.

Intel fought a battle with processing yields from its earliest days.[16] Ron Whittier, the general manager of the Memory Products Division between 1975 and 1983, said that throughout a product's life cycle, wafer yields increased continually as process improvements were developed. Changing the size of wafers also increased the productivity of the factory. This opportunity arose whenever silicon manufacturers developed techniques to grow larger silicon ingots and equipment manufacturers developed machines that could handle larger wafers. As Gordon Moore pointed out, Intel's second source partner in the early days could not capitalize on the opportunity associated with larger wafer size and as a result, Intel was fortuitously left in a de facto sole source position for some time.

Technology-based differentiation and product leadership strategy. Intel's early strategy was to deliver products based on next-generation process technology before competitors. Customers were willing to pay a premium for higher density, higher performance products, especially in the absence of competitive products. Each new generation required a quadrupling of the number of transistors contained on a chip. The driving force behind increased density was the ability to define patterns of ever-narrower dimensions, and to invent creative ways of reducing the required number and size of components per memory cell. Intel's DRAM Technology Development (TD) group was responsible for solving progressive generations of linewidth/density problems. Each new generation reduced the minimum linewidth by a factor of about 30 percent, from 5 microns at the 4K generation. The minimum linewidth was controlled primarily by the resolution capability of the photolithography process, while the maximum chip size was determined by the ability to control the number of random defects on the silicon wafer during manufacturing. While competition was tough even at the 4K density, a series of process innovations kept Intel among the memory leaders through the 16K DRAM generation. Intel developed the strategy of using DRAM as a technology driver. The latest process technology was developed using DRAM and later transferred to other products. Also, being the largest volume product, DRAM served as the foundation for Intel's learning curve.

The technology development–manufacturing integration. From the start, Intel's founders decided to keep the TD and manufacturing activities together at a fabrication site (Fab). Gordon Moore had been dissatisfied with the linkage between TD and manufacturing at Fairchild. He insisted that Intel perform all process technology research directly on the production line. The company then made rapid incremental process changes and stayed ahead of competition using process technology. The approach was especially effective in a firm with relatively few plants operating below full capacity. It was highly successful in the early years. Intel's growth, however, required adding fabs in new locations. The addition of new fabs impeded the transfer of technology as pockets of technical competence proliferated across the different fabs. By 1985, Intel had eight fabs spread over four states (California, Oregon, Arizona, New Mexico) and Israel. Technology transfer between sites became problematic, as engineers tended to trust only processes or equipment that they had personally developed. When a process technology transferred from one fabrication site to another, or from development phase to manufacturing phase, engineers redeveloped the process to fit their own favorite approach. This was internally known as the NIH (not invented here) syndrome. Although management tried to improve the handoff from TD to manufacturing by formal rules, this made the process more bureaucratic and time consuming and did not fundamentally change the behavior of the TD and manufacturing groups.

In spite of the geographical closeness of the TD and manufacturing engineering groups, integrating their activities was a problem. Often process yields that dipped after a transfer from TD to manufacturing would recover only after the receiving engineers learned the process. This effect was internally known as the Intel U. Over time, engineering management attempted to solve the problem by creating strict guidelines and definitions for when one group stopped and another started being responsible for a product's development. One manufacturing engineering manager said: "Part of the problem was that the TD engineers needed to show just five good batches and their job was done." On occasion, the combination of manufacturing's NIH syndrome and the minimal process characterization by the TD group resulted in an Intel U spanning more than six months.

Stage 2: New DRAM Generations and the Emergence of Competition

Some time after Intel's early success, competitors entered the market for DRAM and began to erode Intel's MOS process technology lead. By the mid-1970s, Intel was one of several companies vying to be the first at introducing the new generation of DRAM memories. Every three years, a new generation with four times as much capacity as its predecessor was developed by the incumbents. From the 4K and 16K level on, Intel was struggling to keep up with its competitors. Table 2.1 shows the evolution of worldwide unit shipment and Intel's evolving market share in DRAM between 1974 and 1984.

During the formative years of the DRAM market, the chip design was in rapid flux. A start-up company, MOSTEK, took market share from Intel in the 4K generation by incorporating the peripheral circuitry in its DRAM design that managed the memory on the chip itself, which started a trend in DRAM toward user-friendliness. This led Intel to eventually sell the MSO, since the value added had been integrated onto the chip itself and the majority of DRAM customers had learned how to use DRAM.

Competing on distinctive competence. Attempting to capitalize on its distinctive competence in process technology during the 1970s, Intel competed by developing new processes that enhanced product features. The HMOS (high performance MOS) process enabled Intel to introduce the first 5-volt-single-power-supply 16K

Table 2.1. Evolution of DRAM Volumes and Intel Market Share (1974–84)

			Product			
Year	4K	16K 3PS*	16K 5V	64K	256K	Total Share
Worldwide Unit Shipments of DRAMs (in thousands)						
1974	615					
1975	5,290					
1976	28,010	50				
1977	57,415	2,008				
1978	77,190	20,785		1		
1979	70,010	69,868	150	36		
1980	31,165	182,955	1,115	441		
1981	13,040	215,760	5,713	12,631		
1982	4,635	263,050	23,240	103,965	10	
1983	2,400	239,210	57,400	371,340	1,700	
1984	2,250	120,690	40,600	851,600	37,980	
Intel DRAM Market Share (percent)						
1974	82.9					82.9
1975	45.6					45.6
1976	18.7	37.0				19.0
1977	18.1	27.9				20.0
1978	14.3	11.5				12.7
1979	8.7	4.4	100.0			5.8
1980	3.2	2.1	94.0	0.7		2.9
1981		2.4	66.5	0.2		4.1
1982		2.3	33.1	1.5		3.5
1983		1.9	11.7	3.5		3.6
1984		1.4	12.3	1.7	0.1	1.3

SOURCE: Dataquest.

*16K 3PS refers to the industry-standard, three-power-supply DRAM. The 16K 5V model requires only one power supply.

DRAM in 1979. The new product greatly simplified the user's design and production tasks.

While Intel had lost market share with the earlier 16K products, it was the sole source for the 5-volt device and captured a price premium of double the industry average for its three-power-supply 16K DRAM in 1979. The DRAM TD group focused a significant amount of its resources on developing Intel's third 16K DRAM offering while competitors concentrated on the 64K generation. Intel management decided to focus on the single power supply 16K DRAM for two primary reasons: They projected a relatively long lifecycle for the 16K generation due to the technical challenge in achieving the 64K generation; and they believed the one-power-supply process would eventually dominate the memory industry. They considered it too risky to tackle both the 64K DRAM generation and the single-power-supply technology in the same product. Contrary to Intel's expectations, however, Japanese new entrants began offering standard 64K DRAM products in 1979. The Japanese entrants were large, vertically integrated consumer electronics and computer companies.

Vanishing distinctiveness of competence. The drive toward smaller and smaller geometry was achieved through improvements in both processing methodology and processing machinery. In the early years, some processing steps were considered black magic and defined a company's competitive edge. As time went on, the movement of engineers between chip companies and, more generally, the involvement of equipment manufacturers in process development efforts led to a general leveling of process capability among rivals in the industry. Sunlin Chou, the manager in charge of DRAM TD commented about the trends in processing: "Process technology and equipment had become so complex and expensive to develop that no vendor could hope to do better than his competitors in every process step. The key to innovation was to be on par with your competitors on every process step, but to select one or two or three process features with the highest leverage and focus your efforts to gain leadership there. In DRAM we focused on high-quality thin dielectrics."[17]

During the 1970s, the equipment vendors became increasingly important. Broad process technology leadership was prohibitively expensive as capital equipment costs for a semiconductor fabrication plant rose by a factor of five. Even the largest players, such as IBM, Texas Instruments, Toshiba, and NEC, purchased standard processing equipment from global equipment vendors such as Nikon or Applied Materials. A single semiconductor manufacturer could not rationalize the investment needed to develop new specialized equipment based on its limited production. The locus of process innovation gradually shifted from the chip companies to the equipment suppliers. As a result, the equipment suppliers became a major conduit for the sharing, and hence leveling, of process technology know-how between firms in the industry. As the number of Japanese equipment vendors increased, and given the traditional close relationship between Japanese vendors and customers as well as the strong focus and determination of Japanese DRAM manufacturers, Japanese DRAM manufacturers became the prime beneficiaries of this change.

Regarding marketing competencies, Intel's source of competitive advantage had been in entering and exiting a new DRAM generation early to maximize margins and avoid severe price competition. However, as DRAM moved rapidly from specialty product to commodity, this was no longer working. Already in the 16K generation, while Intel technologists saw the single power supply DRAM as leading edge, the marketing strategy was rooted in attempts to differentiate and create an initial niche product with the hope that eventually the entire market would go for single power supply. When the hope did not materialize, there were severe implications for the sales volumes that could be achieved, and hence for the role that DRAM could play as Intel's technology driver.

Stage 3: Unplanned Products Compete with DRAM within Intel

In the early 1970s, EPROM and the microprocessor also benefited from the constant linewidth reduction driven by DRAM process development. Sales of both products were significant by the mid-1970s. Because of the difficulty of using the new microprocessors, Intel developed design aids to teach its customers how to use the microprocessors. Intel's sales of design aids for its microprocessors exceeded, for a while, the microprocessor sales themselves. By the early 1980s sales of EPROM and microprocessors represented a large share of Intel sales.

Developing new distinctive competencies. Intel had divided its technology development into three groups representing the three major process areas: DRAM, EPROM, and Logic. Competition for scarce resources in the Santa Clara site had led to the decision to separate the groups geographically. By 1984 the three separate technology development groups were in three cities: EPROM in Santa Clara, California; microprocessors and SRAM in Livermore, California; and DRAM in Aloha, Oregon. While development of each technology was independent, top management insisted on equipment standardization. Periodically, the TD groups got together, pooled information on equipment options, and agreed to purchase the same equipment.

The three groups each developed distinctive competencies, which related to their product responsibilities. The DRAM TD group led the company in linewidth reduction. They were already developing a 1-micron process while the logic group was still developing a 1.5-micron process. Sunlin Chou and his group were widely regarded as Intel's best resource for process development. The DRAM group was viewed as different from the other two because of the tight relationship between design and process engineers. The DRAM consists of one structure repeated in a regular array thousands or even millions of times on a chip. Most of the value added remained in optimizing the details of the structure of the repeated cell. According to Dean Toombs, who took over as general manager of the memory products division in 1983: "The DRAM designer . . . focuses on the memory cell and has to understand where every electron in the structure is. . . . The design and the process are developed together. A logic (microprocessor) designer is not as concerned with the details of a transistor's operation. The process is critical, but not as interactive with the design."

In contrast, the microprocessor consists of a more complex interconnection of transistors. The value-added in microprocessor development is in logic design and in being able to interconnect a highly irregular array of building block cells. While process technology skills continued to be very important, the emergence of microprocessors was associated with an increase in the relative importance of design skills. Relative to memory products, microprocessors had a very high design content. The capability for mastering circuit design complexity became as important if not more important than the capability to increase chip density. Thus, in the face of eroding process technology competencies, circuit design became the new basis for Intel's competitive advantage.

Resource allocation: perennially losing DRAM. As new business opportunities in EPROM and microprocessors were pursued and competed for scarce manufacturing capacity, DRAM began to lose out in the resource allocation process. Under the direction of its vice president of finance, Intel adopted a resource allocation rule that shifted resources systematically to products that maximized margin-per-manufacturing activity (or margin-per-wafer start). The rule involved a complex calculation. Each product was assigned a total amount of manufacturing activity based on the number of steps it required. Total manufacturing costs were then allocated to products on the basis of manufacturing activity. For each product, the overall yield (number of good die at final test divided by total number of die on starting wafer) was applied as a divisor to the manufacturing cost to arrive at a total cost per good part. The sales price was then used to calculate margin per part and margin per activity. Table 2.2 shows estimates of accounting data for DRAM, EPROM, and microprocessors in 1985. As a result, manufacturing capacity allocation to DRAM gradually and incrementally declined. In fact, the vice president of finance insisted, at one point, that the DRAM manager sign a symbolic check equal to the margin forgone when high-margin products were bumped by DRAM. Eventually, by 1984, DRAM production was restricted to Fab 5 in Oregon.

Investment in DRAM TD, however, continued to absorb about one-third of

Table 2.2. Sample of Cost Accounting Data for Selected Intel Products in 1985

Product	Process	Raw Wafer Cost	No. Mask Layers	No. of Act.	Cost Per Act.	Line Yield	Cost Per Wafer	Die per 6" Wafer	Wafer Sort Yield	Total Cost Per Die	Package/ Test Cost per Die	Yield at Test	Total Cost per Chip	Average Selling Price	Contribution Margin per Chip
64K DRAM	NMOS DRAM	60	8	30	72.00	90.00%	2,467	1900	90.00%	1.44	0.45	90%	2.103	2.05	-2%
64K DRAM	CMOS DRAM	100	10	38	72.00	84.00	3,376	1806	85.00	2.20	0.45	90	2.944	3.08	4
256K DRAM	CMOS DRAM	100	10	38	72.00	83.00	3,417	922	60.00	6.18	0.65	90	7.585	16.27	53
64K EPROM	NMOS EPROM	60	12	48	72.00	79.00	4,451	1582	75.00	3.75	2.65	90	7.112	8.15	13
256K EPROM	NMOS EPROM	60	12	48	72.00	78.00	4,508	756	60.00	9.94	2.45	90	13.764	21.00	34
80286	LOGIC	60	10	40	7,200	90.00	3,267	172	70.00	27.13	2.00	85	34.273	250.00	86
80386 (est.)	1.5 μ m LOGIC	100	13	50	7,200	90.00	4,111	131	30.00	104.61	15.00	85	140.716	900.00	84

Key

Raw Wafer Cost: Raw wafer cost differs depending on whether or not the process is CMOS.

Number of Mask Layers: Refers to the number of times the wafer goes through the photolithography step.

Number of Activities: Basic unit of manufacturing for cost accounting purposes. Refers to the number of times the wafer is physically altered in the process.

Cost per Activity: An average of worldwide manufacturing costs, including depreciation, materials, labor, and other facilities costs.

Line Yield Ratio: Ratio of wafers started to wafers completed.

Cost per Wafer: Number of activities times cost per activity divided by line yield.

Die per 6 Wafer: Number of devices on a 6" wafer (function of die size).

Wafer Sort Yield: Number of good die divided by total die after all processing is complete and before wafer is sawed and devices are packaged.

Total Cost per Die: Cost per wafer divided by number of good die per wafer at wafer sort test.

Package/Test Cost: Cost of packaging and testing one device.

Yield at Test: Number of devices entering packaging divided by number of devices which pass final test.

Total Cost per Chip: Total cost per die plus packaging and testing costs all divided by yield at test.

SOURCE: Researchers' estimates

Intel's R&D investment. Unlike DRAM wafer allocation, which could be cut incrementally, technology development could not. It made no sense as Andy Grove put it "to have half a team develop half a process." Gordon Moore commented that resource allocation to TD groups did not necessarily parallel the market fortunes of their products: "Allocation of resources to the different development groups was centralized by Andy (Grove) and me. We wanted to maintain commonality. Also, we are old semiconductor guys. . . . Ideally, one of the groups would start a new technology and the others follow."

Efforts to change the capacity allocation rule. Middle-level managers in the DRAM business experienced increasing difficulties in obtaining manufacturing capacity, which, in turn, made it more difficult to compete. These managers proposed that Intel restructure itself to recognize that it was competing in two different businesses: a commodity business (DRAM) and a specialty business (microprocessors). The manager of the Oregon fabrication plant dedicated primarily, but not exclusively, to DRAM proposed a reorganization in mid-1982. At this time, Intel was organized in product divisions responsible for product design, marketing, and sales. Each of Intel's fabrication plants produced products for several product divisions, allocating wafer starts to the most profitable products demanded by customers. The manager of Fab 5 proposed to realign his (mostly DRAM) fabrication facility with the Memory Component Division to create a coherent, dedicated DRAM organization. However, top management did not approve the reorganization and DRAM wafer starts continued to be pressured by the contribution margin decision rule. In early 1984, the engineering manager at the DRAM fabrication plant proposed an investment of $80 million for an upgrade of the fab. This manager's plan was to create a state-of-the-art, dedicated DRAM facility that was cost competitive with any other facility in the world. This manager thought the battle for DRAM should be fought in the manufacturing arena and should focus on manufacturability and cost rather than on the leading process technology edge. But a decision in 1983 to produce leading-edge CMOS DRAM and no longer the NMOS DRAM was supported by top management, and the investment plan for DRAM manufacturing improvements was not approved.[18]

Key technology choices. In addition, technology development decisions made by some key middle-level managers increasingly narrowed the strategic options of the DRAM business. One decision proved especially critical: In 1984, development of the new 386 microprocessor was taking place in parallel with a new "commodity" SRAM process at Livermore (Fab 3) under the direction of Ron Smith, a technical middle-level manager at the time. Although over the years Intel had retained its dominant position in the low-volume, highspeed SRAM segment, it had lost position in the medium-performance, high-volume SRAM segment that required a different, more compact process technology. A new SRAM process development effort was intended to get Intel back into the high-volume commodity SRAM business. Until 1984, both SRAM processes had been similar. Ron Smith viewed SRAM not only as a product line, but as a vehicle for microprocessor development. Process debugging and fault detection were much simpler for SRAM than for logic devices. At each generation of shrinking the process, learning from SRAM development was completely applicable to microprocessor development, since they both used the same six-transistor cell structure. In 1984, the new SRAM process differed significantly from the new microprocessor process: Its four-transistor cell design required building on-chip resistors to very tight tolerances (a difficult technical problem); whereas the new microprocessor process (still six-transistor) required two layers of metal interconnect (also uncharted technical territory). The new SRAM process would not be useful as a development tool for microprocessors. While the group was initially working on both SRAM processes, its manager eventually decided to drop the four-transistor process and go with the six-transistor CMOS SRAM. This meant that Intel would not have a cost-competitive SRAM for the commodity market. Ron Smith recalled: "[We stopped the 4-transistor process development] . . . So that we could focus our attention on the 386 development. Basically, we sacrificed the high-volume SRAM for the 386."

Smith pointed out that Intel bet the company on the 80386 microprocessor and compounded the risk by changing many things at once—both design and process. From his perspective, process technology development for the 386 processor was critical because it involved a team of sixty people, five times the number he had managed before. Smith was under great pressure to come up with a very advanced process and was determined to maintain the consolidation of the SRAM effort with the microprocessor effort. His decision, however, had repercussions for the decision process regarding Intel's participation in commodity memories, including DRAM. As Andy Grove later recalled: "By mid-'84, some middle-level managers had made the decision to adopt a new process technology, which inherently favored logic (microprocessor) rather than memory advances, thereby limiting the decision space within which top management could operate. The faction representing the x86 microprocessor business won the debate even though the 386 had not yet become the big revenue generator that it would eventually become."

Stage 4: Loss of DRAM Leadership Position and Growing Internal Doubts

By the end of 1984, Intel had lost significant market share in DRAM. The first real difficulties had come with the 64K generation. In 1980, Intel's 5-volt 16K DRAM was still a market success due to process innovations, and work was continuing on the 64K generation. DRAM traditionally led the company in new technology development, and the 64K DRAM was no exception.

To make the 64K version, the memory cell size was reduced, but the actual die size still had to be increased significantly. The DRAM TD group calculated that, given current defect levels in manufacturing, the required die size would be too big. Based on the number of defects per square centimeter normally experienced in fabrication, the projected yield on the 64K DRAM would be too low to be acceptable. To boost yield, the group decided to build in redundancy at the chip level. Ron Whittier, the general manager of the Memory Components Division (early 1980s), described the redundancy technology:

> Essentially, you have a row and column addressing system on a memory chip. The periphery of the chip contains logic and refresh circuitry necessary to control and update the DRAM. In the 64K version, Intel added an extra column of memory elements so that in the event of a process-induced defect, the auxiliary column could be activated. There was a physical switch or "fuse" built into each column which could be addressed by the tester machinery. When a bad element was detected, current would be passed through the switch and would blow a "fuse" inactivating the defective column and kicking in the auxiliary column. In this fashion, a defective memory chip could be "reprogrammed" before shipment, and overall yield could be improved.

Intel's redundancy program started out successfully. Two 64K DRAM projects were carried out in tandem, one nonredundant and the other redundant. Prior to production commitment, the redundant design was a clear winner, with yields over twice that of the nonredundant design. But success quickly turned to failure as a subtle but fatal defect in the redundant technology showed up late in development. The fuse technology was less than perfect. The fuse would blow during testing as designed, but a mysterious regrow phenomenon was detected during accelerated aging tests. The problem was symptomatic of the lack of integration of TD and manufacturing engineering at Intel in those days. Sunlin Chou, the manager of the DRAM TD group, later commented: "The failing fuse problem was simply a case of not having done enough engineering early on. We just didn't fully characterize the process technology and the fusing mechanism."

The result was that the switch eliminating the defective column of memory cells was not permanent. In some cases, the device would revert to its original configuration after being in the field for some time—meaning the defective cell would again become a part of the memory. Errors would occur in which the device alternated randomly between the two states, meaning that at any given time the location of data stored in the memory became uncertain. In either case, the failures were not acceptable, and Intel could not develop a quick fix.

While the development team eventually fixed the fuse problem and was the first to introduce a redundant 64K DRAM, its introduction was too late to achieve significant market penetration. Ron Whittier took a one-week trip to visit sales engineers and explain that Intel's 64K DRAM would be late: "The salesforce was very disappointed in the company's performance. Any salesforce wants a commodity line. It's an easy sell and sometimes it's a big sell. That trip was perhaps the most difficult time in my whole career. When I announced we would be late with the product, the implication was that Intel would not be a factor in the 64K generation."

Dean Toombs, the new general manager of the Memory Components Division (after 1983), had worked on DRAM at Texas Instruments (TI) before coming to Intel. This manager said the discussion on redundancy was industrywide. But at TI, engineers had concluded that at the 64K generation redundancy would not be economical and had deferred the discussion until the next generation. For the 64K generation, TI ultimately chose to focus on reducing the defect level in manufacturing. Similarly, Japanese competitors (e.g., NEC, Toshiba, Fujitsu) were also throwing capacity at 64K DRAM and improving the underlying defect density problem which Intel's redundancy program had meant to address. Between July 1981 and August 1982, Japanese capacity for 64K DRAM production increased from 9 million to 66 million devices per year.[19] Intel's redundancy strategy for the 64K, on the other hand was a reaction to the realization that its manufacturing competence was becoming inferior. Instead of focusing on improving the lagging manufacturing competence, Intel's technologists continued to rely, in vain, on the search for sophisticated technological solutions to deal with yield problems.

Having concluded, by autumn 1983, that they were behind in the 64K DRAM product generation and realizing that their manufacturing costs were not competitive with those of the Japanese DRAM suppliers, the DRAM group took another gamble. As noted earlier, the development effort was shifted from NMOS to CMOS. The advantage of CMOS circuitry was lower power consumption and faster access time. Intel defined a set of targeted applications for the CMOS

DRAM technology. In the Memory Components Division the general manager's strategy was to introduce the CMOS 64K and 256K DRAM in 1984. The notion was that by creating a niche market with premium pricing, Intel could maintain a presence in the DRAM market while accelerating forward to regain a leadership position at the 1Meg generation.

Dean Toombs said that by the time he took over the Memory Products Division, things were "clicking along." Demand was on an upswing, and Intel seemed to have a technology strategy which could lead to dominance in the 1Meg DRAM market. Many of the redundant 64K sales in 1983 went to IBM; in addition, Intel sold IBM the redundant 64K production and design technology. Toombs recalled that in late 1983 and early 1984, the silicon cycle was on an upswing and memory product demand was at an all time high. The memory components division's bookings exceeded its billings. However, during the boom of late 1983 and early 1984, all of Intel's factories were running at capacity. Allocation of production capacity between products was necessary. The question facing the Memory Products Division was how to effect the transition from NMOS to CMOS. Toombs said the hard decision was made to completely phase out the NMOS line. As noted earlier, at that time all DRAM fabrication was consolidated in Fab 5 in Oregon. Toombs suggested that the decision to "go CMOS" was consistent with Intel's general philosophy—to exploit new technology and create a lead against competitors based on proprietary knowledge. The development of the CMOS 64K and 256K DRAM took place in a facility adjacent to the Oregon production facility. While the development was not directly on the production line, there was a fairly smooth transition into manufacturing. The 256K chip was well designed and executed. Sunlin Chou commented: "The 256K CMOS DRAM was the first DRAM product, which did not have to go through some sort of design or process revision before or after going to market. With this product, we felt we were regaining our lead in DRAM technology after three generations."

But the CMOS technology was more complex, requiring eleven to twelve masking steps versus eight to nine steps for NMOS. This resulted in a higher manufacturing cost for the CMOS process. The CMOS DRAM products were introduced in 1984 and priced at about one-and-a-half to two times the prevailing NMOS price. DRAM management now deliberately adopted a niche strategy: differentiate the product from other offerings and sell it on features. In addition to the CMOS feature, Intel offered an alternative memory organization which provided performance advantages in some applications. Intel sampled the products broadly to many customers and made many design wins, particularly in situations where other DRAM had inadequate performance. The CMOS DRAM started as a winning product family. Unfortunately, the market softened as 1984 went along. The price of NMOS DRAM fell by 40 percent in one three-month period from May to August 1984: Dean Toombs said that in the scramble and upheaval of the semiconductor market, Intel's differentiation message got lost. All suppliers were pushing product into the market, and Intel's superior product specifications (associated with CMOS) seemed like just another ploy to get volume. By late 1984, Intel's ability to make profits, and, more important, to project future profits in DRAM was limited. Toombs also said: "In a commodity marketplace, your staying power is a function of the size of your manufacturing base." According to Toombs, by late 1984, Intel was down to less than 4 percent of the 256K DRAM market and had lost its position entirely in 64K DRAM.

Nevertheless, the DRAM TD team, considered the strongest TD team within Intel, continued to focus on a process technology catch-up and leapfrog strategy. And the technology strategy seemed to be working, as the first prototype of the 1Meg DRAM was expected in March 1985. The DRAM TD manager indicated that Intel's 1Meg DRAM strategy focused on new thin dielectrics, rapid improvements in lithography (to 1.0 microns), but only incremental changes to the structure of the DRAM capacitor. Dean Toombs believed that the DRAM technology development group had provided Intel with a unique product capability: "The 1 Meg DRAM would have been a technically outstanding product, at least one-and-a-half to two years ahead of any competition in application of CMOS. But the handwriting was on the wall. In order to make the DRAM business go, major capital investment were required and the payback just wasn't there. The issue for 1985 was how to survive."

Stage 5: The DRAM Exit Decision

The exit decision was very difficult for Intel. Even though it had been clear that DRAM products were much less profitable than other products, the Vice President of Sales Ed Gelbach had continued to believe that Intel needed to offer a one-stop semiconductor shopping list of products, including DRAM, to its customers. CEO Gordon Moore had continued to support the idea of DRAM as Intel's technology driver. But, in November of 1984, Intel's top management announced that it would not continue development of DRAM products beyond the current 256K product generation. Intel, the firm which had invented the DRAM less than fifteen years earlier, basically decided to cede the DRAM market to a handful of Japanese and U.S. competitors.

Over the next ten months a number of middle-level managers would make and implement decisions that arose from the original November 1984 exit decision. The cascade of actions required by the November 1984 decision included decisions to redeploy its resources (technologists, manufacturing capacity) and to rationalize its product line offerings while maintaining customer confidence. Interestingly, no single individual or strategic direction seemed to control the array of decisions made in the wake of the November 1984 decision.

Consolidating technology development. Following the November 1984 decision, Intel chose to consolidate its technology development sites. At the time Intel still had three sites—Portland's Fab 5 DRAM development site, Livermore's Fab 3 Logic development site, and Santa Clara's Fab 1 EPROM development site. A combination of factors led to a decision to move microprocessor development from Livermore to Portland. Those factors included Livermore's charter to manufacture Intel's leading-edge microprocessors (the 286 and the 1.5-micron 386 microprocessors), which conflicted with its development role, and Fab 5's approximate twelve months' lead in developing 1-micron technology (for the 1Meg DRAM). Intel needed to develop the 1-micron process for the 386 microprocessor swiftly, because Motorola's 32-bit 68000 chip was gaining wide customer acceptance and Motorola was expected to announce faster versions within a year.

The sinking morale and increasing uncertainty at Fab 5 in Oregon, in the wake of the decision to stop DRAM development, contributed to the decision to consolidate the Fab 3 and Fab 5 technology development groups. To keep Fab 5's highly regarded TD team together and busy, the effort to build a functional 1Meg DRAM chip was allowed to continue. In parallel, the 1-micron 386 microprocessor development effort was moved from Livermore to Portland. There was some initial resistance to this move. The manager of the Livermore (Fab 3) TD group argued against transferring the 1-micron effort to Portland. Based on the not invented here syndrome, this manager predicted that the transfer to Oregon would set back the development of the fast version of the 386 for six to eight months. However, the decision to move this development effort before the technology was too far along reduced the amount of NIH experienced by the Portland team. At the same time, Fab 3's charter (including manufacturing of 286 microprocessors, ramping the 1.5-micron technology for the 386 microprocessor into production, and developing the 1-micron technology for the 386 microprocessor technology) was simplified. By March of 1985, Fab 5 produced the first functional 1Meg DRAM die. A total of five batches were produced that spring before DRAM development ground completely to a halt.

Uncertainty in manufacturing. Although Intel seemed successful in keeping its key technology development and manufacturing resources focused during the transition in late 1984, several implications of the DRAM exit decision were ignored. The charter of the Fab 5 TD team was clear by late 1984, but the associated Fab 5 manufacturing organization was struggling without a mission. The old friction between the technology and manufacturing divisions flared, as each blamed the other for the DRAM failure. Almost a year would pass from the November 1984 decision to stop developing DRAM technology, before a decision was reached to close the Fab 5 DRAM production facility and stop manufacturing DRAM altogether. During 1985, Fab 5 produced primarily 256K CMOS DRAM, and sought to demonstrate its capabilities to produce state-of-the-art products. They scrambled to fill a role at Intel, attempting to qualify as the second source for the microprocessor products currently produced at Fab 3.

Lingering resistance to DRAM exit. From the Components Group's perspective there was still a series of unanswered questions in the 1984–85 period. Jack Carsten, senior vice president and general manager of the Components Group (to whom the Memory Components Division as well as the Microprocessor Division reported), was still not convinced that Intel should discontinue manufacturing the existing generation of DRAMs, but was wondering where it should be done. Carsten had recently suggested that Intel acquire fabrication facilities in Japan to keep Intel in touch with the latest Japanese equipment advances and advances in DRAM manufacture. He also argued that Intel's inability to earn profits on manufacturing DRAM was more a result of the extraordinarily strong U.S. dollar than any Intel failure. In any case, he thought that Intel should utilize the Korean DRAM foundry option.

In mid-1985, as the fate of Fab 5 still hung in the balance, a group in the Memory Components Division evaluated options to outsource Intel's novel 256K CMOS DRAM. In fact, the division's future relied on finding such an outsourcing arrangement. In the summer of 1985, the division evaluated the feasibility of both Japanese and Korean arrangements. Neither Fab 5 manufacturing nor technology development had much interest in supporting an outsourcing alternative. By September of 1985 the outsourcing plan was abandoned; the Korean firms were considered not technologically advanced enough and Intel's top management feared giving competent Japanese competitors either technology or access to Intel's distribution system.

At this point it was clear that Memory Component Division's future as a DRAM organization was ending fast. In the face of lingering organizational resistance, COO Andy Grove took charge of the implementation of the exit decision. He reassigned Jack Carsten to another position and later went to visit the Oregon site, addressing the personnel there with the statement, "Welcome to the mainstream of Intel." By the end of the fourth quarter of 1985, Fab 5 had become a microprocessor fabrication site and some 250 DRAM manufacturing personnel were without jobs.

Going out in style. Memory Products organized an "end of life build" of the 256K CMOS DRAM product at Fab 5, which was being executed well by the lame duck manufacturing organization. Memory Products worked with its DRAM customers, finding alternative sourcing arrangements when possible. By the end of 1985, Fab 5 had built enough DRAM (at record manufacturing yields) to supply Intel's DRAM customers through the transition to other DRAM suppliers. By early 1986 Memory Products had placed its personnel, with the exception of a handful of DRAM design engineers, in new positions at Intel.

Fab 5 was not the only manufacturing facility affected by the 1984 exit DRAM decision. Three Assembly and Test facilities associated with DRAM remained open well into 1986. Barbados was the site of Intel's DRAM assembly operations, with most post-assembly testing done in Puerto Rico or in Santa Cruz, California. Labor costs in Barbados were approximately double those of Asian facilities. Intel management realized that the separation of assembly and test facilities hindered the integration of fabrication, assembly, and testing, and that the long feedback loop between testing and fabrication contributed to a longer development cycle.

Stage 6: Opportunities for Creative Destruction of Organizational Routines

The organizational turbulence generated by the DRAM exit decision, and the lack of decisiveness in making the decision to begin with, made top management more keenly aware of serious problems with the way Intel's strategic development and key aspects of its operations had evolved. Top management had the opportunity to engage in what Andy Grove during one of the interviews called "internal creative destruction" of outdated or simply inadequate approaches, and to replace them with more effective ones. The link between technology development and manufacturing, the company's concept of technology drivers, and top management's approach to strategic planning had been key areas ripe for internal creative destruction.

Improving the TD-manufacturing link. During 1985, Fab 5 (Oregon) was reequipped and redirected to the task of manufacturing microprocessor products. In the midst of a semiconductor recession, during which Intel posted several quarters of heavy losses, the company spent some $60 million to revamp the Fab 5 facility to "Class 10" clean room standards.[20] This helped to effect a 4-inch to 6-inch wafer size conversion and to put in place 1-micron technology capital equipment up-grades. Decisions to convert Fab 5 to 6-inch wafer size and to use a shrink process for the 386 processor as the early test vehicle were made in 1986. The Portland TD group, in the mean time, was "growing up"—learning what it takes to run a fab.

In the spring of 1988, Fab 9.1 in Albuquerque was designated as the first pro-duction facility for the 1-micron 80386. In contrast to the early years, when tech-nology development and production were done at the same site, the development fab and the production fab were now geographically separated. Production engi-neers from Albuquerque were brought to Portland for nine months to participate in process development. Portland team members went up to Albuquerque to help bring up the process. The former system of rules to govern the roles and responsi-bilities of TD and manufacturing which were based on an elaborate system of mile-stone achievement evolved to a system in which the transition points between TD and manufacturing were overlapping. The Portland technology development effort was not considered successful—and the TD team could not start work on the next process—until production ran smoothly at high yields in Albuquerque. Andy Grove had promised shipments within one year, and Fab 5 and Fab 9.1 delivered on the promise.

New thinking about technology drivers. Top management belatedly recognized in 1984 that its small remaining DRAM activity could hardly support further the idea of DRAM as the company's technology driver. On the other hand, it was also clear that microprocessors could not serve as the technology driver either. This was so because of the long and unpredictable design cycle of microprocessors, and be-cause demand for a generation of microprocessors typically ramped up much more slowly than for a generation of memory products and remained low on a unit basis. However, Intel technologists were discovering that the conventional view of a technology driver based on large cumulative volume might be increasingly irrele-vant. Sunlin Chou, the leader of the DRAM TD group, observed during an inter-view in 1989: "You don't learn quickly when you increase volume by brute force. You have to learn by examining wafers. Learning is based on the number of wafers looked at, analyzed, and the number of effective corrective actions taken. Even if you have processed 1,000 wafers, the technical learning probably only came from the 10 wafers you analyzed. Technical learning is time and engineering con-strained, not number of wafers constrained."

Gerry Parker, Intel's vice president of technology development in 1989, had a somewhat different perspective on the issue of technology drivers: "I spend a lot of time now on following what the DRAM people are doing and talking with equip-ment manufacturers. . . . We try to stay in the mainstream by purchasing the most advanced equipment, but then we optimize it to maximum advantage for our products. . . . I certainly don't want to minimize the importance of process development. . . . But, the latest equipment is essential to getting the highest yields."

DRAM epilogue

Intel sold no DRAM products for several years. In 1987 a small Intel group (Components Contracting) worked with Samsung in an effort to obtain a DRAM supply source for Intel resale or Intel internal use. By 1989, Intel Components Contracting sold some $100 million of foundry-built (primarily by Samsung) DRAM profitably. Intel could again serve customers who wanted one-stop shopping or Intel's quality/reliability guarantee. Soon after the failure of the U.S. Memories venture[21] (which was supported by the U.S. semiconductor industry and the U.S. government), Intel signed an exclusive marketing and technology agreement with NMB Corporation in which it agreed to market 100 percent of NMB's DRAM output in exchange for automation technology transfer.[22]

One senior manager mentioned that sometime in late 1988, Andy Grove made a presentation to Intel employees using a chart with the title "Businesses in which Intel has had success and businesses in which Intel had failed." This manager said he cringed at the thought of having to sit through yet another discussion of the failure of DRAM. But he was amazed and surprised when Grove described DRAM as a complete success for Intel. Grove reportedly said that the DRAM business had supported the company for over ten years, had been well managed, and had developed key corporate resources that were redeployed when needed most. Finally, it was a business that Intel exited at just the right time.

IMPLICATIONS

Intel's founding came about, at least in part, because Fairchild Corporation did not want to support the autonomous strategic initiative of Robert Noyce and Gordon Moore that centered around the newly emerging MOS technology. Noyce and Moore saw new business opportunities associated with the new technology that were not apparent to Fairchild's corporate management, or which Fairchild's management was not willing to develop even though the company had spent significant resources on the R&D efforts that produced the new technology. This experience led Noyce and Moore to decide that Intel would not do R&D that is exploratory and not directly related to product development. Intel's founding thus provides additional evidence that unexploited R&D spillovers of established companies

(AT&T's Bell Labs and Xerox's Palo Alto Research Center come most readily to mind) constitute a technological substratum that spawns new variations in the form of start-up companies.

> **Insight 2.1.** High-technology start-ups are often founded as a result of autonomous strategic initiatives that emerged within, but were not supported by, established companies.

The story of Intel's transformation suggests that corporate transformation involves several generic stages resulting from the interplay of internal and external processes of variation, selection, retention, and competition.[23] External variation increased as different sorts of new competitors, some similar (Mostek) but others quite different (vertically integrated Japanese new entrants), offered new products and deployed new competencies. Internal variation increased as new competencies and new products (EPROM and microprocessors) came about. External selection changed with the competitive landscape, but also as a result of suppliers and customers gaining increased bargaining power.

Internal selection changed as competition between existing and new products for scarce resources exerted itself, partly influenced by external selection (for instance through the effect of the manufacturing resource allocation rule, which favored high margin products). External retention was manifest as new winners emerged (the Japanese) and losers (including Intel) exited. Internal retention was manifest in the changing relative importance of different businesses. At the end of the transformation process, both the industry and Intel had completely changed.

> **Insight 2.2.** Corporate transformation involves distinct stages that take shape as a result of the interplay of the key evolutionary processes.

The story of Intel's transformation also suggests that the evolutionary path involved in corporate transformation was not envisaged *ex ante*. Rather, the evolutionary processes shaped it in surprising ways. Top management clearly did not set out to transform Intel from a memory company into a microprocessor company, but eventually realized that Intel had evolved into a microprocessor company.

> **Insight 2.3.** The evolutionary path of corporate transformation is seldom clearly envisaged *ex ante*.

Finally, the story of Intel's transformation shows that the evolutionary path taken did not meet the criterion of "historical efficiency," which views evolution as a rapidly optimizing force.[24] Historical efficiency assumes that evolution brings about empirical regularities as if by a design consistent with a particular theoretical explanation. Intel's transformation clearly did not follow the path of rapid adjustment to external conditions that would be prescribed by traditional strategic management theories and by most management consultants. The evolutionary perspective treats historical efficiency as a hypothesis that is part of the research agenda rather than as an assumption.

> **Insight 2.4.** Corporate transformation seldom follows the optimal evolutionary path prescribed by traditional strategic management theories.

CONCLUSION

Intel's genesis and transformation raise questions that are not usually asked, nor readily answered, by traditional theories of strategic management. For instance, why did Intel's extremely talented and able top management fail to adjust the strategy of its core business to cope better with changing industry forces? Would Intel not have been better off if it had done so? And, why did it take these brilliant top managers several years to come to grips with the reality that Intel had become a microprocessor company? Should they not have been driving strategic change? On the other hand, the organizational ecology view does not provide much insight either. Although suffering from some forms of inertia, Intel was eventually able to adapt and regain control of its destiny.

This chapter provides some evidence that Intel's transformation is best understood in terms of an evolutionary perspective on strategy-making. To be sure, the path of Intel's transformation was not clear *ex ante,* and it did not follow an optimal adaptive trajectory specified by theory. The data show, however, that Intel was able to generate new internal variations that were more viable than existing ones in the external selection environment and to internally select and retain some of these, even without clear and direct guidance of top management. Intel's transformation thus demonstrates the importance of strategy-making as adaptive *organizational* capability, that is, a capability that transcends the traditional view of top management as the prime mover of strategy-making. But this, in turn, also highlights the need to examine in more detail how strategy-making as adaptive organizational capability works. With that in mind, chapters 3–5 revisit Intel's transformation with the help of the tools of the evolutionary research lens.

3 DYNAMIC FORCES DRIVING COMPANY EVOLUTION

If strategy is about gaining and maintaining control over the company's destiny, Intel's defeat in its core DRAM business was an unequivocal failure of strategy. During 1985 and 1986, company revenues fell as top management discontinued several low-margin product lines and reduced the workforce of 25,400 by 7,200. In 1986, Intel incurred a net loss of $173 million—the largest (and last) loss in its history. For many companies, this would have entailed the end of their existence. Yet, Intel was able to rise phoenixlike from the ashes of its memory business and transform itself into a microprocessor company. How did this happen? And why was it possible?

Intel's evolution during Epoch I offers unusually rich data to study a strategic business exit and corporate transformation.[1] Intel's exit from the DRAM business raised the issue of why the evolution of its firm-level distinctive competencies failed to match the evolution of the basis of competition in the DRAM industry.[2] Intel's transformation into a microprocessor company, on the other hand, raised the issue of how its distinctive competencies generated more viable new business opportunities. The study of Intel's evolution during Epoch I, in short, offers insight into the process of dynamically matching distinctive competencies with evolving opportunities, and into the internal and external selection processes through which the mix of businesses in which a company competes changes over time.

The issue of dynamically matching firm-level distinctive competence and industry-level sources of competitive advantage is important for all firms facing structural industry change that causes shifts in the basis of competition. Yet, theory about the coevolution of firm-level distinctive competence and industry-level sources of competitive advantage remains underdeveloped. Existing theory views the development of distinctive (or core) competencies and the matching of distinctive competencies with business opportunities as key tasks of top management, reflecting strategic intent and foresight.[3] The strong normative orientation of this view overlooks the possibility that the matching of competence and opportunity may be governed, to some extent, by evolutionary processes as well as by design.

DYNAMIC FORCES DRIVING FIRM EVOLUTION

The evolution of Intel's DRAM business raised six puzzling questions. First, it was unclear why Intel, the first successful mover in DRAM, failed to capitalize on and defend its early lead. This question focused attention on the changing industry structure and Intel's evolving strategy in DRAM. It required examining why Intel, a company well suited to developing, marketing, and profiting from innovative products, would not or could not effectively compete in commodity businesses. This, in turn, required examining how inertial forces associated with Intel's distinctive competence affected its competitive responses. Second, it was unclear how it was possible that the bulk of Intel's business had shifted away from DRAM and the DRAM market share was allowed to dwindle while top management, even in 1984, was still thinking of DRAM as a strategic business for the company. This question directed attention to sources of inertia in official corporate strategy and to actions by middle-level managers that were not in line with the professed corporate strategy of Intel, the memory company.

Third, it was unclear how middle-level managers could take actions that were not in line with the official corporate strategy. This question directed attention to the role played by Intel's internal selection environment, constituted by its organization structure, its resource allocation process, and its culture of constructive confrontation. Fourth, it was unclear how, if not planned by top management, EPROM and microprocessors came about at Intel in the first place. This question focused attention on the evolution of Intel's distinctive competence, which produced unanticipated innovations, and on its internal ecology of strategy-making through which these innovations became part of the corporate strategy. Fifth, it was unclear why it took Intel's top management almost a year to complete the exit from DRAM after the November 1984 decision not to market 1Meg DRAM. This question helped determine that Intel was not simply harvesting the DRAM business and helped clarify further the intricacies top management faced in determining which key elements of distinctive competence associated with DRAM to retain and how to do so. Finally, it was unclear why it took top management several years to realize that Intel was no longer a memory company and had already transformed itself into a microprocessor company, and how this transformation had happened without a preceding reconsideration of the corporate strategy.

A Framework of Dynamic Forces Driving Firm Evolution

Addressing these questions suggested that the stages in the strategic business exit process could be explained in terms of the framework of dynamic industry-level forces and dynamic firm-level forces—Tool I discussed in chapter 1. The conceptual framework constituted by the five dynamic forces is reproduced in figure 3.1.

Intel's Distinctive Competencies

These three major technological competencies were involved in semiconductor products: (1) circuit design (Can we design it?), (2) process technology development, called TD (Can we make it?), and (3) manufacturing engineering (Can we manufacture it in large volumes with high yields?).

TD was a silicon-based competence: It involved the sequence of physical

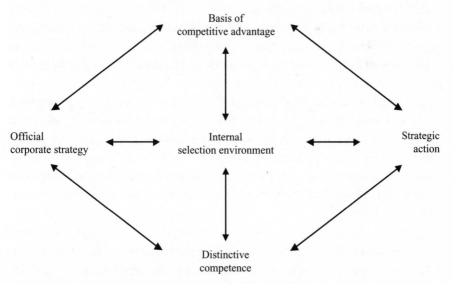

Figure 3.1. Dynamic Forces Driving Firm Evolution. (SOURCE: Adapted from R.A. Burgelman, "Fading Memories: A Process Theory of Strategic Business Exit in Dynamic Environments," *Administrative Science Quarterly* 39 (1994), p. 31.)

steps necessary to put multiple layers of masks on a chip. Circuit design was not a silicon-based competence. It referred to the ability to define patterns on each layer of mask. As Dean Toombs pointed out, DRAM required a very tight relationship between circuit design and TD. TD was also significantly different from manufacturing engineering, which was primarily concerned with reaching high yields of functioning chips. TD activities involved device physics and materials science. TD scientists asked questions such as "Can this material carry enough current?" By defining the process technology, the TD scientists limited the degrees of freedom available to the manufacturing engineers. They set the parameters (e.g., deposition pressure, exposure energy, etch gas mixtures) within which the manufacturing engineers could adjust their process equipment. Manufacturing engineers needed to characterize the product's performance in terms of these parameters. They asked questions such as "How often does this lithography tool need to be realigned?" Or, "How many wafers can be processed in this etch bath before device performance or yield degrades?" And, "What is the mechanism that causes the degradation? How can this mechanism be monitored?"

In the early stage of the DRAM industry, when production volumes and minimum acceptable yield levels were relatively low, the difference between the activities and concerns of TD and manufacturing engineering was not very salient. Intel naturally viewed TD as its distinctive competence because TD made the difference in its initial success. Intel also developed a distinctive competence in integrating TD and manufacturing. From the start, Intel's founders perceived this integration to depend on geographic proximity. They decided to keep the TD and manufacturing activities together at a fabrication facility (fab) and to perform all process technology research directly on the production line. This approach resulted initially in the ability to make rapid incremental process changes and to stay ahead of competition using TD. Intel also developed a distinctive technical marketing competence early on. Top management understood the need to educate customers to help them use the new semiconductor memories in their product development. Intel formed the Memory System Operation, which assembled DRAM chips with the required peripheral controller circuitry for sales to original equipment manufacturers (OEMs). OEMs bought these assemblies and put them together into complex systems for end users.

Dynamic distinctive competencies. Intel's initial success was based on its core DRAM business, but early on, its technological competencies generated two important innovations. EPROMs and microprocessors were unplanned new technologies with major commercial potential. When he invented EPROM, Dov Frohman was trying to understand and remedy a strange phenomenon that was causing reliability problems with Intel's MOS process technology. Even though there were no immediate market applications, CEO Gordon Moore decided to support the new technology.

Microprocessors came about because a Japanese calculator company contacted Intel for the development of a new chip set. Ted Hoff, an Intel technologist, saw the opportunity to build a simple set of a few general-purpose chips that could be programmed to carry out each of the calculator instructions. The new device later became known as the microprocessor. Busicom originally owned the design but eventually sold the right for all noncalculator applications back to Intel. Initially somewhat reluctantly, Intel began to sell microprocessors to other customers for a variety of applications.

Changing relative importance of distinctive competencies. The growing microprocessor business, however, triggered a process of major change in the relative importance of different distinctive competencies within Intel. By the mid-1980s, as Andy Grove put it: "Intel had moved from a silicon-based distinctive competence (TD) in memory products to a distinctive competence in implementing design architectures in logic products." Figure 3.2 provides a rough estimate, informally confirmed by top management, of the relative importance of different distinctive competencies for the memory and microprocessor businesses.

Designing a microprocessor was qualitatively different from designing a memory product. The value added in microprocessor development was in logic design and in being able to interconnect a highly irregular array of building-block cells (product design). Mastering microprocessor design complexity became relatively more important than the ability to increase chip density (process design). The first microprocessor designs had only a few thousand transistors and were designed, developed, and tested manually. Throughout the seventies and early eighties, constant TD advances led to a quadrupling of the "transistor budgets" available to designers every two-to-three years. Gordon Moore pointed out a dilemma: The time consumed by the product design process increased geometrically with the number of transistors in the design. Moore predicted that without dramatic advances in computer-aided-design (CAD) technology, the time to design a microprocessor would quickly become an insurmountable bottleneck in the product development cycle. Under Moore's impulse, Intel embarked on a massive program to build design expertise and CAD tools, investing more than $250 million between 1983 and 1987. A written memorandum stated: "Prior to 1981 our [design] tool mix was 70 percent externally sourced, 20 percent externally sourced and modified, and 10 percent internally developed. . . . By 1985, it was 15 percent, 30 percent, 55 percent." The CAD tools and a growing library of successive genera-

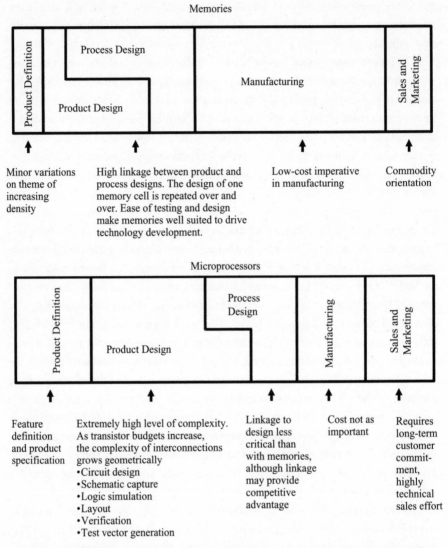

Figure 3.2. Relative Importance of Different Distinctive Competencies for Competitive Advantage: Memories versus Microprocessors. (SOURCE: R.A. Burgelman, "Fading Memories: A Process Theory of Strategic Business Exit in Dynamic Environments," *Administrative Science Quarterly* 39 (1994), p. 39.)

tions of circuit designs constituted new complementary assets supporting Intel's growing skills in implementing microprocessor design architectures.

Figure 3.2 also indicates that the microprocessor business required Intel to reinforce its product definition and technical marketing and sales competencies to get "design wins"—orders from customers who designed Intel chips into their products. As with DRAM earlier on, a key to success was the ability to educate customers on how they could use the new products in their own product design. But the design win in microprocessors was very different from the memory design win because many more factors needed to be coordinated to cultivate a customer relationship. In microprocessors, the customer made a long-term decision about a chip architecture and thereby chose a very limited number of suppliers. In memories, the customer only made a short-term decision because other chip companies were certain to enter with compatible products in all but the smallest niche markets. The mutual commitment between Intel and its customers required Intel to provide customer training and development aids, and to ensure upward compatibility between successive generations of products. The mutual dependence between Intel and its customers grew dramatically over time, requiring high reliability and quality consciousness. Marketing's growing relative strength within the organization was evidenced by an increase in sales, general, and administrative expenditures from 16 percent in 1976 to 19 percent in 1984 (while sales grew sevenfold).

Aggressive task forces helped Intel get many design wins against Motorola, including IBM's selection of the 8088 as the central processing unit (CPU) for its first personal computer. These efforts were significantly enhanced by the availability of development tools for customers, the sales of which exceeded for a while the microprocessor sales themselves, and by Intel's emphasis on showing customers the upward compatibility path of next-generation product.[4]

Process technology (TD), however, remained very important. Intel divided its technology development into three groups that represented the three major TD areas: DRAM, EPROM, and microprocessors. The three groups each developed distinctive competencies that related to their product responsibilities. The DRAM group was viewed as distinct from the other two teams because DRAM TD, as noted earlier, required a very tight relationship between product design and TD. The DRAM TD group led the company in linewidth reduction, which involved the ability to define patterns of ever narrower dimensions and to invent creative ways of reducing the required number and size of components per memory cell. Reduced linewidth allowed greater circuit density and greater performance and thus created higher value. The DRAM TD group was already developing a 1-micron process while the microprocessor TD group was still developing a 1.5-micron process. Both EPROM and microprocessors benefited from the DRAM TD group's distinctive competence in linewidth reduction.

Basis of Competitive Advantage in the DRAM Industry

Shifting basis of competitive advantage. Many of the strategic forces in the DRAM industry changed significantly in the late 1970s and early 1980s.

New entrants. Soon after the successful launch of Intel's 1103 DRAM, competitive product introductions appeared. Texas Instruments and Mostek were early entrants. Mostek, a start-up, challenged Intel's technological leadership as of the 4K generation. Texas Instruments was a manufacturing-oriented company driven by an experience curve-based engineering discipline. More ominously, large vertically integrated Japanese consumer electronics and computer firms targeted the semiconductor memory industry as "strategic" and entered as of the 64K generation with the intention to dominate. At the time, the Japanese companies were on average about an order of magnitude larger than Intel and were excellent in large-scale precision manufacturing. They had reason to be confident they could beat the U.S.-based semiconductor companies just as they had previously beaten the U.S. consumer electronics companies. As noted earlier, this led to aggressive capacity expansion and price competition on their part.

Government as a force: Japan Inc. Although it is too easy to attribute Intel's defeat in DRAM to actions taken by MITI, the Japanese government agency nevertheless played an important role in orchestrating cooperation between the Japanese new entrants. The Reagan administration, which was not strongly focused on antitrust issues, eventually concluded that the Japanese semiconductor companies were actively engaged in dumping practices. Also, Japanese economic policy contributed to the significantly lower cost of capital faced by the Japanese entrants.

Technology. The difference between competitors' product offerings quickly disappeared. Beginning with the 4K generation, Intel's DRAM became the basis for a dominant design.[5] This allowed competitors (initially Mostek) to focus on optimizing the dominant DRAM design. New DRAM generations followed each other in highly predictable two-to-three-year cycles. Personnel migration between semiconductor companies in the United States led to diffusion of the DRAM technology and further leveling of technical competencies, and made it more difficult for companies to build and hold on to proprietary intellectual property in DRAM.

Customers. As the DRAM industry matured, customers demanded tens of thousands of units of a single product. Large numbers of wafers were needed to satisfy OEM customers. Initially, DRAM was sold to engineers in the OEM customer organization, but with the product becoming more widely used and in much larger volumes, professional buyers took over the procurement function. These new customers were no longer willing to accept any batch with a reasonable number of functioning DRAM. They demanded high quantities of DRAM with guaranteed performance, reliability, and price.

Suppliers. Semiconductor equipment suppliers, in particular the photolithography equipment suppliers, became an important source of innovations in manufacturing and the key to increasing yields. Japanese suppliers began to offer superior equipment. Nikon's chief technical officer explained that Nikon's photolithography equipment had a mean-time-to-failure that was an order of magnitude better than that of U.S. equipment suppliers, but Nikon's equipment was not available in the United States until 1986.[6] In the meantime, large Japanese DRAM manufacturers, such as Fujitsu, NEC, and Hitachi, focused on establishing strong relationships with Japanese equipment suppliers. By involving equipment suppliers in the continuous improvement of the manufacturing process in each DRAM generation, top Japanese DRAM producers were able to reach yields that were sometimes 40 percent higher than those of top U.S. companies.

Commoditization of DRAM. The changing industry forces inexorably led DRAM to become a commodity product. As a result the new key factors determining competitive advantage in the DRAM market were manufacturing capacity and manufacturing competence. To be a viable competitor, a company needed to be willing to commit increasingly large capital investments to DRAM capacity, and to develop the necessary discipline in manufacturing to quickly obtain high initial yields and continuous yield improvements for each DRAM generation. This shift in the basis of competitive advantage favored the tightly managed manufacturing-oriented firms over the more innovative but less disciplined TD-oriented Intel.

The changing basis of competition in the memory business strained the relationships between Intel's TD and manufacturing groups and called into question the company's routines for integrating the two groups. The changes made the difference between TD and manufacturing engineering activities salient and important as production volumes in DRAM increased dramatically between the early 1970s and early 1980s. TD scientists continued to see their task in terms of process innovation, revolutionary change, and technical elegance. Manufacturing engineers, in contrast, now saw their task in terms of stability, incremental change, and technical simplicity to reach higher yields. TD scientists were expected to evaluate and introduce new process equipment and materials (e.g., process gases) that enable technical advance. Manufacturing engineers, however, now realized that these changes required recharacterizing the process, a painful and time-consuming relearning of the process parameters and how and when to adjust them.

Increasing the emphasis on large-scale manufacturing engineering competence was difficult for Intel. The early technical heroes at Intel had been TD scientists who understood a fundamental physical phenomenon and converted it into a working product prototype. The line separating TD and manufacturing at Intel was drawn at the point of creating a functioning prototype. Recharacterizing or tweaking the manufacturing processes had been consistent with Intel's strategy of being first to market with premium-priced products. Tweaking had worked in the past and it had been a source of pride for Intel's manufacturing engineers.[7]

Inertial competitive responses. Struggling to maintain a competitive advantage, Intel continued to rely on innovative TD efforts through several successive DRAM generations. For four successive product generations, the DRAM TD group came up with an innovative process solution that was ahead of its time. In 1979, Intel introduced the first 5-volt single-power-supply 16K DRAM. Intel expected the 64K DRAM generation to be introduced later and to be based on single-power-supply. Fujitsu introduced a standard 64K DRAM in 1979, however, and captured a large market share. The single-power-supply 16K DRAM remained a niche product, and Intel fell behind in manufacturing yields relative to top Japanese producers. In 1982, Intel's 64K DRAM with redundancy entered production. Intel expected that redundancy would help overcome its disadvantage in manufacturing yields relative to the Japanese and that the 256K DRAM generation would be based on redundancy. This time, however, its plan was thwarted by Fujitsu and Hitachi, which entered with a standard 256K DRAM in 1982 and captured a large market share. In 1983, Intel decided to produce a Complementary MOS (CMOS) 256K DRAM and to cancel the standard n-channel MOS (NMOS) 256K DRAM effort. In 1984, Intel introduced first a 64K CMOS DRAM and then a 256K CMOS DRAM and was the only supplier of these chips. Intel hoped to offset its manufacturing cost disadvantage with a technically superior product. Intel expected that CMOS would become the standard for the 256K and later DRAM generations, but it did not become the standard for the 256K generation. During mid-1984, the DRAM TD group was working on the 1Meg DRAM generation and focused on an advanced capability in thin dielectrics, which allowed them to reduce minimum feature size to 1 micron instead of changing the entire DRAM cell design. The DRAM TD group estimated its design was two years ahead of the competition.

In each of these instances, however, Intel's innovative TD effort did not produce competitive advantage for the relevant DRAM generation. Intel technologists saw the new technological advances as the leading edge. Marketing people saw them as niche products with higher margins. They hoped that the entire market would quickly go for the new technology. Even the up to double margins available with the niche products, however, were unattractive given the low margins in the commodity markets to begin with. Also, while the market did go for Intel's TD innovations eventually, it always did so for later generations. Intel's inertial competitive responses resulted in the company's losing its strategic position in DRAM over time. By 1980, Intel's market share had dwindled to ninth in the industry.

Official Corporate Strategy

Intel's official corporate strategy was also subject to strong inertial forces. By 1980, the company's total market share in DRAM was less than 3 percent. Yet, rational justifications for staying in DRAM were put forward by CEO Gordon Moore and by Vice President of Sales Ed Gelbach. Moore continued to support the idea of DRAM as the company's technology driver and made sure that Intel continued to fund DRAM TD at the same level as other, more successful businesses. In 1984, for instance, DRAM was estimated to account for only about 5 percent of Intel's $1.6 billion sales revenues. Yet, budgeted expenditures for DRAM TD for 1985 were estimated to be roughly one-third of total R&D. DRAM was viewed as the technology driver because it was still the largest volume product produced by Intel, and was perceived to be the basis of the company's learning curve. This was, in retrospect, a weak justification given that Intel's market share was much smaller than that of its rivals.

Vice President of Sales Ed Gelbach continued to support DRAM based on the idea that Intel needed to offer a one-stop semiconductor shopping list of products to its customers. Given Intel's low market share in DRAM relative to its market share in microprocessors, this was also a weak argument. Gelbach, however, was concerned that Intel had a reputation for moving out of products with declining margins and leaving customers to fend for themselves. This was especially important in DRAM because Intel had been the first and in 1984 was still the only firm offering CMOS DRAM. Gelbach recalled: "In board meetings, the question of DRAM would often come up. I would support them from a market perspective, and Gordon [Moore] would support them because they were our technology driver. Andy [Grove] kept quiet on the subject. Even though it wasn't profitable, the board agreed to stay in it on the face of our arguments."

Emotional attachment by many top managers to the product that had "made Intel" was also part of the inertial force. In the course of the interviews, most managers mentioned emotional factors to explain why it had taken so long for Intel to get out of the DRAM business. One senior manager, for instance, said that Intel had lived on DRAM and that it was therefore difficult to get out: "It was kind of like Ford deciding to get out of cars." Gordon Moore said that Jack Carsten, the general manager of Intel's Components Division, had the strongest feelings about it, because he came from Texas Instruments and was in favor of commodity businesses. Carsten confirmed that it had been an emotional time and that it had been difficult to be rational. He said that his dilemma was excruciating and that he couldn't get the company to make a decision that would allow him to take appropriate actions. In the spring of 1985, it was difficult to get the company to discuss the issue but his business managers were desperately hammering him for decisions while losses were increasing. Carsten said that he tried to get Gordon Moore on one side and Andy Grove on the other. Grove felt very strongly that all resources should be in logic and that he wanted to turn the DRAM TD group into an advanced logic R&D group. Grove's vision for Intel was in microprocessors. Carsten quoted Grove as saying, "Don't worry about the memory business, it is not important to our future." Gordon Moore said that Grove ultimately prevailed, and he himself stepped down in the summer of 1985. Grove then assumed direct operational control. Another middle-level manager also said that top managers were torn by their emotions but that Andy Grove had told him to "make data-based decisions and not to fear emotional opposition."

Bounded rationality in seeing the implications of events signaling strategic change also played a role in the relative inertia of Intel's corporate strategy. Strategic change is usually clearer in retrospect than during the period when it is happening, especially in high-velocity environments. Important events are often the result of the accumulation of smaller steps that are mixed with the multitude of routine events at any given time. Gordon Moore pointed out: "While IBM's use of our microprocessor and our dropping out of the DRAM market seem like independent, dramatic, rapid decisions, they really weren't. They were a series of smaller decisions that ultimately led to a final dramatic outcome."[8]

The decline of the DRAM business within Intel was signaled by an incremental decrease in commitment of manufacturing capacity to DRAM, but the implications of these incremental decisions were not immediately clear to top management. Similarly, the enormous importance of the personal computer for Intel's microprocessor business was not immediately obvious. Intel's list of the top fifty anticipated applications for the 80286 microprocessor, the successor to the 8088 microprocessor chosen by IBM for its first personal computer, did not include the personal computer. Andy Grove later pointed out that if Intel had foreseen the dramatic growth of the personal computer business, it might have been easier to exit from the memory business.

A valid top management concern, however, was that DRAM was viewed as a distinctive technological competence of the company, not just a product. The tight link between product and process design in DRAM made it easier to do failure analysis on memory products than on logic products. Engineers could use the test failure pattern to locate the physical locations of failure on a DRAM device much more quickly than on a microprocessor. In 1984, a new technological development led to a divergence between DRAM, four-transistor static random access memory (SRAM) and six-transistor SRAM technology, and it was unclear to top management which of these memory technologies would best support failure analysis for logic products. Also, as noted earlier, the DRAM TD group was farthest along in linewidth reduction, a critical competence for all products including microprocessors. It was relatively easier to design a leading-edge geometry (1 micron in 1984) in DRAM than to design a leading-edge geometry in microprocessors. Top management was concerned that exiting from DRAM might result in losing the DRAM TD group. Hence, while the exit looks surprisingly slow from the point of view of corporate strategy, it is less clearly so from a distinctive competence point of view.

Recalling how the matter was finally resolved, Andy Grove, Intel's chief operating officer at the time, emphasized the difficulty top managers experience in dissociating themselves from the strategy that made the company successful in the past:

> Don't ask managers, What is your strategy? Look at what they do! Because people will pretend. . . . The fact is that we had become a nonfactor in DRAM, with 2 to 3 percent market share. The DRAM business just passed us by! Yet, many people were still holding to the "self-evident truth" that Intel was a memory company. One of the toughest challenges is to make people see that these self-evident truths are no longer true. I recall going to see Gordon [Moore] and asking him what a new management would do if we were replaced. The answer was clear: Get out of DRAM. So, I suggested to Gordon that we go through the revolving door, come back in, and just do it ourselves.

Internal Selection Environment and Strategic Action

An important administrative element of Intel's internal selection environment was the requirement that product divisions share fabs. Sharing was facilitated by the fact that fabs could, initially, be fairly easily converted from DRAM to EPROM or microprocessor production. DRAM, EPROM, and microprocessors would be given minimum capacity allocations to maintain long-term market position. In times when demand was strong and capacity constrained sales, however, product division managers would get together monthly to decide on how to load the factories based on the rule of maximizing margin-per-wafer-start. The adoption of this rule reflected the fact that Intel's businesses were characterized by high asset intensity, and return on sales was important for profitability. Bob Reed, Intel's chief financial officer at the time, said that the difference between margins for DRAM and for the highest margin products (microprocessors) could be an order of magnitude (see table 2.2).

Incremental decline in DRAM capacity allocation. The rule to maximize margin-per-wafer-start not only guided manufacturing resource allocation but also captured a great amount of information about internal and external conditions. It was clear that high margins reflected Intel's competitive advantage in microprocessors. But the maximize margin-per-wafer-start was a rule that would systematically lead niche markets to be selected over commodity markets. Choosing niche markets was consistent with Intel's historical strategy of premium pricing for leading-edge products. Also, whereas the maximize margin-per-wafer-start rule led to short-term but not necessarily long-term profit maximization, the rapid growth in demand for Intel microprocessors made it difficult for managers associated with the memory business to challenge the internal allocation rule. Within fabs capable of producing both memory and microprocessor products, the allocation rule led to a gradual change in mix in favor of microprocessors. Intel's capital investment in DRAM gradually declined relative to the fast-growing DRAM market and relative to the capital investment in microprocessors. By 1984, DRAM production was restricted to one fab out of a network of eight plants. Microprocessors, in contrast, had become the largest component in Intel's sales revenue by 1982, and continued to grow in relative importance. EPROM still represented more than 15 percent of sales in 1982, but its share in Intel's sales was declining in the period 1982–1985. The strategic position of the DRAM business within Intel gradually deteriorated as a result of the incremental decline in the allocation of manufacturing resources.

These allocation decisions contradicted top managers' beliefs about the importance of DRAM and gradually undermined the legitimacy of the DRAM business in Intel's corporate strategy. As middle-level managers in the DRAM business experienced difficulties in obtaining capital investment—which, in turn, made it more difficult to compete—they proposed that Intel restructure itself. A 1982 proposal to align the Memory Components Division with a dedicated DRAM manufacturing capability was rejected by top management. A 1984 proposal to invest approximately $80 million for a DRAM-exclusive facility was also rejected.

Open debate. An important cultural element of Intel's internal selection environment was the tradition of encouraging open debate about the business merit of different strategic initiatives, constructive confrontation, and the rule that knowledge power should not be overwhelmed by hierarchical position power. Andy Grove maintained that at Intel "no one was ever told to shut up." This made it possible for some middle-level managers of the DRAM business to challenge the way Intel was pursuing the business. At the same time, however, some others were making decisions that implicitly or inadvertently undermined the idea of Intel as a memory company and pushed the company further toward becoming a microcomputer company. While top management continued to view DRAM as a strategic business, and the new corporate strategy of Intel the microcomputer company had not yet become articulated, some middle-level managers made decisions that capitalized on the rapid growth of the microprocessor business and further dissolved the strategic context of DRAM.

Trade-offs in process technology choice. Ron Smith made the key decision to drop work on the four-transistor SRAM process technology and to focus all effort on the six-transistor process technology that would also benefit the 80386 microprocessor development. This middle manager's decision implied that resource trade-offs between the memory and microprocessor businesses now went beyond allocating manufacturing capacity and needed to involve the process technology foundation of the memory business. This decision further contributed to the dissolution of the strategic context for commodity memories, including DRAM. As Andy Grove pointed out earlier, this decision "inherently favored logic [microprocessor] rather than memory advances." It also "limited the decision space within which top management could operate." And, it meant that "the faction representing the microprocessor business won the debate even though the 80386 had not yet become the big revenue generator that it would eventually become." By the end of 1984, top management was finally forced to face up to the dissolving strategic context for DRAM. It was clear in November 1984 that to regain leadership in the 1Meg DRAM implied a capital investment of several hundred million dollars. The 1Meg DRAM investment decision thus forced a test of Intel's real strategic commitment to the DRAM business. Top management decided against it. The November 1984 decision not to put the 1Meg DRAM in production eliminated the possibility of Intel's remaining a player in the DRAM business.

New Strategic Harmony

During the period bracketed by the November 1984 decision not to put the 1Meg DRAM in production and the October 1985 decision to stop producing DRAM altogether, Intel top management struggled with implementing the exit decision. Top management attempted to juggle the need to "stop the bleeding" in DRAM with the need to maintain continuity and take advantage of competencies that would be lost by "cutting off the leg." Some senior managers attempted to take advantage of what Andy Grove called "top management's dancing around the exit decision" by continuing to try to find alternative approaches to stay in DRAM after all. The existing organizational structure impeded implementation, since those who had to make the changes—especially the general manager of the Components Division—were being asked to make themselves less important to the organization. As noted earlier, in the summer of 1985, COO Grove imposed change by restructuring the organization and reassigning senior managers.

The delay in implementation was also at least in part due to top management needing time to sort out and protect the distinctive competencies associated with the DRAM business that were also important to Intel's other businesses. Between November 1984 and March 1985, the DRAM TD group was allowed to continue working on 1Meg DRAM prototypes, thereby preventing the almost certain loss of some of the most important TD talent in the company. Top management also decided in December 1984 to assign the group the task of shrinking the 386 microprocessor to 1 micron, which assured the continuation of technology leadership in microprocessors. Realizing that top management had waited a long time to bring Intel's official corporate strategy in line with the realities of internal resource allocation, COO Grove went to visit the DRAM TD group during the third quarter of 1985. He addressed the group with the unequivocal, "Welcome to the mainstream Intel," thereby forcefully articulating Intel's new corporate strategy as the world's leading microcomputer company.

The exit from DRAM also offered the opportunity for top management to cause what Andy Grove called the internal creative destruction of routines that, while associated with past success, had outgrown their effectiveness and needed to be changed. A key example was the geographical basis of integrating process technology development and manufacturing. By the end of 1985, top management no longer viewed the transfer of process technology from TD to manufacturing as dependent on geographical proximity but, rather, on creating the appropriate incentive system. TD was no longer allowed to start a new process technology until manufacturing was able to get the previous one up and running in the factory with the help of TD.

As noted earlier, Sunlin Chou's group was perhaps the first to realize that learning curve effects could be attained through intelligent statistical analysis of a limited number of wafers as well as through the brute force of large-scale wafer production. And Gerry Parker had decided that working with suppliers of semiconductor equipment had become an effective way to track the advances of the DRAM producers and to make sure that Intel's own manufacturing capabilities for microprocessors remained state of the art. Intel also learned that it could strike effective alliances with world-class, large-scale manufacturers of DRAM, such as NMB in Japan, and sell the devices as part of its product offerings without having to incur the ever-increasing capital investments in fabrication facilities for memory products.

Looking back at the DRAM experience, Intel top management realized that, on balance, the strategic business exit from DRAM had worked well for Intel. Andy Grove could go around the company and retroactively rationalize the strategic exit from DRAM. That is, he confirmed that earlier strategic actions, while not guided by official corporate strategy, had nevertheless been beneficial for the company.

IMPLICATIONS: THE ROLE OF STRATEGY-MAKING IN COMPANY EVOLUTION

Forms of Internal Inertia

Relative inertia in distinctive technological competence. Previous research found inertial tendencies in the strategic responses of companies faced with various forms of technological innovation.[9] Often these companies had to exit certain businesses or, in some cases, they were disbanded. Intel continued to rely on TD competence to compete even though the basis of competitive advantage in the DRAM industry had shifted to competing on manufacturing. Inertia in Intel's technological competence deployment did not preclude it from trying to adapt, but it influenced the trajectory of adaptive efforts. Inertial forces led to adaptive efforts based on TD advances that were, in four successive DRAM generations, too early in relation to industry dynamics. Dwindling market share eventually forced Intel to exit from the DRAM business. Companies thus must take seriously the inertial forces engendered by strong distinctive competencies, which impede the continued matching of competence with the evolving basis of competition in the industry.

> **Insight 3.1:** The stronger a firm's distinctive technological competence, the stronger the firm's tendency to continue to rely on it in the face of industry-level changes in the basis of competitive advantage.

Earlier findings also showed that core competence may become a competence trap or core rigidity.[10]

Inertia associated with strong competence is the bad news. The good news is that strong competence is the wellspring of new possibilities. The productive potential of a company's technological competencies is likely to extend beyond the boundaries set by its product-market strategy at any given time. Deep technological competencies may engender unanticipated innovations that are outside the scope of the official corporate strategy.[11] Through the interaction with the external environment, such innovations may trigger coevolutionary processes that change the mix of the firm's distinctive technological competencies as well as its product-market strategy. Inertia looked at with dismay from current product-market positioning or portfolio-planning perspectives may thus sometimes be looked at more favorably from a resource or competence-based perspective.[12]

> **Insight 3.2:** The stronger the firm's technological competence, the higher the probability that it will generate unanticipated innovations that, if successful, will change the firm's mix of distinctive competencies and product-market position.

Insight 3.2 does not imply that unanticipated technological innovations are necessarily viable, nor that the firm will necessarily pursue them. But it does suggest the need to reexamine the processes driving technological leaders and first movers. It seems quite possible that such competitive stances—often associated with a technology push—may originate from inertial forces associated with the firm's distinctive technological competence as well as from official corporate strategy.[13]

Inertia of official corporate strategy relative to strategic action. There was also relative inertia associated with Intel's official corporate strategy. While Intel is widely regarded as one of the most innovative and adroitly managed high-technology firms, the DRAM exit story suggests that even extraordinarily capable and technically sophisticated top managers, such as Gordon Moore and Andy Grove, do not always have the foresight of the mythical Olympian CEO making strategy. Rational justification, emotional attachment, and bounded rationality, mixed with valid concerns about protecting the core technology of the firm, made it very difficult for Intel's top management to exit from DRAM. At the same time, actions by some middle-level managers responding to external and internal selection pressures had already begun to dissolve the strategic context of DRAM and undermine the reality of Intel, the memory company. Incremental shifts in the allocation of scarce manufacturing resources from DRAM to microprocessors and technological trade-offs favoring microprocessors over DRAM happened before the official corporate strategy was restated. Strategic actions often diverge from statements of strategy,[14] resource allocation and official strategy are not necessarily tightly linked,[15] and strategic actions of complex firms involve multiple levels of management simultaneously. Middle-level actions also provide potentially important signals about the evolution of external selection pressures especially in dynamic environments.

> **Insight 3.3:** In dynamic environments, actions of middle-level managers that diverge from official corporate strategy may signal important changes in external selection pressures.

The Role of Internal Selection

Internal selection prevents the escalation of commitment. To some extent Intel was lucky that their products and fabs were fungible, which reduced exit barriers, and that the maximize-margin-per-wafer-start rule prevented escalation of commitment to the DRAM business during the period that Intel's official corporate strategy was in flux.[16] This short-term oriented rule, in isolation, might equally well have thwarted development of new technologies or strategic thrusts, but this rule was only one element of the internal selection environment created by top management. The maximize-margin-per-wafer-start rule required product divisions to compete for shared manufacturing resources and forced open debates concerning resource allocation. The criteria governing these debates were constructive confrontation based on knowledge rather than hierarchical position, and economic performance in the marketplace rather than success in internal politicking. These criteria ensured that the internal selection processes accurately reflected the competitive pressures faced by different businesses in their external environment. They became the focal point around which the organization came together and prevented the coevolution of its distinctive competence and the basis of competition in the DRAM industry before the official strategic decision to exit from DRAM had been made.[17]

Once established by top management, the internal selection environment constrained the purposeful behavior of individual participants.[18] It was difficult, even for the top managers themselves, to deviate from the criteria constituting the internal selection environment. As DRAM began to lose out in the resource allocation process, middle-level managers of the DRAM business attempted to change Intel's structural context and lobbied for their own manufacturing resources to compete better as a commodity business. But they could not escape thorough debate and could not win their case. Even though top management continued to invest heavily in DRAM TD, it did not interfere with the manufacturing capacity allocations that were decided at lower levels in the organization. Eventually, CEO Gordon Moore and other top managers accepted the results of the internal selection processes.

Insight 3.4: Firms whose internal selection environment accurately reflects external selection pressures are more likely to strategically exit from some businesses than firms whose internal selection environment does not accurately reflect external selection pressures.

Internal selection links competence with new opportunity. The dissolution of the strategic context of DRAM was facilitated by the emergence of new distinctive competence-based business opportunities within Intel. Internal entrepreneurial initiatives brought competition for resources within the boundaries of the firm and forced it to make strategic choices. By favoring microprocessors over memories, the internal selection environment reinforced the coevolution of distinctive competence and the basis of competition in the microprocessor industry, before the new strategy of Intel the microcomputer company was in place. The strategic choices shifted resources away from the memory business to the microprocessor business, thus causing strategic renewal. Strategic renewal, in turn, made it easier to exit from the memory business.

Insight 3.5: Firms that have new businesses competing with existing businesses for relatively scarce resources are more likely to make a strategic exit from existing businesses than are firms that are not confronted with such strategic choices.

Earlier research on the restructuring of the global petrochemical industry and the steel castings industry in the United Kingdom suggested that financially strong and diversified companies are often the first to exit.[19] Also, diversification through internal entrepreneurship may motivate firms to evaluate the opportunity cost of existing businesses and activate divestment processes.[20]

Internal selection depends on strategic recognition capacity. To some extent, Intel was also lucky in having a distinctive competence base capable of generating new, high-growth business opportunities that provided alternatives to the DRAM business. But Intel's top management needed to be able to recognize their importance and support them in-house. Gordon Moore allowed Dov Frohman to pursue the EPROM development before there was a clear market need for it. Top management responded to Ted Hoff's championing by buying back the rights to the microprocessor before microprocessors were established in the market. Later on, although top management had not yet redefined Intel's corporate strategy in terms of the microcomputer company, it resisted the efforts of some middle-level managers to redefine the strategic context of DRAM within Intel and to commit the company to competing on the terms required by a commodity business. Top management recognized that Intel was neither oriented toward nor equipped for competing in a commodity business. Thus, determining the strategic context for a new business (microprocessors) and dissolving the strategic context for an existing one (memories) depended critically on top management's ability to see the broader strategic implications for the firm of initiatives of middle-level managers before market signals definitively confirmed their strategic importance. Strategic recognition implies the possibility of self-reflexive evaluation of means and ends in the light of changing circumstances but without having to resort to foresight or grand strategy. It also does not assume that top management is necessarily the prime mover in strategy. Rather, it is predicated on strategic initiatives of middle-level managers that top management can assess and support or not support. Strategic recognition augments the adaptive value of the internal selection environment.

> **Insight 3.6:** Firms that have top managers with strong strategic recognition capacity are more likely to make strategic exits from businesses than firms that have top managers with weak strategic recognition capacity.

Strategic recognition capacity must, of course, be established independent of a given strategic exit decision. A top manager's record in supporting and rejecting previous middle-level strategic initiatives could measure that person's strategic recognition capacity, for instance.

Internal selection produces organizational learning. The dissolution of the strategic context for DRAM concluded with retroactive rationalization efforts by top management. The exit decision had required top management to examine DRAM strategically, from a distinctive competence perspective as well as from product-market and financial results perspectives. Retroactive rationalization affirmed that the outcomes of the strategic exit were beneficial from the firm's point of view and explicated why that was the case. Top management now took the explicit position that strategic exit was a natural part of competing in high-velocity environments. Once top management had brought the official corporate strategy back in line with the realities of viable strategic actions by middle-level managers, the strategic learning process continued. Top management was now ready to examine the other semiconductor memory businesses in light of the new official corporate strategy of Intel as a microprocessor company. It was ready to set the stage for the strategic exit from EPROM manufacturing, thereby further freeing up resources for the microprocessor business. Exiting from memories had required top management to consider why staying in the microprocessor business was more attractive. Top management understood more clearly that, as Andy Grove put it, Intel's distinctive competence now resided in implementing design architectures in logic products.

> **Insight 3.7.** Firms that have strategically exited from a business are likely to have a better understanding of the links between their distinctive competence and the basis of competition in the industries in which they remain active than are firms that have not strategically exited from a business.

Alternative Conjectures

What would have happened if Intel's top managers had understood more quickly that DRAM were no longer viable and had actively sought to diversify their business portfolio? Would they have done better? Or suppose Intel had more closely tracked the evolving basis of competitive advantage in the DRAM industry. Would it have done better? These questions cannot be answered definitively in the context of this study because it was not possible to set up an experiment. But they raise important issues concerning alternative concepts of corporate strategy and forms of adaptation. From a portfolio-planning perspective, the delay in exiting the DRAM business could be viewed as a manifestation of crippling inertia, but such a perspective does not consider the implications of exit for the firm's distinctive competencies. While the study confirms that business exit is viewed by top management as an investment decision, it also suggests that top management is concerned with identifying the elements of distinctive competence associated with the failing business that have the potential to be transferred to new businesses.[21] As noted earlier, this requires time and a capacity for recognizing the important aspects of competencies as well as appreciating the financial performance characteristics of different businesses. The conjecture supported by previous research is that Intel would probably have done worse if it had simply divested the DRAM business and entered new businesses through acquisition.[22] Intel would have dissolved the strategic context for DRAM too soon and thereby failed to capitalize on the full potential of its distinctive competencies in DRAM. Some of these competencies could be effectively deployed in the microprocessor business, which represented an opportunity for strategic renewal for Intel. Hence, the time involved in dissolving the strategic context for DRAM helped prevent strategic change that might have been too rapid.[23]

Adaptation through strategic renewal is quite different from adaptation through tracking the basis for competitive advantage in the industry. Intel did not closely track the basis of competitive advantage in the DRAM industry. If Intel's top managers had chosen to follow the logic of competitive advantage in the DRAM business, they would have had to commit hundreds of millions of dollars to a commodity market characterized by relatively low and highly volatile margins. Again, the conjecture is that Intel probably would have done less well.

CONCLUSION

During Epoch I, Intel transformed itself from a memory company into a microprocessor company. This transformation did not follow the path prescribed by traditional approaches to strategic management. Top management did not have a grand strategic plan for the transformation that could be implemented through an induced strategy process. The transformation happened as a result of various, seemingly somewhat uncoordinated, actions. Some of these involved autonomous strategic initiatives; some others were responses to the company's structural context. Most of them had unanticipated consequences that helped the transformation process along. And it took top management a fairly long time to realize that the transformation had actually happened.

Several lessons about the role of strategy-making in a company's evolution can be learned from Intel's transformation during Epoch I. The first lesson is that the strategic business exit has implications for a company's distinctive competencies as well as for its product-market position. This implies that company leaders need to understand the linkages between a firm's businesses in terms of distinctive competencies and should view a strategic business exit as part of the learning process. While some have made the normative case for this, this chapter shows that it is quite difficult.[24] Gordon Moore and other top leaders were worried that selecting against the DRAM business unit would also select against the distinctive competencies associated with that unit. It took them a while to find ways to selectively retain and redeploy the competencies while selecting against the organizational unit that contained them.

The second lesson is that Intel was able to transform itself from a memory company into a microprocessor company because its distinctive competencies generated alternative business opportunities. This suggests that top management should nurture the development of the company's distinctive competencies and be willing to transfer key competencies to new product-market activities before these product-market activities have become powerful in the firm. Again, this seems to be sound normative advice. But this chapter indicates that this is particularly difficult if the new opportunities are outside of the scope of the corporate strategy as defined by top management at the time of their occurrence. While hard to believe in retrospect, this was the case with microprocessors at Intel in the early 1970s.

A third lesson is that Intel was able to transform itself because top management had evolved an internal selection environment that was more adaptively robust than the official corporate strategy. The implication of evolving such an internal selection environment is that strategic actions by middle-level managers will sometimes diverge from official corporate strategy and may signal important environmental changes. Top managers must develop a capability for strategic recognition to guide the organization. They must guard against approaches that will mask or eliminate disharmony without addressing the underlying divergences that cause it.

A fourth lesson is that as time goes by, top management's beliefs about the strategic situation facing the company and the reality of that strategic situation are highly likely to diverge in important ways. Even extraordinary, talented top managers such as Gordon Moore and Andy Grove were subject to this, at least for a while. A fifth and related lesson, however, is that a strategic business exit is not equivalent to failure and that new leadership does not necessarily imply new leaders. Andy Grove understood that Gordon Moore and he could walk through the revolving door, retake charge, and do the difficult job of exiting from DRAM themselves. But the implication here is that top leaders must be willing and able to break with the past—sometimes their own illustrious past.

Finally, this chapter provides insight into strategy-making as adaptive organizational capability needed for long-term survival. Dynamic competence that generates new variations, internal selection that correctly reflects external selection pressures, and top management's capacity for recognizing and retaining viable strategic initiatives are key components of such organizational capability. Strategy-making as adaptive organizational capability results in the timely expansion and contraction of internal support for different businesses. This, in turn, leads to the firm's entering into and exiting from businesses on the basis of its evolving distinctive competencies and the evolving basis of competition.

4

COEVOLUTION OF

GENERIC AND

SUBSTANTIVE

STRATEGIES

Exiting from DRAM taught top management why the microprocessor business was more attractive than the semiconductor memory business and top management acted accordingly. This exit from DRAM also taught top management that strategic exit was a natural part of competing in dynamic environments.[1] Once top management had brought Intel's official corporate strategy back in line with the reality of strategic action, the learning process continued. Top management was now ready to examine the other semiconductor memory businesses in light of the new official corporate strategy. Intel still retained its strategic position in electrically programmable read-only memory (EPROM) and had also begun developing a new semiconductor memory called Flash. The exit from DRAM had revealed a deep and persistent tension within Intel. This tension existed between those who favored continuously moving toward product markets that valued leading-edge technology highly and those who argued that Intel should learn to compete better in existing product markets as competition intensified rather than exit and move on.

The tension arose from the divergence of Intel's generic and substantive strategies. Generic strategy and substantive strategy are two facets of a company's corporate strategy. *Generic* strategy refers to the way in which a company competes. Differentiation and cost leadership are generally recognized as the most important types of generic strategy.[2] *Substantive* strategy refers to the specific product markets that a company competes in. At founding, Intel's generic and substantive strategies were congruent. In principle, generic and substantive strategies should coevolve commensurably. Throughout Epoch I, Intel's generic corporate strategy remained based on differentiation: to maintain and exploit technical leadership and to sell leading-edge products that could fetch premium prices. Intel's substantive corporate strategy, however, changed significantly during Epoch I from memory products to microprocessor products.

THE EVOLUTION OF EPROM AND FLASH MEMORY AT INTEL

The study of the evolution of Intel's DRAM business suggested a framework encompassing the six stages discussed in chapter 2. These are (1) initial success in the emerging industry, (2) competitive challenges and response, (3) internal competition for resources, (4) growing internal doubts about the viability of the business, (5) strategic exit decision and implementation, and (6) internal creative destruction of obsolete routines. While these stages were not neatly separated, they served to bracket key events and strategic leadership challenges. This framework also serves to examine the evolution of EPROM and Flash memory.

Stages in the Evolution of EPROM

Stage 1: Development of EPROM and initial success. Dov Frohman invented EPROM. As a recent hire from Fairchild in 1969, Frohman was assigned to help understand and remedy a strange phenomenon that was causing reliability problems with the MOS process. Frohman saw that the phenomenon could be explained by the existence of an unintentional "floating gate" within the MOS device (the floating gate is the structure in an EPROM device that allows a memory cell to be programmed and later erased). He realized that if a floating gate were intentionally constructed, a new type of programmable memory, which would permanently store information, could be built. Frohman's story has become legendary at Intel. He not only invented the product, he also described the physical phenomenon, saw that it could be applied to a memory device, designed the first part, and fabricated the first device. Frohman recalled: "We put together a 16-bit array with primitive transistor packages sticking out of the 16 sockets, an oscilloscope and pulse generator, and we carted all this into Gordon's office. There were red bulbs to indicate the bits. This was all new to us, and we were thrashing around. We showed Gordon that by pushing the button you could program the device, and we demonstrated that it would hold a charge."[3]

Later, it was discovered that ultraviolet light could be used to erase the memory. Gordon Moore committed Intel to the production of the EPROM even though no one could tell where the device would have applications.

No one foresaw that microprocessors would create a booming market for EPROM. The original four-chip design for the 4004 microprocessor, Intel's first microprocessor, was general purpose except for the read-only memory (ROM) which had to be customized at the factory for each application. The EPROM could substitute for the ROM and provided two advantages: the designer of a custom product could develop and revise the ROM-resident microprocessor programs quickly; and smaller applications, which could not afford the expense of a custom ROM, could substitute off-the-shelf EPROM.

Intel's distinctive competencies in EPROM. Intel stayed in the lead with new EPROM generations and gained and retained a majority market share until the late 1970s. Competitors had trouble imitating Intel's floating gate process. Ron Smith, manager of the SRAM and microprocessor TD group in the early 1980s, said: "If a device physicist were confronted with the EPROM out of the blue, he might be able to prove that it won't work. The EPROM process has as much art as science in it, not only in the wafer fab but in the packaging, testing, and reliability engineering." In 1977, Intel introduced the 16K EPROM, which was compatible with any microprocessor system. All alone with the floating gate process, Intel enjoyed a boom in EPROM for several years. As Gordon Moore pointed out, the somewhat fortuitously expensive EPROM was not designed out by Intel's OEM customers and remained its most profitable product line until 1985.

Stage 2: Competitive threats and responses. By 1981, however, the industry faced a cyclical downturn, and Intel's virtual monopoly in the EPROM market was challenged by several competitors, including NEC and Hitachi. The industry average selling prices for the 16K EPROM dropped by 75 percent in 1980. Intel management responded by accelerating the introduction of the 64K EPROM. Intel decided to retrofit the new Fab 6 at Chandler, Arizona, with a new photolithography technology called stepper alignment.[4] Fab 6 had just come on line and was idle. The gamble was significant, involving a new plant, a new product, a new process, and lots of new people. But the 64K team met the very aggressive yield goals, and Intel was again leading the world in EPROM sales. By mid-1981, Fab 6 had produced hundreds of thousands of units and output was doubling every quarter. In 1986, Intel commanded a 21 percent market share of the $910 million market versus 17 percent of a $860 million market two years earlier. In 1989, EPROM was manufactured in five of Intel's fabrication sites. Intel's continued dominance in the EPROM business arose partly from a successful legal battle, during the mid-

1980s, against Hitachi and other Japanese companies accused of selling EPROM below cost in the United States.

In September 1986, Intel's top management asked a middle-level manager to prepare a study of the memory business and to make recommendations for Intel's long-term strategy. This manager recommended that Intel maintain its position in the EPROM business, in part because it was an important technology for a new form of memory called Flash. Intel decided to keep the EPROM operation for two major reasons: as a relatively high-volume product to drive learning and as an enabling technology for the microcontroller business.

Keeping us honest. Craig Barrett, executive vice president and general manager of the Microcomputer Components Group, who had been put in charge of manufacturing at the time of the implementation of the DRAM exit decision, commented on the importance of large-volume products for Intel in 1989. Barrett observed that staying in EPROM might be important, not so much because EPROM provided scale advantages for learning, but because this product provided a critical linkage between Intel and its competitive environment—a reality test of sorts. Barrett explained that Intel had learned to appreciate the limits of volume as a technology driver, but nevertheless valued having some high-volume products. He said:

> I think that the industry used the notion of technology driver as a crutch. We were late in waking up to the fact that we did not need to run volume in order to learn. There are other ways to be intelligent. You don't have to depend on volume if you depend on good engineering.
>
> We have data to show that our learning as represented by lowering defect density has actually accelerated in the past two generations when plotted either as a function of time or as a function of cumulative wafers put through the fab. For each generation since 1985—1.5 micron, 1 micron, and most recently 0.8 micron—each defect-density trend line is downward sloping with the most recent generations having the steepest slopes.
>
> While we have some volume from our EPROM line and we make lots of efforts to transfer learning from one facility to another, we focus on basic techniques to accelerate learning: design of experiments, statistical process control, and just plain good engineering.
>
> While we do have a lot of high-margin wafer starts, we still have a significant mixture of products. We have 256K EPROM, 1Meg, 2Meg, and just recently 4 Meg in addition to our microcontrollers which are all very cost sensitive. We chose to stay in those commodity businesses partly because it does "keep us honest." Of course, it also represents a

significant part of our revenue and it helps to amortize R&D expenditures.

Initial symbiosis with microcontrollers. Intel had developed a line of microcontrollers that integrated logic and memory (both SRAM and EPROM) to provide a self-sufficient, one-chip computer. The microcontroller business had products in the 4, 8, and 16-bit market segments. They were used to control everything from house fans to complex satellites. Their prices ranged from one dollar to several thousand dollars per chip. Gerry Parker, Intel's Vice President of technology development in 1989, suggested that integration of EPROM technology with microcontrollers was an effort to lift EPROM from a commodity product status. Parker mentioned that Intel had developed a modified EPROM process, which allowed some logic to be added to the periphery of the device. This was another effort to lift EPROM from its commodity product status.

Stage 3: Internal competition for manufacturing capacity. EPROM faced internal competition from other products, first microprocessors and later Flash memory.

Internal competition from microprocessors. While there was a symbiotic relationship between the EPROM and microcontroller businesses, Intel's fast-growing microprocessor business required some trade-offs in capital allocation. At the end of 1985—in part because Dov Frohman had moved his technology development work to Israel—Intel converted the new fabrication site there that was originally designed for EPROM to the new 386 microprocessor products. This was done to support the "sole source" strategy, which Intel had adopted for its new 386 processor (see chapter 6).

Gerry Parker suggested that the same "death spiral" which had been responsible for killing the DRAM business—financial and marketing focus on more profitable products, manufacturing's preoccupation with the sexier devices, budget cutting, and some execution problems—might be happening to Intel's EPROM business. He said Intel was trying to find more profitable niche markets for EPROM, while ignoring severe manufacturing issues at the main plant that produced EPROM. The EPROM plant was Fab 7 in Albuquerque, New Mexico, which was built several years earlier ("a dog fab"). In the vicinity of Fab 7 was Intel's showcase Fab 9, which had just been started up to produce the 386. Even though the processing for the 386 microprocessor was significantly more complex, the yield figures coming out of Fab 9 were better than those from the EPROM plant. Parker said he told Andy Grove that the only way to improve Fab 7 was to get new furnaces—the ones there were originally for 4-inch wafers, later converted to

6-inch, and not state of the art. He said Intel could not hope to be competitive as EPROM became a commodity, because the competition was using state-of-the-art facilities.

Internal competition from Flash. As of 1988, Flash memory, a new form of nonvolatile semiconductor memory, started to compete for resources with EPROM. Flash's primary use was to replace EPROM in specialized applications where a service call by a technician was difficult or expensive. Though relatively low volume, these early applications supported high margins because of the value of avoiding a service call. Over the next three years, the market grew quickly. Flash used the same process technology as EPROM. As demand began to increase, Flash began to substitute for EPROM production.

Stage 4: Growing internal doubts about EPROM. At the beginning of 1989, doubts about the future viability of EPROM in Intel's corporate strategy were growing. Andy Grove, during an interview in January 1989, said that EPROM was a useful capability for Intel: "But the question is, am I the best in the technology. If the answer is yes, I will fight tooth and nail. (In DRAM we weren't anymore.) That is why we decided to get out of DRAM. It could happen in EPROM as well."

In an interview later in the year, Grove said that he anticipated perhaps only one more generation of EPROM as a separate technology at Intel: "The margins are not good. The technology development costs are rising. The market is not large enough to amortize the investment. In addition, EPROM used to be an enabling technology for the microprocessors. But now they are again on their own." Commenting on how he reconciled the anticipation of not continuing a business with the need to convince people to keep working on it, Grove said:

> Not very well! It's a very ambiguous, sensitive deal. You need to be able to be ambiguous in some circumstances. You dance around it a bit, until a wider and wider group in the company becomes clear about it. That's why continued argument is important. Intel is a very open system. No one is ever told to shut up. But you are asked to come up with better arguments. People are allowed to be persistent. In EPROM, for instance, "X" [a manager who strongly believed that EPROM technology was important for a new form of memory called Flash] will work even harder to show you wrong. . . . It is always easier to start something than to kill something.

In 1990, however, it was clear that a relatively low margin business generating only about $200 million per year in revenue could not support all the associated development costs (informally estimated to be about $65 million a year). In late 1990, the vice-president in charge of all commodity chips proposed a new state-of-the-art EPROM-only plant. A compromise counterproposal involved a mixed charter (microprocessors and EPROM), but this executive believed that mixing commodity production and microprocessor production was tantamount to slow death for EPROM.

Stage 5: The EPROM exit decision. In early 1991, senior management decided not to go ahead with the EPROM-only plant. Instead, they decided to work with manufacturing partners in Japan to outsource production of EPROM while remaining involved in the design and technology development efforts for future generations. Later in 1991, Intel moved the whole EPROM team to Flash.

Stages in the Evolution of Flash Memory

Stage 1: Flash development. In 1983, Intel researchers were among the first to develop Flash memory technology. However, while Intel was a leader in Flash memory technology from the beginning, it was not given much attention during the early years of its development. Throughout the mid-1980s, Intel focused a great deal on electrically erasable programmable read only memory (E²PROM), a form of ROM that could be erased electrically (instead of with ultraviolet light) and reprogrammed at the user's factory. Flash was similar to E²PROM, except that it was less flexible; entire blocks of data must be erased and reprogrammed as a group—a more complicated process. Flash's advantage, however, was that it was much cheaper to produce.

Origin in skunk works. While work progressed on E²PROM, a small team of researchers continued to pursue Flash as a skunk works project with little top management support and a small budget. By 1986, E²PROM efforts had still not been able to produce a low-cost solution. Dick Pashley, the leader of the E²PROM development effort and general manager of the Flash Division in 1993, explained "That was when we decided that we should take another look at Flash." Reflecting on Flash in 1993, Andy Grove said: "Flash was a skunk works when the official strategy was E²PROM. We blew [a lot of money] on E²PROM. McCormick was the champion and wanted to supplant E²PROM. But EPROM (at the time) barely got capacity and Flash had to borrow from EPROM."

Serendipitous application for Flash. Flash was originally predicted to overtake rotating discs as the primary means of storing large quantities of data in a computer. As disk drive manufacturers continued to improve the performance of their drives, this prospect still seemed a long way off in the early 1990s. However, because Flash was a semiconductor device, it required much less power than a rotating disc. As Flash memory became denser and more affordable, it was increasingly used with low-power mobile computers. CEO Andy Grove noted: "We justified pursuing Flash because it was going to replace disc drives. Nobody ever talked about mobile computing. The market for Flash is taking off, but it is in a different market than we anticipated." In 1993, Grove said: "Now, Flash gets to be a big deal, but not as a substitute for disc drives. It is not a replacement product. So, it starts fitting into the corporate strategy. We have put $100 million per year to update the factories for Flash, but there has not yet been a big capital investment."

Stage 2: External competition. Determining the strategic context for Flash within Intel was in some ways easy, even though initially top management favored E²PROM. Vice president Gerry Parker explained in 1989: "Flash was a natural extension of EPROM; it was an improvement rather than a 90-degree turn." On the other hand, while Intel had some patent position in Flash, it was expected there would be intense competition. This raised the issue of whether Flash was compatible with Intel's differentiation-based corporate strategy. Parker also said: "So, is this going to be another DRAM scenario? It will be difficult to compete because you must be willing to lose a lot of money to conquer the market. Intel traditionally does not want to do that. It is a continued internal debate between those who want us to learn to compete and those who advocate a strategy based on value added through technology."

On the other hand, Flash became an important product for laptop PCs. As an enabler of mobile computing the strategic context of Flash within Intel became clearly established. As a result, as Andy Grove pointed out, Flash had started fitting into the corporate strategy.

Stage 3: Flash encounters internal competition. Like DRAM and EPROM, Flash had to compete for internal resources.

Flash wins internal competition from EPROM. In 1988, Intel introduced its first significant part, a 256K Flash memory. As noted above, Flash's primary use, in the first two years, was to replace EPROM in specialized applications where a service call by a technician was difficult or expensive. Though relatively low volume, these early applications supported high margins because of the value of avoiding a service call. Over the next three years, the market grew quickly. Flash used the same process technology as EPROM. As demand began to increase, Flash substituted for EPROM production. In 1991, the entire EPROM development team was redeployed to focus on Flash.

Internal competition from microprocessors in the late 1990s. Competition in Flash was intensifying in the late 1990s. This put pressure on margins and instigated a battle for market share. Intel's prospects in this business were diminishing, leading Flash to experience the selective pressures of the maximize margin-per-wafer-start. In an interview in August 1997, Craig Barrett, Intel's COO at the time, mentioned that the tension between commodity and specialty businesses within Intel was alive and well. He said:

> Last Friday, I got an e-mail about capacity allocation to Ron Smith's Semiconductor Group (where Flash was situated). It pointed out that if we upgraded the capacity and gave it to microprocessors, we would save a very large amount of money. However, if we want to be there, either we have our own capacity or contract it out. The long-term contract solution is not better in financial terms than owning it, because the depreciation must be paid for. We can afford to invest. We maintain the tension. Nobody will be happy. That's good!

STAGES IN STRATEGIC BUSINESS EXIT: A BRIEF COMPARISON

DRAM–EPROM Comparison

The stages of strategic business exit were roughly the same for EPROM, but the time taken by the different stages was generally somewhat different. Like with DRAM, Intel was the first successful mover in EPROM (stage 1). For EPROM, the competitive challenge (stage 2) came much later than for DRAM, in part because the knowledge about the physical phenomenon underlying EPROM and the technical knowledge involved in EPROM was more tightly contained within Intel. The competitive challenge in DRAM turned out to be overwhelming, in spite of Intel's ability to introduce technological advances that were ahead of the competition. Intel's success in resisting the competitive challenge in EPROM was, except for the 16K generation in the early 1980s, complete. As Gordon Moore, CEO at the time, put it, "Intel never missed a step" in the technology development for the various generations of EPROM products. Also, Intel benefited more from the semiconductor industry's successful efforts to mobilize the help of the U.S. government against the alleged dumping practices of the Japanese in the EPROM case than in the DRAM case. This offered some relief of competitive pressure from the Japanese for a while, and the company used this time to reestablish its leadership position.

While DRAM was the perennial loser in the internal competition for resources, EPROM continued to secure capital investment in spite of smaller margins than microprocessors beyond 1985, in part, because EPROM was an enabling technology for microprocessors. Like DRAM, however, a middle manager's proposal to invest in a new EPROM dedicated plant was rejected (stage 3). The period of growing doubts (stage 4) was longer for EPROM, in part because Intel still valued the relatively large production volumes involved and because of the initial symbiosis with microcontrollers. In the late 1980s, it became clear that EPROM had become a commodity product. EPROM had lost its role as enabling technology for microprocessors, and faced additional competition for manufacturing capacity from Flash. After it became clear that EPROM could not be sufficiently profitable to warrant further capital investment, top management was swifter to decommit to EPROM manufacturing than they had been with DRAM. Given the importance of the link with Flash, top management decided to keep funding, for a while, the EPROM design and technology development capability. Funding ended, however, in 1991, thereby completing the exit (stage 5). The exit from EPROM did not involve to the same extent creative destruction of obsolete routines. It also did not require a major reconsideration of the corporate strategy. Hence, stage 6 was not part of the EPROM exit process.

EPROM-Flash Comparison

Flash, too, seemed to go through the same stages as DRAM and EPROM. Flash replaced EPROM as Intel's main memory product in the early 1990s. But during the 1990s, Flash faced intense competition in the market and margin pressure. In the late 1990s, the reasons for staying in Flash had become strategic rather than financial. Top management continued to believe that competing in a commodity market helped keep the company honest about its real manufacturing prowess. In a session for Intel executives in fall 1997 when asked why Intel was staying in the Flash business, Andy Grove said: "It is important to have product lines that are not protected; where we must rely on raw manufacturing skills. Flash and microcontrollers are such product lines. You cannot just cherry pick the industry."

But it remained to be seen whether Flash would survive the continued pressures in Intel's internal selection environment. As the earlier reported quote from Craig Barrett indicates, Intel's internal selection environment continued to put pressure on commodity products, and it required top management decisions to prevent Flash from being systematically denied manufacturing capacity.

COEVOLUTION OF GENERIC AND SUBSTANTIVE CORPORATE STRATEGIES

Tension between Specialty and Commodity Products

During the late 1980s, Gerry Parker was worried that EPROM would suffer the same fate as DRAM. Parker believed that Intel should learn to compete in commodity businesses. During an interview in late summer 1989, Parker suggested that the trade-offs in capital allocation imposed by the internal selection environment illustrated Intel's attitude toward commodity businesses. He said: "There is a continued internal battle between some who want Intel to learn to compete [through manufacturing] and others who emphasize a focus on value added [through technology]."

Les Vadasz, senior vice president and general manager of Intel's System Business, confirmed that Intel's generic strategy was based on differentiation. During an interview in early summer 1989, Vadasz said: "The guiding question at Intel is where can we add intellectual value? Some semiconductor people used to grow crystal ingots (raw material for semiconductors), but they found they could not add value there. . . . DRAM has become like that. . . . The lowest value-added component in the chain always tends to spread, so you get perfect competition in that area."

Gerry Parker, however, expressed concern that Intel's systematic bias toward specialty products would narrow its manufacturing base and reduce the company's strategic flexibility:

> Just going with proprietary technology leaves you vulnerable. Customers may not like Intel's lock on them. . . . We could now manufacture everything in one and one-half plant! That's obscene. You need a broad product base—EPROM is natural because of its importance for microcontrollers—which allows you to keep more factories open. So you can switch if you have a proprietary technology winner. You are more flexible that way.

Divergence of Generic and Substantive Strategies

The tension between specialty products and commodity products is reflected in the divergence of the generic and substantive facets of Intel's corporate strategy during Epoch I. If everything had remained the same during Epoch I, no tension would have arisen between Intel's generic (differentiation-based) strategy and its substantive (semiconductor memory-based) strategy. Of course, everything did not remain the same. First with DRAM, then with EPROM, and later with Flash the tension between the generic and substantive strategy facets arose each time that the products involved became commodities. This tension thus became an enduring feature of Intel's strategy-making.

IMPLICATIONS

In principle, the generic and substantive facets of corporate strategy should be consistent with each other. During Epoch I, this was initially the case at Intel. The subsequent evolution of the generic and substantive facets of its corporate strategy, however, was not a smooth continuous process of mutual adjustment. The stages of strategic business exit show the emergence of misalignments between generic and substantive strategies. These misalignments resulted from the dynamic interactions among the forces that drove Intel's evolution.

Generic strategy is the most general and abstract facet of corporate strategy. It reflects the company's distinctive competencies and becomes embedded in its internal selection environment.

> **Insight 4.1.** A company's generic strategy derives from its distinctive competencies and is reflected in its internal selection environment.

Substantive strategy is the expression of generic strategy in a particular product-market domain. The endurance of substantive strategy depends primarily on how successful it is in the external selection environment. But it also depends on the capacity of the internal selection environment to correctly interpret the signals about the changing fortunes of the substantive strategy in light of the changing basis of competitive advantage. These signals drive the company's strategic actions.

> **Insight 4.2.** A company's substantive strategy changes as a result of external selection pressures, reinforced by the internal selection environment.

Accurately reading the signals about the competitive reality facing different businesses was an important feature of Intel's internal selection environment. But this would probably not have been enough to save the company during Epoch I. The internal selection environment also drove Intel toward a new, more viable substantive strategy that was consistent with its generic strategy. It could do so because Intel's dynamic distinctive competencies had generated more attractive options than those encompassed by the existing substantive strategy. DRAM withered away in the internal competition for resources because the internal selection environment favored the more externally viable options (EPROM, microprocessors). If those options had not been available, Intel would have had to hold on to its substantive strategy and its only alternative would have been to try bringing its generic strategy in line with the changing basis of competition in the DRAM industry. Given the association of generic strategy with distinctive competencies and its strong embedding in the company's internal selection environment, however, successful substantive strategy changes are likely to continue to reflect the generic strategy. In other words, when the external selection environment drives generic and substantive strategies apart, it is more likely that the substantive strategy will be changed consistent with generic strategy rather than the generic strategy being changed to fit with substantive strategy.

Insight 4.3. Successful changes in substantive strategy continue to reflect the company's generic strategy and its distinctive competencies.

Changes in substantive corporate strategy are difficult because substantive strategy is most readily associated with the company's identity in the external environment and people's emotional attachment. This was nicely expressed by a senior Intel executive who said that getting out of DRAM was for Intel like getting out of cars would be for Ford. Also, the DRAM case indicated top management's realization that substantive corporate strategy was no longer consistent with the generic corporate strategy took a fairly long time to take hold. This suggests a great amount of inertia associated with substantive corporate strategy. Eventually, however, substantive corporate strategy was changed but generic corporate strategy was not. Hence, generic corporate strategy is more enduring and may be an even stronger source of strategic inertia.[5]

Insight 4.4. Generic corporate strategy is likely to be more enduring than substantive corporate strategy, and also a stronger source of strategic inertia.

CONCLUSION

Intel's transformation involved a major change in the company's substantive strategy. Yet, the new substantive strategy was based on the same generic strategy as the one it replaced. A complete analysis of a company's evolution thus requires paying attention to both the generic and substantive aspects of corporate strategy. Considering only the generic aspect of Intel's corporate strategy would overlook the fundamental corporate transformation (from memory to microprocessor company). On the other hand, focusing only on the substantive strategy would overlook the remarkable continuity in the company's generic strategy (product leadership). Recognizing both facets of corporate strategy helps understand better the underlying dynamics of the tension that arises within the company's strategy-making process when specialty products become commodity products, as they almost always eventually will in dynamic industries.

Being alert to and resolving the strategic dissonance arising from diverging substantive and generic corporate strategies is an important strategic leadership challenge for top management. Top management can meet this challenge better if the internal selection environment correctly registers the changing competitive reality faced by its different businesses in the external environment. As the DRAM case shows, top management must be aware of the strong inertia associated with deployment of distinctive competencies. The increased awareness produced by the DRAM experience led top management to more quickly disengage in the EPROM case, resolving thereby the strategic dissonance. Top management's decision to stay in Flash and make the organization live with tension was also deliberate. It was to a large extent motivated by the desire to keep the company involved in an intensely competitive business to hone the company's competitive skills.

Viable new substantive strategy is likely to be consistent with a company's generic strategy and based on its distinctive competencies. For Intel, this meant that new business opportunities had to offer product leadership opportunities. Hence, while Intel's distinctive competencies during Epoch I were a strong inertial force from the perspective of the semiconductor memory based substantive strategy, they also turned out to be a source of tremendous dynamism generating a potentially new substantive strategy. Maintaining the generative potential of the company's distinctive competencies, as well as developing the capability to take advantage of them, are major strategic leadership challenges.

5

INTERNAL ECOLOGY

OF STRATEGY-MAKING

Intel's transformation, which marked the start of Epoch II, was remarkable because it was not the result of top management strategic intent as commonly understood. Rather, it was an outcome of the interplay of dynamic external (evolving basis of competition) and internal (evolving distinctive competencies) forces mediated by the company's internal selection environment. To be sure, top management played a crucial role in assembling the distinctive competencies and creating the internal selection environment in the first place, and in resolving the tensions that came about as the external and internal forces produced unexpected problems and opportunities. But levels of management below the top also made critical contributions to strategy-making. Intel's strategy-making during Epoch I could thus be usefully described in terms of adaptive organizational capability.

As is sometimes the case, insights derived from new and somewhat unusual research fit most readily, if unexpectedly, with theory that exists outside received theory in the field. In this case, the link is with the organizational learning and organizational ecology perspectives of evolutionary organization theory.[1] The organizational learning perspective of evolutionary organization theory focuses on how organizations search for and use information to try to adapt, that is, proactively manage their fit with the external selection environment, through internal variation, selection, and retention processes. While organizational learning does not necessarily lead to organizational adaptation—organizations can learn the wrong lessons—this perspective leaves room for cognitive processes and knowledge development that is purposeful, even if only myopically so, in driving organizational change. Strategy-making as adaptive organizational capability is one manifestation of the organizational learning perspective in evolutionary organization theory.

The organizational ecology perspective, on the other hand, suggests that organizational change must be understood at the level of entire populations of similar organizations, and as the result of replacement and selection rather than adaptation. Incumbent companies fail in the face of environmental change because inertia prevents them from adapting; new companies can replace them because they do different things or the same things differently or simply better in the eyes of the majority of customers. The study of Intel's exit from the DRAM business adds empirical evidence in support of organizational ecology, which leaves little room for adaptation based on strategy. Yet, strategy-making processes clearly helped Intel transform itself from a memory company into a microprocessor company, thereby preventing its demise. Hence, organizational ecology does not always provide a complete explanation of organizational change.

Established companies continue to remain subject to the selection force of the external environment. Many do in fact succumb to it in the long run.[2] But established companies have also gained the opportunity to substitute, to some extent, internal selection for external selection. This is the central idea of the internal ecology model of strategy-making.[3] An established company is an ecological system in its own right, and its survival and continued success depend on the functioning of this internal ecology. While ecological processes at the level of organizational populations (industries) involve organizational founding and disbanding rates, the internal ecology of strategy-making involves entering new businesses and exiting from failing businesses over time. Different parts of the internal ecology of strategy-making can be linked to different forms of adaptation, and this helps reconcile opposing ideas about various consequences of strategic change.

INTEL'S INTERNAL ECOLOGY OF STRATEGY-MAKING

Intel's Internal Ecology

Intel's evolution from a memory company into a microprocessor company during Epoch I is illustrated in figure 5.1, reflecting the outcomes of Intel's internal ecology of strategy-making. Logic (microprocessor-based) products gradually replaced memory products. At founding, Intel's vision was to be a leading semicon-

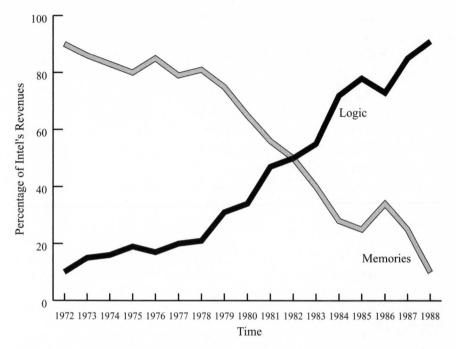

Figure 5.1. Intel's Evolution from Memory Company to Microprocessor Company. (SOURCE: R. A. Burgelman, "Intraorganizational Ecology of Strategy Making and Organizational Adaptation: Theory and Field Research," *Organization Science* 2 (1991): p. 241. Based on Andy Grove, Intel Corporation, presentation to New York Society of Analysts, February 1988, Figure 11.)

ductor memory company. In the early stages of the company's existence, memory products accounted for 90 percent of sales volume, and logic products accounted for only 10 percent. EPROM and then logic products began to crowd out DRAM in manufacturing during the late seventies. By 1982, logic products surpassed memory products in Intel's total sales, and continued to grow in importance relative to memory products. In 1984–85, Intel went through the traumatic experience of exiting from its core DRAM business. The success of the microprocessor business continued to crowd out EPROM. In the mid-1990s, Flash was struggling with the same forces.

Induced and Autonomous Strategy Processes

Figure 5.2 casts the variation, selection, retention, and competition processes of evolutionary organization theory in terms of the induced and autonomous strategy processes of Tool II. Variation corresponds to induced and autonomous strategic

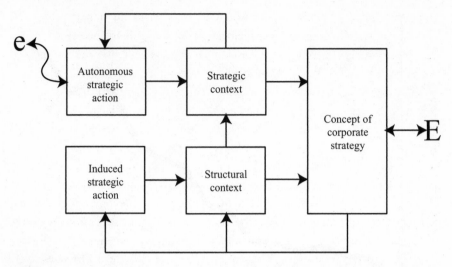

Figure 5.2. An Evolutionary Framework of the Strategy-Making Process in Established Firms. (SOURCE: Adapted from R. A. Burgelman, "A Model of the Interaction of Strategic Behavior, Corporate Context, and the Concept of Strategy," *Academy of Management Review* 8 (1983): p. 65.)

action; selection corresponds to the structural and strategic contexts; and retention corresponds to the concept of corporate strategy. The induced and autonomous strategy processes are simultaneously in play at any given time and are important determinants of a company's evolution. To the extent that a company's resources are limited, there is internal competition between induced and autonomous strategic initiatives.

Through the induced process, a company's strategic actions are joined over time, distinct patterns of company-level strategy are realized, the organization's character is maintained, and the company successfully reproduces itself over time in its familiar environment (**E** in figure 5.2). In a sense, the induced strategy process is a company's genotype: its genetic inheritance and makeup.

If genotype is a metaphor for a company's induced strategy process, mutation is one for its autonomous strategy process. Autonomous strategic action involves internal entrepreneurship. Internal entrepreneurs explore the boundaries of the company's competencies and opportunities. Without internal entrepreneurs, a company cannot know what it might be able to do. This does not imply of course that it should do all those things. Like most mutations, most autonomous initiatives do not survive—most new ideas are bad ideas—because they cannot continue to obtain resources. But like some mutations, some autonomous initiatives are important for the company's continued evolution. The selection of appropriate autonomous strategic initiatives for corporate support is an important but ill-understood function of senior management. At Intel, the emergence of the microprocessor was the most important autonomous strategic initiative during Epoch I, the story of which is told in detail below. Autonomous strategic action typically originates in relation to unfamiliar, emerging environments (e in Figure 5.2). Microprocessors initially had limited applications but eventually found an enormous application in microcomputers. Flash was originally viewed as a potential substitute for magnetic memory, but found an unanticipated major application in mobile computing (chapter 4).

Most of the time, autonomous strategic initiatives originate at lower levels in the organization, from persons close to the frontiers of technology, customers, and markets. But this is not always the case. Sometimes such initiatives originate at the top of the organization, in particular when company leaders believe that the company needs to match some important variation in the environment. Usually, but not always, top-driven autonomous initiatives involve acquisitions. Intel's acquisition of Microma, a solid-state watch company, in 1972 is an example (see below).

INTEL'S INDUCED STRATEGY PROCESS

Intel's Concept of Corporate Strategy

In the late sixties and early seventies, Intel was a successful start-up. Whether initial success is the result of competence or luck, top management's role is to articulate a corporate strategy that will help secure continued survival. Such a strategy is based, at least in part, on retrospective sense making and attempts to capture learning about the basis of the company's success. Of course, a corporate strategy largely based on retrospective rationality does not preclude prospectively rational efforts on the part of top management. One upper-level manager at Intel expressed this as follows in the context of the DRAM exit: "Grove has been preaching: Make the tough decisions! Don't do something tomorrow because you did it today." However, as we saw earlier, Grove himself was aware of how difficult it was to change what he called the "self-evident truths" that underlie a company's concept of strategy.

The self-evident truths that underlie a company's concept of strategy are top management's beliefs about four factors. These factors, together, constitute organizational learning. The first factor concerns distinctive competencies: what top management has learned the company can do better than others, which also determines its generic strategy (differentiation versus cost leadership). A second factor concerns the product-market domain: the competitive arenas where top management has learned the company can win, which constitutes its substantive strategy. A third factor concerns core values: principles of behavior that top management has learned to associate with the company's survival and success. A fourth factor concerns the company's objectives: financial and other ones that top management has learned are effective in providing guidance for strategic action.

Distinctive competencies. Describing how Intel tried to understand the factors underlying its success in the early days, Les Vadasz, a top-level manager, recalled in 1988: "Intel was a successful start-up in the late '60s and one of the first things I did [when asked to think about strategic planning] was to try to understand what led to Intel's success. The reasons for success were embedded in the combined talents of the group that was in charge. We had a sense about the technology and the business, which led to a series of correct decisions."

Having a sense about the technology meant that Intel's top management, who were among the leading experts in the world on integrated circuit technology, understood that silicon was the key material for semiconductor memories and that process technology was the driver of the semiconductor memory business. In fact, it was innovative MOS (metal oxide semiconductor) process technology combined with sufficient skills in manufacturing that made it possible for Intel to succeed with DRAM where other memory start-ups (such as Advanced Memory Systems) had previously failed. Gordon Moore recalled in 1999: "We made just the right technology choice in the early days—silicon gate MOS. This was a new version of MOS. To make complex circuits required several steps, and it took real work to get by. We had seven years using this technology without competition, and this really helped us financially. We did a variety of different memories, and we were first to market with each major memory technology." Intel's distinctive process technology competencies focused on how to get more transistors on the same amount of silicon real estate. The ability to make smaller and denser integrated circuitry resulted from Intel's R&D and was kept proprietary.

Product market domain. Intel's choice of product-market domain was determined by its distinctive competencies, which led the company to create new types of memory products that competed with the standard magnetic core memory. Intel was the first company to manufacture and market DRAM successfully and viewed itself as the memory company. As one manager put it, "In a way, DRAM created Intel." Gerry Parker, an Intel executive vice president in 1999, who for many years had been in charge of Technology and Manufacturing, echoed this point. In an interview in 1999, when asked how Intel was going to be able to get into new businesses, Parker said that it was no different from when Intel was founded:

> Robert Noyce and Gordon Moore started the company. They only knew that they were going to do integrated circuits—bipolar and MOS. That was the core competency and it drove the general direction of the company. Our competencies had to be built. We hired people from Texas Instruments and Fairchild. The first MOS chips didn't work, but they knew that they had to make MOS work. That resulted in a sequence of products that came from these competencies. DRAM became the driver. The microprocessor was a little product that we let develop . . . I joined Intel in 1969 and Gordon [Moore] had me work on LED.

Craig Barrett, Intel's CEO since 1998, provided a similar perspective:

> In the first part of our history we had integrated circuit expertise and we were looking to apply it. We discovered applications by happenstance—the DRAM and others. We had solutions looking for problems. We had the IC gurus and they were dealing with systems people. We were functionally oriented, with fuzzy business units. Test & Development, Manufacturing, Sales, etc. all responded very much to what customers were driving us to do. We were responding rather than driving the industry.

Intel's success with semiconductor memories set the stage for a fundamental transformation of the computer industry. But such transformation was not the founders' original purpose. They simply saw and pursued the entrepreneurial opportunity of offering replacement parts for mainframe computer memories. Gordon Moore recalled in 1999:

> We started out wanting to find a hole in the product line of established companies, especially Texas Instruments and Fairchild. We wanted to do something different, and not compete directly. We saw the opportunity to do something in semiconductor memory to make a complex chip. This was very difficult to do economically. TI and Fairchild both were making simple chips. We saw memory as a function used in all digital systems. We thought that semiconductors would be very competitive for small memories where magnetic core memories didn't compete well, so we started out making memory circuits.

Core values. Intel's core values were shaped by the behavior of the members of the founding team. They had a deep appreciation of the importance of technical excellence and depth. They insisted on discipline in thinking and action. They were focused on results. They wanted to create an egalitarian meritocracy in which knowledge power was not subjugated by position power. They created a culture of openness that encouraged ferocious intellectual debate and focused on substance rather than style. They instituted power sharing as exemplified in the two-in-a-box management system (a technical-oriented and a business-oriented manager share the leadership task of their unit). In a 1996 internal videoconference, Andy Grove responded to a question about what kind of company Intel would be in twenty years. He pointed out that it was impossible to know what products Intel would bring to market then, but he said: "Intel will still be a technical company; disciplined and results oriented; wholesome."

Objectives. Throughout its history, Intel always had a strong profit and shareholder-value orientation. This is reflected in the prominent position—an equal partner to operations—that the finance function had held throughout Intel's history. Andy Bryant, Intel's chief financial officer in 1999, pointed out:

> Finance should mirror operations. For instance, everyone who reports to Craig Barrett (CEO in 1999) has a finance person next to him. The finance person is a quasi-assistant general manager, with complementary skills. The finance people's first job is to look out for the shareholders, second for finance, and third for operations. This is somewhat overstated because the natural orientation is to focus on operations, given the force of proximity. Most general managers accept the finance person as a teammate, even though they will always complain about "finance."

Intel's Structural Context

As Les Vadasz's quote above suggests, when Intel was a start-up the founders and key team members all understood what the tasks implied by the corporate strategy were and simply devoted themselves to accomplishing these. The link between concept of corporate strategy and strategic action was immediate and direct. As the company grew large and more complex, however, the link between corporate strategy and strategic action became necessarily less immediate and direct. In response, top management evolved a structural context. Structural context refers to administrative and cultural mechanisms that help maintain alignment between strategic action and corporate strategy. Organization structure, strategic planning systems, resource allocation rules, recruitment and promotion systems, measurement and reward systems, and principles guiding behavior are all part of the structural context.

Organization structure. Early on, Intel had a structure based on product divisions, each of which had its own technology development and marketing group, but which shared a common sales force and manufacturing. Later on, Intel developed into a matrix structure with product groups and functional groups as the key structural building blocks. A key feature of Intel's organization structure was its fluidity. Intel continuously reorganized its product groups to match the structure with the changing product-market environment. The functional groups, on the other hand, remained more stable. In part because of this, organizational positions and titles did not carry much weight. People moved from positions of higher formal authority to lower formal authority and back without any stigma being attached to it. Far more important than position power was influence power, which reflected a person's standing and reputation based on his/her knowledge and content expertise.[4]

Strategic planning. Another key element of the structural context was the strategic planning system. In 1988 Dennis Carter pointed out that:

> Historically, the process was basically informal or "bubble up." An engineer or marketer would come up with an idea and try to sell it to upper management. If successful, top management would fund the idea. If not, the person with the idea might leave.
>
> As the company grew, the informal process became too difficult to manage. Les Vadasz implemented a formal centralized planning system called SLRP (strategic long-range planning). Each organization in the company had a strategy subcommittee. Each subcommittee would go through a yearly process of developing a long-range strategic plan. The plans would be submitted to Vadasz for funding approval. Over a period of years, the system lost effectiveness. Yearly long-term strategy presentations became repetitive and lacked the innovation or renewal anticipated.

Andy Grove added, "New ideas tended to be co-opted and molded by powerful organizations and were not allowed to develop freely." Commenting (also in an interview in 1988) on the evolution of Intel's Strategic Long-Range Planning Process (SLRP), Les Vadasz said:

As the company grew, we tried to replicate the environment that led to making correct decisions by forming relatively small business units and creating a bottoms-up strategic planning system. However, that became very unwieldy. The notion of pushing decisions down may have been a good one, but the task-relevant maturity was not great enough. Managers started gaming with the system. One key symptom was that new ideas were often co-opted by groups and molded to fit immediate needs rather than developed as originally intended.

Vadasz also pointed out at the time that the system had been changed in the mid-1980s:

The system is now more top-down. A high-level group sets the corporate strategy, and business units operate within that locus. Business units must focus on a few things and do them right. Neither the old nor the new system is perfect. . . . Some managers complain that their "sandbox" is too well defined.

Resource allocation. Rules concerning manufacturing resource allocation were a potent part of Intel's structural context. The maximize margin-per-wafer-start was the key allocation rule. This rule reflected Intel's differentiation strategy and profit orientation. The maximize margin-per-wafer-start rule had been initiated by Intel's first vice president of finance, Bob Reed. Reed insisted, at one point, that the DRAM manager sign a symbolic check equal to the margin forgone when high-margin products were bumped by DRAM. Given the relative size of the capital investments involved (hundreds of millions of dollars), this was extremely important.

Intel had traditionally operated with a zero-based budgeting approach. While, as will be documented in later chapters, the system was very much in force in 1999, Andy Bryant (who had joined Intel in 1981) nevertheless felt that: "It used to be tighter, but the company has become too large. There is sometimes more of a broad-brush approach than before. But in some places, the discipline has lived on." Top management controlled R&D resource allocation. In 1989, Gordon Moore said: "Allocation of resources to the different technology development groups is centralized by Andy and me." As documented in the DRAM case, this could lead temporarily to a discrepancy between the performance of a business and the share of R&D resources that it obtained. These R&D allocations kept alive the mythology—the self-evident truth—of Intel the memory company during Epoch I.

Recruitment and promotion. Another important aspect of the structural context concerned the recruitment of new employees and the promotion of people to positions of leadership. The rigor of the recruitment process and the probing of technical depth and competence during the process were legendary. Intel has traditionally paid great attention to hiring people compatible with its culture. The importance of recruitment of new people and the associated skill sets is perhaps best demonstrated by the fact that Andy Grove personally interviewed all the exempt employees until the early 1970s. In an interview in 1999, Grove said:

> For many years I was part of the hiring process for every exempt hire. That's 25 years gone. (But) that influenced generations of hiring managers. We still select people pretty damn well. People may look very differently, but they all have some affinity. The first time someone argued with this was in 1971. But we still retained more of the characteristics than we lost. . . . As managers, we tend to replicate ourselves. Not automatically; but we hire people that plausibly will reinforce it. It is cultural reproduction—controlled by other employees.

Asked about the selection criteria, Grove said: "I could say all the usual things. Results orientation. Openness. Dealing with issues aggressively. It's all true, but it somehow falls flat. People bring their own personalities. The characteristics look different in each person. . . . It's quite instinctive."

The subsequent socialization process was equally strong. Regarding the importance of promotion of managers to senior positions, Andy Grove said: "There are two key things. Who you hire and who you promote. Who you promote is probably even more important, because it is the most visible statement that you can make about the selection environment."

Measurement and reward systems. The same rigor that went in recruiting and promoting people also permeated the process involved in measuring and rewarding managerial performance. Intel used a form of management by objectives whereby an employee identifies some ten objectives with quantifiable measures. Performance against those objectives was the basis for the measurement of performance.

To measure performance, Intel used a ranking and rating system that was applied by each manager to all of his or her direct reports. The process started early in the calendar year and concluded sometime in April, with each employee receiving an "outstanding," "successful," or "improvement required," rating arrived at through an exhaustive process of comparisons during review meetings. Dennis Carter, vice president and director of corporate marketing, said: "It is taken bloody serious. If you are unprepared in a review meeting to talk factually about the employees you are reviewing, you are bludgeoned. I don't think anything we do is taken more seriously." Carter also pointed out that "Reviews should be nonevents because the review process between the manager and his or her direct reports should be ongoing throughout the period. So there should be no surprises—positive or negative."

Compensation, which included salary, executive bonus, and stock options, was tightly linked to the ranking and rating process. According to Carter:

> There are guides provided by corporate for pay raises. If the overall pay raise for the company is × percent, then perhaps "outstandings" will get 2× percent, "successfuls" will get .5× percent, and "improvement requireds" will get 0% raise. . . . Executive Bonuses (EB) were started in the mid-1980s by Andy Grove in order to provide pay flexibility and reinforce the meritocracy. . . . They are based on a complex calculation. The possible range is 0–125 percent of salary. . . . Salary and EB are based on actual performance. Stock options depend also on expectations about potential.

Principles guiding behavior. Finally, Intel's structural context reflected its core values, which created a culture of openness and willingness to engage in "constructive confrontation." While it is difficult to provide a full explanation of how such a culture actually comes about, the role of Robert Noyce, Gordon Moore, and Andy Grove was important in setting the initial tone and maintaining continuity. The influence of top management in strategy-making at Intel was undeniably very strong, but there was also a perception on the part of most managers that, most of the time, knowledge and facts win over positional power at Intel. Asked about how Intel resolved the tension between tolerance for dissent and the need for directed action, Grove said: "We allow a period of dissent where we forcefully debate issues, and then we follow this period of debates with clear, crisp decisions. We're probably better at the former than the latter. Sometimes the decisions are not as crisp as you would like. But I think if you compare us to [other companies] there is a huge difference."

In other words, during the period of debate, disagreements are forcefully aired (sometimes resulting in shouting matches that could easily be misinterpreted by those not familiar with the culture), but once a decision has been made those who still disagree are expected to commit to making the decision work. "Disagree and commit" complements constructive confrontation.

Induced Strategic Action at Intel

The structural context was created to couple strategic initiatives at operational levels with the corporate strategy through shaping managers' perceptions about which types of initiatives were likely to be supported by the company. As Les Vadasz's comments about the SLRP process suggest, the induced strategy process had a variation-reduction effect on the strategic initiatives that the company spawned. Of course, this does not imply that there was no planned variation in the induced process. Clearly, there remained room for core technology advances, new product development for existing product families, new approaches to marketing and manufacturing, and so on. Hundreds of examples of such variations could be documented at Intel. And these planned variations were not always small; for instance, new plant and equipment required very large investments.

INTEL'S AUTONOMOUS STRATEGY PROCESS: THE EARLY STORY OF MICROPROCESSORS

Intel's top management quite naturally created an induced strategy process to pursue its opportunities in semiconductor memories. But unplanned variations decisively shaped the evolution of the company and its corporate strategy during Epoch I. The most important of these variations was the microprocessor. In 2001, Intel is clearly the leading microprocessor company in the world. Yet, the microprocessor was not developed as the outcome of deliberate strategic planning. The story of the microprocessor provides insight into the role of the autonomous strategy process in Intel's internal ecology of strategy-making during Epoch I.

Four-Bit Microprocessors

Ted Hoff, who had joined the company as an integrated-circuit designer in 1969, invented Intel's first microprocessor. The Japanese firm Busicom had approached Intel to design and build a set of chips for a number of different calculators. Busicom had envisioned a set of around fifteen chips designed to perform advanced calculator functions. Hoff suggested building a simpler set of just a few general-purpose chips, which could be programmed to carry out each of the calculator functions. He was the architect of the chip set that Federico Faggin and a team of designers implemented. The set included four chips: a central processing unit (CPU) called the 4004, a read-only memory (ROM) with custom instructions for calculator operation, a random access memory, and a shift register for input/output buffering. It took nearly a year to convince Busicom that the novel approach would work, but by early 1970 Intel signed a $60,000 contract, which gave Busicom proprietary rights to the design. The CPU chip was eventually called the microprocessor. While Intel produced chips for Busicom, which were successfully made into 100,000 calculators, a debate within Intel developed about whether the company should try to renegotiate the rights to the chip design. Hoff believed that Intel could use the devices as a general-purpose solution in many applications ranging from cash registers to streetlights, and he lobbied heavily within the company. Eventually, Intel decided to offer reduced prices to Busicom in exchange for noncalculator rights to the design. Busicom, in financial trouble, readily agreed to the proposal. Top management, however, did not yet understand the full potential of the microprocessor. Ed Gelbach, senior vice president of sales at the time, remembered the decision: "Originally, I think we saw it as a way to sell more memories and we were willing to make the investment on that basis."

The 4-bit 4004 microprocessor was introduced in 1971. It contained 2,300 metal oxide semiconductor (MOS) transistors and could execute 60,000 instructions per second. Its performance was not as good as custom-designed logic, but Intel believed there was a significant market for it. Early on, it became apparent that Intel would have to educate its customers to sell the 4004. As a result, Gelbach's group developed the first of Intel's development aids, which were programming tools for customers. By 1973, revenues from design aids exceeded microprocessor sales.

Eight-Bit Microprocessors

In April 1972, Intel introduced the 8-bit 8008 microprocessor that was custom designed for Datapoint, a computer terminal company. Datapoint, however, eventually rejected the chip because it was too slow and required twenty support chips for operation. Intel was able to get back the rights to the 8008. After announcing the 8008 in 1972, Intel reportedly disbanded its design team and planned to focus on its much larger and fast-growing semiconductor memory business. The 8008, however, generated an enormous amount of interest on the part of engineers seeking to use microprocessors in numerous computer applications.[5] In the meantime, Intel's advancements in static and dynamic RAM had provided a new process technology that increased speed. This process technology was applied in the 8080 microprocessor that could execute 290,000 instructions per second and was ten times as fast as the 8008. In addition, the 8080 required only six support chips for operation. Ted Hoff and Stan Mazor developed the instruction set. Federico Faggin and Masatoshi Shima, an extremely talented young Japanese designer, did the circuit design.

The introduction of the 8080 in April 1974 heralded the beginning of a new age in computing. The markets for microprocessors exploded as new uses were developed. Intel was one year ahead of Motorola's introduction of the 6800 microprocessor and eventually took nearly the entire 8-bit market. Even though the 6800 used an architecture more familiar to programmers, Intel offered more effective development aids and support systems. Besides Motorola, Intel also faced Zilog as a competitor. Federico Faggin, Masatoshi Shima, and another Intel design engineer had formed Zilog as a start-up in 1974. (Andy Grove later commented that the loss of those engineers set back Intel's microprocessor program by as much as one year.) Intel offered licenses to produce the 8080 to several integrated circuit companies to assure customers of a second source of supply. Ed Gelbach remembered the mid-1970s as the good old days: At an initial selling price of $360 per chip, Intel paid for the 8080 R&D in the first five months of shipments.

Sixteen-Bit Microprocessors

At this stage in their development, Intel's microprocessor strategy bifurcated between two architectures: a completely new and more complex architecture mandated by top management (the 8800) and a new but simpler architecture that continued to be compatible with the 8-bit 8080 microprocessor.

The 8800 architecture. The 8080 microprocessor was very successful with numerous applications but at the time did not make inroads into the computer business itself—mainframes and minicomputers. To try to remedy this, a frustrated top management mandated the development of a radically new 16-bit architecture, the 8800, in 1975. This architecture was very complex, attempting to provide performance features that only much later would become feasible. In typical Intel fashion, the development of the architecture was doggedly pursued. But the end was never clearly in sight. This did not help the legitimacy of the microprocessor business within Intel, which was still very much a memory company.

In addition, the delays experienced with the 8800 architecture threatened to create openings for competing microprocessor architectures, notably those of Motorola and Zilog. Fortunately for Intel, the strategic situation facing its microprocessor business was clearly recognized by Bill Davidow, who had joined Intel in 1973 and had been co-general manager (with Les Vadasz) of the microprocessor division in 1976. Davidow suggested that Intel should continue to pursue the work on the 8800 (perhaps to placate top management) but that it should also develop an intermediate product to fend off the competition—in a hurry.[6]

The 8086 architecture. Driven by the urgency of the situation, Intel's 16-bit microprocessor, the 8086, again was first to market by about one year when it was introduced in June 1978. Intel management decided that upward compatibility would be a critical feature of the 16-bit chip. While the 8086 could operate software developed originally for the 8080, it employed a new architecture requiring new software for full exploitation. A lower-priced version of the new architecture, the 8088, was also introduced for the segment of the market that wanted to move up to 16-bit processing but found the price of the 8086 too high. The 8088 had the same 16-bit engine of the 8086, but used an 8-bit bus to communicate with memory and peripheral devices. Buyers could use the 8088 to fairly easily upgrade old 8-bit systems.

For two years, Intel did not meet its sales forecasts for the 8086 microprocessor family as customers purchased only sample quantities and worked on a new generation of software. In the meantime, Motorola introduced its own 16-bit microprocessor, the 68000, and appeared to be gaining momentum in the market. Winning the Apple Computer account, in particular, was a signal event. Recognizing that the 68000 represented a critical threat that could lock Intel out of the 16-bit market segment and potentially the next generation as well, Intel created a task force to attack the 68000. The project was called Operation CRUSH—crush the competition.

Operation CRUSH. By late 1979, Intel was under full siege in its microprocessor business. This was particularly threatening, because a number of multimillion-dollar Intel businesses depended on the 8086's success. These were difficult times for Intel (remember that the company's DRAM business was already in decline). In the face of numerous customer defections, the microprocessor marketing and sales group was suffering from low morale. Bill Davidow reports a catalytic event that triggered strong top management action:

> Management encouragement had been ineffective at correcting what was becoming a destructive situation. In late November Don Buckout, an Intel field engineer on Long Island, sent management an incisive and desperate eight-page telex. The discussion of Buckout's telex at the executive staff meeting the following Tuesday couldn't have been more

unpleasant. By the end of it I had either volunteered or been asked by Grove to run a marketing task force charged with solving the 8086 problem. This was the beginning of Operation CRUSH.[7]

The effort was intense: The task force set out to generate 100,000 sales leads, which were reduced to 10,000 qualified leads resulting in a target of 2,000 design wins in 1980. (A design win involved the choice by a customer to design their product based on the 8086 chip.) SWAT teams of engineering, applications, and marketing people were mobilized to travel anywhere in the world whenever a design win was threatened.

According to Davidow, Intel provided strong team-based incentives. These, in turn, created extremely strong peer pressures to attain the design win targets. But the foundation on which these sales efforts rested was the concept of the 8086 as a complete product—one that satisfied the total customer need—rather than simply the best device. Hence, the CRUSH campaign emphasized Intel's system approach. And it was successful. It produced 2,500 design wins in the first year.

The IBM design win. The most notable design win was IBM's decision to use the 8088 in their first personal computer in 1981. IBM planned an open-architecture personal computer, and Intel's 8086 family defined the software standard. Intel sales representatives knew they won the IBM account several months before it was made public when the IBM Boca Raton office started placing orders for Intel's ICE–88 development systems. It was not, however, until Intel was asked to provide a second-source supplier for the 8088 that the company realized that their microprocessor was going to go into IBM's first personal computer.

IBM's decision to adopt Intel's 8088 microprocessor was a fortuitous turn of events for Intel, but not a random draw of luck. As told in a narrative reconstructing the development of the first IBM PC,[8] some engineers in an IBM skunk works had already been building prototypes of microcomputers based on Intel microprocessors that became precursors to the IBM PC. Out of this came a motherboard-based system that proved to be a good match for the 8088 chip. In addition: "The chip was one of the few microprocessors of the time to have its own full suite of native assemblers, compilers, linkers and editors—a whole applications design environment. Hardware support was equally broad: timers and a host of controllers for interrupts, floppy disks and parallel serial ports, with support for the Intel mode bus, were available from many suppliers."[9]

The IBM PC sold 500,000 units in its first two years, and some 80 percent of these machines used an Intel microprocessor as CPU. (The rest came from the second sources upon which IBM had insisted when picking Intel.) As one IBM engineer put it, Intel was "just another component supplier." [10] In 1981, 13 percent of Intel's sales were to IBM. Interestingly, Intel did not immediately see the implications of the IBM design win. In 1999, Gordon Moore recalled the IBM PC design win: "Any design win at IBM was a big deal, but I certainly didn't recognize that this was more important than the others. And I don't think anyone else did either."

The project to develop the next generation x86 microprocessor began in 1978. The 80186 and 80286 were designed to be upwardly compatible with the 8086. The 80286 was designed to operate with as few as four support chips. The 286 team developed product features through extensive field interviews, and created a list of more than fifty applications ranging from business systems to industrial automation. Ironically, the applications list did not include personal computers, which later became the single largest application. According to Gordon Moore: "The application of the 80286 microprocessor in the personal computer, for example, wasn't even mentioned in our early market studies." [11]

The 80286 was the most ambitious design effort ever undertaken at Intel. The chip contained 130,000 transistors (versus 29,000 for the 8086). The design team worked feverishly for three years to develop the first prototype. That device did not operate with enough speed. Gradually, all the bugs were worked out, and only one hurdle remained: developing the methodology to test the chips as they came off the production line. Production was ready to start making the 80286 six months before the testing procedure could be developed. Intel had to develop computer tools to design the tests. The chip was introduced in 1983, eighteen months later than originally planned. It became the CPU for the IBM AT (advanced technology) personal computer.

In the meantime, Motorola was regaining momentum with its 68000 architecture. According to Dennis Carter, who worked on marketing the 286:

> The 68000 came out after the 8086 and it was having some success in the marketplace, but we weren't particularly concerned because we knew the 186 and 286 were on the horizon. We believed we would announce the 286, and everyone would flock to our door. But when we introduced it, the world perceived the 286 not as a powerful monster machine, but as a slight continuation of the 8086. It also seemed that a lot of startups were using Motorola, and that was real scary because that's one indication of where the future is going to be.

Operation CHECKMATE. Operation CHECKMATE paralleled the earlier Operation CRUSH in concept. CHECKMATE task force members gave a series of 200 seminars to 20,000 engineers around the world. Rather than emphasizing pure performance specifications that Motorola could also use to their advantage, the seminars stressed features which had been included at the request of the market-place in 1978. These included "virtual memory addressing" (which allows the microprocessor to handle many users at the same time without confusing each user's tasks) and multitasking (the ability to manage more than one task simultaneously that is embedded in the chip's architecture). Dennis Carter recalled: "As a result, the design wins completely turned around. When we went into CHECKMATE, some market segments were three or four to one in favor of Motorola. By the time we finished, it had turned around the other way."

By the mid-1980s, Intel had been able to decisively shape the basis of competitive advantage in the microprocessor industry by gaining very large market share for the x86 architecture. With the 8086 microprocessor family Intel had won the first major competition between architectures in the microprocessor industry against Motorola and Zilog. Zilog's prospects looked very dim. Motorola, however, having gotten the Apple Computer design win, was still a player to reckon with in the future.

8800 epilogue. The 8800 was renamed the 432 architecture and introduced in 1981. But its impact on the company's fate was minuscule compared to that of the 8086 microprocessor family. Andy Grove later pointed to the irony that the only microprocessor architecture that was ever mandated by top management ended up in relative failure (personal communication). One senior executive pointed out in 1999, however, that several of the Intel Fellows—Intel's top scientists—had been associated with the 8800 effort and had made important contributions to the Intel Architecture.

Autonomous Strategic Action at Intel

Autonomous strategic action can originate at all levels of management. But it is most likely to emerge at a level where managers are directly in contact with new technological developments, new customer needs, and changes in market conditions. Hence, as a company grows, even a company such as Intel where top executives have strong technical backgrounds, autonomous strategic action is increasingly likely to emerge at levels below top management.

This was clearly illustrated in the emergence of the microprocessor. Ted Hoff's solution was based on his extraordinary technological competence deployed in response to a new customer need. It was also a response, in part, to Hoff's realization that implementing the customer's initial design concept was impractical because of Intel's internal resource constraints (not enough engineering resources available to design the large number of chips involved). While Intel's top management was eager to oblige a new customer, strategic planning did not drive the origin of the microprocessor. In fact, for many years, the legitimacy of microprocessors within Intel—the memory company—was precarious.

Autonomous strategic action often emerges fortuitously and is difficult to predict. But it does not usually emerge randomly because it is rooted in and constrained by the company's distinctive competencies at any given time. For instance, in the case of microprocessors, it is quite plausible that Busicom chose Intel to develop the chips for its new calculator product because of Intel's demonstrated competencies in circuit design and miniaturization. The success of microprocessors and the accompanying shift in relative importance in Intel's product-market domain from memory (low-design content) to microprocessor (high-design content) had important consequences for the evolution of Intel's distinctive competencies. As differences in process technology leveled among competitors in the industry, distinctive competence in circuit design increasingly became the new basis for Intel's competitive advantage. And, as customers needed to be taught what the powerful microprocessors could do for their own products, it also led Intel to develop new distinctive technical marketing capabilities, especially application engineering.

Dennis Carter highlighted the great diversity of Intel's businesses during the first epoch of its history and explained how Intel's technical marketing capability helped link diverse customer needs to the company's technological capability to provide solutions for these needs. This, in turn, generated new, sometimes unanticipated business opportunities:

> In the 1970s and early 1980s, Intel had a unifying focus, but many different products and business lines, more like HP. Intel had many general managers and people empowered to make decisions. It had strong R&D that generated many new ideas. The business divisions were more autonomous. And the sales force provided information about customer needs. This allowed us to spontaneously take advantage of new opportunities. . . .
>
> Fifteen years ago, the organizational power was in the factories and sales force. The sales force was very powerful. Product success depended on field support. They were in direct contact with customers, and served as a lightning rod for information. They provided input about the market and customer needs and gave feedback to the product planning groups. This was not planned or intentional, but it still happened. You could not make a product successful without the support of the sales

force. They represented the perspective of the customer. They were a unifying force across the various divisions.

The general managers were not that great—they were not market focused—but they relied on the field sales people. And that worked. The field sales force was made up of two types. Field sales engineers, who were more typical salespeople, and field applications engineers, who were incredibly technical. They had to have been design engineers before they became field applications engineers. They were very hands-on and very sophisticated technically. They could sit down with the customers' engineers and help them to design in new products. They were incredibly valuable. And they knew where the technology had to go. They connected with the manufacturing people. They became informally part of the development process and provided input to the design teams. They had great influence—they told you because of their expert power, not because of their position power.

We had tens of thousands of customers then. All the business units were dovetailed, yet independent. For instance, the microprocessor business unit (which was a couple of hundred million dollars then) was coupled with the microprocessor development systems business (also a couple of hundred million dollars). The sales force would unify them, discipline them.

While autonomous initiatives initially do not require large amounts of resources, they do need some resources to get started. This requires some external support, as with Busicom in the case of the microprocessor, or some budgetary discretion as in the case of the skunk works that kept the Flash initiative alive (see chapter 4). Asked how autonomous initiatives can get started at Intel, one senior manager (in the late 1980s) said he kept the process fluid by "carving out a certain amount of resources for unplanned things. Usually you need no more than a million dollars to get something going." Hence, the availability of uncommitted resources is an important factor affecting the rate at which autonomous strategic action can be supported.

Strategic Recognition and Strategic Context Determination at Intel

Successful strategic context determination for microprocessors. The development of the microprocessor business was the outcome of an unplanned initiative outside of the scope of Intel's memory product-oriented corporate strategy in the early 1970s. Top management recognized the microprocessor as a major technical breakthrough, but initially there was less confidence in its commercial potential. As Ed Gelbach pointed out, microprocessors were initially supported to help sell more memory products. Microprocessors faced the problem that their position relative to Intel's memory-oriented corporate strategy was initially indeterminate. In earlier chapters I have called the process through which this indeterminateness is resolved strategic context determination, and showed that this process is highly dependent on top and senior management's capacity for strategic recognition.

Strategic recognition and strategic context determination are high-level, cognitive, and political processes. They involve reflective learning and the cognitive ability to put the outcomes of internal and external selection in context. They require thoughtful approaches for suspending the fairly crude rules of resource allocation and for questioning the existing corporate strategy. They involve high-level political activities to convince peers to support a new strategic thrust.

Strategic recognition and strategic context determination were illustrated by the microprocessor story. Ted Hoff and Federico Faggin recognized the strategic importance of the microprocessor for Intel's future. While Gordon Moore was enthusiastic about its technical possibilities, it took intensive championing on their part to convince top management of the strategic importance of microprocessors for Intel's future. These efforts led top management to provide resources to buy back the rights to the microprocessor from Busicom. This gave microprocessors a chance to demonstrate their viability as a new business for Intel. Hence the impetus for making microprocessors a more central part of Intel's corporate strategy came from senior managers, not top management initially. Later on, Bill Davidow and other senior managers recognized that the new 8800 architecture, mandated by top management, would not be ready to face the challenge of Motorola's new microprocessor. Their strategic recognition and championing efforts helped determine the strategic context for the 8086 microprocessor architecture at Intel. Once their strategic context had been determined, 8086 microprocessors became an integral part of Intel's corporate strategy—though not yet the dominant part. Andy Grove then put his considerable competitive energies behind Operation CRUSH for the 8086 microprocessor, which gave the campaign its decisive force.

In addition to having been a fortuitous development for Intel, the concept of a general-purpose microprocessor had also been a radically new approach in the emerging semiconductor industry. In a presentation to security analysts in 1980, Andy Grove reflected on the strategic recognition involved in this. He pointed out that the decade of the '70s started with all of metal-oxide-semiconductor large-scale integrated circuitry to be implemented in the form of custom circuits. He noted that if the customized approach had continued throughout the 1970s, electronics would have been far less prominent by 1980 because there simply wouldn't have been enough circuit designers to keep up with the growth in demand for customized circuitry. He said: "Instead, some of us naively barged onto the scene with a different approach. We said 'we will not provide you with a custom capability. We will build you a microcomputer, say the 4004, and we know it is not the particular microcomputer you want, but it is the microcomputer that you can get. You can get it today and you can get it at a reasonable cost. Use it, you will learn to love it.' It worked."[12]

Failed strategic context determination for PCs. The microprocessor eventually found its killer application in the personal computer. But, as we saw earlier, the PC was not on the top fifty applications list for the 286 microprocessor. Just as initially top management had not recognized the business potential of the microprocessor, they did not recognize the importance of microprocessors for personal computers. This, in spite of Gordon Moore being the originator of "Moore's Law," and the fact that Intel had developed operating system software that allowed third parties to write software applications. Recalled Gordon Moore: "In the mid-1970s, someone came to me with an idea for what was basically the PC. The idea was that we could outfit an 8080 processor with a keyboard and a monitor and sell it in the home market. I asked, 'What's it good for?' And the only answer was that a housewife could keep her recipes on it. I personally didn't see anything useful in it, so we never gave it another thought."

One senior manager recalled the circumstances that caused the idea of Intel's entry into the PC business to be shot down: "A guy called X was hired to work on a proposal for getting Intel into the PC business. . . . He was very much into Altair computers and developed a presentation for a big planning meeting trying to convince management that we should go into the PC business. He was a real enthusiast, but he came across as such an amateur. . . . the word came down that management decided that PCs would never be more than Heathkits." This executive also pointed out: "I was real disappointed, and X soon left the company . . . I believe it wasn't long after that Gary Kildall came to us to try to sell us CPM, and we turned him down, paving the way for Microsoft's current success. . . . Gary Kildall did our ISIS development system OS for us, so we already had a business relationship with him."

Andy Grove had mentioned earlier that Intel had actually developed a form of operating system software to run on the microprocessor, but that its importance was not understood. Reflecting on Intel's strategy-making process in a Stanford MBA class in 1990, Grove used missing the PC opportunity as an example of the failings of Intel's strategy-making process. He said: "Intel at its worst is when we lose opportunities because top management doesn't have the clear options to decide—if we are not forced to make the choice. For instance, we were supplying PCs before anybody else. Yet, we did not realize the opportunity." Grove also said that if Intel had anticipated the personal computer and the growth opportunity it implied for the microprocessor business, exit from DRAM would have been easier (personal communication).

The story of Intel initially not capitalizing on the PC business opportunity associated with the microprocessor highlights the importance of top management's belief about the company's appropriate product-market domain. Intel was truly a hardware-oriented semiconductor component manufacturer. Getting into operating system software as a business would have been a great stretch. Getting into a business that required integrating all of the major hardware and software components of personal computers would probably have been an even greater stretch. The story also highlights how core values may affect strategic choice. The person who made the pitch for entering the PC business did so in a way that was not viewed by top management as consistent with Intel's core value of disciplined thinking. This not only affected top management's perception of the person but also the idea that this person tried to champion. The most important aspect of this story from our perspective is that it underscores how much strategic context determination is dependent on the capacity of senior managers to make a compelling case for a new business to top management—to present top management with clearly articulated options. No one really knows whether top management would have ultimately chosen to enter the PC business if there had been a compelling case made for it. But it is clear that failing to make a compelling case reduced its chances to zero and made it easier for top management to decline pursuing the opportunity. This implies that senior managers involved in autonomous strategic initiatives should resist going in front of top management until they are confident that their strategy for the new business is clear and robust, and they are ready to face skeptical and incisive questioning.

Difficulties facing strategic context determination. Les Vadasz, who was responsible for Intel's internal corporate venturing efforts in the early 1980s, commented on some of the difficulties faced by managers trying to determine the strategic context for a potential new business at Intel. He mentioned that these efforts sometimes required alternative avenues for obtaining resources so that the new business has a chance to demonstrate its viability.

Intel's add-on boards venture. The difficulty of determining the strategic content for a new product is illustrated with Intel's add-on boards venture. In the early 1980s, some middle-level managers wanted to develop add-on boards for personal computers. The induced strategy process initially rejected the idea because channels of distribution were too different. The idea, however, received support through Intel's internal corporate venturing program and became a separate business. After success of the business became evident, the venture was folded back into Intel's Systems business.

The Intel data also reveal that, in some instances, the failed attempt on the part of a new business initiative to determine its strategic context within Intel nevertheless led to a sharper articulation of the company's strategy.

Application specific integrated circuits (ASIC).   An example of such a failed attempt (in this case resulting from imitation) concerns the ASIC venture. Intel had been late moving into ASIC in the early-1980s. Tens of millions of dollars were invested for a fast ramp up, and a separate division was established. However, top management soon realized that ASIC was simply a delivery vehicle for circuit designs. As one middle-level manager observed: "In ASIC the customer added all the value. So we realized that we should add the value ourselves." The separate division was eventually folded back into Intel's mainstream as the corporate focus on design as a competitive advantage was adopted by the entire organization. Later on, Intel disengaged from ASIC, in part, because its own distinctive design competencies were different from those employed in ASIC.

Sometimes, autonomous initiatives have the potential to cannibalize an existing business, which makes it difficult to determine their strategic context.

Flash.   The potential to cannibalize is illustrated in the Flash venture, which had started as a skunk works in the early 1980s (chapter 4). The manager who championed Flash at Intel in the late 1980s suggested at the time that Flash might ultimately provide a replacement for microprocessors. Asked to describe life as a champion at Intel, this manager said: "You have to be naive, but mature enough to realize that the process takes a long time. You have to be sensitive to political toes. You have to be a religious zealot, but not too religious because then you lose your credibility. Finally, you have to succeed. . . . It is most difficult to champion a product that threatens the company's (current) business."

Spin-off may be the right outcome of strategic context determination. The history of Silicon Valley is testimony to the difficulties in determining the strategic context for autonomous strategic initiatives in established companies. Such initiatives often result in the creation of new firms, rather than in new businesses for the firms where they originated. Internal entrepreneurs often leave reluctantly because of lack of support. In the Intel case, one example, among others, concerned the group involved in E^2PROM. As mentioned in the Flash story, a majority of top management eventually, if reluctantly, determined that the business potential of

E²PROM was too small and specialized. The team involved subsequently left Intel and formed a venture called Xicor. This was probably the right outcome for both Intel and the internal entrepreneurs.

Strategic context determination and dissolution as learning opportunities. The dissolution of the strategic context of DRAM and EPROM—which were core businesses—produced important learning for Intel. Similarly, the dissolution of the strategic context for failed autonomous strategic initiatives produces lessons about what types of initiatives not to pursue again.

Microma. A poignant case is Intel's foray into digital watches in the early 1970s, a move into consumer electronics that was clearly outside of the scope of Intel's memory product-oriented corporate strategy, even if at the time it didn't necessarily look that way to top management. Intel's 1972 acquisition of Microma, a solid-state watch company, was based on top management's belief that consumer electronics products such as watches would become an important outlet for Intel's EPROM chips with growing volumes and fast-declining prices. Intel found out, however, that chips for watches rapidly became a commodity product—hence inconsistent with the differentiation-based generic strategy. They also found out that marketing to consumers was very different from marketing to engineers, extravagantly expensive and intractable—hence inconsistent with its distinctive competencies and core value system. Top management decided to quit the watch business in 1977. In fall 1988, Gordon Moore referred to the Intel digital watch that he was wearing (he also had a Busicom calculator on his desk) as his "$15 million watch." He said: "If anyone comes to me with an idea for a consumer product, all I have to do is look at my watch to get the answer." It was clear that it would be hard to try to determine the strategic context for another consumer-related product at Intel for a long time to come.

A related insight is that autonomous strategic initiatives are not always good for the company. Autonomous initiatives can potentially have a dissipating effect on the company's resources. Also, distinctive competencies can be diluted or lost if an autonomous initiative is not internally supported and important talent decides to leave the firm—often with the help of venture capital. (Gordon Moore, at one point, called it vulture capital, and it is interesting to note that Intel significantly increased its legal staff during the 1980s to protect its intellectual property.) Autonomous strategic initiatives may also potentially undermine the company's established strategic position. (An example, discussed in chapter 6, is the dangerous conflict that RISC-based microprocessor efforts created within Intel.) Autonomous strategic action, however, is very difficult to suppress and its existence should be considered a fact of life and a strategic leadership challenge in high-technology companies. Strategic context determination and dissolution help top management learn more about their implications.

Amending Intel's Corporate Strategy

Through the process of strategic context determination, the corporate strategy can be amended to legitimate and embrace new businesses that originated in autonomous strategic action. But this implies some flexibility in the corporate strategy. During Epoch I, Intel's corporate strategy was characterized by such flexibility. This was, in part, related to the fact that integrated circuit technology was still quite young, with many unexplored and unexploited product applications. Intel's strategy-making during Epoch I was thus very much driven by the opportunities generated by the company's distinctive competencies. The earlier reported quotes from Les Vadasz, Gerry Parker, Craig Barrett, and Gordon Moore support this view and dovetail with Dennis Carter's quotes that reflect the marketing and customer-based perspective. The situation depicted by Dennis Carter is one of intense interaction between a great variety of customers and Intel's technical people, and suggestive of a very strong inbound technical marketing capability. The inbound technical marketing capability increased the chances of identifying new, unanticipated opportunities. This situation was very conducive to autonomous strategic action.

As a result, Intel's corporate strategy by the end of Epoch I had been amended in several ways. First, as seen in chapter 3, the company's distinctive competencies had been broadened and the relative importance of different competencies had changed. As Andy Grove put it: "Intel had moved from a silicon-based distinctive competence in memory products to a distinctive competence in implementing design architectures in logic products." This nontrivial change had big implications for Intel's incumbent senior managers. Andy Grove quoted Gordon Moore warning the top management group at the time of the DRAM exit: "You know, if we're really serious about this (becoming a microcomputer company), half of our executive staff had better become software types in five years' time."[13] In response to this warning, Grove reports that he started to visit software companies to reeducate himself.

Second, the company's product-market domain had been broadened to encompass logic (microprocessor-based) products as well as memory products, and the center of gravity of the company lay now in microprocessors. Third, the company's core values still remained in place. Intel continued to be a very technical and differentiation-oriented, as well as a disciplined and results-oriented company. Finally, the company's emphasis on financial objectives and shareholder value creation remained in force.

The Situation in the Late 1980s

While Intel's history in Epoch I was clearly shaped by autonomous strategic action, by the late 1980s there was also a sense emerging that the induced strategy process was becoming more dominant. Chairman Gordon Moore addressed this issue in relation to Intel's strategy-making in 1989:

> We started out with deciding to develop technology for semiconductor memory. We did not choose between bipolar and MOS, so we tried both. Over time, however, Intel has narrowed and narrowed its technical interests. We are now strictly focusing on versions of CMOS. Andy (Grove) has been instrumental in this. For instance, take E^{2}PROM. We were after it for a long time. It was not becoming a large business as thought, but it was a reasonably large niche. We had very interesting technology, but we decided it was a sideline and chopped it off painfully. This narrowing is fine as long as the market gets bigger. But it could be a problem if it doesn't because then you could find yourself in a backwater.
>
> We can do variations on present businesses very well, but doing something new is more difficult. Today, the likelihood of someone killing an effort like Dov Frohman's (inventor of the EPROM) is very high, because you need a well-defined application to a market from the outset. This is especially so because we are not looking for additional opportunities. There is still a lot of evolution left in the current technology. If you consider the possibilities with reducing linewidth, you can see another twelve years of evolution along the same curve.

Moore's observations also imply that the strength of top management's emphasis on the induced strategy process depends on the growth opportunities remaining in the mainstream product-market domain. To the extent that these growth opportunities are perceived to be strong, top management is more likely to continue to favor induced strategic initiatives.

INTEL'S INTERNAL ECOLOGY OF STRATEGY-MAKING: FOUR FORMS OF ADAPTATION

While Intel's evolution from memory company to microprocessor company was strongly influenced by changes in the external environment, the microprocessor and Flash stories show that strategy-making processes also played an important role. The way Intel's strategy-making processes worked during Epoch I was somewhat different from the traditional textbook approach to strategic management, with strategic recognition playing a more prominent role than strategic planning.

Together, the induced and autonomous strategy processes constituted Intel's adaptive organizational capability during Epoch I, and these processes can be linked to four forms of adaptation: (1) strategic inertia, (2) strategic adjustment, (3) strategic reorientation, and (4) strategic renewal.

Strategic Inertia

Overcoming the liabilities of newness requires companies to develop a capacity for reliability and accountability in their transactions with the external environment. But, doing so creates inertia. Paradoxically, adaptation to existing environmental demands may reduce a company's capacity to adapt to future changes in the environment or to seek out new environments.[14]

The induced strategy process is likely to produce strategic inertia. Strategic inertia means that the rate of strategic change that the company can implement will, in the long run, be lower than the rate of change in the environment. Because the corporate strategy is rooted in a company's experience and learning, top managers are reluctant to change it. So it is plausible, especially in dynamic environments, to expect the evolution of a company's strategy to be inert relative to the accumulation of environmental changes over time.

The study of Intel provided insight in this. First, Intel's differentiation-based generic corporate strategy led the company to gradually fall behind in DRAM against new companies that competed on cost and quality. Second, the explicit change of substantive corporate strategy in terms of microprocessor leadership versus memory leadership came almost five years after the company had stopped being a major player in DRAM. Andy Grove recognized how difficult it had been to make the company see that the self-evident truth that Intel was a memory company was no longer true. It took top management several years to finalize a decision that had been in the making since the early 80s. Several managers pointed out later that the exit decision could and should have been made sooner. The delay occurred in part because some managers sensed that the substantive corporate strategy was no longer adequate but there were competing views about what the new strategy should be. There was still an important group of managers who believed that DRAM was critically important to Intel for technical and commercial reasons.

Strategic Adjustment

Tendencies toward strategic inertia in the induced strategy process do not preclude strategic adjustments.[15] Strategic adjustments involve deliberate changes that leave the overall strategy in place and may temporarily result in improved performance. Again, as we saw in earlier chapters, Intel made several strategic adjustments to try to stay viable in the DRAM business. These involved efforts to continue to differentiate Intel's products in the face of DRAM becoming a commodity product and were based on inertial deployment of the company's circuit design and process technology competencies. None of these adjustments was sufficient to make Intel's DRAM strategy viable again. Eventually, the decision to exit became unavoidable.

Strategic Reorientation

Organizational ecologists predict that major strategic change reduces the probability of a company's survival. This is so because such change "sets back the clock" and subjects the company again to the liabilities of newness and the associated powerful environmental selection pressures.[16] Other researchers, on the other hand, suggest that strategic reorientation, which implies a major change in the corporate strategy, is an integral part of a "punctuated equilibrium" model of company evolution. Punctuated equilibrium simply means that a company's evolution is characterized by extended periods of equilibrium that are interrupted by relatively short and sudden periods of large-scale change. Punctuated equilibrium theorists argue that firms that do not reorient when major changes are necessary or reorient when the need for such changes is not compelling will see their life chances reduced.[17]

How does the internal ecology of strategy-making help sort out this theoretical debate? The internal ecology perspective agrees that major changes in the corporate strategy are indeed likely to upset the induced strategy process in fundamental ways. The necessity of such change suggests that selective pressures coming from environmental change have made adjustments largely irrelevant. As an initial response, "threat-rigidity" effects may lead top management to reaffirm familiar approaches.[18] Threat rigidity refers to the likely behavioral responses of companies to threats. For instance, some researchers have found that established firms confronted with the threat of radically new technologies were likely to increase their efforts to improve the existing technology rather than switch to the new technology even after the latter had passed the threshold of viability.[19] To some extent, Intel's continued reliance on process technology competencies to compete in the face of a change in the basis of competition in the DRAM industry could be viewed as a manifestation of threat rigidity. Other research shows that established companies also have great difficulty coping with disruptive technologies, because misleading feedback from existing customers leads the sales force to erroneously dismiss the strategic importance of these technologies.[20]

Eventually, however, confronted with chronic low performance, top management is likely to take major risks by making extreme and vacillating changes in the strategy, potentially involving a complete change of domain.[21] When a company finds itself in a precarious situation, top management may perceive strategic reorientation as necessary to maintain or regain viability and better than doing nothing. One leading organization theorist however, has observed, that: "Organizations facing bad times and therefore following riskier and riskier strategies may simultaneously increase their chances of survival through the present crisis but also reduce their life expectancy: . . . for those organizations that do not survive, efforts to survive will have speeded the process of failure."[22]

Strategic Renewal

So, why did Intel's transformation during Epoch I—from memory company to microprocessor company—not lead to its demise? Was Intel perhaps simply lucky? The internal ecology of strategy-making resolves the apparent contradiction between organizational ecologists and punctuated equilibrium theorists in terms of the role of the autonomous strategy process. Strategic reorientation is implemented through the induced strategy process. Strategic reorientation involves "betting the company" because it eliminates a good deal of its cumulative learning. Consistent with the view of organizational ecology, environmental selection is expected to govern strategic reorientation.

Intel's transformation from a memory company into a microcomputer company seemed at first to have been a rather abrupt company-level strategic reorientation taking place in the 1984–85 time frame. However, as shown in figure 5.1, the company-level change was the culmination of a gradual replacement of memories by microprocessors as the core business of Intel. A closer look at the corporate transformation revealed that different levels of management played an important role in this gradual replacement, and that it took top management a relatively long time to come to grips with it. Figure 5.3 shows an overlay of the punctuated equilibrium view on the internal ecological view of Intel's corporate transformation. Intel's transformation was the result of strategic renewal through the autonomous strategy process, not a strategic reorientation.

A perspective of strategy-making as an internal ecological process calls into question the universal applicability of the punctuated equilibrium model, and helps

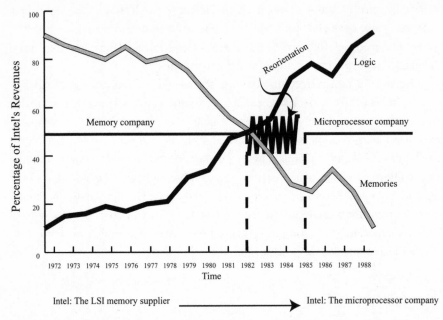

Figure 5.3. Intel's Evolution from Memory Company to Microcomputer Company.

establish more precisely how and when strategic change takes place. Strategic change may be taking place before it is recognized or acknowledged as such by top management. As Andy Grove has pointed out "the senior management in a company is sometimes late to realize that the world is changing on them—and the leader is often the last to know."[23]

Changes in the corporate strategy via the autonomous strategic process need not be completely governed by external selection processes. Autonomous strategic initiatives, as seen in the Intel case, offer opportunities to open new niches or provide early warning of impending radical, external changes. A company may learn new capabilities and skills in anticipation of making major changes in its strategy but without knowing in advance how it should be changed. Changes of this sort form the basis for strategic renewal: Major strategic change preceded by the internal experimentation and selection that takes place in the autonomous strategy process. In the Intel case, EPROM and microprocessors, as well as Flash memory, were unplanned developments. But Intel management recognized the importance of these developments after they had occurred and kept them inside the firm through shifts in resource allocation. Strategic renewal is the critical outcome of the autonomous strategy process through which a company can indefinitely remain adaptive. Table 5.1 summarizes the analysis of the induced and autonomous strategic processes and their proposed ties to modes of adaptation.

Table 5.1. Intraorganizational Ecology of Strategy-Making and Organizational Adaptation

Intraorganizational Ecological Processes

	Variation	Selection	Retention	Ties to Adaptation
Induced	Strategic initiatives seeking resources for projects that correspond to internal selection pressures of structural context, fit with the current organizational strategy, and offer access to regular opportunity structure for career advancement. Originates at operational-level but intended to be driven by top management's ex ante vision. Enhanced by availability of growth opportunities remaining in current action domain Radically new induced initiatives from top management	Initiatives selected through administrative mechanisms (e.g., strategic planning) and/or cultural influencing (e.g., reference to key values). Differential allocation of resources to different areas of strategic initiative. Key is that internal selection reflects current external selection pressures. Major changes in structural context.	1. Organizational learning about bases for past/current survival (variously embodied). 2. Distinctive competencies (variously embodied). 3. Organizational goals. 4. Organizational action domain. 5. Organizational character. All of these elements integrated in ex ante vision. Major changes in the dimensions of organizational strategy.	1. *Relative inertia.* Organizational survival is due to a good fit of internal selection processes with the environment. Survival motivates conservatism on the part of top management and desire to leverage existing organizational learning through induced process. Reluctance to change organizational strategy. 2. *Adjustment.* Relatively minor changes in strategy to accommodate environmental change. 3. *Reorientation.* Major changes in strategy in response to major environmental change.
Autonomous	Strategic initiatives outside scope of current strategy. Driven by operation-level managers seeking to use their skills in new combinations with organization's distinctive competencies and, in some cases, seeking career advancement through alternative opportunity structure. Enhanced by availability of unabsorbed slack.	Defining strategic context for new initiatives through: • Finding resources outside regular resource allocation processes • Demonstrating viability in external environment through entrepreneurial activity • Mobilizing internal support on the part of upper level managers • Developing new competencies/skills • Setting stage for an amendment in the organizational strategy.	Changes in organizational learning, distinctive competence, and relative importance of new activities in total domain activity, which, cumulatively, lead top management to recognize that a major change in strategy is necessary and feasible. Lead to new ex post vision. Once formally ratified, new vision becomes part of the basis for the induced process.	4. *Strategic renewal.* Major change in organizational strategy preceded by internal experimentation and selection offers organization possibilities for anticipatory adaptation to new environmental demands and/or to enter new niches.

SOURCE: R. A. Burgelman, "Intraorganizational Ecology of Strategy Making and Organizational Adaptation: Theory and Field Research," *Organizational Science* 2 (1991): p. 254.

IMPLICATIONS

The study of the evolution of Intel during Epoch I suggests an important role for both the induced and autonomous parts of a company's strategy-making process. Companies overcome the liabilities of newness by accumulating learning and leveraging what they have learned—in particular about their distinctive competencies and product-market domain—in their induced strategy process. This eventually results in strategic inertia, but strategic adjustments based on incremental learning and implemented through the induced strategy process can keep a company adaptive over some range of environmental change and over a certain time horizon. The autonomous strategy process, on the other hand, helps companies generate, select, and retain radically new learning. This process leads to strategic renewal and thereby offers companies the possibility to remain adaptive over a wider range of environmental change and a longer time horizon.

While clearly demonstrating a degree of strategic inertia during Epoch I, Intel's strategic decision to exit from DRAM was not too late. Intel lost a lot of money in DRAM, but the hemorrhage was stopped before the company's viability became threatened. Intel's relatively low strategic inertia was, in the first instance, not due to a prescient or exceptionally agile top management. Rather, it was due to the way in which the internal selection processes were allowed to work themselves out. Intel survived as an independent company, in part, because it was able to recognize important internal variations that were externally viable and to allocate resources to these through the internal selection mechanisms—almost in spite of the pervasive desire to continue to be a memory company. Although Intel went through a major change in substantive corporate strategy—from memory company to microcomputer company—it did not do so through a dramatic and sudden strategic reorientation. Instead, unplanned, autonomous initiatives were allowed to run their course, with some losers and some winners. As the winning autonomous initiatives continued to survive and grow in the internal selection environment, strategic renewal gradually took shape. By the time top management recognized the company's transformation, its ratification had already become a reasonably safe bet. Also, the new substantive corporate strategy was consistent with the generic corporate strategy based on differentiation.

Internal Selection and Company-Level Adaptation

Intel's internal ecology of strategy-making suggests that selection and adaptation are complementary rather than alternative processes if it is recognized that they take place at different levels: Intracompany-level selection processes help produce company-level adaptation.[24] But the Intel case also indicates it is critically important that the internal selection environment should reflect the selective pressures of the external environment. This provides a reality test for the corporate strategy. The discrepancy between the outcomes of internal selection and official corporate strategy in the DRAM case suggests that strategic action in the induced strategy process may be impacted more by the structural context than by the corporate strategy.[25] This is somewhat surprising, especially in a company with unusually strong and articulate top managers like Gordon Moore and Andy Grove. And it has important implications. It suggests that induced strategic action can continue to be effective if the internal selection environment correctly reflects the selective pressures of the external environment, even while becoming decoupled from the official corporate strategy. In this situation, a company can continue to perform well and thereby gain a time cushion for bringing corporate strategy in line with the reality of the external environment. The opposite does not hold. Internal selection coupled strongly to corporate strategy but not correctly reflecting the selective pressures of the external environment may lead to rapid failure.

The importance of linking the internal selection environment directly to external environmental pressures as well as to corporate strategy nuances the traditional view that structure should follow strategy.

Insight 5.1. The adaptive organizational capability associated with a company's internal ecology of strategy-making depends more on the internal selection environment correctly reflecting the selective pressures of the external environment than on the link between the internal selection environment and corporate strategy.

An additional and perhaps somewhat surprising implication is that in established companies short-term profit orientation should guide strategic action as long as a company's existing corporate strategy is in doubt and no compelling case for a clear strategy has been made.[26] In that case, short-term profit orientation helps secure and avoids dissipation of resources, and this helps maintain the company's degrees of freedom. This does not imply of course that top management should not worry about strategy as long as short-term profits are available. Rather, it implies that the burden of proof regarding long-term profit potential should probably be on strategy if strategy implies not maximizing short-term profit.

In the autonomous strategy process, top management's role is strategic recognition rather than strategic planning. Top management needs to facilitate the activation of strategic context determination processes to find out which of the autonomous initiatives have adaptive value for the company and deserve to become part of the corporate strategy. This requires some looseness in the coupling of strategic action and corporate strategy through the structural context so that strategic context determination processes can be activated. It also requires that top management accepts some ambiguity in the corporate strategy so that there is room for amendments, even though such amendments are difficult to achieve.

> **Insight 5.2.** The adaptive organizational capability associated with a company's internal ecology of strategy-making depends on the possibility to activate strategic context determination processes and to amend the corporate strategy to accommodate successful autonomous strategic initiatives.

Process Generates Content; Content Disciplines Process

The internal ecology of strategy-making also provides a framework for integrating the process and content aspects of strategy, which sometimes have been viewed as distinctly separate. The Intel study illustrates that strategy process generates strategy content. Intel deployed its distinctive technological competencies in new, unplanned directions, which generated new strategic content, notably new product-market opportunities related to the microprocessor. The Intel study also illustrates that new strategic content, in turn, disciplines the strategy-making process. The new microprocessor product-market opportunities forced the allocation of manufacturing away from DRAM, and the cumulative effect of these allocation decisions led Intel to exit from the DRAM business.

> **Insight 5.3.** Companies that are relatively successful over long periods of time, say, ten years or more, will be characterized by a top management that is concerned with building the quality of the company's induced and autonomous strategy processes as well as with the content of the strategy itself.

Simultaneity of Induced and Autonomous Strategy Processes

Combining induced and autonomous strategy processes gives companies a chance to outsmart or outrun the selective pressures associated with environmental change. Companies have to keep both processes in play at all times, even though this means that the company never completely maximizes its efforts in the current domain (it always has some uncommitted resources available to support autonomous initiatives). This also implies that strategic intent and internal entrepreneurship, separately, are not sufficient for organizational survival. Both are needed simultaneously. Research of failing corporations suggests that they miss the ability to maintain these different concerns simultaneously. They tend to operate either in an inactive (no strategic change) or hyperactive (excessive and vacillating strategic change) mode.[27]

> **Insight 5.4.** Companies that are relatively successful over long periods of time, say, ten years or more, will be characterized by maintaining top-driven strategic intent while simultaneously maintaining bottoms-up driven strategic renewal.

The simultaneity of induced and autonomous strategy processes also implies that a sequential approach to strategic change involving periods of convergence strictly punctuated by strategic reorientations may not be optimal in the long run. As the analysis of Intel's transformation indicates, internal variation and selection processes involving autonomous strategic initiatives preceded the company's successful transformation.

> **Insight 5.5.** Successful strategic reorientations are more likely to have been preceded by internal variation (experimentation) and selection processes than unsuccessful reorientations.

These insights do not imply of course that there is only one way to organize strategy-making or that top managers should get overly absorbed in the details of these processes. Also, there is no fixed optimal ratio of emphasis on the induced versus autonomous strategy processes. At different times in a company's development a different emphasis on these processes may be warranted, and there may not be a fixed life cycle characterizing a company's evolution. Old firms may continue to be able to act like young ones, even though young ones may not be equally able to act like old ones. The renewal capacity associated with the autonomous strategy process may enable companies to negate the inevitability of aging and decline. By the same token, it may expose them again, to some extent, to the liabilities of newness.

CONCLUSION

This chapter examined Intel's strategy-making process through the lens of the internal ecology model—Tool II—that distinguishes between induced and autonomous strategy processes. Strategy-making that involves induced and autonomous processes balances variation-reduction and variation-increasing mechanisms. The induced strategy process accommodates incremental adjustments, but also eventually leads to strategic inertia. The autonomous strategy process expands the firm's domain and augments the organization's distinctive competence base, countering strategic inertia and serving some of the functions of a reorientation. At Intel, during Epoch I, there was a close correspondence between the internal selection environment and the external selection environment: Resource allocation in the induced process favored business activities that were able to get high returns in the current external environment. At the same time, Intel kept open the possibility to activate processes of strategic context determination through which new, autonomous strategic initiatives got a chance to obtain resources to demonstrate their viability.

Given dynamic distinctive competencies, companies naturally generate autonomous strategic initiatives that create internal variation. Microprocessors were an important example among many at Intel during Epoch I. As a result of internal and external selection, some autonomous strategic initiatives may win and others may lose. But the genius of surviving companies lies in their ability to benefit from both winning and losing autonomous strategic initiatives. This suggests a company-level analogy to societal-level processes documented by economic historians, who have provided insight in how western capitalism has used decentralized entrepreneurialism. Western capitalism has allowed innovators to bear the losses of failed experiments and to gain the profits of successful ones, and it has benefited from both in terms of growth.[28]

The analogy, however, is not perfect. First, autonomous strategic initiatives usually turn out to have some interdependencies (sometimes interference) with various activities in the induced strategy process, which have to be managed. The success of autonomous strategic initiatives depends on a proactive learning process based on strategic recognition and resulting in strategic context determination, which involves multiple levels of management. Also, like their external entrepreneurial counterparts, internal entrepreneurs make a rational assessment of the available opportunities for career advancement in the company relative to outside opportunities. This raises questions about how incentives may need to be different in the induced and autonomous strategy processes and how changing incentives may affect a company's capacity to adapt. Intel was able to retain many of its internal entrepreneurs because they were offered stock options in the company. The company's rapidly rising, if fluctuating, stock price offered the prospect of significant individual wealth accumulation and thus provided "strong incentives" for staying with the company, independent of operating in the induced or autonomous process.[29]

A related issue concerns the effects that external and internal resource constraints may have on the degree to which induced and autonomous strategic initiatives are supported by top management during any given period in a company's history. For instance, if the remaining growth opportunities in an organization's familiar environment are plenty, top management may be less inclined to support autonomous initiatives. At Intel this possibility was foreseen, correctly as it turned out, by Gordon Moore in 1989 (see chapters 6 through 9 concerning Epoch II). The availability of uncommitted resources, on the other hand, may stimulate the emergence of autonomous initiatives. Rather than simply being driven by these sorts of natural forces, deliberately balancing the emphasis on induced and autonomous strategy processes throughout a company's evolution is an important strategic leadership task. As the study of Intel's Epoch II will show, it is very difficult to meet this strategic leadership challenge.

In conclusion, this chapter shows that the opposite views of blind natural selection or prescient and comprehensive strategic planning are both too narrow to act as the basis for understanding organizational adaptation. The pure environmental selection view misses the additional insights that can be obtained from considering the internal ecology of strategy-making. The pure strategic planning view misses the ecological components altogether. An internal ecological perspective on strategy-making thus provides a useful input to organization theory as well as a tool for thinking differently about the role of strategy in a company's evolution.

Epoch II:
Intel the Microprocessor Company

Let Chaos reign, then rein in chaos.

Intel CEO ANDY GROVE, 1994

6   CREATING A

STRATEGY VECTOR:

INDUCED STRATEGIC

ACTION

Why are some firms extraordinarily successful during part of their history? Organizational and strategic management researchers are mostly concerned with studying ordinary states, and they expect regression toward the mean to wash out fluctuations over time, but the phenomenon of periods of extraordinary success is interesting. They usually depend on the confluence of external and internal forces that are mostly not under the organization's control. Nevertheless, such periods are often also associated with leaders who seem to have an outstanding ability to make the organization exploit its fortuitous circumstances, seemingly approximating the ideal of the rational actor model of strategy-making.

The rational actor model is often held up as the ideal, but few studies have actually documented its successful realization. In fact, organizational and strategic management researchers have long highlighted the difficulties leaders encounter in aligning organizational action in the pursuit of deliberate strategic intent. The cumulative evidence suggests relatively modest prospects for top management being able to set clear strategic intent and getting the organization to fully and effectively implement it. Studying the rare cases in which leaders are able to achieve this improbable state of affairs helps produce useful insights into the role of strategic leadership. Andy Grove's decade as CEO of Intel Corporation was a rare case in which a company leader successfully set strategic intent and created a process for its relentless and successful pursuit.

In 1987, Gordon Moore passed the CEO mantle to Andy Grove who remained in the position until early 1998. During the years of Grove's tenure as CEO, Epoch II in Intel's history, Intel established itself as the leading microprocessor company in the world. Intel's performance during that period was nothing less than spectacular. Between 1987 and 1997, the company's revenues increased from $1.9 billion to $25.1 billion, an increase of 29.4 percent per annum. Net income grew from $248 million to $6.9 billion, an increase of 39.5 percent per annum. In 1997, $100 invested in Intel stock in 1987 would have been worth $2,078. In 1997, Intel was the sixth most profitable company in the world, and its net margin of 28 percent was 2.5 times higher than any other company in the top ten.[1] Sales of Pentium microprocessors and related board-level products comprised about 80 percent of the company's revenues and a substantial majority of its 1997 gross margin. In 1998, reflecting on his tenure as Intel's CEO, Grove said: "The most significant thing was the transformation of the company from a broadly positioned, across-the-board semiconductor supplier that did OK to a highly focused, highly tuned producer of microprocessors, which did better than OK."[2]

Grove described his strategic leadership approach as *vectorizing* Intel's strategy-making process. A vector—a quantity having direction and magnitude, denoted by a line drawn from its original to its final position (*Oxford English Dictionary*)—seems an apt metaphor for Grove's efforts to align strategy and action to secure and exploit Intel's preeminence as supplier of microprocessors in the PC market segment. By creating a strategy vector, Grove was able to drive Intel in the intended direction with a total force equal to all the forces at its disposal. Grove's strategy vector created an exceptionally strong induced-strategy process, which gave Intel the opportunity to become a key driver of the development of the PC market segment.

GAINING PREEMINENCE IN THE INTEL ARCHITECTURE MICROPROCESSOR MARKET SEGMENT

Intel's Opportunity in the Horizontal PC Industry

The microprocessor was a truly disruptive technology.[3] Initially, microprocessor-based personal computers couldn't do what mainframes and minicomputers were able to do, but they found a new group of customers for whom the functionality they offered was good enough. The microprocessor was subject to Moore's Law and made possible a revolutionary decline in price/performance of computing—a greater than "10X" change. Before long microprocessor-based computers would be good enough to perform an increasing number of tasks hitherto performed by minicomputers and even mainframes.

The success of the Apple II microcomputer in the late 1970s signaled that a new, microprocessor-based computing architecture had arrived. By 1979, IBM felt the need to respond and engaged in a crash effort to develop and market its first PC. As discussed in chapter 5, IBM chose Intel's 8088 microprocessor and Microsoft's MS-DOS operating system as the key components of its PC. IBM's choice of an open-system architecture for its PC was no doubt motivated by the need to move fast in the face of Apple's surge. But it also established that the vertical, proprietary system model of mainframes and minicomputers was giving way to a horizontal, open-system model in the personal computer industry. Microprocessor technology and operating software technology were major components that were now being developed by different companies in distinct horizontal industry layers, and the co-ordination of these rapidly evolving technologies between layers would take place primarily through market mechanisms rather than hierarchical ones (vertical inte-grated companies).[4] The implications of this fundamental change for IBM and the component suppliers were initially not quite clear. At first IBM was very suc-cessful with the IBM PC. Apple had welcomed the entry of IBM into the personal computer industry as a legitimizing force with big advertisements in major news-papers. But by 1984, it was IBM not Apple Computer that had become the standard in the PC industry.

The horizontal PC industry was governed by "increasing returns to adoption," a new economic force that was not well understood initially by most of the indus-try participants.[5] Increasing returns to adoption meant that a technological plat-form, such as Intel's x86 microprocessor architecture, became increasingly valuable as more and more people were using it. Achieving a high installed base was the key to setting in motion the virtuous circle associated with increasing re-turns to adoption. The high installed base of a technological platform motivated the development of software applications. The availability of software applications in-creased the value of the platform. The increased value of the platform attracted more users and hence increased the installed base. Increasing returns to adoption created a winner-takes-all competitive situation.

The strategic position of the x86 architecture. By the mid-1980s, Intel deci-sively shaped the basis of competitive advantage in the microprocessor industry by gaining a very large market segment share for the x86 architecture in the booming personal computer industry. With the help of the CRUSH and CHECKMATE cam-paigns (see chapter 5), Intel's 8086 microprocessor product family had won important battles in the "between-architectures" competition in the microprocessor industry against Motorola, Zilog and others (like Rockwell). The prospects of Zilog and other microprocessor manufacturers relative to those of Intel looked dim in the mid-1980s. Having obtained the Apple Computer design win, Motorola was still an important player to reckon with in the future. The main battle for Intel in the mid-1980s was about gaining greater share for itself in the Intel Architecture market segment. Indeed in 1984, when the Intel Architecture accounted for 59 percent of all 16-bit microprocessors, Intel's own market segment share was much lower.

Intel had to fight this battle against the traditional licensees of its x86 architecture, and these still included Japanese companies such as NEC and Fujitsu. In fact, the threat of the Japanese in the mid-1980s loomed as large in microprocessors as it had in DRAM. By the mid-1980s it appeared that the worldwide unit market segment share of Japanese owned companies would surpass that of U.S. owned companies during the late 1980s. This is clear from Figure 6.1. The change in the trajectories of the U.S. and Japanese companies beyond 1985 was almost completely due to Intel's new corporate strategy and its flawless execution.

New Corporate Strategy Reflects Top Management Learning

In 1985, Intel's top management officially recognized the reality that microprocessors were the company's new core business. The new corporate strategy affirmed that microprocessors, which had originated in Intel's autonomous strategy process,

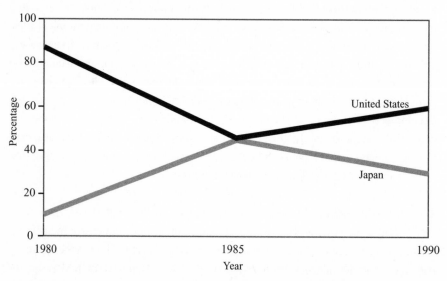

Figure 6.1. Microprocessors Worldwide Unit Market Share (United States-Owned versus Japan-Owned Companies). (SOURCE: International Data Corporation.)

were now the central focus of the company's induced strategy process. The new corporate strategy was based on three cornerstones: (1) maintaining Intel's architectural leadership in the microprocessor market segment, (2) becoming sole-source supplier of 386 and future generations of Intel Architecture-based microprocessors, and (3) becoming a world-class manufacturer. The new corporate strategy also recognized that personal computers would be the most important application for Intel's x86 microprocessors.

The cornerstones of Intel's new corporate strategy reflected key lessons that top management had learned from the DRAM exit. These cornerstones were a reaction to the organizational trauma caused by losing a core business. Intel did not want to experience this trauma again. In the context of a case discussion in an MBA class at Stanford Business School in the early 1990s, Andy Grove pointed out: "We learned that we had to get around the companies that had subjugated us in DRAM. We learned that high market share was critical for success, and that to get market share we had to be willing to invest in manufacturing capacity. Such investments involve big bets because they have to be made in advance of actual demand. We learned that commodity businesses are unattractive, so we didn't want to license out our intellectual property anymore."

Architectural leadership: design plus process technology. The design of the 386 was a step-function improvement over that of the 286. Design competencies, however, would not be sufficient to assure lasting architectural leadership. Process technology competencies—especially linewidth reduction (shrink)—were extremely important for continuously achieving increases in performance and integration of new features, and lowering unit costs. As a result of the exit from DRAM, Andy Grove moved Sunlin Chou and his DRAM technology development group—Intel's most advanced group, working already on 1.0-micron technology at the time—to the 386 microprocessor. They helped shrink the 386 microprocessor, which allowed more space to integrate features. Jack Carsten, a former vice president and general manager of the Components Group at the time of the DRAM exit, said in 1988: "Lots of people talk about the design team that developed Intel's 386 chip. It's a great product. But, the great unsung heroes at Intel are the people who successfully developed the shrink technology for the 386. That reduction in geometry led to higher performance parts as well as to higher yields."

World-class manufacturing and vendor relations. The success of a sole-source strategy would critically depend on building world-class manufacturing competencies, something that Intel clearly lacked during Epoch I. A major cause of Intel's poor manufacturing lay in the lack of standardized interface between process technology and manufacturing. A key decision therefore was to change the routine for transferring process technology to manufacturing. The introduction of the Copy Exact approach prevented the Intel U from recurring in microprocessors (see chapter 2) and enhanced speed as well as quality in manufacturing ramps. Developing world-class manufacturing competencies also required improved management of relationships with equipment suppliers. Equipment suppliers in the semiconductor industry continued to be driven by the needs of the DRAM producers who were the biggest equipment purchasers.

Sole-source strategy. In retrospect, the decision to become sole-source supplier—aside from a licensing agreement with IBM—was the most important strategic decision Intel made. Dennis Carter, however, recalled that the initial decision was not to become the sole-source supplier, but simply to make sure that Intel was getting a fair return on its increasingly large investments in chip design:

> In the early days of the microprocessor market segment, there emerged a plethora of new architectures. The key in those days was to get design wins from the engineers in the OEM-customer organizations, and then to license your design to several second-source manufacturers—form a coalition of companies—in order to become the preferred standard. The competition was intense. For instance, Intel's 8080 lost out as the design standard to Zilog's Z80 and we only regained it with the 8086—we had a dozen or so licensees for the 8086. . . .
>
> However, we noticed that designing the next-generation chip and getting design wins was becoming more and more expensive. The cost of the 386, for instance, was over $100 million compared with about $50 million for the 286. The value added of design had become larger than the value added of manufacturing. Yet, the second-source manufacturers did not have to incur any of these design-related costs. So, we decided we were not going to give away the design anymore; we wanted to sell it to the second-source manufacturers. But nobody was interested!

The situation was exacerbated by the fact that, while the 286 had again been selected by IBM for its next generation PC, demand for the 286 had been less than forecast. According to Gordon Moore,

> The 80286 was introduced in 1982, and we were given huge forecasts. This was a new generation of products, and we had IBM using several other things, too. It looked like we would need more than we would be

able to make ourselves. So we ended up sourcing the 286 technology very widely. We had AMD in the United States, Fujitsu in Japan, and Siemens in Europe. We did lots of sourcing. The actual demand was about one-third of what we had been led to believe, so this turned out to be a very competitive business. We essentially gave away the profits on several generations of product.

During previous x86 generations, Intel had engaged in a broad cross-licensing agreement with Advanced Micro Devices (AMD) in which AMD acted as a second source and promised to provide development of support chips. Intel's top management believed that AMD had not lived up to its promise. With the arrival of the 386, top management decided that if AMD did or could not perform under the existing agreement, Intel would become sole-source supplier. In 1989, Craig Barrett, executive vice president and general manager of the Microcomputer Components Group, described some of the factors that figured in the decision:

Basically, Intel got to the point where it could generate enough customer confidence to pull it off. There were at least several factors at work. Our quality thrust of the early 80s began to pay off in improved consistency on the manufacturing line and overall better product quality. In addition, customer-vendor partnerships became more prevalent throughout our business. . . . We also decided to pursue a "vendor of choice" strategy in 1984, which led to improved customer satisfaction. Finally the experience with earlier x86 generations led us to believe that we could accurately forecast demand for the 386 and put sufficient manufacturing capacity in place. . . . And, as our second-source deal with AMD came unraveled, we put in the capability to never miss a shipment by adding strategic inventory and redundant capacity.

Intel's decision led to a widely publicized legal dispute with AMD that was only settled in the mid-1990s. Bob Reed, Intel's chief financial officer in 1989, underlined the importance of intellectual property to Intel. He pointed out that Intel's legal department had grown from five to twenty internal people in the past five years, and that in addition they retained outside counsel. In 1986, a court had ruled that microcode can be copyrighted and that Intel's copyright was valid, in response to a lawsuit brought by NEC. Reed concluded: "We vigorously pursue anyone who infringes on our intellectual property rights."

In a Stanford MBA class in 1999, Andy Grove impressed on the students how difficult the decision to become sole source actually had been. He said:

You're sitting in a room with IBM purchasing executives who purchase more of any one item in one month than all of your total production for the year, and they ask, "Who is your second source?" Weigh in the balance: what good is the 386 if IBM doesn't adopt it?

Further reconstructing Intel's strategic logic, Grove continued:

[We realized that] the factor that determined the potential outcome didn't depend on Intel but on the customers. If the industry dynamics in the PC industry are competitive, with backward compatibility being important, then the purchasing people at IBM will get overruled by the marketing people.
We were chewing our nails until 1986, when Compaq adopted the 386. IBM adopted it the next year.

The Success Story of Intel's 386 Microprocessor

The shipment of the 386 microprocessor was announced during the same week in October 1985 when Intel made the decision to close the last DRAM fab in Oregon. The 386 microprocessor embodied a discontinuous improvement in the x86 architecture over the 286, and paved the way for PCs to become a serious alternative to centralized computing for an increasing number of applications. The electronics industry received the 386 microprocessor with great enthusiasm. Just one year later, in the third-quarter of 1986, OEM customers completed development of new products, and the first products to contain the 386 microprocessor were shipped. By then, the new microprocessor had garnered over 200 design wins by virtue of its upward compatibility with existing personal computer software and its broad applications in other markets.

The role of compatibility in the success of the 386. Before the 386, the importance of compatibility had not been clearly understood at Intel. Dennis Carter provided insight in the strategic recognition of the importance of compatibility: "We had planned for the 80186 to be the next winner in the x86 market segment. But the 186 didn't go anywhere. IBM didn't like the 186 because it didn't run 8086 software. Design changes in the I/O system made it incompatible with the operating system. The 286, on the other hand, was designed primarily for the high end and was not expected to be a winner. But since it was really designed as two-machines-in-one, it could actually run 8086 software."
Paul Otellini, executive vice president in charge of Intel Architecture, ex-

plained in 1999: "We didn't really understand the importance of compatibility between different generations of processors. I remember a meeting in 1982 with Don Estridge who was running the IBM PC division. We had just finished the 286 and were shipping it to IBM. Estridge called Gordon [Moore] and me up to San Francisco and lectured us on the importance of compatibility—the 286 was not strictly compatible with its predecessor. As a result of this experience, we finally got it. Backward compatibility is really critical."

The 386's ability to leverage previous software led to the most rapid ramp up of production for any microprocessor in Intel's history. By the end of 1987, just two years after introduction, Intel had shipped an estimated 800,000 units as compared to 50,000 units for the earlier 8086 at two years after its introduction. In 1989, analysts estimated that the 386 and its support chips generated nearly $1 billion, or between 30 and 40 percent of revenue for the company in fiscal year 1988.

Intel's sole source and upward compatibility strategies fundamentally changed the basis of competition in the Intel Architecture-based microprocessor market segment to the company's advantage. While the Intel Architecture had won the lion's share in the 16-bit microprocessor generation against other architectures, Intel's share of the market tended to decline precipitously over time in previous product generations. In 1987, the company's market share for 8088 chips (introduced in 1980) was about 30 percent; and for 80286 chips (introduced in 1983) the company's market share was about 65 percent. For 80386 chips (introduced in 1985), however, Intel still had 100 percent market segment share in 1987.

The importance of end user-oriented marketing. Nevertheless, the 386's share of the fast-growing total microprocessor market segment was fairly flat until 1989. This led, for the first time, to the strategic recognition of the importance of marketing to end-users in addition to the technical marketing efforts oriented toward OEM customers. Intel's Corporate Marketing Group (CMG) got its start in the early 1980s as a division of the Microprocessor Group (MPG). The End-User Marketing Group in CMG was a small team of "guerrilla marketeers." Several smaller-scale advertising programs had been used to encourage end-users to adopt the latest Intel technology. Dennis Carter pointed out:

> The 386 was perceived as a high-end product: too expensive and more appropriate for workstations. So in 1989, we brought out the 386SX, which was a cheaper version because it was easier to manufacture. It had basically the same cost as the 286. [Note: SX is the same basic processor design but without an on-chip math-coprocessor (floating-point).]
>
> Yet, the OEMs did not push sales of the 386SX because end-users

were still happy with 286-based machines and the OEMs were getting high margins on these. So we decided we ourselves needed to tell the end users—at this time, these were the IT managers in large corporations and the hobbyists. This led to our Red X campaign in 1989 in which we placed billboards along highways that showed the 286 crossed out by a large red X and replaced with the 386SX.

The Red X advertising campaign was a vivid signal that Intel was ready to cannibalize its own products, and that the end-users, and by implication the OEMs, should follow Intel's lead. It worked. The annualized run rate of Intel's 386 microprocessor increased from about 4 million units in 1989 to about 18 million units by mid-1991, after which time it began to decline rapidly in the face of competitive pressures.

Competition emerges in the 386 market segment.   Intel was able to serve as sole source for the 386 for four years. But, having introduced its first Intel-compatible 386 microprocessor in 1990, AMD became the 386 market leader by 1992. AMD's AM386 processors accounted for more than 50 percent of the 386 market in 1992. AMD achieved this position in the face of severe price cuts by Intel. From a $299 price at launch, the average price of the 386 had dropped to $91 by 1993.

The Success Story of Intel's *i*486 Microprocessor

The *i*486 microprocessor was introduced in April 1989. With more than 1 million transistors the *i*486 contained nearly four times the circuit elements of the 386. The *i*486 had taken a total of 130 human/years in design effort, compared to 80 for the 386. It had benefited from a fourfold increase in proprietary specialized design tools created by Intel. The overall investment in the *i*486 development had been more than $200 million. In keeping with its strategy of backward compatibility, Intel had designed the new product offering to run software developed for its predecessors. The *i*486 was expected to be especially important for the growing market of a new class of servers. These servers could store information for an entire corporation, and send it out as needed to PCs in response to queries from different types of users (engineers, accountants, marketing specialists, senior executives, and so on). In 1990, the market for servers was projected to grow from $4 billion to $12 billion in 1994.

The importance of the Intel Inside campaign.   In April 1990, under the impulse of Dennis Carter, Intel launched its first Intel Inside campaign. Aimed directly at end users, rather than Intel's traditional OEM customers, the campaign sought to influence customers to ask specifically for Intel microprocessors when they purchased a PC. This was a bold move with few precedents.[6] This effort, which had been hotly debated in the industry, was the most noticeable effect of the changes brought about by Intel's Corporate Marketing Group. CMG became committed to transforming Intel from a microcomputer company that marketed primarily to a small number of engineers, to a branded products company that marketed to both the traditional technical customers (its OEMs) as well as a mass, nontechnical audience. CMG oversaw all Intel communications programs aimed at end users, except those related to Intel's retail products marketed by the Intel Products Group (more on IPG in chapter 9).

From 1990 to 1993, CMG invested more than $500 million in programs designed to increase Intel's brand equity with end users. Intel Inside was the largest and most visible of these investments. It was composed of two broad thrusts. The first involved advertising and merchandising activities with OEMs. This included cooperative advertising with OEMs that displayed the Intel Inside logo in their print ads and product catalogs. In addition, promotions for OEMs displayed the Intel Inside logo (usually a sticker) on their point-of-sale displays and packaging materials. The second thrust was a series of print and TV ad campaigns focused on Intel Inside and the associated brand promise, which were placed directly by Intel. These print and television ad programs stressed Intel's guarantee of safety and advanced technology. Safety was seen both as software compatibility and upgradeability. Ads also emphasized Intel's latest technology.

According to Intel's market research, the Intel Inside campaign significantly increased end-user awareness of the Intel brand name and enhanced the perception of Intel as a technology leader versus competitors such as AMD and Cyrix. However, not every OEM welcomed Intel Inside with open arms. Major OEMs such as Compaq and IBM were less enthusiastic about the program and refused to participate in some elements. These OEMs thought that Intel Inside decreased their ability to differentiate their products from the competition.

Closing holes in the product offering. In late 1992, Intel announced plans to introduce more than 25 versions of the i486 during 1993. Albert Yu, general manager of the Microprocessor Product Group, noted "Our competitors seek niches initially and then expand out of them." Another senior manager added "AMD and Cyrix got into the 386 market because we left gaps. . . . We've worked to minimize holes in the i486 processor family." Tom MacDonald, director of marketing for the 386 and i486 processor families elaborated:

We knew there were holes in the 386 but we focused more on the 486. Once the 386 was designed, it was finished. We didn't add additional features. Our strategy for the 486 is to cover all the holes. We have a number of design teams working on a wide range of proliferations of the basic 486 design. The versions differ based on the speed of the processor clock (MHz), the package type, and other features (e.g., lower operating voltage, and the inclusion of power management features). Our design goal is to be the fastest processor at a given MHz (clock speed) and to offer the most MHz.

In terms of pricing, AMD and Cyrix tend to charge slightly less than Intel with slightly more MHz. For example: AMD initially offered a 45MHz AM386DX for slightly less than an Intel 33MHz 386DX. [Note: In contrast to SX, DX stands for the high-end processor version, which includes an on-chip math-coprocessor.]

Competition emerges in the *i*486 market segment. Intel was able to be sole source for the *i*486 for four years again. It took until the summer of 1993 before AMD launched its first 486-compatible processors. The new chips were delayed over six months by the legal dispute about AMD's right to use key Intel intellectual property. AMD initially lost a court decision on the matter; however, the decision was overturned in May. Immediately following the reversal, which was appealed by Intel, AMD announced that two 486-compatible processors were entering production. In July, AMD announced a new set of 486 compatibles that utilized internally developed microcode and didn't rely on the Intel intellectual property in question. AMD expected to achieve a 5 percent of the 486 market segment in 1993, and a 20 percent share by the end of 1994. Industry analysts expected AMD's short-term ability to gain market share to depend, in part, on its ability to add new manufacturing capacity. AMD's prices matched corresponding Intel parts. This was not surprising because Intel had been unable to fully meet demand for the *i*486 throughout the first half of 1993. In early October, Intel announced plans to drop fourth-quarter prices for some *i*486SX processors by 20 to 30 percent.

Cyrix, a start-up founded in 1987 by a group of Texas Instruments engineers, entered the microprocessor market segment in 1991 with the Cy486SLC. Fitting into a 386 socket and incorporating many features found in the *i*486 family, the Cy486SLC was more powerful than any member of the Intel 386 family of processors, but not as powerful as the *i*486SX25, Intel's entry-level 486. Late in May 1993, Cyrix introduced a line of six Intel 486SX-compatible processors. The products were priced comparably with Intel's processors. Cyrix depended on two large semiconductor partners for production capacity and access to crucial intellectual property. Cyrix did not have the rights to manufacture and sell Intel-compatible microprocessors. However, rights to key technologies necessary to duplicate the Intel Architecture were widely cross-licensed during the late 1970s and early 1980s. Texas Instruments (TI) and SGS Thomson Microelectronics, each of whom had rights to the necessary Intel technology, served as Cyrix's manufacturing and marketing partners. While these rights were initially challenged by Intel, U.S. courts upheld Cyrix's ability to design and market processors manufactured by its partners. However, Cyrix managers publicly complained that they were not able to fill orders for their 486s because TI was not making enough production capacity available for Cyrix's products. Cyrix managers confirmed that TI was preparing to use most of its microprocessor production capacity for its own line of 486-compatible processors.

IBM, the world's largest PC maker in 1993 and Intel's largest customer, manufactured versions of Intel's microprocessors under license from Intel. IBM's license allowed it to alter Intel's designs to increase performance or to add features. Historically, IBM used this license to differentiate its PC product line from other OEMs. In 1993, IBM's microelectronics division had begun selling components outside of IBM for the first time, and was actively seeking to supply other PC makers with its enhanced Intel-compatible processors. These processors were being positioned directly against those of Intel.

The Strategic Situation in the Early 1990s

By the early 1990s, Intel had established a preeminent position in the personal computer microprocessor business based on the Intel Architecture. Every manufacturer of advanced IBM-compatible personal computers—except IBM—had to purchase the 386 or i486 microprocessor from Intel. Similarly, those manufacturers or their customers had to purchase operating system software from Microsoft Corporation to maintain backward compatibility with the thousands of programs already developed for the PC market. During 1990, NCR had been the first Intel customer to decide to use Intel microprocessors throughout its entire product line. AMD had successfully entered the 386 market segment in 1990, and together with Cyrix also entered the 486 market segment in 1993. But Intel had been able to achieve high growth and very high margins by being first to market in each generation and holding competitors at bay for several years each time.

Key Strategic Insight: The New Computer Industry

By the early 1990s Intel, and Andy Grove in particular, had begun to realize that the microprocessor had fundamentally changed the computer industry. Grove was perhaps the first CEO to clearly see the strategic implications of the transformation of the computer industry from vertical to horizontal. Grove clearly understood that the strategic imperative implied by increasing returns to adoption was to achieve and maintain the preeminence of the Intel Architecture in the microprocessor layer of the PC industry because this created a virtuous circle: Intel's microprocessors became more attractive to end users the more they were adopted. Grove also clearly understood the implications that this imperative had for the way in which Intel's strategy-making process needed to be managed.

INTEL'S INTERNAL ECOLOGY OF STRATEGY-MAKING: RISC VERSUS CISC

While Intel established itself as the preeminent supplier of Intel Architecture-based microprocessors for the booming PC industry in the late 1980s, engineering workstations created a new market segment for microprocessors. This market segment required high-performance graphics and intensive computation. Sun Microsystems, a start-up company in the early 1980s, had pioneered an open systems approach in this market segment. In some of its early systems, Sun had used the Intel 386 chip, but instead of Microsoft's MS-DOS operating system had chosen the UNIX operating system. Scott McNeally, Sun's president believed that Intel was charging too much for its 386 processors, so he initiated the development of Sun's own microprocessor based on the RISC architecture.

The Intel Architecture was based on Complex Instruction Set Computer (CISC) design. Sun's new microprocessor was based on Reduced Instruction Set Computing (RISC) design. *Reduced Instruction Set Computing* was a term describing a microprocessor design philosophy that emerged in the mid-1980s.[7] Microprocessor instructions are the lowest level commands processed by a microprocessor and include functions such as "retrieve from memory" or "compare two numbers." RISC processors support fewer instructions (70–80) than CISC (100–150). As a result, RISC chips offered better performance over a narrow range and could be optimized for a specific purpose. Also, RISC processors were much simpler to design and much cheaper to manufacture.

RISC had been developed in IBM's research labs in the early-to-mid 1970s, but it was MIPS Computersystems, a Silicon Valley start-up that attempted to commercialize the technology in the mid-1980s for workstation computers. Soon several other companies, including Sun, HP, IBM, and DEC began work on their own RISC architectures.

In an exploratory meeting with Andy Grove in August 1988 about writing a case on Intel, one of the strategic issues on Grove's mind was whether Intel should start a "RISC branch."[8] Grove seemed to be leaning fairly strongly against starting such a new branch. So it was a bit of a surprise when the front page of Intel's *1989 Annual Report* actually showed a picture of the *i*860 RISC chip. Afterward Grove explained that the *i*860 chip was the outcome of a strategic initiative started by an engineer in Intel's design organization who had acted quite autonomously in pushing the development of the new chip.[9]

Autonomous Strategic Action Generates the *i*860 RISC Processor

The story of Intel's entering into the RISC processor business details the emergence of a new product family, which ultimately challenged Intel's core microprocessor strategy. It illustrates the ability of an astute technologist to test and to modify the boundaries of Intel's official corporate strategy.

In the late 1980s, Intel's official corporate strategy was *not* to enter the RISC business, but rather to focus on the extremely successful x86 (CISC) architecture. Intel's top management called RISC "the technology of the have not." And the strength of the organization's aversion to RISC architectures was demonstrated by the corporate argot, YARP, for Yet Another RISC Processor. Yet, a young engineer by the name of Les Kohn had been attempting to get Intel into the RISC processor business ever since joining the company in 1982.

While talking in understated terms about his approach, it appeared Kohn had a deliberate strategy, which could be viewed as somewhat surreptitious from the perspective of corporate strategy. He mentioned that there was some realization at levels below top management that Intel needed to broaden beyond the x86 (CISC) market, but that there was no agreement on what to do and how to do it. He also intimated that there were various contending architectures at different points. From a technical point of view, Kohn believed that RISC architecture had intrinsic advantages over CISC architecture. However, he had learned from several more straightforward attempts at the product approval process that an approach that supported rather than challenged the status quo would be more likely successful. Also, the investment needed was too large to do it under the table. His solution was to disguise his product. Kohn said:

I joined the company in 1982 after working for National on their 32000 processor. At that time, I realized that RISC architecture had some definite technical advantages. That was very difficult to see from Intel's perspective of the x86 architecture. So even at the technical level, there was no clear consensus that RISC was the right approach.

Between 1982 and 1986, I made several proposals for RISC projects throughout the Intel product planning system, but I wasn't successful. RISC was not an existing business and people were not convinced that the market was there. Also, the company had had a bad experience with a new architecture, the 432, which was not commercially successful. Experience makes skeptics. The design would have been way too big to do in a skunk works.

In 1986, I saw that our next generation processors would have 1 million transistors, and I started working on the idea of a RISC-based processor that would take full advantage of that technology. This proposal had more aggressive goals and was more convincing than previous ones. Several people, including a divisional general manager, got interested in the idea, and we drafted a product requirement document that outlined market size, pricing and rough development cost. Then we had several breaks that made the project go.

First of all, we positioned it as a coprocessor for the 80486 and made sure that it could be justified on that basis. We designed it as a stand-alone processor, but made it very useful as an accessory to the 486.

We made sure it was very different from the x86 family so that there would be no question in the customer's mind of which product to use. The real fortuitous part came when presentations to several large customers generated a lot of positive feedback to senior management. Feedback helps because at a technical level, senior management are not experts.

There were also a whole group of customers who did not previously talk to Intel, because they were more interested in performance than compatibility. 3D graphics, workstation, and minicomputer accounts all got very interested. In the end it looks like the *i*860 will generate a whole new business for Intel.

Kohn also pointed out that the 64-bit *i*860 chip (Intel's other microprocessors were 32-bit) utilized design concepts found in supercomputers. The *i*860 would be the brains for extremely powerful workstations that would bring the computing power of a Cray-1 supercomputer to the desktop. The design team wore T-shirts with a miniaturized Cray supercomputer icon resting on a chip. It was the first microprocessor to break the 1 million-transistor barrier. Commenting on their efforts to produce a 1 million-transistor RISC chip, Kohn said that to do it on schedule required a very close working relationship between technology development and the design team. He also mentioned the importance of advanced CAD tools in which Intel had made a strategic investment.

Strategic Context Determination of the i860

The RISC story shows how successful autonomous strategic action by internal entrepreneurs may lead to a change in corporate strategy. Andy Grove said that Kohn sold the design to top management as a coprocessor, rather than a stand-alone processor. He pointed out that this was possible because of the difficulties top management faced in assessing the advanced technical aspects of what Kohn was proposing. By the time top management realized what their "coprocessor" was, Kohn and two other champions had already lined up a customer base for the stand-alone processor that was different from the companies that purchased the 486 chips. Thus the i860 team could argue that they were broadening Intel's business rather than cannibalizing it. Even though top management had not officially sanctioned the development of the i860 as a stand-alone processor, Intel did in fact introduce the product as a stand-alone RISC microprocessor rather than as a coprocessor in February 1989. At that time, Andy Grove was quoted: "We had our own marketing story for the chip, but our customers changed it. They said, 'Listen, this isn't just a coprocessor chip. This could be the central processor of a super technical workstation.' Occasional jibes aside, we're in no position now to dump on RISC as a technology. Our chip shows what the real potential of RISC is." [10]

As Kohn pointed out, the i860 also had important implications for Intel's distinctive technological competencies in microprocessor design. In addition, the i860 story is important because it shows how the autonomous strategy process allows a company to become more clearly aware of, and prepare itself to cope with, environmental variations that have already come into play and might potentially threaten its competitive position. In 1989, Craig Barrett, a top-level Intel manager, pointed out that RISC was still viewed as relatively less important than CISC in Intel's strategy, but that its availability made it possible for Intel to be a strong competitor in what might become an important new market: "Intel's bread and butter are in the x86 product family. There is a 586 on the drawing board and a 686 planned to follow that. If there was ever any question of which comes first, it could be answered quickly. But if there are enough people out there who want to buy YARPS, then . . . the i860 . . . is the highest performance RISC processor on the market." Kohn's autonomous efforts made it possible for Intel to be prepared in case RISC would ever pose a threat to CISC.

Strategic Context Dissolution of the *i*860 RISC Processor in 1991

The threat of RISC, however, took a different form than envisaged by Kohn and his supporters within Intel. With the 8088 and 80286 microprocessors, Intel had clearly established itself as the architectural leader in microprocessors for the IBM-compatible PC market in the early 1980s. With the arrival of the 80386-micro-processor generation imminent, Intel had made the bold strategic move of declaring a sole-source strategy, no longer licensing the Intel Architecture (IA) microcode to other suppliers such as AMD. With Compaq becoming the first manufacturer to offer a 80386-based PC (IBM was delayed, in part, by trying to come up with a better 286 processor in-house), and clone manufacturers following suit, Intel (together with Microsoft) had begun to wrestle control of the PC industry away from IBM. The sole-source strategy for the 80386 processor was spectacularly successful, and the industry began to refer to Intel-compatible PCs rather than IBM-compatible PCs. Leveraging off increasing returns to adoption, Intel became the driving force of a fast-growing ecosystem involving independent software vendors (ISVs) that wrote applications programs for Intel-compatible PCs.[11] With the upcoming 80486 microprocessor, Intel was poised to further strengthen its strategic position as the architectural leader in microprocessors for PCs in the early 1990s.

During the late 1980s, however, the much smaller workstation industry (hundreds of thousands of units compared to the millions of units in the PC industry) had settled on RISC-based machines, and technologists like Les Kohn had become convinced that the performance advantage of RISC would eventually make CISC obsolete. Dennis Carter, Intel's vice president of corporate marketing, confirmed that in the late 1980s Intel was perceived as a technology laggard and that this hurt the company's growth in the workstation market. Some industry observers interpreted the introduction of the *i*860 as a signal that Intel was endorsing RISC. For instance, the *Wall Street Journal* published an article in February 1989 under the title, "Fast, Costly Chip From Intel Signals Firm's Endorsement of RISC Design."[12] This, however, could confuse Intel's existing PC OEM customers, who might fear that Intel would reduce support for the x86 architecture in the future.

That fear was not unfounded. Kohn's championing efforts within Intel had created a strong following. Distinct CISC and RISC camps—situated on different floors of the same building—had formed and they were competing for the best engineering talent of the company. Dennis Carter said that the RISC effort siphoned off hundreds of people just on the marketing side. Claude Leglise who headed up engineering and marketing for the *i*860 started working with ISVs to get the Unix operating system ported to the *i*860, as well as to write basic software such as compilers and tools. Andy Grove indicated that by 1989, RISC-based processor development had begun to absorb almost 50 percent of the total resources allocated to microprocessor development. He also said that people were drawing up a development trajectory showing the Intel Architecture transitioning to RISC after the 486. To facilitate the transition, RISC proponents were proposing that Intel develop 486c (CISC based) and 486r (RISC based) processors simultaneously. This alarmed Dennis Carter: "From a marketing perspective, this became a major issue for me. . . . Despite the similarities in the proposed names, the two chips were not at all compatible! This would destroy everything that we had created. I became pretty hysterical about it. In the end, the *i*860 was launched at the same time as the 486, but nothing about the x86 was associated with it. The key issue was don't confuse the brand!"

The two camps were also trying to gain allies in the industry. Andy Grove said: "Our allies at the time were Microsoft and Compaq. The *i*860 team went to Microsoft and talked them into supporting them. Microsoft was doing NT at the time and they wanted to port NT to the *i*860 first! Microsoft asked us to increase our investment in the *i*860. Compaq had always been straightforward and said we don't want the *i*860. If you do we will invest in other microprocessor makers (such as NexGen)." Grove later said that by 1989, the battle between CISC and RISC within Intel had turned into civil war. In February 1991, reflecting the considerable ambivalence experienced by top management during this period, Andy Grove said to a Stanford MBA class, which had just discussed the case about the *i*860:

> Three weeks from now I am giving a speech to 2,000 software developers in San Francisco. Probably 1,200 or so are dedicated to CISC; some 300 are dedicated to RISC; and the others are waiting to hear what Intel is going to do. What should I tell them? I have three options. I can tell them that we lean heavily on x86, that the x86 is forever. Or I can tell them that RISC is important and that Intel wants to be the premier company in RISC. Or I can tell them we will support both CISC and RISC and let the marketplace sort it out, just trust us.

Shortly after the February 1991 class, Grove sent me a freshly published article by a well-known computer architect turned consultant that he had just received. Grove had marked a paragraph concerning Motorola's struggle with the same issue, which he felt illustrated the danger associated with not taking a clear stand on the RISC versus CISC debate. The article reported:

The 88000 (RISC) further weakened Motorola's position. Inside and outside the company, the 88000 competed with the 68x0 (CISC). Motorola management did not establish clear directions for their products. Customers felt stuck. What would Motorola do long term? Would they dump the 68x0 and support the 88000? Would they attempt to support both? . . . Even if they were long-time customers, once they opened their decision process to accommodate different microprocessors from Motorola, they might as well open the decision process slightly more and consider microprocessors from other vendors as well." [13]

Referring to actions taken later in 1991, Dennis Carter recalled: "In the end, Andy (Grove) resolved the debate. He essentially did a compromise that favored CISC."

Denouement. Eventually, the *i*860 was not successful because demand for it petered out as every workstation vendor decided to develop its own RISC processor (which lead to the use of MORP—my own RISC processor—jargon within Intel). According to Claude Leglise: "It turns out that there was a lot of hype, and we got caught up in it. The reality is that there was not enough business to sustain the investment necessary to be competitive. . . . We won a number of deals, but all of them were low volume. We won Stratus Computer, which was a pretty big deal. We won every high-end 3D-graphics accelerator deal. But at the end of the day, there was no volume."

By 1993, Kohn and most of his technical team had left Intel. However, Intel succeeded in retaining most of the other people associated with the program. The ability to retain competencies by redeploying human resources is an important aspect of Intel's structural context. Claude Leglise explained: "After the *i*860, I shut down the operation and found jobs for everyone else. Andy [Grove] says that most CEOs move money around, but not people. We've institutionalized the redeployment of people. We move people around. I went from 225 employees to 3 in about 90 days. This was a very interesting experience, and it's something that Intel does quite well. This leads to less fear in the organization of doing something risky."

Darwinian Strategy-Making Process or No Strategy?

In a Stanford MBA class in February 1991, Andy Grove examined Intel's strategy-making process in light of how the company was dealing with the *i*860. He said:

The strategic process reflects the company's culture. You can look at it positively or negatively. Positively, it looks like a Darwinian process: we let the best ideas win; we adapt by ruthlessly exiting businesses; we provide autonomy and top management is the referee who waits to see who wins and then rearticulates the strategy; we match evolving skills with evolving opportunities. Negatively it looks like we have no strategy; we have no staying power; we are reactive, try and move somewhere else if we fail; we lack focus . . .

One year later, in another Stanford MBA class, Grove commented on the dangerous situation created by the *i*860 for Intel's existing strategic position: "It was a confusing period for Intel. . . . The *i*860 was a very successful renegade product that could have destroyed the virtuous circle enjoyed by the Intel Architecture. . . . Intel was helping RISC by legitimizing it. . . . We were dabbling in it and were trying to be the best of the second best."

For Grove, a key lesson was that "not all paradigm shifts are paradigm shifts." Having concluded that RISC did not constitute a paradigm shift strengthened his determination to fully exploit Intel's favorable strategic position. He said: "The commitment to the x86 architecture vectorized everybody at Intel in the same direction."

CREATING A STRATEGY VECTOR:
ALIGNING STRATEGY AND ACTION

The emergence of the *i*860 (RISC) microprocessor during Epoch II showed that Intel's autonomous-strategy process was still active in the late 1980s. The significance of the rise and fall of the *i*860 microprocessor, however, lies primarily in illuminating how Intel under Andy Grove's leadership was able to significantly strengthen its induced-strategy process. Grove's efforts to do so reflected his understanding of the strategic imperative to retain Intel's preeminence in the microprocessor market segment of the PC industry. Grove's efforts to vectorize everybody at Intel in the same direction turned Intel's internal ecology of strategy-making into a planned economy. This had implications for strategy-making as adaptive organizational capability at Intel. On the one hand, it created an induced-strategy process superbly suited for exploiting the rich opportunities in the PC market segment of the microprocessor industry. On the other hand, it set Intel on a course that narrowed the company and would make it more difficult to move into new businesses. But, as Gordon Moore had insightfully observed in 1989 (see chapter 5), the growth potential of the core microprocessor business would not make that a problem in the next twelve or so years. In many ways, Andy Grove was the right man for that long season.

Andy Grove's Strategic Leadership

Luck and strategic recognition. Observers sometimes point out that Intel was lucky to invent the microprocessor as a result of the Busicom contract, and even more lucky to obtain the IBM design win for the first PC. Both events were fortuitous, but they were not random. Busicom probably went to Intel because Intel had a reputation for being a world-class leader in circuit design and miniaturization. Part of the reason that IBM went to Intel was perhaps that Apple Computer had already signed up Motorola to supply its microprocessors. But the main reason was that Intel provided the most complete product and made extraordinary efforts to convince customers of this (Operation CRUSH). Given that Intel was nevertheless indeed somewhat lucky, it was *ex post facto* strategic recognition of the importance of these fortuitous events that set Intel on its highly successful course. An article in the *New York Times* in 1988 pointed out that it was "irksome to competitors . . . that there is a fair amount of luck involved in all of this [Intel's success]." Andy Grove responded: "There is such a thing as luck and then you grab it and exploit it." [14] Grove sometimes also called it "earned luck." [15] Ted Hoff, Federico Faggin, and other senior technical managers' early strategic recognition of the importance of the microprocessor helped set Intel on the course of transforming itself into a microprocessor company. But it was Andy Grove's forceful articulation of the need to capitalize on the opportunity in microprocessors and his capacity for getting the entire company to focus on executing the new corporate strategy that made the transformation successful.

Focus on execution. Andy Grove is well known for the expression, "Only the paranoid survive." Perhaps the first time that he used the expression was in his concluding remarks at the Annual Shareholder Meeting of March 26, 1985, which referred to the newly adopted corporate strategy: "We at Intel know that this industry is one where only the paranoid survive. We are running harder than ever; we are working our tails off. We are determined that we will come out of this period stronger in architectural leadership, in our position with our customers, and as a manufacturer." [16]

The expression has stuck with him, perhaps because he always manifested unusual intensity and diligence in pursuing matters important to Intel. Gordon

Moore is probably in the best position to describe Grove's leadership style. In 1995, Moore recalled: "Andy always made it hard on me. I would be all excited that we were under budget or ahead of schedule on a product—and he'd ask why we couldn't do it faster and cheaper. He got very interested in the art of management, and that served us very well."[17]

Looking back in 1999, Moore described how he, Noyce, and Grove had complemented one another:

> We generally complemented one another pretty well. With Bob Noyce and me, Noyce was more outside, while I was more inside. For example, he organized the second and third financing rounds completely by himself without any real input from me. I focused on the technology and the products, and I had a sound feel for the products and the markets. The thing about Bob was that everyone liked him. He had a tremendous personality, he was very bright, and he was full of ideas. The tough thing was that these ideas were usually too good to ignore. . . . Noyce was what I consider to be a real leader. He would suggest the right things to people and then go away. Andy is a true manager. He's very detail oriented. He has strong follow-up—he never trusted that anyone would do what they were asked unless there was follow up—and he is strongly data driven. I was somewhere in the middle.

When Andy Grove became CEO, Gordon Moore remained chairman. Grove and Moore worked closely with each other in running Intel. Moore explained how they complemented each other:

> Andy tends to see things in black and white, whereas I tend to see things in delicate shades of gray. In running the company, he was a very good amplifier for me, and we had a good relationship. He ran everything internally, and I worked through him and others. . . . When he became CEO, he really jumped on the opportunity to organize the industry. I wasn't so inclined to do this. He likes public exposure more than I did, and he has a stronger feeling about where it fits in. . . . Andy has had a tremendous impact on what's going on outside. He needed someone who was focused internally, and that's where Craig [Barrett] came in.

Andy Grove confirmed: "At no point in Intel's history has it been a solo show. It's never been only one person leading the organization. Our tradition is somewhat of a shared power structure." Nevertheless, Grove's impact on Intel's strategy-making process was decisive.

Sharp strategic insight. Current and former executive colleagues invariably expressed admiration for Andy Grove's mental abilities and his extraordinary capacity to focus his attention and energy. One senior executive, who had been in several intense and difficult strategy discussions with Andy Grove said, "When Andy gives a speech, it feels like he is probing your mind. He will find that one lazy synapse. . . . It's a very cerebral experience. . . . It is profound how capable he is." Grove's intellect was also manifest in the MBA elective case-based course he has cotaught at Stanford Business School since 1992. Always well prepared, Grove has the analytical ability to see the relevant pattern in a sea of data and to cut through to the heart of the matter. He combines this with the ability to synthesize the essence of a situation with apt expressions that reveal his facility with words. Having obtained sharp insight in a strategic situation he typically pursues a line of thinking quite forcefully driving others to see the point. Grove's early understanding of the competitive dynamics of the new horizontal computer industry and the importance of the virtuous circle enjoyed by Intel's x86 architecture were key in keeping Intel focused and in resolving difficult strategic dilemmas such as the one posed by the *i*860 microprocessor.

Careful listening. Andy Grove listens intently. One can literally see him absorb the input, almost never jumping in with a response before his interlocutor is finished. Having processed the information, his response is to the substance of what is said, not to how it is said. He likes economy of speech and directness and has the ability to reduce circuitous answers to their simple meaning, sometimes with acerbic wit. (In one memorable instance he responded to an academic giving a long-winded answer to a question by simply saying "I hear no!").

Demanding but fair. Some former Intel executives pointed out that Grove occasionally could be intimidating and verbally aggressive. One former Intel senior executive was quoted at the time that Grove took over as CEO: "Andy is so incredibly articulate and so powerful that he can tear somebody apart."[18] This executive also said: "Those close to him know he is very sensitive to people, but he won't let friendship get in the way of demanding peak performance."[19] Several executives who had left Intel to join other companies pointed out that some of the most memorable and useful developmental events in their careers had been one-on-ones with Andy Grove.[20]

Data-based, crisp decisions. Andy Grove is not comfortable with mushy strategy statements, statements which, in his words, "are somewhat right but mostly wrong." One Intel executive said: "It's important to get a sense of Andy's mood. If he is confused, he gets tougher. He then bulldozes everything that's in his way and tells anyone who's not in his way to [get lost]." Another executive pointed out that once Andy had made up his mind, it was difficult to change. And if he did, he sometimes did so without acknowledging it. Grove was therefore at his best in situations where he could unravel the complexity of a strategic situation, frame the problem or issue clearly based on data and arrive at what he calls a crisp decision, one that has direct action implications. As noted earlier, Grove felt that to force top management to make crisp, actionable strategic choices, it was extremely important that senior management confront top management with clearly articulated options. This emphasis on clarity, data-based decision-making, and action readiness pervaded Intel's culture and worked very well for executing Intel's crystal clear, microprocessor-focused corporate strategy. It was less hospitable, however, for autonomous strategic initiatives, which inevitably are more ambiguous and for which the strategic context remains to be determined.

Strategy by speech. Throughout his tenure as CEO, Andy Grove was a very articulate spokesperson for Intel and became one of the most quoted CEOs of the late 1980s and 1990s. He was featured as one of the top CEOs in the United States by numerous business publications throughout the 1990s. For instance, *Financial World* chose him as Man of the Year in 1990, stating that Grove had transformed Intel into the most profitable semiconductor company in the world.[21] The culmination of Grove's fame came in 1997 when *Time* chose him as Man of the Year.[22] These accolades were no doubt highly personally satisfying for Grove as an individual. But he was also keenly aware of the great opportunity the business press offered him to communicate Intel's strategic intent to the world as well as to Intel's employees.

One senior Intel executive called Grove's conscious use of the media to make Intel's strategy stick in the external environment "strategy by speech." By articulating the same strategic intent over and over to a great variety of audiences, Grove capitalized on the potential to create a self-fulfilling prophecy—given that Intel's strategic intent was based on real strengths. Grove's credibility with the media was, in part, based on his willingness to speak with remarkable candor about some of Intel's failures. For instance, in a *Wall Street Journal* article in April 1991, he spoke about Intel's misfortunes with the *i*860 RISC microprocessor: "We were mesmerized by the technological power of the 860," concedes Andrew Gove, Intel's president and chief executive. "We confused ourselves as much as we confused the rest of the world."[23]

At the same time, Grove was equally confident in affirming Intel's competitive strengths. For instance, Grove was confronted with the formation of the so-called ACE-consortium in 1991—an alliance of Compaq, Microsoft, Mips and many other players intent on developing a new RISC standard. The *Wall Street Journal* reported: "However, Intel's Mr. Grove says few competitors can afford the huge investments his company is making. He adds that Intel isn't afraid of the Compaq–Microsoft–Mips alliance because computer buyers, not such groups set the kind of standard Intel has become. 'Volume begets standards, not the other way around,' he says."[24]

Grove also saw great internal benefits to Intel from sharing his views with the media. He was convinced that Intel's employees were more likely to believe statements about Intel's culture when they saw them published by outsiders (personal communication). Grove consistently emphasized the openness of Intel's culture. For instance the *Financial Week* article featuring Grove as Man of the Year in 1990 reported: "This is where Andy Grove 'debates,' as he puts it, peppering customers and associates with a machine gun-like volley of questions, theories and ideas. Employees might use the word 'interrogate.' Grove refers to the process as 'intellectual honesty.' 'Anyone can ask any question,' he explains. 'We have probably shaken loose a lot of bad ideas that way. I don't see a lot of companies carry it to the degree we do."[25]

Teaching strategy. Andy Grove loved to debate strategy and took strategy as an intellectual discipline seriously. Busy as he was, as CEO of one of the fastest-growing high-technology companies during the 1990s, Grove nevertheless made time to study the subject of business strategy. As Intel's strategy-making process was becoming highly centralized at the top during Epoch II, Grove became concerned that there was room for strengthening Intel's strategic thinking capability at levels below top management. This led to intensive executive programs being developed internally to stimulate and augment middle and senior management's capacity for strategic thinking. In 1994, Grove initiated a course on "Strategy and Action in the Information Processing Industry" for senior executives. Between 1994 and 1999, roughly 300 of Intel's most senior executives took the course. Hence, while strategy-making became highly centralized during Epoch II, Grove himself helped create a countervailing force not only by making it acceptable for senior executives to challenge corporate conventional wisdom but also by providing them with the concepts and tools—and a vocabulary—to actually do so.

Strengthening Intel's Induced-Strategy Process

The evolutionary framework of the strategy-making process—Tool II—serves to summarize Andy Grove's efforts to strengthen Intel's induced strategy process during Epoch II.

Solidifying Intel's microprocessor-focused corporate strategy. Executing the transformation from memory to microprocessor company in the mid-1980s had posed severe strategic leadership challenges—cognitive as well as emotional. Grove had been the first among top management to recognize the need for strategic change. He needed to solidify the changes in the key beliefs about distinctive competencies and product-market domain that had guided the company's strategy for a long time. He also needed to overcome the lack of excitement for the new strategy on the part of some incumbent senior managers and get the organization's commitment to the new strategy.

Focused distinctive competencies and resources. Under Andy Grove's direction, Intel began to intensely focus its process technology competencies and manufacturing resources on the microprocessor business. Gordon Moore recalled: "With the decision to drop out of DRAMs, the technical teams were increasingly diverging. . . . We had three generations of products in three product categories (DRAM, EPROM, and microprocessors). In DRAMs, we were out. In EPROMs we were pushed out. So we had three groups to focus on the microprocessor business. The timing of that focusing was very fortunate, given the big growth in the microprocessor business."

Focused product-market domain. Grove's strategic approach during his tenure as CEO can be cast in terms of hedging or betting; that is, putting your eggs in multiple baskets to reduce the risk of losing all or putting all your eggs in one basket and trying to win big. Grove chose betting. Quoting Mark Twain, he loved to say "Put all your eggs in one basket, and then watch that basket!" Grove made Intel focus intensely on the PC industry as its product-market domain. In his strategic long-range planning kickoff presentations in the late 1980s, Grove started using a picture that showed Intel as a medieval fortress besieged by various enemies, all keen to steal the company's microprocessor crown jewels. In 1997, Grove still used the picture to keep track of the various competitive forces that Intel had to cope with. He defined competitive forces as "anything that affected Intel's future and could derail the company's initiatives."

Focused corporate objectives: Job 1. Intel's strategic focus became ingrained in the strategy-making process through the setting of clear objectives. In 1997, objective 1 was still to strengthen the number 1 position of Intel microprocessors in the new computing industry. Objective 2 was to "make the PC it" and establish Intel as the leading PC-communications company. Intel made a distinction between Job 1 that encompassed everything having to do with making the Intel Architecture more successful and Job 2 that involved the development of new businesses around the core business. The distinction between Job 1 and Job 2 became pervasive in Intel's internal selection environment and served as a key organizing principle for strategic long-range planning (SLRP) meetings. For instance, in the fall of 1997, Andy Grove still organized his SLRP kickoff presentation along this distinction: Job 1–related initiatives had the highest priority in everything Intel planned to do.

Focused leadership: getting commitment to the new strategy. Grove also needed to help the company refocus all its intellectual and emotional energy on the microprocessor business. This meant getting organizational commitment to the new strategy. He said:

> The Grove leadership approach consisted of trying to persuade and sell the new strategic approach to the management team. . . . After some period of time, the new strategy had traction with some managers and it did not have traction with some others. The people who did not get traction—they may have provided lip service to the new strategy, but their actions were not so supportive—the approach was to remove these people from positions where they could choke progress. We moved them around to other positions where they couldn't impede progress. This worked for a period of time. But when it became obvious that they were in a position that was not so important or influential, several of them left. We didn't actually have to fire anyone, nor were we happy that they left. But they were not happy being in a non-core activity.

Grove continued:

> In substance, the new strategy touched on a number of things, for instance what programs to fund; what the willingness of managers was to learn about microprocessors. As a top manager you have to have a high-level understanding and then let people do the implementation. They do or they don't. You see whether the detailed decisions they make meet the requirements of the new strategy or not. It was not that some didn't understand the strategy, or even that they disagreed with it; it was more like they didn't get excited about it.

Highlighting the "genetic" impediments to strategic change, Grove recalled:

> I remember a discussion I had with (the CEO of a major computer company). He said to me "Andy, we've learned to bend sheet metal. We're good at bending sheet metal. We love bending sheet metal. You are telling me not to bend sheet metal. But I want to bend sheet metal." You

cannot win this argument as a cognitive battle. It's part of his genetics, and the genetics of the company.

Revising the structural context. Besides clearly articulating Intel's new concept of corporate strategy, Grove also streamlined Intel's structural context to secure alignment between the stated strategy and strategic action. Asked in early 1999 what particular organizational and managerial tools (e.g., measurement approaches) he had used to implement the new strategy, Grove said that he had used major changes in the company's strategic long-range planning process (SLRP) to help execute the transformation.

The dialectic of SLRP. In the early 1970s, Les Vadasz had been put in charge of creating a SLRP process that was initially a bottoms-up process driven by middle-level managers but was changed in the mid-1980s to become more top down. In an interview in 1988, Andy Grove had already elaborated on the problems of letting middle-level managers drive the induced strategy process in the face of unclear top management strategic intent. At that time he said: "The SLRP process turned into an embarrassment. Top management didn't really have the guts to call the shots, so we were trying to get middle management to come up with strategies and then taking pot shots at them. It wasn't clear whether middle management had either positional *or* informational power."

Grove had also pointed out in 1988 that to keep things from getting out of hand top management instituted a rule that everyone who took a pot shot would have to put one dollar in a jar. And Grove had continued: "In addition to being unpleasant, the system resulted in unrealistically high projections. One year, someone had the idea to put all the previous SLRP forecasts for unit sales on one chart along with the actual growth for the same period. The result was a series of "hockey sticks" which demonstrated the ineffectiveness of the process."

In 1999, revisiting and further reflecting on the importance of the changes in the SLRP process to execute Intel's transformation, Grove said:

> In 1987, we blew up the SLRP process. Formerly it had been a very bot-
> toms-up process, but there was no strategic framework. Each of the dif-
> ferent groups was supposed to come up with the strategy for their group,
> and then we would try to piece them together like a jigsaw puzzle. By
> '87, I was so frustrated with the whole thing that I started the process of
> turning the SLRP process on its head. I said, 'I'm going to tell you what
> the strategy is.' I started with a detailed discussion of the environmental
> issues, which led to a series of strategic mandates. I did not consult the
> organization. I did this myself, along with the help of my TA at the time,

Dennis Carter. . . . I became very directive in prescribing the strategic direction from the top down. This defined the strategy for all of the groups, and it provided a strategic framework for different groups at different levels of management. It's very hard to reach through several layers of management to communicate the strategy and the vision. SLRP became a tool for doing that.

Continuing, he said:

It's not always clear why you do certain things. You do a lot of things instinctively, without knowing why you're doing it. I knew we had to get out of DRAM and put all of our best and brightest on microprocessors. It was easier for people to accept that we had to get out of memories, than it was to face what that meant. It was easier to convince people that we needed to focus on the microprocessor business, than it was to get them to face what that meant. We eventually put people in places where they would have a good chance of achieving the strategic objectives. I screwed around for about a year trying to make the existing incumbents in the organization work.

The revised SLRP process from then on took place in two major stages: In April, three-day meetings were devoted to strategic analysis and discussion of key areas of opportunity and threat facing Intel in the next three to five years. In October, the meetings were implementation oriented, with strong emphasis on resource allocation. The first stage of the process involved a kickoff by Andy Grove followed by a two-hour presentation in which he addressed Intel's strategic challenges, presented his vision of what was happening in the industry, and identified high-level trends.

In 1997, Grove's technical assistant explained how Grove prepared for his SLRP presentations:

I go to all the strategy meetings that Andy attends during the year. I keep a logbook of his ideas that pop up in the general strategy review meetings and corporate strategic discussions. Andy and I work through these and talk about them. We continuously scan the business press for relevant articles. This leads to a list of the hot topics, for instance the importance of "segment zero" (the low end of the microprocessor market segment). For every SLRP meeting, I also pull out the record of the last three ones. I then prepare a preliminary draft of the presentation, with slides. Once he sees it on paper, his brilliance shines through. New ideas pop up. He draws graphs on the board, makes lists of people and things that are important. Then he develops some hypotheses, and we look for data to test these, including historical Intel data. Then I work in my own ideas and other people's ideas.

The remainder of the spring SLRP meeting involved presentations by Intel's senior executives concerning specific issues and topics. They worked across product and functional groups to put their presentation together, with the help of a staff member. These executives had been given their assignment without knowing in advance what Grove was going to present. Because of the lack of strategic context in which to prepare, this was a tough assignment—dreaded by some. Dennis Carter pointed out that as a result of this approach instances of strategic dissonance surfaced immediately.

Carter's observation was very much confirmed when an outsider was invited to sit in on the April 1993 SLRP meeting and could observe Andy Grove and Intel's executive staff meeting in action for the three days of the meeting. Grove did the kickoff presentation for the meetings and then got deeply involved in the various presentations delivered by senior executives. Here are some observations:

(1) Grove had a keen understanding of the strategic evolution of Intel; he seemed to operate on the principle that you need to understand the past if you want to understand the future. For instance, in his 1993 opening statement, he used the metaphor of Intel's "journey" to the center of the new computer industry (NCI) to interpret past actions and to determine what the company would have to do to remain in the center of the NCI. The interpretation was candid: pointing out where Intel erred (e.g., underestimating the rate of growth of the PC industry) and where it did well (e.g., always able to respond quickly). His interpretation conceptualized Intel's strategic evolution: from being a large-scale integrated circuits company to being a microcomputer company to becoming a "branded product" company. Grove observed that the Intel Inside campaign had educated the end users on the "goodness" of Intel's technology. He also observed at the time, "We get credit, but also the blame. We should anticipate this!" (This was a particularly prescient observation in light of the Pentium flaw crisis that would strike in November 1994.)

Grove also conceptualized the factors that provided the basis for Intel to differentiate itself throughout its strategic evolution. The differentiators in the various stages of Intel's evolution comprised silicon technology competency (1970s), design competency (mid-1980s), intellectual property (late 1980s), and brand preference (1990s). Grove observed that the increasingly large capital investments necessary for new generation microprocessors had become a new differentiator. He noted that these investments had to be made several years ahead of demand and asked: "Who is going to invest \$5 billion on speculation?" To underscore the degree of uncertainty, he noted that "Intel knew only 80 percent of the required features of the Pentium processor two-and-a-half years ago."

(2) Grove showed that he kept himself informed by closely following the business press. For instance, in his opening statement he referred to articles in the *WSJ* (on the importance of making the PC more user friendly—plug and play); *Business Week* (on the transformation of the old computer companies into systems integrators); *Time* (on the revolution in telecommunications and the information highway); and *Fortune* (comparing investments made by local phone companies and cable companies). He used the *Time* and *Fortune* articles to support his vision of the new communications industry. His vision was one of horizontalization of the telecommunications industry, similar to what had happened in the computer industry, and of a future of free bauds (units of speed of telegraphic transmission). He was keen on articulating Intel's role in the new computer and communications industry.

(3) Grove derived clear strategic mandates for Intel from his analysis of the past and the future. In 1993, he gave Intel senior management four mandates: Mandate 1 was don't botch up on microprocessors. Mandate 2 was don't let the hardware-software spiral stop. Mandate 3 was learn to integrate technology. He pointed out that technology integration was and would be a difficult task because "it's not instinctive for Intel." He also asked to what extent Intel's P&L organization was hindering the integration process. Mandate 4 was marry our application vision and the free bauds to grow the demand for mips and volume. He concluded that "The only thing bigger than PCs is phones."

(4) During the subsequent presentations of Intel senior executives, several instances of strategic dissonance surfaced. One, involving the executive in charge of corporate marketing and the executive in charge of non-microprocessor products, was particularly intense. The conflict involved the director of CMG, and the general manager of IPG, the non-microprocessor products. It flared up during the CMG director's marketing SLRP presentation. The CMG director pointed out that there was a need for a consistent "brand promise." He proposed that the product business plans, which were owned by the product divisions, needed to be guided by the business plans made up by CMG—that CMG needed to define the rules. Here are excerpts from the exchange between the key players, and how Grove settled the matter:

> GENERAL MANAGER: I need to decide on my own promotion.
> GROVE: [The marketing director's] leadership is stronger toward MPG than toward IPG. . . . It cannot be so clear as with finance, because the markets are different.

GENERAL MANAGER: Promotion is to be determined by the divisional people, while recognizing the overall Intel approach . . .

GROVE TO MARKETING DIRECTOR: You tried to fill his channel because you didn't understand his business.

MARKETING DIRECTOR: Forget about me; let's take the position of CMG. Why should CMG not do the promotion? It is a different discipline from doing the business.

GENERAL MANAGER: You need intimacy between the 4Ps within the business to be efficient . . .

MARKETING DIRECTOR: Looking forward, I can see that everybody will be spending lots of money; more than on 'Intel Inside.' That's a dilemma . . .

GROVE: The manufacturing capacity allocation rule was instituted [for these kinds of decisions]. Why is it not like wafer loading? . . .

GENERAL MANAGER: [The marketing director] is concerned with the big picture stuff. We deal with the concrete stuff, for example, the price of Flash [memory] . . . We must react fast . . .

GROVE TO GENERAL MANAGER AND MARKETING DIRECTOR: You guys have had three months to work on this . . .

MARKETING DIRECTOR: What we don't agree on is that it is a looking forward problem. We are flooding the channels with advertising. The advertising will in sum be confusing. . . .

GENERAL MANAGER: Policy violations versus business level decisions must be separated.

GROVE: These are lasting and fundamental differences between these two groups. Joint psychotherapy must [make them] surface first.

OTHER EXECUTIVE: Get together—the two of you—rather than do it in this group. You will regret this [because] Andy will decide.

GROVE: I cannot. The distinctions are too subtle.

GENERAL MANAGER: Give us six months to work it out.

MARKETING DIRECTOR: You have already improved in some areas.

Grove ends the debate by telling the marketing director: "The Marketing SLRP team is alive until the reorganization can be agreed on. Show accomplishments. Issues to be worked on must be highlighted. Spell out what needs to be done. Write a three-page memo that focuses on the branded products–corporate marketing dialectic." Grove then wrote his ruling down in a notebook to remind him to ask for follow-up.

(5) Grove asked most of the penetrating questions during these presentations. He refused to answer questions that he felt others should answer. He insisted on keeping the discussions on track at any given time by focusing on interrelated issues. He always seemed to be looking to crisply identify conflicts or tensions in a particular situation. He used analogies to sharpen insight in a situation. He demonstrated strong intuition of the way the PC industry works by occasionally coming up with clever marketing themes. He tried to move the discussion from *maybe* to *yes* or *no*. He helped determine what the right sequence of steps would be to deal with an issue, and showed a keen sense of the importance of timing in execution. At the conclusion of the discussion of a particular set of issues he would assign responsibility to specific individuals for the follow up by a certain date, and he would make a written note of that assignment.

At the end of the spring 1993 SLRP, the forty-plus senior executives present at the meeting apparently felt that real progress had been made—new strategic insight gained—as a result of the discussions. It was also clear, however, that Andy Grove had been the center of intellectual energy in the meeting, with the discussion of strategic issues naturally gravitating toward him for resolution.

Looking back in 1999, Grove felt that the dialectical approach to SLRP had been helpful because his vision was initially not so clear. He said he only knew that Intel had to get out of memories and do the best they could in microprocessors. Grove also mentioned that the SLRP process had recently been fine-tuned, with the presenters now knowing in advance what the new CEO, Craig Barrett, was going to say. He said: "[My assistant] feels that all the drama is taken out of it. But if it's boring, that's OK; having the right strategy is most important."

Resource allocation in support of Job 1. During summer, the SLRP directions coming out of the April meeting were taken by different groups within Intel and translated into Product Line Business Plans (PLBP), which were road maps for implementing the SLRP. Originally, SLRP tried to use a five-year time horizon. But in light of the rate of change in the industry this was changed to a two-to-three-year time horizon. PLBPs had a time horizon of about eighteen months. During the fall, the resources required and costs of implementing the PLBPs were determined. These plans were then presented to Andy Grove, Craig Barrett, sometimes Gordon Moore, and Andy Bryant (CFO). One senior executive observed:

> You almost always get something cut, but you end up with the same goals nonetheless. Then you figure out what you can do with what you're given. The plan is hard-baked in December, and this leads directly into establishing the Employee Bonus (EB) objectives.

A common complaint about EB is that you end up throwing the plan out of the window in the first quarter. If things change in the environment, you change the plan accordingly. You end up doing planning month by month. You spend most of your time looking at the modified plan, not the original plan.

Another important implementation mechanism was the Plan of Record (POR), which was done quarterly. POR was considered by many the most important plan. The senior executive continued: "You sit before Andy Bryant and Craig [Barrett], and review the numbers and the plan. Usually the controller from your division, and the division heads sit in on the meeting. Ultimately, the budgeting process and POR are more of a quarterly process, in spite of all the effort that goes into the annual plan."

The resource allocation process strongly favored Intel's core microprocessor business. One executive observed in 1999:

[As long as I've been here] we've applied the POR process to establish budgets for all our projects. We start with sales and marketing projections, and this drives the expense requirements. Virtually every single quarter, the requests outweigh the willingness to spend. We would end up ZBB-ing [zero-based budgeting] the lower ROI projects. The larger ROI projects were almost always related to the mainstream CPU (microprocessor) business. Therefore, if you were not part of the mainstream business, you needed to be very spirited and very perseverant to drive your projects through that POR process every quarter. I knew they were great businesses by any other metric, just not compared to the microprocessor business.

Three or four years ago, I took a senior management course at Intel. At the end there was a question and answer session with Craig Barrett. I asked Craig, "Shouldn't we be diversifying more?" His answer was "Absolutely not. It takes every bit of our energy to execute on the microprocessor business." That was about three years ago. If you were in a non-CPU business, it was tough.

Recruitment and promotion. In the mid-1980s, Intel's top management group—the Executive Staff (ESM)—consisted of the general managers of the business divisions (about eight) and the heads of the functional groups. One of Andy Grove's key personnel decisions was to promote most of the senior managers of the microprocessor division to the ESM. This signaled the importance of micro-processors in Intel's corporate strategy.

Measurement and reward system. Intel always had a very rigorous perfor-mance measurement system, which was tightly coupled to the compensation sys-tem (see chapter 5). The strong tie between the EB and POR strongly motivated managers to try to achieve their goals. This was particularly important given the dependency of Intel on basically one single business and the interdependencies be-tween the various groups responsible for executing the strategy.

Intel also offered all employees stock options. Given the enormous increase of Intel's market capitalization during the 1990s, this was a very strong incentive. Intel was viewed by the capital market as a hot growth company, and entrepreneur-ial individuals could easily justify working for Intel and passing by the stock op-tions offered by start-ups.

Organization structure. During Grove's tenure as CEO, Intel's organization structure was highly centralized. In the words of one senior executive, "Intel was organized around funneling things up to Gordon, Andy, and Craig."

Intel continued to be structured as a matrix, with various product groups on one side and various corporate functions on the other. Each product group carried profit and loss responsibility for its respective market, but no product group con-trolled all of the resources needed to execute its strategy. The functional groups were responsible for supporting the product groups and for cultivating necessary expertise across the organization. Given the importance of microprocessors in Intel's new corporate strategy, and the relentless pace with which new product gen-erations needed to be developed, manufactured, and marketed, coordination among all the groups was critical.

Principles guiding behavior. Given these interdependencies, delivering on one's commitments was absolutely crucial for everybody, and the measurement and reward system was unforgiving for those who didn't. To get things done, how-ever, measuring and rewarding was not enough. Managers needed to build working relationships based on trust and respect. As one member of the executive staff de-scribed it: "Hallway conversations are important. Power at Intel is not based on po-sition. It is influence power, based on content rather than style, an ability to attract people, and a reputation for being able to make things happen. If you don't have in-fluence power, people just don't listen to you."

Although Intel was an extremely disciplined organization, managers were en-couraged, as this senior executive put it "To do what was right, not what you were ordered to do." And, because of the constant questioning by top management and the norm of open arguments, "Managers were forced to rethink their plans to make them work, to scrape around to make the most of their available resources."

Induced Strategic Action Dominates

Andy Grove's efforts to clearly articulate Intel's corporate strategy and to stream-line the structural context to secure alignment between stated strategy and strategic action worked. During Epoch II, Intel's induced strategy process overwhelmingly dominated the company's strategy-making.

Horizontal product-market strategy. Having made the explicit strategic choice that its core business was developing, manufacturing, and selling general-purpose microprocessors for the PC industry, Intel became extremely adept at executing a horizontal product-market strategy: delivering new microprocessor generations to the entire PC market segment. Intel's horizontal product-market strategy was reflected in its powerful microprocessor road map, which laid out several genera-tions in advance of what the performance characteristics of new microprocessors would be. Implementing this road map required large investments in R&D and Plant and Equipment. Initially, new generations were brought to market roughly every three or four years. Intel's decision to invest $600 million in R&D in 1991— a recession year—demonstrated its determination to maintain leadership. Remem-ber that these investments had to be made several years before there was certainty about the demand for new processors. Few companies as large as Intel are as de-pendent on one product family for their revenues and profits. For instance, industry analysts estimated that by 1993, Intel's 486 microprocessor accounted for 75 per-cent of the company's revenues and 85 percent of its profits.[26] By 1997, sales of Pentium microprocessors and related board-level products comprised about 80 percent of the company's revenues and the overwhelming majority of its profits.[27] The potential of the horizontal product-market strategy clearly warranted the strong emphasis on building the company's induced strategy process.

Short-term responsiveness. While the long-term development trajectory of the company was not easily changed, Intel put mechanisms in place that allowed very quick response to short-term contingencies affecting the road map. Dennis Carter explained: "There is also the powerful microprocessor road map, which is difficult to change to accommodate certain types of change, such as longer-term demographic shifts in how the technology gets used, etc. At the same time, we are extremely capable of exploiting opportunities such as linewidth reduction, proces-sor speed, Moore's Law, etc. We can make very rapid adjustments to new techno-logical developments in the familiar space. So, Intel becomes more and more focused."

Top-driven strategic action. The parallel stories of Andy Grove's efforts to get Intel to focus on the microprocessor business, and in particular on its extremely valuable Intel Architecture franchise, and the unexpected rise and fall of the *i*860 RISC processor indicate that Intel's internal ecology of strategy-making could not be easily suppressed. There was a time lag between the strategic intent of top management to drive the organization in a certain direction and the organization's response. In many companies top management's strategic intent is never fully realized because of the relentless top management efforts required to see it through. The failing of many CEOs lies in their inability to get their organization to execute. Andy Grove, however, was highly successful in getting Intel to turn the new strategic intent into vigorous strategic action. After the internal battle between the x86 and *i*860 had been resolved, Intel became strongly focused on further securing the continued success of the x86 during the remainder of Grove's tenure as CEO. To implement the horizontal product market strategy, Intel created a highly centralized organization geared toward turning top management's strategic intent into strategic action. As one senior executive looking back on Andy Grove's tenure as CEO pointed out: "Decisions are mostly bumped to the top. Most corporate decisions are pushed to Andy and Craig, and they make the decisions." As a result, Intel achieved top-to-bottom strategic alignment during Epoch II. Some top executives of suppliers and customers dealing with Intel reveled at the degree of alignment they sensed throughout Intel's management ranks: Managers at all levels seemed to be reading from the same page and telling the same story.

DISCUSSION AND IMPLICATIONS

During Epoch I, Intel's strategy-making process resembled the internal ecology model: strategic action was distributed throughout the organization, and induced and autonomous strategic initiatives were going on simultaneously. Strategic action was not always strongly aligned with official strategy. During Epoch II, Intel's strategy-making process moved toward the rational actor model: strategic decision-making became concentrated at the top of the organization, in particular in CEO Andy Grove. Intel's capacity for simultaneous strategic action throughout the organization remained intact but became far more integrated because of Grove's successful efforts to vectorize everybody in the same direction. The distinction between the induced and autonomous parts of the strategy-making process became much more pronounced. Official strategy and strategic action became strongly aligned. The analysis of CEO Grove's efforts yields several insights into the role of strategic leadership.

Formulating a Winning Strategy

Finding a new way to win . . . It is easy to underestimate how traumatic Intel's defeat in its core DRAM business had been. Top management had had to lay off almost 30 percent of the workforce and Intel was expecting to lose several hundred million dollars in 1986. The bleak situation in DRAM was exacerbated by 1985 when the Japanese competitors seemed to be inexorably moving toward dominance in the microprocessor business as well (figure 6.1). It was crucial for Intel's top management to put the company on a new strategic course that would give it the opportunity to win again. By 1985, Andy Grove had concluded that the strength of Intel's strategic position in microprocessors for the IBM PC, the importance and enormous growth of which Intel's top management had not anticipated, offered such a new course.

> **Insight 6.1.** The role of strategic leadership is to identify a business in which the company can be a winner.

By capitalizing on luck . . . Grove recognized that Intel had been lucky to invent the microprocessor, to get the IBM PC design win, and to not yet have licensed the intellectual property associated with the 386 microcode to other companies. He recognized that it was paramount for Intel to understand that "there is such a thing as luck and then you grab it and exploit it." This motivated Intel's bold move to become sole-source supplier of the 386 microprocessor and to do what was needed to make that move stick. In 1985, Intel was ready to heed the hard lessons it had learned from the DRAM experience, in particular about the importance of protecting intellectual property and the need to make investments in manufacturing capacity to secure the company's strategic position.

> **Insight 6.2.** The role of strategic leadership is to understand the sources of a company's good and bad luck, and to use this insight to formulate a winning strategy.

And moving the organization from understanding to action. In one of his MBA classes at Stanford, Andy Grove observed that "strategy cannot be better than its execution." And, execution would depend on middle and senior management levels. Grove knew that it was not enough for managers at those levels to understand the new corporate strategy; they had to be excited about it and commit themselves emotionally as well as intellectually to making it happen. So he needed to make the hard decisions of moving senior managers who were not excited by the new strategy out of positions in which they would be in the way of executing force-fully. This required high-level understanding of the requirements of the new corporate strategy on his part and the ability to ascertain whether lower level strategic actions contributed to, slowed, or hindered its execution. Grove's decision to move the senior managers of the Microprocessor Group to the top positions in the company (the executive staff) was a clear signal to the rest of the organization. It also put in place a key mechanism for securing implementation of the corporate strategy at the highest level of the company.

> **Insight 6.3.** The role of strategic leadership is to place into key positions managers who are enthusiastic about implementing the strategy and to remove managers who are not.

Creating a Strongly Focused Induced-Strategy Process

Continuously looking for the strategic truth. Grove's decision to play an active role in the SLRP process and to make that process a dialectical one was motivated by the need he felt to clarify the new vision and strategy. Taking the lead in SLRP forced him to become extremely well informed about the dynamics of the microprocessor market segment of the PC industry and to sharpen his insights into the competitive challenges facing Intel. Because Intel's strategy was narrowly focused on microprocessors and the PC market segment, Grove felt that he could be more deeply knowlegeable about substantive strategic issues than CEOs of multibusiness companies (personal communication). Grove developed detailed knowledge about Intel's major customers, competitors, and suppliers, and kept himself well informed about industry trends. He was perhaps the first person in the computer industry to conceptualize the difference between the old/vertical and new/horizontal computer industries, and to clearly see the strategic implications. Over time, he gained strong intuition for where the strategic forces affecting Intel's initiatives were headed. Such strong intuition was necessary because in Intel's culture of open debate Grove would not be able to hide from incisive questioning. The confrontation of Grove's best effort to analyze Intel's overall strategic situation with other senior Intel executives' independent efforts to analyze particular aspects of that situation, provided the best guarantee for finding the strategic "truth" facing Intel.

> **Insight 6.4a.** The role of strategic leadership is to create a strategic planning process that maximizes the company's chances to continue to find the truth regarding the strategic situation.

Insight 6.4b. The search for the strategic truth is facilitated if the CEO has deep intuition based on substantive knowledge of the strategic forces facing the business.

Gaining confidence to bet. Grove's insistence on clarity of thinking and incisive analysis—moving his managers from *maybe* to *yes* or *no*—reflected his distaste for hedging. Grove believed that to win big, Intel needed to be willing to bet. And the ability to make successful bets, in his view, was a function of the clarity of thinking about a strategic situation. Intel's various forums for strategic discussions (SLRP, General Strategy Reviews, and Corporate Strategic Discussions), where senior executives' strategic arguments had to confront Grove's incisive questioning, became an integral part of the internal selection environment. Managers that survived these intellectual ordeals could be confident that their proposed bets had a good chance of winning.

Insight 6.5. The role of strategic leadership is to create selection mechanisms that give rise to confident managers who make crisp, actionable decisions rather than hedge.

Tying measurement and rewards to strategy execution. Intel's measurement and reward systems always reflected the company's emphasis on disciplined thinking and result orientation. Under Andy Grove's strategic leadership, however, the measurement and reward system became tightly linked to executing the microprocessor strategy. In particular, tying the executive bonus (EB) to the plan of record (POR) made sure that managers at all levels and in all functional areas and product groups were motivated to reach their objectives. All these objectives combined to secure timely implementation of the microprocessor strategy. Grove's efforts were strongly helped, of course, by the rapid and sustained increase in Intel's stock price, which provided very strong incentives for everybody at Intel to pull his/her weight in the same direction.

Insight 6.6a. The role of strategic leadership is to tightly link metrics of performance and rewards for performance to strategy execution.

Insight 6.6b. The CEO's efforts to get the organization to execute on the corporate strategy are significantly helped by the availability of strong, market-based incentives.

Maintaining Focus: Staying the Winning Course

While Grove's actions strengthened Intel's induced strategy process, autonomous initiatives—initiatives outside the scope of the x86-focused corporate strategy—continued to emerge in the late 1980s. The emergence of the *i*860 RISC chip, in particular, posed a significant strategic leadership challenge.

Top managers are paid to be sure. The *i*860 had emerged from new design competencies within Intel and was beginning to drive the company in a new, unplanned direction by 1990. The potential strategic importance of the *i*860 was enhanced by the fact that its development seemed to correspond to the growing importance of the RISC architecture in some market segments of the computer industry. This posed a difficult challenge for Intel's top management, which had to decide whether to continue to support the *i*860 development efforts. The challenge was not simply one of allocating scarce resources among internally competing but otherwise independent initiatives. Intel's support for the *i*860 was also support for the RISC architecture, which was competitive with Intel's highly successful x86 CISC architecture. In 1990–91, it was by no means clear which architecture would come out as the winner, and there was considerable strategic dissonance within Intel about this matter. Ultimately, Andy Grove had to resolve the dissonance. To do so, he needed to resolve whether RISC-based microprocessors represented a real paradigm shift. Considering whether RISC microprocessors on their own would be able to take over the lion's share of the PC market segment sharpened his analysis. He also considered whether further support for the *i*860 might help create a self-fulfilling prophecy that would undermine the virtuous circle enjoyed by the x86 architecture. Grove's deep intuition based on substantive knowledge of the industry forces was again a critical factor in the resolution of the strategic dilemma. Grove's appreciation of the strength of the virtuous circle of the x86 architecture in the PC market segment gave him the confidence to make the difficult decision in favor of the x86 architecture and to convince the overwhelming majority of the organization to fall in line behind that decision.

> **Insight 6.7a.** The role of strategic leadership is to be sure about when to stay the course in the face of internal and external challenges and to convince the organization to support the decision.

> **Insight 6.7b.** A CEO's confidence about staying the course depends on his or her deep intuition based on substantive knowledge of the strategic forces facing the business.

Vectorizing the strategy-making process. The i860's challenge as a seemingly viable alternative microprocessor architecture was a watershed event that forced difficult strategic choices. Working through the challenge posed by the i860 confirmed the strength of the strategic position of the x86 architecture in the early 1990s. At the same time, however, it revealed the dangers posed by autonomous strategic initiatives that detracted the organization from its singular focus. CEO Grove concluded that Intel's Darwinian approach to strategy-making was actually a guise for lack of strategic direction. This conclusion motivated him to further strengthen Intel's induced strategy process. Vectorizing everybody behind the x86 architecture became Grove's key strategic leadership objective as of 1991. Even more than before, everything that Intel did had to be tied to furthering the core microprocessor business—Job 1. The efforts to vectorize everybody at Intel contributed to Intel's spectacular success in the product and capital markets. These positive results, in turn, created a powerful positive feedback loop that further strengthened the induced strategy process and the focus on microprocessors.

> **Insight 6.8.** Strategic leadership efforts that vectorize the strategy-making process and achieve strong positive results in the external environment create a positive feedback loop that further strengthens the induced strategy process.

CONCLUSION

The relatively narrow focus of Intel's corporate strategy during Epoch II provided Andy Grove the opportunity to concern himself with strategy content as well as strategy process. Grove was able to develop comprehensive knowledge of the microprocessor business and the PC market segment and deep intuition for its evolving threats and opportunities. This, combined with his extraordinary mental abilities and forceful personality, made substantive strategy-making at Intel increasingly gravitate toward him. Andy Grove became Intel's prime mover. With substantive strategy-making concentrated at the top and an execution capability unrivaled in making the various parts of the organization act simultaneously in concert, Intel's strategy-making process during Epoch II became the paragon of the "rational actor" model. Seldom has a CEO achieved such complete success in aligning strategy and action. Strategy-making as practiced under Grove's leadership during Epoch II is often viewed as the ideal form of adaptive organizational capability. And it did indeed work extremely well. Grove's success in vectorizing Intel drove the company's spectacular success in the product and capital markets, and the company's success in the product and capital markets, in turn, reinforced Grove's vectorizing efforts.

The study of Andy Grove's approach as CEO during Epoch II yields useful insights into the art and science of strategic leadership, some of which are captured by the insights offered above. The actions, of course, reflect the professional persona of Andy Grove. Without falling into the trap of the great man or woman theory of strategic leadership, it is useful to recapitulate some of the manifest personal characteristics that made it possible for Grove to decisively shape Intel's strategy-making process. From the intellectual point of view, Grove's strategic leadership approach was informed by his relentless emphasis on data-based decision-making and incisive analysis. He spent significant effort on identifying the threads that linked past and current actions to future possibilities and constraints. He had a real knack for finding meaningful analogies and juxtapositions to illuminate a strategic situation. From the perspective of character, Grove's strategic leadership was based on single-minded purposefulness, dedication, and diligence in following up with everyone all the time. He was able to make the organization follow through from strategic analysis to unified, forceful execution. His ability to listen intently showed respect for everyone, independent of position and without prejudice, and implied an expectation that the speaker knew what he or she was talking about. Grove didn't suffer fools very long. He ruthlessly but objectively assessed and moved managers based on performance. As a result, while he may have occasionally made a type one error (rejecting someone who was actually competent); he rarely if ever made a type two error (accepting someone who was actually not competent). Overall then, Grove's strategic leadership approach allowed him to project confidence based on deep insight and strong will.

Grove's success in vectorizing Intel's strategy-making process produced spectacular financial results for the company, its employees, and shareholders. It also, however, created an exceptionally strong focus on Intel's induced-strategy process (which became known as the *blue process*). Later chapters will document some of the systemic problems this created for Intel's autonomous-strategy process (which became known as the *green process*). But first, chapter 7 provides insight into how Intel's stubborn autonomous-strategy process continued to work in the face of Andy Grove's strategy vector.

7

FACING A STRATEGY

VECTOR:

AUTONOMOUS

STRATEGIC ACTION

During Epoch II, CEO Andy Grove created an extremely strong induced strategy process focused on Intel's core microprocessor business. Yet, in the early 1990s, there still remained some room for autonomous strategic action, which is well illustrated by the development of Intel's chipset businesses. The chipset venture succeeded within Intel even though top management viewed chipsets initially as a strategic support for microprocessors but not as a new business in its own right.

This chapter draws on data from interviews with most of the key players involved in the chipset venture to describe and analyze its development within Intel.[1] Key managers involved in the chipset venture included Ron Smith, vice president and general manager; Eric Mentzer, responsible for marketing; Randy Wilhelm, responsible for engineering (validation); and Andy Beran, responsible for finance. Gary Thomas, responsible for engineering (design), was mentioned by the others as an important team member but was not interviewed. Additional data were obtained from senior and top executives. Ron Smith reported to Paul Otellini and Albert Yu, the two-in-a-box who were responsible for the Microprocessor Group.[2] Otellini and Yu, in turn, reported to Craig Barrett and Andy Grove. Most of the interview data cover the period 1992–96—from the inception of the chipset venture to its recognition as a strategic business for Intel.

The chapter uses Tool III—the process model of internal corporate venturing (ICV)—to explain the development of the chipset venture in Intel's corporate context. Figure 7.1 shows the ICV process model (Tool III).[3] The ICV process model

		Venture Level		Corporate Level	
		Core Processes		Overlaying Processes	
		Definition	Impetus	Strategic Context	Structural Context
Management Levels	Corporate Management	Monitoring	Authorizing	Rationalizing	Structuring
	Senior Management	Coaching Stewardship	Organizational Championing Strategic Building	*Selecting* Delineating	Negotiating
	Venture Manager and Team	Technical & Need Linking *Product Championing*	Strategic Forcing	Gatekeeping Idea Generating Bootlegging	Questioning

Figure 7.1. A Process Model of Internal Corporate Venturing. (SOURCE: Adapted from R.A. Burgelman, "A Process Model of Internal Corporate Venturing in the Diversified Major Firm," *Administrative Science Quarterly* 28 (1983), p. 230.)

considers three generic levels of management: (1) venture team, (2) middle and senior management, and (3) top management. It also considers two generic levels of strategy: (1) corporate-level strategy, and (2) venture-level strategy. Corporate-level strategy encompasses the structural context and strategic context (overlaying processes). Venture-level strategy encompasses definition and impetus (core processes). To visualize the two generic strategy levels, it is useful to think of them as two triangles: corporate strategy resembles a big triangle moving with a certain speed and force and direction. New venture strategy represents a smaller, emerging triangle moving with its own speed and force and direction. For the venturing process to be successful the small, emerging triangle must become part of the big triangle at some point in the future. This is illustrated in figure 7.2.

A major challenge for the different management levels involved in the process is to make the integration of the new business into the corporate context happen. This is inherently difficult because these different levels of management have different perspectives on the strategic situation. Each level faces different strategic forces. In contrast to the core business, strategic action in a new venture is initially not clearly aligned, or at least not perceived by top management to be clearly aligned, with the corporate strategy.

Tool III helps zoom in on the set of strategic leadership activities involved in developing the chipset venture and in bringing the venture-level strategy and the corporate-level strategy together. The strategic leadership activities involved in new business development in the corporate context are building blocks of strategy-making as adaptive organizational capability.

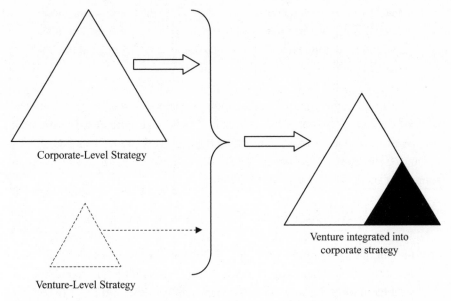

Corporate-Level Strategy

Venture integrated into
corporate strategy

Venture-Level Strategy

Figure 7.2. Levels of Strategy-Making in New Business Development.

A PROCESS MODEL ANALYSIS OF THE CHIPSET VENTURE

Antecedents

By 1990, Intel had been active in the chipset business for some time but more or less as an ancillary activity in support of its core microprocessor business. When it provided the 8088 microprocessor for IBM's first PC, Intel also supplied all the support chips necessary to build the PC motherboard. For subsequent generations of microprocessors, however, Intel no longer developed the support chips. This provided opportunities for new companies, such as Chips & Technologies, to integrate the support chips into a low-cost chipset that was fully compatible with the IBM PC and to sell these to the clone makers. In an interview in 1999, Paul Otellini, executive vice president and general manager, Intel Architecture Group, recalled the origin of the chipset business at Intel:

> We opened a site in Folsom [in 1985]. This was a bubble memory fab. We ended up moving the Flash business there. We also moved the peripherals business there, and that was the beginning of the chipset business. . . .
>   We built discrete components, including chips for I/O, memory

management, keyboard control, etc. Chips & Technologies came along and did a high-level integration of these components . . . Intel didn't because we did not understand the market and did not understand the importance of compatibility.

While the availability of low-cost chipsets enabled the fast growth of the PC market segment, it also put some severe constraints on performance. In particular, the Industry Standard Architecture (ISA) bus was very slow.[4] This bus slowed down everything that was connected to it. In the mid-1980s, IBM decided to do something about it. According to Paul Otellini:

[In 1987] IBM introduced the Micro Channel Architecture (MCA) bus. We decided to clone IBM's Micro Channel and use the technological discontinuity to compete with Chips & Technologies. I did Micro Channel without corporate support. Andy [Grove] wouldn't let us go public with the project, because he was concerned that we would upset IBM. The code name for the project was Zebra. We had stickers made up that said, Free the Zebra.

Paul Otellini continued:

For a variety of reasons, Micro Channel bombed. (But) we found another discontinuity—Compaq's move to the Extended ISA (EISA) bus. This was the first chipset business that made lots of money. We were the only EISA supplier.

However, nobody cared much about the battle between MCA and EISA because the performance improvement of both was small. Most manufacturers stayed with the cheaper ISA bus, and the PC industry remained stuck with a slow bus.

Paul Otellini pointed out that Intel's senior management had begun to recognize the need for the PC bus to evolve to higher performance, but that the OEMs were unwilling to do it. He said, "So we did it ourselves." During the 1990 Strategic Long Range Planning (SLRP) meetings Intel senior managers discussed the potential problem associated with the system architectures that Intel's customers were using. While the performance of Intel processors had advanced at a steady and rapid pace, the PC bus had not changed in more than a decade. One Intel manager explained: "It was like we were putting a Ferrari engine in a Volkswagen. We realized that we had to take more of a leadership position in the industry. Originally, IBM and other OEMs had set system design standards. With OEMs under extreme pressure to cut costs, most aren't thinking about this—they are focused on executing today to survive. Only a handful of OEMs has the ability to do research on next generation system architectures."

Intel Architecture Labs (IAL), an Oregon-based research group formed to develop technologies aimed at facilitating industry acceptance of Intel's microprocessors, introduced the PCI (Peripheral Components Interconnect) bus in the early 1990s. The PCI bus improved bus speeds by a factor of four to five and overall system performance. It was Intel's intent to make the PCI bus technology widely available for free to the PC industry and thereby turn it into a standard. This, it was hoped, would help chipset manufacturers develop chipsets that would be an enabling factor in the adoption of Intel's increasingly powerful microprocessors. One technical manager explained: "We developed PCI technology, and are giving it to the industry. While PCI as an architecture does not directly generate significant revenue for Intel, it is an important enabler for Intel's next generation high-performance CPUs."

Paul Otellini had become technical assistant to Andy Grove some time in 1989, but he had spent only about nine months in that capacity when Grove asked him to take on the leadership of the Microprocessor Group (MPG) together with Albert Yu. At the time of becoming Grove's TA, Otellini had passed responsibility for the chipset business to Ron Smith. While viewed as strategic by Intel's top management, chipsets were not considered as a new business. The development of the PCI bus, however, provided an opportunity for Intel to develop the chipset business. Ron Smith saw and acted on that opportunity. The chipset venture's new strategic direction based on PCI technology started around mid-1991 at the time that Ron Smith took over as general manager of the Integrated Microcomputer Division (IMD), which reported into the Microprocessor Group directed by Otellini and Yu.

Process Model of the Chipset Venture

In the process model, the chipset venture team encompassed Eric Mentzer, Randy Wilhelm, and Andy Beran, as well as Ron Smith. (Gary Thomas, who was not interviewed, belongs here, too.) The middle management level involved Albert Yu and Paul Otellini. Top management involved Andy Grove, Craig Barrett, and the Executive Staff (ESM). Given that Intel was strongly integrated around its core microprocessor business and used a matrix structure to coordinate the allocation of critical corporate resources to the different business groups, the generic levels of management were somewhat less clearly differentiated than in a diversified, multi-divisional company. Hence, Ron Smith bridged the venture and middle levels of management; Yu and Otellini bridged the middle and top levels of management (both were members of the Executive Staff at the time of the venture development). On the other hand, the strategy-making levels in the chipset case were straightforward: the PCI chipset venture-level strategy and the corporate-level strategy.

Major Forces at Work in the Chipset Venture Process

Structural context. The top-down force of Intel's structural context was very strong. Intel as a corporation was doing extremely well in the early 1990s. Top management's strategic imperative was to protect and expand Intel's core microprocessor business—Job 1—and they were intensely focused on the impending launch of the Pentium processor in 1993. A key aspect of Intel's structural context was the rule used to allocate scarce manufacturing capacity. The "maximize margin-per-wafer-start" rule continued to be an important part of the structural context. The very high margins commanded by microprocessors in the early 1990s gave them virtually absolute priority in the allocation of scarce manufacturing resources. Also, Intel's top management was concerned that pursuing chipsets as a business could potentially endanger the relations with the OEMs and the carefully built brand image supporting the microprocessor franchise.

Defining the opportunity and forming the team. The bottom-up force of IMD, on the other hand, was initially very weak. IMD faced a dim future in 1991 as existing business was in decline. Following Intel's corporate strategy of integrating peripheral functions with the microprocessor, they had tried to do something similar at the desktop level but soon realized that customers were not willing to pay for the integration. Facing low margins, they eventually abandoned the effort. They were left with an existing chipset product—the EISA chipset, which was a niche product—and with a bunch of older products that were profitable but without much growth potential. To survive they had to take risks and pursue new opportunities.

When Ron Smith took over as general manager in mid-1991, he realized IMD's predicament and told the group: "There is no sunrise if we don't go do something different and make it successful." He motivated the team to: One, survive and then, two, rally around a new mission and thrive on it. Through interactions with the OEMs, Smith had learned that not all peripherals would be put on the motherboard and that there would be demand for non-motherboard chipsets based on the new PCI bus standard. Smith decided to embrace PCI. In defining the opportunity, Smith tried to anticipate how it could be linked to Intel's corporate strategy. He decided to build the venture's chipset solution from the ground up for the Pentium processor. He saw that this would give them an advantage because the other chipset makers were not ready to commit to the Pentium until they saw the market develop. Smith realized that the PCI chipset could be an important solution to ramp up the Pentium, and that a successful Pentium ramp, in turn, would help his business: "We may help drive the Pentium into market and get our product swept along with the ride."

Smith renamed his unit the PCI division.[5] He realized that to succeed with the new mission, PCI needed to change some of the division's personnel. On the finance side, he recruited Andy Beran. On the marketing side, he recruited Eric Mentzer, who decided to join because: "There definitely was a vision, and the vision was huge. And there were very few people that even comprehended the vision. . . . I am an optimist, and I got really excited in talking with Ron about what we could do with this. . . . Ron said we can become the world-class leader, and be in the strategic heartland of Intel."

Mentzer, in turn, made several changes to the venture's marketing department. He brought in new people with a different attitude. He wanted people who, as he put it, "were committed to the success of the venture before they were really confident that it was going to work out."

Key Strategic Leadership Activities in the Chipset Venture Development

Technical and need linking: An iterative team effort. Smith had been able to recognize the strategic opportunity associated with PCI. But pursuing that opportunity successfully involved developing a product that would capitalize on the new PCI technology while meeting OEM customers' needs. This required careful technical and need linking activities on the part of the venture team.

On the technical linking side, Randy Wilhelm referred to early discussions he had with the people from IAL who had developed the PCI technology. These discussions focused on the advantages that PCI would have for graphics applications. He said: "They came to us (to discuss) this new bus strategy, and it made sort of sense, as much as I hate to admit it. . . . We started looking at it (and asked) what kind of product should we do around this? The focus was on graphics. . . . Clearly, graphics sitting on the EISA bus was not getting any advantage. . . . So we started looking at this . . . I think just after this Ron Smith took over the division." Mentzer said that he agreed with Wilhelm that graphics was the most important advantage for PCI.

Randy Wilhelm pointed out that the technical people initially did not get much help from the marketing side, and that it was not clear which features to put into the product: "Marketing lacked the tools and the capability to help. . . . Engineering figured out what not to put into the product. I mean, every OEM said, yes, that's important. I have got to have it. Well, in reality, we couldn't balance the cost with the desire." He also pointed out: "Ron was very much in the mindset that, in the end, we are probably the best judges of what to go put into the platform."

Developing a new technical capability. Ron Smith recognized that there was an opportunity in understanding better than the OEM customers themselves how to design chipsets: "We learned that OEMs didn't give you that much feedback about how good your chipset was. . . . They only had a limited capability of validating that systems environment. And we saw that and I jumped on that and said we're going to develop our own system validation. And that will differentiate us from everybody else."

Smith recalled that Randy Wilhelm questioned him on the aggressive stance that he was taking relative to the OEMs:

> I remember Randy coming to me one day and saying, "OK, Ron, if you want to do this, do you realize what it's really going to take?" I said no, but you own it; so you go out and put a claim on it and you show me what it's going to take. . . . He said "We need this and this. . . . Are you ready to do this?" And I said, "Yeah, go do it." I think he was shocked because he expected me to nickel and dime him, but I didn't. I said go do it, but I want it by tomorrow. I want it more aggressively than what you're proposing. . . . I supported him and held him accountable. . . . He did an excellent job of it. We made that one of our competitive differentiators.

Developing a complete product. On the need linking side, Eric Mentzer said: "My piece of it was to get the technical marketing group to figure out how to make the product complete—more than just a chip."

Mentzer pointed out that an important shift in orientation was necessary on the part of the technical marketing group to develop the right product:

> The first thing was setting the kind of subvision for the marketing department. I remember telling my team this hundreds of times: that we can't be chip-heads. We needed to be smarter at designing systems; better than our customers. If we knew how to design systems better than our customers, they would value us and we could help them use our product right.

Continuing, Mentzer said:

> So there was a huge challenge to get our team that was used to just think-
> ing bits and bytes to think at a system level. . . . This implied that they
> had to learn how other products—even those that we did not sell like the
> hard disks or the graphics subsystem—worked with the chipset.

Mentzer explained further why he had to change the orientation in his group from technical marketing to applications engineering:

> What I was thinking was that we're not going to get any help from the
> rest of Intel, and we're not going to get any help from the customer. If we
> have one piece of the puzzle and the other five or six pieces aren't there,
> we can't sell our product. Nobody was going to step up and own the is-
> sues to make sure everything came together; we had to put in place this
> capability ourselves. . . . So one of the things that I wound up doing was
> to put about two-thirds of my resources in applications engineering.

Mentzer pointed out the importance of making the product easy for customers to use:

> I was going to customers . . . and it's incredible the number of barriers
> that they threw up. What we had to figure out was what they were really
> saying. What they're really saying is that their engineering resources
> were limited. They're not sure about the PCI thing and they don't want to
> go throw a bunch of people at it. But if I gave them a solution that was
> complete and had no loose ends, they would probably go do it. So we ac-
> tually started [with] these applications engineers telling them to learn the
> system, learn super I/O.

Fostering team effort. Mentzer explained the importance of making sure that Randy Wilhelm and his validation engineers and Gary Thomas and his design engineers would back him up when he asked for help from the lab: "We weren't compartmentalized. . . . Randy knew my issues, and I knew Gary's issues." To achieve this, Mentzer created what he called war room meetings every week, to bring everybody together so that everybody knew what everybody else was work-ing on. In these meetings, Mentzer said: "I had to be the voice of the customer. . . . And part of the thing that I had was figuring out how to position our product. . . . At the same time, going out and winning customers."

Product championing: Gaining control over our destiny. The venture had to overcome several major internal roadblocks to get the resources needed to realize PCI's new mission. First, because the chipset products could not hope to get the high margins that microprocessors typically enjoyed, they could not get internal manufacturing capacity allocated to their products. According to Andy Beran (Finance): "We never would have gotten into the business if we had to fight for internal capacity. . . . It always would have looked like a lower [return] to the processors." Ron Smith confirmed: "We were told there was no internal capacity."

Second, top management believed that Intel should do everything to get the PC industry to adopt the PCI standard. Andy Grove favored using an industry consortium and was doubtful that Intel could do it by itself by growing its own PCI chipset business in a major way. Ron Smith recalled: "Andy Grove told me that we had no damn business doing PCI. . . . That was early on. . . . He and I had a heated discussion about it. . . . He basically said something to the effect of who do we think we are, a chip company thinking we're going to go drive an I/O bus standard." Even though top management did not shut the initiative down, Smith said: "The Executive Staff . . . viewed us as just another chipset vendor and one, quite frankly, who started with only 3 percent market share when all we had was the EISA niche." Top management was ready to support other competitors, if necessary. According to Smith: "When we ran into some supply issues and people perceived that could stop the processor shipments, the Intel sales force was engaged to go help sell our competitors' chipsets."

According to Eric Mentzer: "They said, we don't believe you guys are going to be successful, so we don't want you going into those accounts. . . . The processor division was out telling the field sales force and the customers, don't use this; use the low-risk thing."

Randy Wilhelm said: "There was some doubt, I think, in certain parts of Intel that we were able to push a bus standard, whereas in the past we had always had key OEMs pushing the bus standard."

Paul Otellini also mentioned that below top management there was doubt about Intel's chances to be successful in the chipset business: "Some people at Intel did not believe that Intel could be successful in the chipset business. X (a senior Intel manager) used products from Chips & Technologies rather than Intel. His job was to move processors, not chipsets. This created some tension."

And Albert Yu recalled:

[We] ran into lots of resistance in investing in this area, because of our lack of success for many years of pouring resources into different chip sets with little return. Several of us (Paul Otellini, Ron Smith and myself, among others) persisted and were able to find resources to design the first PCI chip set for the 486 processor to test-market the concept. Ron moved rapidly to design that chip set—called Saturn—and demonstrated a fully functioning PC system by Fall Comdex [the major trade show for computer dealers] in November 1992.[6]

The venture manager as strategist. Ron Smith understood that at the venture level it was strategically important for PCI to gain control over its own destiny in the face of limited corporate support. In his words:

> "The other thing was to control your own destiny. You don't wait for Moses to come off the mountain with the Ten Commandments. . . . Well . . . we were not only not blessed from the top, we had people from the top telling other people in the corporation to go help our competition."

But Smith was also an adept corporate strategist. He understood that the roadblocks associated with the corporate context—lack of manufacturing capacity and top management's ambivalent attitude toward the chipset venture—made sense at that level and simply represented strategic challenges for the PCI division rather than things to be discouraged and whine about. According to Smith:

> The biggest single thing I really imparted to the group was: Look, let's stop lamenting the fact that we weren't given this charter or weren't given that role. . . . There was really the feeling of second-class citizenship relative to microprocessors, which is not hard to figure out why. Okay, I said, look we need to, as a group, get control of our destiny. I harped on that a number of times. I kept saying, this business is going to be what the people in this organization make it, period.

Going outside for manufacturing resources. As noted earlier, a big challenge the venture team faced was that there would be no internal manufacturing capacity available for their products. Andy Beran noted: "The constraint for Intel was not so much R&D dollars, but competing for manufacturing capacity."
Ron Smith said:

> We went for the first time ever to outside suppliers for an Intel component, instead of doing it at Intel factories . . .
>
> It took a lot of negotiation. It took a lot of paradigm shifting among our engineers. And it took a few people in the engineering group who

were willing to bet their careers on it and champion it. And we just started doing it.

Smith explained that later on the venture was able to get access to manufacturing capacity, which became idle as microprocessors moved off a technology:

> Then the manufacturing guys embraced us. (They said): "Why are you doing all of this stuff outside? Why don't you bring it inside?" Well, it just so happened at that time we needed more supply, so we did bring some stuff inside. And to keep the suppliers honest, the next chipset we did, we did both external and internal.

Paul Otellini also mentioned the importance of going outside Intel for manufacturing capacity, underscoring his and Yu's support for the venture: "Andy [Grove] asked me to run the Microprocessor Group with Albert Yu. We took manufacturing for the chipset business outside of Intel. Our mentality was that this shall not be stopped. This stood Manufacturing on its head. We ended up bringing it back in-house pretty quickly."

Securing financial resources. To pursue the PCI chipset opportunity also required resources for product development. But given the relatively low margins forecasted, it would have been difficult to secure corporate resources for their product development. Andy Beran explained the problem:

> Probably the other biggest thing was just securing resources from the corporation. And fighting for investment dollars through the product line, which is an ongoing finance activity. We do a ZBB [zero-based budgeting], which is a concept of rank ordering of product averages from top to bottom across the company. . . . Again, we were looking at a relatively low margin product line and a high spending rate. . . . I spent a lot of my time . . . to make sure that it was a good idea to spend the money.

Beran explained how they were able to do it:

> So here you are in meetings with senior management, saying, yes, I know it doesn't look like it's the highest potential return, but we still think it's a good idea; we still think we need the money. We tried a lot of different tactics, including [that] Ron seemed to really think—and it actually got quite attractive to say—[that] at some level the company won't ship a processor without a chipset.

Beran explained, however, that top management allowed them to hold on to the financial resources they were still able to generate with their old business:

> The PCI division . . . at that time . . . consisted of . . . this older, mature collection of cats and dogs, all these old micro-controller products, and keyboard controllers. . . . The old stuff . . . was reasonably profitable, making 40 percent margins. . . . It was a cash cow. . . . We were basically subsidizing all the chips and development with that cash cow. . . . And then the corporation kind of turned a blind eye to it. . . . The corporation did let us subsidize the development with that cash. At the point where that wasn't enough, we were already successful enough to keep going.

Building the team . . . fast. Referring to his efforts to augment the applications engineering capability of the venture team, Mentzer said: "I don't believe Ron at the time . . . understood the value of what I was trying to do . . . because he basically put me under a flat headcount on engineering. I grew it real quick before he realized what was going on, and then he just totally stopped me for a long period. . . . The issues were mushrooming and our team wasn't growing and we were frying people. . . . The resource issues we had were in accepting that charter of: 'We'll do anything.' "

Selling internally: Tapping into relationships. As mentioned earlier, Mentzer had changed the orientation in his group from technical marketing to applications engineering to get a better grip on the real needs of the OEM customers. But these applications engineers had to get access to the customers, and access was controlled by the Intel field sales force. Mentzer emphasized the importance of his good connections to this resource that was outside his control:

> I went out to the field and negotiated . . . to get a team dedicated to the chipset and the IHVs, the graphics card vendors.[7] So, I actually got resources within Intel; [it] was a lot of work to get anybody to give you any resources for this stuff. . . .
>
> It was a [sales] team that I came from, and it was really the relationship that I had. I called up my buddies that I had worked with. I said, "Look man, I just moved out here. You need to give me a hand here. Help me, personally, do me a personal favor, and help me get into some of these accounts and figure out what we need to do." Now they did that, but they wanted me to be real credible. . . . I was totally honest with them. I never held anything back. . . . I really built trust with them, so they knew that I wasn't going to go off and shine them.

Explaining how he tried to work with a field sales force that had gotten instructions from top management to support the competitor's chipsets to protect the Pentium launch, Mentzer said:

> I spent 50 percent of my time with all the Intel internal groups trying to convince them that this was good for them. Now, we created a slogan, Ron and I just said it hundreds of times, "The best way to make Pentium happen is to make PCI happen." Eventually we turned it into a value proposition for them saying, "Look, you've got three hundred people here who the only thing they want to do is ramp Pentium; and by the way, we have the exact same goals as you do as a stockholder."

Strategic forcing: Focus on growing the business. Scavenging the resources to develop a complete product, outsourcing the manufacturing to Japanese suppliers, and negotiating help from the field sales force to get access to customers provided a basis for developing the business. But the venture team knew that they would only have a business if they were able to get customers to buy their product. Eric Mentzer was fully aware of this:

> We needed customers, real simple. . . . We were going to be successful if we won some customer business. And we weren't going to win customers' business because they read some ad in a magazine, or whatever. So we really got focused, we picked an account, it was Alpha, and we just totally smothered them. We were going to go and win them.

Mentzer also explained:

> Now, the first thing we realized was that we weren't going to win the big boys. . . . So what we needed to do was focus on the risk takers, the guys who were trying to win from [Delta and Gamma].[8] And at that time that was [Alpha]. . . . But we also needed to win the masses. And so one of the things that we did was put together a program, and I actually hired a really strong guy . . . just to win APAC. What you do for the big customers [is] you smother them with love. What you do for the other customers is make it so cookbook that anyone can use your product.

Chasing the right rabbits. Mentzer further explained:

> The first thing we did is we put together this war room. . . . We looked at the detailed status of all our target accounts. . . . This got formalized

over the years and we called it afterburner . . . We had this big black-
board up, and we had every single design tracked. We knew what graphics they were using. . . . We knew what their launch date was. . . . We
used this to make sure the applications team really understood the business. We needed them to work on the problems for the accounts that really mattered. We had the applications engineering team track the rabbit
chart, which was our list of must-win accounts in priority order.

Ron Smith confirmed how they had converged on certain OEMs as their first
target customers to put pressure on the leading OEMs, but he pointed out that it was
important to also put pressure on the first OEMs by going to Taiwan:

We said we need a rabbit. We need somebody to get out there and embrace PCI and make it available in the market quickly. We looked at the
channel, we said the telemarketers, [Alpha and Beta], they are faster to
implementation and faster to actual sales time. So, we said we're going
to win one or both of them . . . [Beta] felt they were an up-and-comer.
They felt they were ready to go from just a demand fulfiller to a technology leader. And (Alpha) was actually kind of skeptical . . . but we managed to get them once we showed them the quality. . . . So, those two
[were putting pressure on] the [Gammas and Deltas] of the world. Then
we said, well, maybe we need [pressure] on these guys too. So, let's go to
Taiwan.

Creating pull by helping customers sell.   Mentzer pointed out the importance
of spending effort to help their customers sell the PCI chipsets: "Nobody knew
how to sell it (PCI). Our customers didn't know how to sell it. I had just moved to
California, and I remembered seeing this program called Help-You-Sell to help
you figure out how to sell your house. So I said, we need a Help-You-Sell for PCI."
Ron Smith confirmed the importance of Help-You-Sell:"

We did this thing called Help-You-Sell kit, where we put in . . . all the
benefits we're bringing. . . . We basically did first-level merchandising
for our customers. It was amazing . . . [Alpha], for example, took clips
out of that and put it verbatim in their advertising. And some of the same
things happened at [Beta]. . . . We learned that . . . these guys are just
like us. They're low R&D, low marketing, and so on. If we can just make
it easy for them, they just go sing our story for us, and they did. And it
created pull.

Getting the Intel labs to help with customer technical issues. During the definition part of the chipset development process, the venture team had worked closely with IAL when the lab was developing the PCI specifications. But after that there had been a quiet period in the collaboration, with the venture team focused on developing their chipset product. Successful strategic forcing efforts, however, produced a rapidly increasing number of customers, each of whom brought specific technical issues and problems that the venture team needed to solve. To do so, the venture needed to be able to draw on technical resources in the lab, over which it had no direct control. According to Mentzer:

> It became obvious to me that I wasn't going to get all the resources to do everything, because . . . it was just mushrooming . . . as more and more products were coming out. . . . All of a sudden we were winding up with ten different vendors doing graphics. . . . I remember kind of coming to an agreement with the labs that they would pick it back up. . . . It was real frustrating because the labs . . . didn't want to get their hands dirty with this grunt work.

To get the labs involved again, Mentzer created the idea of a "plug-fest:"

> We were in total fire-fighting mode. So we created this idea of a plug-fest. I remember the first was when we got a couple of people together and we said, You bring your motherboard, you bring your graphics card, and we'll sit there and have a plug-fest and plug these things in. And the labs came back in to really partner with us at that time . . . doing these plug-fests.

Working with internal customers. Mentzer also mentioned the importance of the OEM products and services division (OPSD) for the chipset venture's strategic forcing efforts. To get OPSD to collaborate, however, he had to convince them that the collaboration would serve the corporate interest—the paramount reason for collaborating—as well as their own, narrower interest:

> OPSD really hadn't made a commitment to PCI. They were trying to build their own business. . . . They wound up [winning a lot of the early design in the 486]. . . . We treated OPSD as a customer in 1993–94. OPSD was actually our toughest customer because they take the gloves off and tell you how it is. They don't have to feign any kind of customer relationship . . . [because] we're all Intel. . . . We were trying to con-

vince them [that] we've got a real big potential here. If we work together on this PCI thing, it's not only a market opportunity for Intel chipsets, but it's also your way to really establish yourself as the big [mother] board company in the industry.

Mentzer concluded that PCI and OPSD maintained a love-hate relationship, both needing the other, but also wanting to work with outside customers: "They made it real clear to us that they were going to use our chipset, but they were also going to use other peoples' chipsets."

Working around the Intel brand policy . . .   In their attempts to market the PCI chipset product, the venture team ran into resistance from Intel's corporate marketing group that was very protective of the Intel brand. Ron Smith said: "We not only didn't get any brand support, when our internal code name for the part started to be used by our customers and people started saying they had the Triton-based . . . chipset . . . the branding people stopped us from using it. Even after it was widely disseminated."

Eric Mentzer explained the venture team's approach: "Most of Intel marketing wouldn't give us the time of day . . . [Yet] I wanted somehow to create awareness for this stuff. . . . Triton became our first real home-run Pentium chipset. We basically did a channel marketing program. . . . We were doing umbrellas, T-shirts. . . . We were effectively creating awareness for this product name in the channel, and that's like a big no-no within Intel." Mentzer pointed out that Ron Smith probably knew about it, but never actually authorized it, and just let him decide whether he wanted to take the risk.

And working around the Intel quality standard.   Andy Beran pointed out: "The real issues were related to quality standards. . . . Are we shipping Intel quality? Who [cares]? . . . We [ignored] Intel quality standards and held our breath. But the market . . . complained rarely. . . . The product was so much in demand that it tended to pull itself through the channels."

Committing to demanding sales targets.   Mentzer explained how he and Smith went about setting sales targets for the venture:

> In '94 when we said we were going to do 10 million—Triton— . . . I remember just thinking . . . no way, what's he smoking? But we all said OK. I remember thinking, well, if I had to do that, what would it take? How many would I need in APAC? I don't have [Alpha]. . . . If you keep it a big number, you'll never know what to do. So we had the team break it down between the four geographies. . . . We did a quota negotiation. . . . We created a team called market development. . . . I assigned some-

one to each geography and said you own APAC. And by the way, your number is 5 million. So come back and tell me how you're going to do it. It really was a great tactic.

Mentzer also explained that Ron Smith kept everybody involved by letting them know what the business plan was, what the costs were, and what the engineering investment R&D dollars were: "One real positive thing he did, he almost had everybody thinking like the business manager. . . . I felt like I was thinking like the GM . . . It gave a lot more commitment and assumed ownership."

Maintaining the pace. Ron Smith emphasized the importance of capitalizing on the validation capability that they had built, and moving the learning that came from the validation upstream into the product design process to stay ahead of the competition: "It had a fast time-to-market. And [we were] able to go to [our] customers and say if It says Intel on it, you know it works and you can use it and get to market."

Smith also described the intensity of the strategic forcing efforts:

Every freaking design went out there as a must win. We just flogged ourselves, we kept track of it, developed strategies by account. We figured out where we needed to do a technical sell at the engineering ranks; where we needed to do an executive sell at the management ranks; where we needed to do both and who was going to be responsible for what.

Referring to the enormous pressure they were under to make the Pentium ramp happen Smith also said:

It wasn't a question of sitting around debating whether it can be done or not. It was a question of . . . we have to do this, there's no alternative, this just has to happen. People . . . were making a huge impact on the corporation at that point. They also felt that if we didn't do it, Intel was going to turn off this business forever and go on to produce a different model. So, we're going to execute on this and put our head down, and [we] did it. But we also said, "We're not going to leave any stone unturned. We're not just going to say, oh yeah, we're under pressure here to make this happen. But the pressure is so intense let's stop winning designs." We said, "No, we want it all." We kept going for it and that was the focus. I think the key thing I did was just driving people to control their destiny and make that happen.

Exceeding expectations. The results were impressive. According to Ron Smith: "I'm not sure I remember what the revenue was for '91, since I was only here for half a year. But for '92 our total revenue from all the products and the full cornucopia of stuff was around $240 million. In '93 it dropped to around $200 million. In '94, with the new chipset coming out and everything, we raised it to $400 million. In '95 we did over $700 million and in '96 we did about $1.3–1.4 billion." Smith explained that the planned revenue expectations that they set were always short of actual revenues.

Coaching versus strategic building: capitalizing on learning. While the team was doing the strategic forcing, Smith was also concerned about keeping track of what was being learned and getting the team to capitalize on that learning, in order to sustain the strategic forcing efforts. This effective coaching was, in part, possible because the PCI chipset opportunity was big enough by itself to continue the impetus of the venture in the corporate context. This allowed Smith to focus totally on the efforts of the venture team to grow the chipset business and did not require him to spend much time and effort engaging in strategic building: trying to find other products to add to the venture's portfolio to achieve critical mass.

Looking for an encore: "Concurrent PCI." Smith tried to create a process in which the venture team was constantly learning and then applying that learning to keep moving forward:

> The key lessons were stay focused; rapidly apply the learning as you're going, and increase our design capability [and] our validation capability. When we tried something [that] worked, we institutionalized it. I'll give you an example. We had all these blue granules in the chipset. When we went to (Delta) we put a story together as to how these were different and how this other chipset that they had selected couldn't keep up. We had a graph there . . . that showed how performance dropped off with loading and where ours was and why it was better. . . . These guys bought it and we turned the design around. Well, once we got a win like that we went and made that part of our collateral. We made sure everybody heard that story. . . . We called it concurrent PCI. . . . Next thing you know, there were articles in *PC Week* that were saying you need concurrent PCI in your next chipset. . . . Every time we found something that worked, we made it purr away, we did business and tried to build on it. We tried to get that kind of infectious success going. And we had fun with it.

Smith explained how he went about inculcating the team with this learning orientation: "Every manager was very hands-on. But the worst thing that could happen [was] you come to a staff meeting and I knew more about what was going on than you did. Boy, people stayed on top of things because they didn't want to have to deal with that."

Andy Beran had a slightly different perspective on Ron Smith's leadership style:

> Ron's staff meetings were like a series of one-on-ones. You would watch him have one-on-one with everybody around the table. But there wasn't a lot of staff interaction. . . . [When he left on sabbatical] we were dependent on each other, and we learned to work with each other a little better. Then he came back and pretty much claimed that we had all [screwed] up while he was gone. And luckily he came back just in time. But I think the bonding, I hate to use that word, but just the ability that we found to work with each other, [helped us] survive.

Eric Mentzer emphasized the important coaching role Ron Smith played in teaching him how to deal with senior management: "I remember Ron really coached me when Albert [Yu] came down. . . . I didn't know how to present to Intel management. And I remember Ron really working with me [to teach me what] you say to an Intel vice president, and how you present to him, and what they are looking for. Because I remember always going into a sales mode, because I was a sales guy, but you don't try to sell Intel senior management."

Delineating: Intel's strategic position in the chipset market segment. The chipset venture team ultimately delineated Intel's position in the chipset market segment. As noted earlier, from the beginning Ron Smith knew that there was no clear corporate strategy guiding the chipset venture. In fact, the corporate strategy was initially experienced as an impediment rather than a facilitator. But, as also noted earlier, Ron Smith told his team from the outset that it was the venture team that was going to determine what the business would be: "It's not going to be what the Pentium processor folks say. It's not going to be what our sales force says. It's going to be what we go and do. And it's up to us, one, to make it a successful business and, two, make it strategic to Intel. We've just got to execute."

Developing a leadership mentality. Eric Mentzer explained that after they had overcome the initial internal and external hurdles their mentality changed to that of a market leader: "We really needed the group to think like we were the leader in the PC industry. . . . We said, boy! That was kind of neat with PCI. We created this and established ourselves with it. What if we started creating these inflection points ourselves? So we moved from chip-head to system-level thinking about everything. And then we moved from system level to thinking about the market and the end user."

Mentzer said he felt that they had moved from a situation in which they were used to just following the OEMs to one in which they felt they could have a decisive impact on the industry. He said: "I think we changed the overall market where chipset guys used to just follow the OEMs. . . . With PCI we did a consortium . . . I remember thinking . . . we don't need to rely on the OEMs to tell us what to design. . . . Of course ultimately you need them because if the standard is not open, nobody will use it. But we knew we had an advantage."

Organizational championing: activating corporate interest. By this time, the venture had gained critical mass in its external environment. Now the key question was whether top management would also be willing to make it part of Intel's corporate strategy. Top management, of course, would reach its own conclusion independently. This would be a test for the strategic premise on which Ron Smith had based the venture's development.

Linking the venture strategy to corporate strategy. Ron Smith had anticipated that the PCI chipsets would be strategically important for the launch of the Pentium processor. Smith had made sure that the new PCI chipset product was built from the ground up for Pentium. He had anticipated that by helping drive the Pentium processor sales, the PCI chipsets would be "swept along for the ride."

Randy Wilhelm confirmed Smith's concerns of tying the PCI chipset product to the Pentium processor: "How could we make sure that we had a business solution for the Pentium when it came on board? . . . Ron's term was . . . a *snowplow.* It was sort of like helping to pave the way for the Pentium. Wilhelm also pointed out how Ron Smith had taken advantage of the negative results of the sales force's efforts to encourage OEMs to use other companies' chipsets to show the strategic importance of chipsets for the corporation: "There were a tremendous number of bad experiences, where the customer was told by Intel [to] go use another solution [and it] backfired on the customer. . . . This is when Ron was probably at his height saying, look how strategically important we are."

Gaining key senior managers' support. Smith pointed out the difficulties the chipset venture encountered in Intel's corporate context, in particular corporate marketing, but he also recognized that there had been significant support from the key senior managers in the Microprocessor Group and from Craig Barrett: "I'm not going to say that there was no support at all from the Executive Staff. . . . That wouldn't be fair. Paul [Otellini] was kind of a personal champion of chipsets. . . .

But that was after the ball was rolling. . . . And Craig Barrett was for it as well at that point. Although Craig was also the guy that authorized the field [sales force] to go out and sell competitors' [chipsets] when he didn't think we had enough supply."

Andy Beran had again a slightly different perception of the situation. He pointed out that Craig Barrett had been Smith's mentor and had stood up for him and gave him the benefit of the doubt: "The way the venture was funded. . . . [Ron] tended to fly under the corporate radar, either by using the cash cow subsidy or by going external for capacity. We never went up against hard decisions, tough scrutiny. And when we had to, Barrett . . . let us get by."

Retroactive rationalization: Linking with corporate strategy. Top management allowed the chipset venture to fly under the corporate radar, but nevertheless subjected the venture to rigorous strategic reviews. Top management did not stop the venture's activities, but also did not embrace them until their viability and strategic importance had become clear.

Surviving general strategy reviews (GSR). As noted earlier, initially the venture team ran into great skepticism on the part of top management. This was made clear to Randy Wilhelm and Ron Smith when they gave a GSR presentation to the Executive Staff concerning the impact the PCI chipset was going to have on the chip business. Wilhelm said:

> Andy [Grove] gave Ron and me a very hard time. . . . He was civil about the whole thing but he thought [that] it was far to the left field, and he absolutely wanted no Intel name to be associated with this. . . . He wanted it to be a consortium activity. . . . This is long before Triton. . . . This is before I could even deliver the first Saturn, the first snowplow. . . . This is the same year we want to go to COMDEX and make a big deal, but Andy wants the consortium effort. He does not want Intel beating its chest saying, "We think this is the right thing." . . . So Andy rags on us for about two hours.

Wilhelm, however, also mentioned a personal discussion with Andy Grove right after the GSR session in which Grove signaled his readiness to defer to the judgment of the venture team:

> I think Andy was implying, don't let all that beating you up [discourage you from] going off and trying to build your business, which I found kind of refreshing. Because you could have come out of there very disil-

lusioned. . . . I felt very good when Andy said, don't take it too seriously; like if you still have conviction and you still think you can go do something to build the business, and build this thing up. . . . [But] just be careful about how you take Intel's name to it.

From flying under the corporate radar . . .   Hence, while top management did not actively support the chipset venture, they also did not kill it. Not having active top management support actually helped the venture in some ways. Reflecting on the venture's success, Ron Smith said: "I think what made us successful in part was we weren't on the Executive Staff radar screen. As a result, there was an expectation that we do something but it wasn't, okay, we've blessed this, we've endorsed it, we agree it's a great idea, now why isn't it a billion dollar business overnight?"

To joining the induced process.   Eventually, top management came to view the chipset venture as strategic to Intel. Ron Smith said: "But once they realized what share we had, once they realized what influence we had, once they started reading all kinds of articles in the press, once they went to Comdex and saw PCI was more visible at Comdex than the Pentium was, we started getting real attention." Smith also recalled that Andy Grove wanted to let him know that he had been right to stay the course in the face of top management skepticism: "I had this one headline from an article that said PCI proliferates profusely, circled by Andy [Grove], sent to me with a note that said 'And I said it couldn't be done.' " Reflecting back on the struggle for legitimacy, Smith said: "We didn't let the chief executive officer of the company tell [us] something we believed in couldn't happen."

Once top management had come to view the chipset business as strategic for the company, it became part of Intel's induced-strategy process. Top management, and in particular Andy Grove, now began to drive the strategy for the chipset business. Andy Bryant, Intel's CFO, recalled how Grove had intervened when the motherboard division decided that Intel's chipsets were too expensive and wanted to source them from the outside:

> At a time when motherboard pricing was extremely competitive, the motherboard division decided not to use Intel's chipsets because they were more costly than third-party alternatives—even though they provided superior performance. Again, Grove said that the key mission of the group was to move advanced technology into the marketplace, and that saving $10 a board to ship inferior technology was unacceptable [it should be noted that this was a substantial portion of the margin on certain boards]. If Intel's motherboards, which were targeted for high-end

PCs, had the superior performance, the rest of the market would need to respond with similar high-technology products. Finance made a presentation that supported the use of the cheaper chipset. Short-term profitability would be enhanced by cost cutting. Grove ruled that the long-term interests of the company required moving advanced technology into the marketplace, and that we would forgo short-term returns for the long-term benefits.

Top management's commitment to the chipset business was further demonstrated by the 1997 acquisition of Chips & Technologies for about half a billion dollars. This acquisition provided Intel with the opportunity to significantly strengthen its capabilities in the graphics market segment. In 1999, some observers estimated that Intel's chipset business generated around $2 billion of revenues for the company.

DISCUSSION AND IMPLICATIONS

Figure 7.3 conceptualizes the discussion of the chipset venture development in terms of the ICV process model. As shown in figure 7.3, the process model of the evolution of the PCI chipset venture in the early 1990s tracks the behavioral patterns identified in the process model of internal corporate venturing (figure 7.1) quite closely. The top-down force associated with the structural context, and the bottom-up force associated with the definition of the new business opportunity, were clearly present in the chipset case. As the venture team successfully pursued the opportunity, impetus was gained and the initial resistance and lack of active support of top management were overcome. As the strategic context for the chipset venture became clearly defined, top management integrated the chipset venture into Intel's induced strategy process and began to drive its strategy to correspond with that of the core microprocessor business.

The study of the chipset venture corroborates the usefulness of several of the rudimentary categories of strategic leadership activities identified in the ICV process model: technical and need linking, product championing, strategic forcing, organizational championing, delineating, and retroactive rationalization. On the other hand, the analysis also reveals some differences in the relative importance of different key strategic leadership activities in the chipset venture case. Strategic building was less important, but coaching and, to some extent, negotiating, were more important in the chipset venture. These differences probably reflect to some extent the differences between the highly centralized and focused Intel Corpora-

	Business Strategy Level		Intel Corporate Strategy Level	
	Definition	Impetus	Strategic Context	Structural Context
A. Grove Corporate Management C. Barrett	Monitoring	Authorizing	Retroactive Rationalization Strategic Recognition	Structuring
P. Otellini and A. Yu Senior Management R. Smith	Coaching*		Organizational Championing Delineating	Negotiating
Venture Team A. Beron E. Mentzer R. Wilhelm G. Howard	Technical and Need Linking	Strategic Forcing	"Flying Under Radar"	Questioning

*No need for strategic building.

Figure 7.3. A Process Model of the Chipset Venture.

tion and the more decentralized and diversified companies that were the subject of the original ICV research.[9] But they also reflect that the chipset business opportunity was quite large by itself.

The chipset venture illustrated some, but not all, of the generic problems encountered by new ventures in the corporate context. The venture had to cope, to some extent, with the vicious circle associated with resource access. Initially, it could not get internal manufacturing capacity. On the other hand, it was lucky that top management allowed it to use the resources generated by its old products. The venture did not experience the typical strategic leadership dilemmas triggered by the pressures for growth, because the chipset business opportunity was large enough by itself. The venture did experience the problem of indeterminacy of strategic context since top management saw PCI initially as a PC industry-enabling technology, rather than as a basis for developing Intel's own chipset business in a major way. Finally, the problem of incomplete structural context was not strongly manifest in the chipset venture for several reasons. First, the venture was a separate business unit within MPG. Also, the venture team was comprised of Intel managers with a strong track record and a network of relationships across the various functional organizations, making it possible for them to get access to critical resources within Intel's matrix structure. Furthermore, senior MPG management was supportive of the venture and protected it from too much top management pressure early on. Finally, the incentives of the chipset venture personnel were strongly aligned with the rest of Intel.

Implications for Theory and Strategic Leadership Practice

The power of the structural context. The process model analysis of the chipset venture shows the impact of Intel's structural context. It confirms the powerful control exerted by the "maximize margin-per-wafer-start" rule over access to manufacturing capacity within Intel. To survive, the chipset venture was forced to go outside for its manufacturing needs. It also shows the powerful effect of zero-based budgeting (ZBB) on financial resource allocation within Intel. The chipset venture was lucky to be able use its old products as a cash cow (with the approval of top management) to sustain its initial development. Without this source of cash the chipset venture would probably not have survived. The process model analysis also highlights the constraints imposed by corporate marketing on the use of the Intel brand by new ventures. The marketing people of the venture team needed to be willing and able to work around these constraints. Finally, the analysis shows the constraints associated with Intel's matrix structure, which is strongly focused on executing the microprocessor strategy and does not leave much slack for autonomous strategic action. This was clearly manifest in the difficulties that the chipset venture encountered in getting access to OEM customers, which was closely guarded by the field sales force.

> **Insight 7.1.** A strongly selective structural context, linked to a highly focused corporate strategy, makes it difficult for autonomous strategic initiatives to gain impetus within the company.

The need for general management skills. The evolution of the chipset venture indicates the importance of having the venture led by a middle-level manager with strong general management skills and credibility with senior and top management. The venture manager must be a good strategic thinker, who understands what it will take to gain and maintain control over the venture's destiny, and one who can execute. This was especially important in Intel's matrix organization and because the business opportunity was initially perceived as not quite fitting with the corporate strategy (or it was unclear whether there was a fit). In the chipset venture case, Ron Smith was able to define a new compelling mission for the venture. He was able to recognize the strategic importance of the venture's success for the corporation's success before top management did. He was able to reconcile the different strategic perspectives and interests of different levels of management. For instance, he was able to accept that Craig Barrett both supported the venture and at the same time instructed the field sales force to recommend other vendors' chipsets to OEMs to protect the Pentium ramp. He was able to overcome the unavailability of internal manufacturing capacity by going outside, getting around the constraints imposed by ZBB to develop the product, and getting around the constraints imposed by CMG on the use of the Intel brand.

At the same time, the general manager must be able to keep the team focused on the business success of the venture. Smith did it by keeping the key team members in the various functional areas all involved in and informed about the venture's progress. As Eric Mentzer aptly put it, he made all the key team members adopt a general management perspective.

> **Insight 7.2.** A new venture needs a leader with strong general management skills to overcome the selective effects of the company's structural context while keeping the venture team focused on the venture's strategy.

The need for a well-connected team within the company. Resources to support the venture's development must be obtained from a variety of sources within the corporation. Yet, the natural tendency of a new venture team that is trying to do something different is to isolate itself from the rest of the corporation. This, in turn, often leads to the adoption of an us-versus-them attitude that reduces the venture team's chances to get cooperation from others who control critical resources. Intel's chipset venture development process underscores the importance of forming a team of key players in the different functional areas that are well connected to others within the company who control critical resources. This was, again, particularly important in Intel's matrix organization. The chipset venture team was able to tap into relationships with the field sales force, get IAL to help with customer technical issues, and work together with an internal customer (OPSD) that was very demanding.

> **Insight 7.3.** To overcome the selective effects of the company's structural context, a new venture needs team members who can access various types of resources located in and controlled by different parts of the company.

Technical and need linking provide a foundation. The chipset venture case also underscores the importance of thoroughly understanding the customers and their needs and being able to provide a complete product. If "need linking" and "technical linking" are not performed well and together, all the rest does not matter. The chipset venture team was able to clearly understand the OEMs' needs. They understood the OEMs' technical resource limitations and the importance of fast time-to-market for the OEMs. They also had an astute understanding of the dynamics of competition among the various OEMs, which provided clarity regarding which customers they needed to win first. They quickly understood the importance of developing a new technical "validation" capability to increase the dependency of the OEMs on Intel. These were all quite demanding tasks, both in conceptualization and execution. The story of the chipset venture also clearly indicates the strong drive and determination that are required to actually stay ahead of the customer.

> **Insight 7.4.** A new venture's success depends critically on the ability of the venture team to link technological solutions to ill-defined customer needs. This requires strong intuition and relentless efforts to understand the customers' needs on their terms.

Flying under the radar for a while to build on the foundation. The chipset venture case also shows that it is important to allow the venture to fly under the corporate radar for a while to give it the opportunity to establish a viable business foundation *at its own pace*. This is so because once top management starts focusing on the new business the pressures to grow big fast are enormous. And, if the venture cannot meet top management's expectations, disenchantment is likely to set in quickly. Flying under the radar requires that some senior managers shield the venture from top management by carefully managing their expectations.

> **Insight 7.5.** New ventures that are outside of the scope of the current corporate strategy need a quiet period out of top management's immediate line of sight to build a business foundation that will allow the venture to manage top management expectations later on. Such protection must be provided by some member(s) of senior management (but preferably not the CEO).

Winning inside by winning outside. Paul Otellini and Craig Barrett shielded the chipset venture from the Executive Staff's considerable doubts. They could continue to do so because Smith consistently delivered on his promises. The chipset venture could be a winner inside Intel because it was winning outside Intel in the marketplace. To maintain control over its destiny, the venture manager had to stay ahead of top management's expectations. This is the main reason why successful strategic forcing is central to the continued viability of a new venture in the corporate context.

> **Insight 7.6.** Successful strategic forcing—winning in the marketplace—provides the basis for the venture's continued impetus in the corporate context.

A big opportunity helps. Another lesson from the chipset venture is that if the opportunity is big enough, management of the venture can be more focused and spend more effort on coaching—helping the team with its strategic forcing efforts—and less on strategic building. Strategic building was not necessary in the chipset venture because its business potential was sufficiently large that there was no need to broaden the strategy of the venture to include other, related products. Not having to engage in strategic building left Smith with more time and energy to coach the venture team. It allowed him to stay closely involved with the team and drive its strategic forcing efforts to make the PCI chipset successful in the marketplace. Later on, he was clearly looking for an encore, but by that time the venture's strategic context within Intel was already determined.

> **Insight 7.7.** The larger the business potential of a new venture, the more the venture leader can focus on building the venture around that opportunity through strategic forcing, and the less need for strategic building.

The need to determine the strategic context of the venture. On the face of it, the chipset venture may seem to be a somewhat special case because by 1994 it had become clear that PCI chipsets would be very helpful in the launch of the Pentium processor. This was particularly important in light of the recalcitrance of some OEM customers to get behind Intel's efforts to launch the Pentium processor. Hence, to some extent determining the strategic context for the chipset venture may seem to have been a less difficult task than for a new venture that must get top management to recognize its strategic importance based only on its own merit. There is little doubt that the chipset venture's strategic importance to the core microprocessor business helped determine its strategic context within Intel.

Yet, reconstructing the strategic context determination process of the chipset venture in this chapter indicates that such retrospective assessment is also somewhat misleading. The data indicate that Intel initially simply wanted to deliver the new PCI technology to the PC industry with the help of a consortium-based effort, and to leave the design and manufacture of PCI chipsets mostly to the incumbent chipset makers. Ron Smith had to overcome at least some senior and top managers' belief that pursuing chipsets as a business was perhaps too big a stretch for Intel and potentially an unwise competitive move. Smith was successful in determining the strategic context for chipsets as an Intel business because he had anticipated that chipsets would be strategically important for the Pentium processor ramp. His strong conviction, supported by real success in the marketplace, gave the venture impetus and led some top managers to protect his efforts until its strategic context was determined.

> **Insight 7.8.** The leader(s) of a new venture outside the scope of the corporate strategy must set the stage for determining the strategic context of the venture from day one. Conceptually, this requires understanding the importance of the venture for the company's development before top management does. Politically, this requires building a growing network of support among senior and top management.

Top management's strategic recognition and follow through. The process model analysis of the chipset venture suggests that it is important for top management not only to be hardheaded while the venture is trying to achieve viability but also to recognize the venture's achievement when its success shows that their skepticism is no longer warranted. Andy Grove's note to Ron Smith is a nice example of such top management strategic recognition.[10]

Finally, the analysis of the chipset venture shows the importance of top management capitalizing on the work done by the organization. Once Andy Grove recognized that chipsets were strategic for Intel, the full force of execution was brought to bear on its further development. There is little doubt that such top management follow-through is one of the greatest forms of satisfaction that corporate entrepreneurs derive from their efforts.

> **Insight 7.9.** The major role of top management in new venture development is to recognize when the corporate strategy should be amended to accommodate the new business, and then to put the resources of the corporation fully behind that recognition.

CONCLUSION

Tool III—the process model of internal corporate venturing—was used to diagnose how the autonomous strategy process involved in the chipset venture at Intel actually worked. The analysis has corroborated insights derived from earlier work on internal corporate venturing, but has generated some new ones as well. The process model analysis of the chipset venture suggested several conditions that increase the chances for venture success. These include:

1. A venture manager with strong general management skills.
2. A venture team well-connected with the rest of the corporation.
3. Careful technical *and* need linking in defining the opportunity.
4. Protection of the venture for some time from close top management scrutiny to build a viable business foundation.
5. Winning inside by winning outside through strategic forcing.
6. Identifying an opportunity that is big enough by itself so that no inordinate effort is needed to find complementary opportunities to reach critical mass.
7. Being concerned with strategic context determination—the tie-in with corporate strategy—from day one.
8. Top management having the capacity to recognize, retroactively, the strategic importance of a new business and a willingness to then commit the corporation.

If one of these conditions is missing, the venture's chances of successfully overcoming the selective effects of the company's structural context are significantly reduced.

The fact that the chipset venture's business potential was sufficiently large that no additional business opportunities needed to be found to reach critical mass, and that it was fairly quickly recognized as strategically important for the company's core microprocessor business made it a somewhat special case. In ventures in which these two conditions are not met, senior management's capacity for strategic building and organizational championing becomes crucially important for venture success. Strategic building requires the agglomeration of additional business opportunities through internal transfer of projects and/or through carefully targeted acquisitions. Organizational championing requires convincing peers as well as top management that the venture's success is in the interest of the corporation. Strategic building and organizational championing are difficult, both conceptually and politically. Hence, while the chipset venture offers considerable insight into the challenges associated with new business development at Intel, the process model shows that it is also somewhat incomplete. It will be necessary to examine other ventures, ones that also require strategic building and more intense organizational championing, to more completely test Intel's new business development capability. Intel's networking business, discussed in chapter 9, served that purpose.

Besides its diagnostic usefulness, Tool III helps executives conceptualize in a fairly parsimonious way the strategic leadership activities and challenges involved in the autonomous part of the strategy-making process. The process model captures the essence of what the various actors in the chipset venture actually did in the form of a concise story. The story of the various activities, approaches, practices, and techniques used by the venture's protagonists, provides perhaps the best available tool for learning about new venture management. The process model helps to construct the narrative by putting together the key actions of these protagonists in a coherent way, while preserving some of the organized anarchy that is inherent in innovation.

One of Andy Grove's favorite expressions is, indeed, to "Let chaos reign, then rein in chaos." The story of the development of the chipset venture offers some illustration of this maxim. The story shows that during the late-1980s to mid-1990s there was still room for entrepreneurial managers to pursue autonomous strategic initiatives within Intel, in spite of the very focused induced-strategy process that CEO Andy Grove had created. As a result of the chipset venture's success, Intel amended its corporate strategy in at least two ways. First, the newly achieved prominence in the chipset product market led top management to expand its views concerning Intel's legitimate product-market domain. Second, the successful efforts to build a validation capability led top management to expand its views concerning Intel's distinctive competencies. By the same token, the chipset venture developed in accordance with Intel's core values of discipline and results orientation. And, it clearly advanced the corporate objectives. The story of the development of the chipset venture thus illustrates the vigor and resilience of the autonomous strategy process as a key part of strategy-making as adaptive organizational capability.

8

COEVOLUTION OF STRATEGY AND ENVIRONMENT

By the early 1990s, microprocessors and closely related products were the dominant source of Intel's revenues and profits.[1] The key to regaining and maintaining control over its destiny was Intel's ability to capitalize on the success of the x86 architecture as the preeminent microprocessor architecture in the fast-growing PC market segment. Gordon Moore pointed out that Intel was able to become a major driving force in the development of the PC market segment. Craig Barrett, who was named Intel's new CEO in early 1998, also emphasized that during Epoch II Intel was intensely focused on shaping the industry to the advantage of the Intel Architecture (IA):

> We've had two hugely different environmental periods. In the first case, we had IC expertise and we were looking for a place to apply it. We were looking for problems to which we had the solution. . . . In the second case, this evolved into a focus on the microprocessor business. Quickly, the environment changed to where we knew as much about the system and platform as the customers. We became the industry driving force rather than just facilitating the industry with our technology. . . . With this, we became much more verticalized behind IA and related businesses.

It is against the backdrop of the coevolution of its microprocessor strategy and the PC market segment that Intel's strategy-making during Epoch II can be further illuminated.[2] Andy Grove was able to vectorize everybody at Intel in the same direction, in part, because that direction had become quite clear by the early 1990s. Intel realized it had the opportunity to take command of the evolution of the PC market segment because it supplied the most valuable component of the PC. Intel's top management recognized that, in contrast to the vertical mainframe and minicomputer market segments, the PC market segment was characterized by a horizontal industry structure. Initially ill understood by most industry participants, increasing returns to adoption manifested itself as a powerful dynamic force in some of the horizontal layers of PC industry, including the one associated with microprocessors. Since the installed base was the main driver of increasing returns to adoption, the preeminence of Intel's x86 microprocessors in the PC market segment and the associated virtuous circle provided the company with a very strong strategic position.

In retrospect, Intel's success during Epoch II might thus seem all but inevitable. Yet, a quick perusal of the business press covering Intel in the early 1990s reveals that industry observers and some knowledgeable company leaders were doubtful that Intel would be able to maintain its large market segment share during the 1990s. For instance, in *Financial World,* December 1990, Cypress Semiconductor CEO T. J. Rodgers compared Intel's situation to that of General Motors in the 1970s, and predicted "a decade of eroding market share" for Intel.[3] In April 1991, the *Wall Street Journal* published a lead article, "Intel Faces Challenges to Its Dominance in Microprocessors" as rivals were cloning its main chips and the ACE industry alliance (in support of the RISC architecture) took shape.[4] Some three years later, in February 1994, the *Wall Street Journal* asserted that "Intel is no longer having it all" and asked "Has the world's most dominant maker of microprocessor chips hit the wall?"[5] Intel's spectacular success during Epoch II thus needs to be examined against a background of perceived as well as real competitive threats.

Internally, in spite of his efforts to vectorize everybody at Intel in the same direction, Andy Grove continued to face strategic leadership challenges as well. Reflecting, in October 1993, on what he called "weaknesses of Intel" Grove said: "People are rushing about. They don't think things through. We are torn by the immensity of the opportunity. We suffer from 'imperial overreach.' I worry that we will implode! We are not taking initiatives at the time that we can. . . . I am giving too many speeches. . . . We are teetering on the edge of disaster." Continuing he said: "The ramp-up of the Pentium is key. We need first-class execution. Why do they not pick up on the ramp-up of the Pentium? How to bring up the 'business communication' stuff is a second worry." Grove also said: "There are no discontinuities envisaged. But the Pentium versus the imitators, and the P6 (Pentium Pro architecture) versus RISC, are determining battles." Given the external and internal challenges, the fact remains that the opportunity existed and was Intel's to lose, but Intel didn't.

COEVOLUTION OF INTEL'S STRATEGY AND THE PC MARKET SEGMENT

Complementary Strategic Thrusts

Intel's role as driver of the development of the PC market-segment came about as the result of several complementary strategic thrusts. Intel was able to build brand with end users and to set the pace at which new generations of microprocessors were introduced into the PC market segment. The company also vertically integrated into system-level products and developed and disseminated other new technologies into the PC market segment that paved the way for adoption of new, more powerful generations of microprocessors. Finally, the company became the center of an ecosystem comprising independent software vendors (ISV) that created new applications for the increasingly powerful new microprocessors. These complementary strategic thrusts redefined the relationship between Intel and its OEM customers and underscored the importance of Intel's relationship with complementors, companies that provided products that increased the value of Intel's microprocessors in the eyes of its customers. The most important complementary relationship in the PC industry existed between Intel and Microsoft.

These complementary strategic thrusts did not reflect a comprehensive, *ex ante* formulated strategic plan to take control of the PC market segment. Intel's decision to become sole-source provider of 386 microprocessors was initially motivated by the desire to protect its ability to obtain an acceptable return on its investments in microprocessor design and development. After making this watershed decision, however, Intel's microprocessor strategy coevolved more strongly with the PC market segment. Intel's microprocessor strategy became more sharply articulated as the coevolutionary process unfolded, reflecting strategic recognition on the part of top management. This formed the basis on which top management developed Intel's deliberate strategy to drive the PC market segment during the latter part of Epoch II.

The Success Story of Intel's Pentium Processors

New branding strategy: From x86 to Pentium processor. Intel's successful microprocessor strategy continued unabated in the years 1993–97, supported by the

Intel Inside marketing campaign. However, the numeric names associated with the x86 architecture were not properly trademarked, and competitors offering Intel-compatible processors could use the same name convention. After an unsuccessful legal effort to prevent other suppliers from using the 386 name, Intel commissioned the search for a new name that could be protected as a trademark. From several alternatives, the name "Pentium processor" was chosen, in part, because Andy Grove felt the name associated well with the idea of Intel processors as a key ingredient of personal computers. Intel's considerable marketing resources were henceforth deployed toward gaining end-user recognition of the Pentium processor brand. The Pentium processor was launched in March 1993.

Technology leadership: Pacing the race. Intel's strategy was to continually introduce higher performance microprocessors, and the company did so at a relentless pace. Between 1989 and 1999, Intel launched members of the i486 family, the Pentium processor family, the Pentium Pro processor, the Pentium processor with MMX technology, the Pentium II processor, and the Pentium III processor (see Appendix II, figure A-II.6). While there typically had been a time lag of about four years between microprocessor generations, by the late 1990s the pace had picked up. Intel's Microprocessor Group (MPG) was responsible for developing the next generation microprocessors. In 1993, MPG had new development efforts underway for both P6 and P7. Microprocessor Division 6 (MD 6) was readying the P6 (the Pentium Pro), the sixth generation Intel processor. MD 5, 7 was working on the Pentium (P5) and P7, Intel's seventh generation processor (the Pentium II). The use of overlapping development teams for subsequent generation microprocessors was put in practice after the i860 RISC processor development was halted. Each of these product groups contained their own design engineers and marketing resources, and maintained matrix relationships with other groups such as the Sales organization, Technology and Manufacturing Group (TMG was responsible for developing process technology and managing production facilities), Finance, and others. Product group general managers maintained profit and loss responsibility for their product lines.

Albert Yu, senior vice president and general manager of MPG in 1993, provided some background on microprocessor design:

> Versions of each generation of the microprocessor architecture follow a road map, which usually contains three dimensions: Performance,[6] Packaging,[7] and Features. Performance and Packaging are rather obvious. Features are much less obvious. These refer to specific functions, which may be included on the microprocessor chip which aren't neces-

sarily part of the core processor. Our products serve three markets, Servers, Desktop PCs, and Mobile Computers. These markets look similar, with many of the same players (OEMs). However, the details (feature set required) are very different.

Emphasis on product quality. Along with continued emphasis on increased microprocessor performance, managers in MPG also sought to improve the reliability of new processors. Vin Dham, a senior technical manager who was in charge of the development of the Pentium processor, explained in 1993:

> This was a big shift in focus from the 486 to the Pentium processor development efforts. We were lousy in quality and support to our customers. When the 486 came out, there were many bugs—bad bugs— which we didn't catch. One bug that was found by a customer, surfaced after we had begun production—50,000 486s became key chains instantly—that's a lot of very expensive key chains! We were at our customers' mercy—they were finding the errors in our products. We were depending on them for our quality assurance.
>
> For the Pentium architecture . . . I offered to pay anyone $100 on the spot if they found a bug—I paid out a few hundred dollars. This was a lot cheaper than finding the bug later—or having a customer find the bug for us. With the Pentium processor, no bugs have gone to customers.

Emphasis on customer support. Vin Dham further explained the increased importance of customer support:

> In the past, we have, at times, provided lousy customer support. We designed the CPU and gave it to our customers to design their systems. We began to change this for the first time with the 486DX2/50.[8] We got much more involved in their design programs, as they transitioned to higher-end systems. We are also focusing on providing a more complete solution to our customers. For the Pentium architecture we provided a very comprehensive solution. We even designed and built some of the first Pentium processor based systems. This allowed us to benchmark our customers and say "Hey guys, we can build a system that performs better than yours—here's how you can improve."

Investment in design tools. Intel bought off-the-shelf tools for designing standard elements of the microprocessor, but for the most complex and innovative elements, Intel developed its own design automation tools. Intel made large investments to develop these tools, and this gave Intel an important advantage. According to Albert Yu: "We have made a big investment in proprietary design tools. For the last decade we have led the industry in the complexity of logic design. When we were putting 1 million transistors on a logic chip, the industry was at 500K. We have no choice but to do our own tools. This is also an advantage over our competition—they have to either build their own or work with less advanced, generally available tools."

Investment in manufacturing. Intel's TMG, led by Gerry Parker, was a functional organization that managed Intel's manufacturing sites, or fabs. TMG engineers were closely matrixed with MPG's product groups because of the close link between product and process design. One of the imperatives associated with the sole-source strategy for the 386 had been that Intel needed to become a world-class manufacturer. Under the leadership of Craig Barrett and Gerry Parker, Intel had become renowned for its ability to manufacture its chip designs. Having learned the lessons from the DRAM debacle, Gerry Parker had given TMG the mandate of optimizing the manufacturing process for a given chip, and then rolling out that process to Intel's other fabs using the principle of Copy Exact. In addition, Intel had closely integrated product design with process development. According to Albert Yu:

> Having in-house manufacturing is very important. Design engineers in MPG work very closely with TMG to integrate the design and manufacturing process. . . . This is a key element to success—the heart of the business. This is important to our ability to get the most into the smallest chip. If you look at our competition, the ones with their own manufacturing have chips that are compact and well designed. Competitors who don't [have their own manufacturing] have bigger chips.

Gordon Moore also spoke of the importance of manufacturing and process technologies:

> One of the amazing things about our industry is that the next generation of technology is always much more cost effective than previous generations. Making things smaller makes everything else better simultaneously. That's a pretty unique characteristic with important implications. If you stop spending during a slow down, it's a big drawback if you get behind. We have a saying, "you never get well on your old products."

We've been able to continue the march forward. Other companies have been in the same vein of technology, but nowhere near as successful. Over the years, we have made more profits than the whole industry combined.

To implement its microprocessor strategy, Intel continued to aggressively invest in manufacturing capacity for its high-performance chips. Intel's capital investments in property, plant, and equipment had grown from $302 million in 1987 to $4.5 billion in 1997, three times that of any other chipmaker in the world.[9] Production investment decisions were usually made long before demand for these chips could be ascertained. The willingness to build manufacturing capacity ahead of demand set Intel apart from its competitors. In 1997, Intel president Craig Barrett was quoted in *Business Week:* "It's a risk to go out and spend billions of dollars on these manufacturing plants. But if we didn't, we couldn't possibly reap the benefits. We're going down the road at 150 miles per hour, and we know there's a brick wall someplace, but the worst thing we can do is stop too soon and let somebody else pass us."[10]

In a Stanford MBA class in November 1994, Andy Grove pointed out that the rule in high technology is that whatever you can do somebody else can do too. So do it as soon as you can! Grove, however, also pointed out the financial ramifications of correctly timing Intel's huge capital investments. Intel's top management had developed a strong intuition for making these decisions. Grove, for instance, had learned from studying the data that the peak-to-peak production across microprocessor generations in the past had been three years. Based on this, he was willing to assume that the next generation would follow the same time pattern.

A Brief Hiccup: The Pentium Processor Flaw

Inertial response to a consumer marketing crisis. After introducing the Pentium processor in March 1993, in spite of the increased attention to product quality and Vin Dham's assertions about a bug-free Pentium processor, Intel discovered that the chip had an obscure flaw that caused extremely rare computation errors when performing certain mathematical calculations. In the tradition of its excellent, time-tested OEM marketing approach Intel had evaluated the flaw and determined that the average user would encounter the problem only once every 27,000 years or so. As a result, it was extremely unlikely that most users would ever encounter the error and this so-called floating point flaw was not considered particularly significant or urgent (the flaw was in the processor's floating point part used only for very complex calculations). After all, microprocessors were extremely complex chips with millions of transistors and they commonly had bugs, especially when they were initially released. Intel had been far more careful and concerned about product quality with the Pentium processor than it had with any previous processor. Relatively speaking, the Pentium processor flaw looked quite innocuous. This bug could be corrected in later versions of the chip as part of the normal succession of changes that were made to reduce the chip size or cut manufacturing costs.

However, in October 1994 a mathematics professor discovered the bug, and a week later hundreds of users had posted messages to Internet news groups discussing the problem. Intel agreed to replace the chip with a corrected one for heavy-duty users likely to be affected by the flaw. For the typical user, Intel explained how unlikely it was for the error to surface, and offered to provide a detailed white paper that explained its analysis. Initially, Intel's approach seemed to be working. Then on November 7, 1994, the *Electrical Engineering Times* ran a cover story on the Pentium processor flaw. On November 22, CNN ran a feature story that discussed the issue in depth. On December 12, IBM announced that it had stopped shipments of all Pentium processor-based computers, claiming that errors due to the flaw were more common than Intel had reported.

Intel initially refused to go beyond remedial action on the technical side, viewing the problem as strictly a technical matter. In response to some who claimed that they could generate the error much more frequently than Intel was willing to admit, Andy Grove suggested that someone who wants to get hit by a meteor—and knows where it will hit—can always go stand in that place. In spite of Intel's efforts to play down the importance of the situation, however, the ensuing publicity caused call volumes to Intel's customer support lines to skyrocket. The complaint problem would not go away, even though shipments of Pentium processor-based machines continued unabated. On December 19, Intel's board met to discuss the issue, and decided to reverse the old policy and replace any Pentium processor affected by the flaw regardless of the user. Intel took a $475 million charge against earnings for the quarter to cover the expense.

Intel, the branded products company. The success of Intel's marketing campaigns—Intel Inside and the Pentium processor branding efforts—had helped make Intel into a consumer products company rather than just a semiconductor component supplier. Used to working with engineers in OEM-customer organizations, Intel now had to deal with, and was unprepared for, the less than strictly rational approach of the average end user/consumer. The Pentium processor flaw crisis made this transition and the lag in end-user marketing competencies painfully manifest. Intel learned the hard way that in consumer space: reality =

perception. An unexpected benefit of the Pentium processor crisis, however, was that Pentium suddenly had become a household name. Both on the technical side and on the marketing side Intel took action to reduce the chances that this type of crisis would come about again.

Loss of innocence. The Pentium processor crisis happened during the time that Andy Grove was coteaching an elective course in the Stanford MBA Program. On the Tuesday after the CNN story broke, he asked the students what he should do about the crisis. One student suggested that Intel needed to move fast to limit the damage to its reputation because Intel was now viewed by many in the computer industry as a powerful, unstoppable juggernaut. Grove seemed to be genuinely surprised by this answer and replied that he never thought of Intel as a juggernaut but still as the start-up company that he had helped found. There was first some incredulous laughter in the room, but then everybody realized that Grove was quite sincere. People suddenly realized that in some way the Pentium processor crisis also had brought about a loss of innocence for a hardcore high-tech company that was now and forever caught up in the vagaries of the consumer market.

Redefining the Relationship with OEMs

Intel's strategic imperative. To support its microprocessor strategy, captured in its microprocessor road map, Intel needed to invest multiple billions of dollars in plant and equipment several years in advance of demand. While these capital investments were difficult for competitors to match, they also created very high-risk exposure for Intel. The Pentium flaw highlighted these high risks: even a relatively small glitch could potentially delay the adoption of a new microprocessor with disastrous financial consequences. More systematically and dangerously, Intel had to make vast capital investments in manufacturing but was highly dependent on the OEMs to deliver the new generation microprocessors to the market. It was a strategic imperative for Intel to reduce this dependency.

Sole source strategy and OEM bargaining power. Intel's decision to become sole-source supplier of its microprocessors in 1985 had the potential to fundamentally change the bargaining power between Intel and its OEM customers. Initially, however, there was little room to take advantage of the new situation. This was clearly illustrated by IBM—still the most powerful company in the computer industry at that time—which retained the right to manufacture its own Intel Architecture-based microprocessors and to enhance their design for its own purposes. Intel's opportunity to strengthen its bargaining power with OEM customers, however, was enhanced with the emergence of new entrants into the fast-growing PC industry, the so-called clone makers whose products were highly dependent on Intel's microprocessors. These new entrants, of course, did not come about as the result of strategic choices by Intel. Rather, they emerged because these companies valued the opportunity to participate in the fast-growing PC industry and saw access to Intel's microprocessors as one of the enablers to do so. (Microsoft's MS-DOS operating system was another critical enabler.)

Intel provides system-level products to help new OEM entrants. Once they had entered, these new companies became quite dependent on Intel. This was, in part, because of Intel's highly successful marketing programs that targeted the end user and reduced the OEMs' ability to differentiate their products. But another important factor was the fierce competition among the PC makers, which rapidly lowered the cost of systems based on Intel's processors and reduced their margins. PC system manufacturers (OEMs) faced one of the most intensely competitive markets in the world. Major OEMs had seen gross margins decline between 35 and 45 percent in 1990 to the mid-20 percent range in 1993. For example, Compaq saw gross margins fall from 43 percent in 1990 to 24.1 percent in 1993. Major OEMs such as IBM and Compaq spent most of 1992 and 1993 in a price war with several rapidly growing, low-cost manufacturers such as Dell Systems, Gateway 2000, and Packard Bell. Several medium-size OEMs and several smaller players either entered bankruptcy, sold out, or merged with a competitor. In one such transaction, Tandy, a pioneer in the PC industry and eighth largest vendor, sold its PC operations to AST Corp., the number seven player. Noted one Intel manager in 1993: "All the major OEMs are struggling to survive on very thin margins. There's no money left in most of these guys to do advanced development. Instead of thinking about where next generation systems are going, they're trying to figure out how to survive next quarter." And *Infoworld* reported: "Most manufacturers, Compaq and AST included, angrily reject that term [commodity] and point to the ways their systems differ from others. But Dell president Joel Korcher said the term is entirely correct for systems that can be sold over the phone and shipped out by mail. . . . We're about two steps up the food chain from rice. This is a commodity business and we like it just fine. Only a moron would say PCs aren't commodities."[11]

The OEMs' slim margins were not directly caused by the high prices charged by Intel for its microprocessors. Even if Intel had lowered its prices, the intense competition among the OEMs would most likely have led them to compete the increased margin potential away. The slim margins enjoyed by the OEMs as a result of the structure of competition also made it increasingly difficult for them to innovate. This provided an opportunity for Intel to step into the breach and to increasingly drive innovation in the PC industry beyond innovation in microprocessors. In particular, Intel became a major innovator in chipsets and motherboards—system-level products—that were enabling technologies for the OEMs.

Influence through innovation. Intel's increased role in innovation at the systems level had great strategic value; it gave the company the ability to significantly influence the pace of the introduction of new generation microprocessors. Intel's strategy was not always well-aligned with OEM manufacturers, who were often content to extend the life of a processor generation, especially if they had invested significant R&D in the development of their own systems for that generation. At the time of the Pentium launch, Intel had experienced recalcitrance on the part of IBM and Compaq to bring the new microprocessor to market. With its systems business, Intel enabled many OEMs, who otherwise would have been unable to compete, to introduce their own PCs with leading-edge systems sourced from Intel. Dennis Carter recalled: "With the introduction of the Pentium processor, the motherboards became a big deal. Both Compaq and IBM decided not to design Pentium processor-based systems for the consumer segment. We had a motherboard which enabled smaller companies to introduce Pentium processor-based systems, who otherwise wouldn't have been able to. Despite IBM and Compaq, we sold lots of them in 1994, the year of the Pentium processor ramp."

In 1997, Intel expanded its vertical integration strategy by acquiring Chips & Technologies, Inc., a supplier of graphics chips, for more than $400 million. By becoming a major player in the market for chipsets, motherboards, and even complete computer systems, Intel was able to support OEM manufacturers who were less competitive in these areas, improving their time to market, reducing their R&D requirements, and allowing them to focus resources in other areas. This leveled the playing field among OEM manufacturers, and it offset some of the power and competitive advantage of the major OEM manufacturers.

Integrating functionality at the microprocessor level. Besides increased vertical integration at the systems level, Intel increasingly incorporated greater amounts of functionality into its microprocessors, allowing it to add more value and capture a higher percentage of the total value of a computer system. Albert Yu, vice president and general manager of the Microprocessor Group, explained how the increasing number of transistors allowed Intel to incorporate increasingly more functions on a chip. In 1991, Yu said: "Intel only integrates functionality on a chip if it has become 'mundane,' that is, not much innovation is taking place in that function."

Looking back in 1999, Gordon Moore observed: "One of the really amazing things about this industry is that we assimilate the value add of our customers and give it back to them for free. The ones that recognize this force do well. The ones that don't, and try to protect their little niche, get steam-rolled. The technology is phenomenal in terms of the economics. It commoditizes everything."

Intel's ability to influence design standards impacted the balance of power in the industry. A case in point is Intel's entry into the server market segment. In 1996, Compaq earned 27 percent of its sales—and all of its profits—from server sales, based on the success of their unique system designs. These systems cost between $10,000 and $20,000, and add-on processor cards cost about $16,000 more. When Intel entered the server market segment with proposals for comprehensive system design standards, the playing field quickly leveled. By 1999, dozens of OEMs using Intel technology offered multiprocessor servers between $5,000 and $10,000, with add-on processor cards at about $2,500.[12]

A positive feedback loop: Influence breeds more influence. Through its brand strength, its influence over design standards, its vertical integration into chipsets and motherboards, and its ability to integrate more and more functionality into its microprocessors, Intel became increasingly more central to the PC industry during Epoch II. Some analysts likened the OEMs more to distributors than technology companies. According to Tom Yuen, cofounder of PC maker AST Research: "You no longer buy a Compaq computer, you buy an Intel computer from Compaq."[13] And according to Paul Otellini, executive vice president and general manager, Intel Architecture Business Group: "In a sense, PCs are now commodities, because most of the intellectual property is now tied up in the microprocessor."

Consequences of acquiring strong industry influence. The positive feedback loop associated with the coevolution of Intel and its OEM customers, which increasingly shifted the center of industry influence to Intel, had potentially important consequences. One consequence was growing resistance on the part of some OEMs to Intel's strategic leadership, which sometimes led to legal disputes. These disputes shed light on the scope of strategic information controlled by Intel.[14] Intel's top management was strongly aware of its leadership position in the PC and workstation market segments and of the potential for the organization to cross the line of acceptable influence behavior. In view of this, top management had established training programs throughout the company to instruct employees on antitrust compliance and was widely considered exemplary in this regard.

Another consequence of Intel's increasingly central role in the evolution of the PC market segment and the growing asymmetry in influence between Intel and the PC OEMs concerned its impact on the future of the relations with the OEMs and with Microsoft. Andy Grove illuminated these issues during a 1996 Stanford MBA class discussion focused on Intel's strategy to enable Packard Bell and Dell to bring out Pentium processor-based systems in the face of recalcitrance to do so on the part of Compaq and IBM. One student observed that this strategy would force Intel to do more and more R&D because the OEMs themselves would not be able to do so. Grove responded by saying: "Yes. So where will that lead Intel? If it strengthens Intel but weakens the customer, what would competitive strategic analysis suggest here? What is the danger if this goes on? How does this look to Microsoft because the OEMs are their customers, too? Will this help or hinder us vis-à-vis Microsoft?"

While Grove did not answer these questions in class, they indicate that he was seriously thinking about the implications of Intel's growing influence in the PC market segment. Neither Intel nor Microsoft would benefit from a situation where all the OEMs were too weak to contribute to the innovation process that would keep PC technology at the system level moving forward. Hence, it would not be advantageous if the OEM customer base became too fragmented, with a more or less uniform size distribution. On the other hand, having a very small number (say, only one or two) of very powerful OEMs would not be advantageous either.

Still another consequence of Intel's ability to strongly influence its OEM customers concerned the effect this was having on Intel's strategy-making process. In his summary of the 1996 MBA class discussion, reflecting on Intel's ability to manage the OEM relationship, Grove observed: "There is a hidden danger of Intel becoming very good at this. It is that we become good at one thing only."

Providing Enabling Technologies to the PC Industry

Noblesse oblige Throughout Epoch II, Intel had very high stakes in the continuation of the dynamism of the PC market segment. Yet, the relatively low margins of the OEMs in the highly competitive PC market segment made it difficult for them to support innovation. A consequence of Intel's growing prominence was that the burden of innovation increasingly fell on its shoulders. An important aspect of strategic value associated with Intel's ability to lead innovation in the PC industry came from providing new technologies to the industry that enabled the adoption of next generation microprocessors by increasing the ability of computer systems to take better advantage of performance improvements. This required Intel to develop a new R&D capability.

The role of Intel Architecture Labs (IAL). While developing the 1990 Strategic Long-Range Plan, Intel top management saw a problem. Intel's microprocessors had steadily increased in sophistication and performance, but the system architecture Intel's OEM customers were using had changed little in nearly a decade. To address this problem, several small research departments from the product groups were brought together to form Intel Architecture Labs. IAL's first goal was to bring new technology into the systems around Intel microprocessors, ensuring Intel-based PCs would remain competitive with other platforms such as Apple's Macintosh. The second goal was to chart the path of future technologies related to the PC and help eliminate roadblocks to the development of leading-edge applications for the PC.

IAL was composed of both hardware and software researchers. In 1993, Richard Wirt, a high-level IAL manager said: "Most people don't realize Intel employs over 1,000 software engineers. That would make us the tenth largest PC software house if they were broken out. . . . Increasingly our focus is on providing basic software technology that allows operating systems and applications to take advantage of leading-edge microprocessor capabilities."

From 1990 to 1993, IAL proposed a series of basic hardware and software enhancements to the PC architecture. These included, among others, the new PCI bus standard,[15] new compilers,[16] and a digital video standard.[17] To be sure, not all of Intel's evangelizing efforts were successful. The digital video standard, for instance, did not become the standard as was hoped in the early 1990s. The key factor is that by the early 1990s, Intel was generally in a position to strongly enable its OEM customers in the PC market segment toward adopting its new generations of microprocessors.

Emergence and Support of an Ecosystem around the Intel Architecture

Role of independent software vendors (ISVs). Demand for Intel's increasingly powerful microprocessors depended on the availability of new software applications that required lots of MIPS (millions of instructions per second), a key indicator of microprocessor performance. As independent software vendors were attracted by the rapidly growing installed base of Intel Architecture-based PCs, an ecosystem consisting of ISVs interested in writing applications for the PC emerged. Intel was quick to recognize the strategic importance of gaining and maintaining the "mind share" of the ISVs. Throughout the 1990s, Intel continued to work actively with development partners, providing them early access to new technologies so that Intel's new products would have strong applications that supported them at launch. Intel pursued strategic alliances with developers of multimedia and communications applications, as well as computer-based video games.

Capitalizing on a new, unplanned capability. Ironically, Intel's capability to work with the ISV community arose in part from the earlier efforts of the *i*860 RISC group to get applications developed for their new processor. Dennis Carter recalled in 1999:

> Claude Leglise headed up marketing for the *i*860. He headed the team getting ISVs to write software for the *i*860. What started as Industry Software Marketing became what is now the Content Group. Claude had been marketing manager for the 386. He had run the Indeo video standard efforts. Then he was brought into my group. With the Pentium processor coming about, most of the software had been optimized for the 486, and we needed to get the ISVs to move faster to develop software optimized for the Pentium. We realized we had this valuable resource in Claude's group, so we reallocated these people to recruit ISVs, especially those that were developing CD-ROM-based applications. From the work that they did with the *i*860, they developed a framework for working with ISVs, and this became a crucial capability for the core business.

Claude Leglise added:

> Today we have over 200 people that are working with the software community worldwide. The first effort was for the Pentium processor. We had nine or ten applications packages about one year after the launch of the Pentium. For the Pentium processor with MMX, by the day of launch we had twenty packages available. For the Pentium III, at launch there were about 300 packages. The effort has grown and we have improved. Most of the software is bought in the first twelve months of a new microprocessor product. Therefore, there is an advantage for them to be available up front.

The role of corporate business development. Intel's efforts to support the ecosystem of its microprocessor products went beyond working with ISVs to include strategic investments in smaller companies that were potentially useful in helping develop the PC industry. Intel's Corporate Business Development (CBD) group, led by Les Vadasz, performed an important function by doing acquisitions or making equity investments in such companies. The importance of CBD for developing Intel's ecosystem was still growing during the mid-1990s.

Continued Competitive Threats

In spite of Intel's growing centrality in the PC market segment during Epoch II, the company's microprocessor business continued to experience significant competitive threats during 1993–97. These threats came from rivals within the Intel Architecture as well as from RISC-based rivals. Some of these threats were perceived but did not materialize. Others remained largely unnoticed until they did in fact manifest themselves. In the early-to-mid 1990s, the most important perceived threat came from the PowerPC—a joint venture between Apple Computer, IBM, and Motorola—but this threat did not materialize. In the mid-to-late 1990s, the most important perceived threat came from the new network computing paradigm, and the much-hyped NC (network computer). This threat also did not materialize. An unanticipated surge in the demand for PCs costing less than $1,000 did materialize and posed serious strategic challenges for Intel in 1997–98.

Within-architecture competition. Throughout the 1990s, Intel continued to compete with AMD and Cyrix for market segment share in the PC industry.

AMD. AMD introduced its 486-compatible processor in 1993, and its Pentium-compatible processor, which it dubbed K5, in 1994. AMD, however, had traditionally had great difficulty in transferring its processor designs from the lab to the factory floor. This was one of the causes for the relative failure of the K5. In 1996, AMD acquired NexGen, Inc., whose president, Vinod Dham, had been a senior technical manager at Intel. The combined company collaborated on the K6 processor, with which AMD had some success, gaining design wins with Digital Equipment Corporation and IBM, among others. Aggressive pricing was a key element of AMD's strategy, and AMD's stated goal was to achieve 30 percent market segment share in Intel-compatible processors by 2000, up from its 1997 share of approximately 15 percent.

Cyrix. Cyrix also introduced a 486 processor and a 586 (Pentium compatible) processor. In February 1997, Cyrix introduced the Cyrix MediaGX Processor that reduced system costs by incorporating multimedia and systems functions on the CPU—a first for the industry. This innovation enabled the introduction of a complete multimedia system with a 180 MHz processor, monitor included, for $999. Cyrix outsourced the production of its processors to IBM Microelectronics and SGS-Thompson, providing Cyrix with access to leading-edge process technology and volume capability. In 1998, Cyrix was acquired by National Semiconductor. However, in 1999 National decided to divest Cyrix and to focus on its areas of strength.

Intel's competitive response. The long and bitter legal battle with AMD in the 386 and *i*486 microprocessor generations was settled in 1995. According to Intel's 1994 *Annual Report:* "Intel licensed AMD to copy the microcode in the Intel 386 and Intel 486 microprocessors. However, AMD agreed that it has no right to copy the microcode in the Pentium processor and future microprocessors. The net effect of this situation . . . is that . . . future imitations are not expected to be as close an imitation as were AM386* and AM486* products from AMD."

Intel's leadership position and Pentium processor brand name permitted it to pave the path of new product introductions while charging a slight premium for its products. In a SLRP session in 1997, Andy Grove observed that AMD and Cyrix had contributed little to the development of the PC industry, but "they snap at our heels, so they make us go faster." The relentless pace of product introductions accompanied by steep price decreases for previous-generation products put enormous pressure on its rivals. AMD's 1996 *Annual Report* stated:

> Intel Corporation's dominant market position has to date allowed it to set and control x86 microprocessor standards and thus dictate the type of product the market requires of Intel's competitors. In addition, Intel's financial strength has enabled it to reduce prices on its microprocessor products within a short period of time following their introduction, which reduces the margins and profitability of its competitors, and to exert substantial influence and control over PC manufacturers through the Intel inside advertising rebate program.

As noted earlier, Intel had strengthened its position in the PC market segment relative to the OEMs by manufacturing and distributing chipsets and motherboards with its microprocessors. This turned out to also be a strong competitive weapon against its competitors. AMD and Cyrix had to source chipsets and motherboards from other vendors who often lagged Intel in producing such components since Intel had proprietary technology attached to these integrated components. Thus, AMD and Cyrix had to form relationships with third-party designers of core-logic chipsets, motherboards, BIOS (basic input-output system) software, and other components.

Between-architecture competition. In the early-to-mid-1990s, RISC-based microprocessors of several vendors attempted to get a foothold in the PC industry.

Silicon Graphics (MIPS). In 1991, MIPS, then an independent company, had helped found the ACE consortium. MIPS, Compaq, and Microsoft led ACE, which stood for Advanced Computing Environment. The purpose of the alliance was to advance personal computers by moving from Intel's CISC processor architecture to MIPS' higher performance RISC architecture. MIPS got involved because the company had come to the realization that it would not be able to sustain itself as a supplier of RISC processors for the workstation market segment only. Compaq's motivation was presumably to expand its product line to high-end desktop systems, in part to reduce its dependence on the low-end market segment, which had become commoditized. Microsoft began development on Windows NT with the commitment to support both the Intel (x86) and MIPS architectures. Microsoft was presumably worried that if RISC processors were to become successful in the PC market segment, they would bring the Unix operating system with them. This would allow Unix to attack Microsoft in its core business. In 1992, however, Compaq withdrew support for ACE, announcing that it would remain committed to the Intel Architecture because it believed that Pentium, and future generations of the Intel Architecture would offer comparable performance to RISC architectures. ACE fell apart shortly after Compaq's announcement, and MIPS, nearing bankruptcy, was bought by Silicon Graphics, a leading workstation vendor and consumer of its microprocessor technology. MIPS remained an independent division of Silicon Graphics, after its purchase in 1992. MIPS was a design center that relied on partners to manufacture and sell its products. The market penetration of MIPS-based systems, however, remained small. And, in the mid-1990s, Silicon Graphics increasingly lost market share in the workstation market segment against systems based on the combination of Intel's Pentium Pro processors and Microsoft NT. After Silicon Graphics decided to adopt the Intel Architecture for some of its product lines in 1997, it divested itself of MIPS.

ALPHA. Digital Equipment Corp. (DEC), also sponsored a strong Pentium competitor. Its Alpha 21064 processor, introduced in late 1992 as the first of the Alpha architecture, was then the most powerful processor in existence. Having initially introduced Alpha in their workstation product line, DEC eventually planned to base its entire product line (mainframes, minicomputers, workstations, and desktop PCs) on the Alpha architecture. Of particular importance to DEC was the transition of its VAX product line, the world's leading minicomputers (and DEC's traditional core product) to Alpha processors.

DEC's Personal Computer Business Unit, which mounted a large thrust to make DEC a major player in the PC business in the early 1990s, continued to offer Intel-based PCs as its primary product line. Desktops and servers based on Alpha and Pentium processors running Windows NT were added at the top of the line in early 1994. Alpha-based systems, however, remained a small niche throughout the mid-1990s. In 1997, DEC sued Intel for alleged misappropriation of intellectual property associated with the design of its Alpha microprocessor. Intel subsequently purchased Digital's semiconductor manufacturing operations for about $625 million. Intel would serve as the foundry for multiple generations of Digital's 64-bit Alpha microprocessors while Digital retained the Alpha technology and Alpha-related semiconductor design teams to develop future generations of the microprocessor. In February 1998, Intel announced that it had signed an agreement with Digital's Advanced RISC Machines (ARM) to license ARM's CPU architecture. Later in 1998, Compaq acquired DEC but Intel retained the rights to manufacture and sell StrongArm. Ron Smith, vice president and general manager of Intel's Computer Enhancement Group, believed that the high-performance, low-power StrongArm processors had tremendous potential, especially in the market for portable devices and other consumer electronics applications of the future.

PowerPC. In the early summer of 1993, IBM, Motorola, and Apple announced the PowerPC 601, the first microprocessor to emerge from their joint venture formed three years earlier. The 601 was advertised to provide comparable or superior performance to the Pentium processor for less than half of the price. Having cost the partners nearly $1 billion, the PowerPC development program was lauded by many industry analysts as a very well-managed joint venture. The PowerPC 601, remained on schedule and delivered impressive performance. The Somerset design center, which housed more than 300 engineers from the three companies, was recognized as a world-class R&D center. PowerPC's manufacturing capabilities were also considered to be world-class, with both IBM and Motorola serving as foundries for various parts of the PowerPC product line. Initially, IBM would be the only producer of the 601 because it was designed in conjunction with a proprietary IBM manufacturing process. Motorola announced that it would come on-line with several follow-on products in 1994. Motorola planned a full line of PowerPC processors for applications ranging from microcontrollers to workstations to powerful servers.

Both Apple Computer and IBM committed to bringing out systems based on PowerPC. From the beginning, Apple announced that it would transition its entire Macintosh product line from Motorola's 68000 microprocessor architecture to PowerPC. By 1996, PowerPC was supporting the majority of the Macintosh product line. While IBM did not commit to move its PC product line away from the Intel Architecture, it had big plans for PowerPC as well. IBM's first PowerPC systems were released in September 1994. These first systems were high-performance technical workstations running IBM's AIX operating system (a version of UNIX). Because IBM's workstation products, and AIX, were based on the RS/6000 architecture, from which the PowerPC had been derived, few changes were needed to integrate PowerPC systems into this product line. IBM also announced its intention to use PowerPC as the basis for systems ranging from powerful massively parallel supercomputers, to minicomputers, to workstations, to desktop PCs, to handheld computers and consumer devices.

At the time of the PowerPC launch, the IBM PC Company announced its intention to continue to manufacture systems based on the Intel Architecture. This was not surprising, since IBM had a $10 billion IA-based PC business, and the group selling IA-based PCs was not about to roll over and play dead. Another source of ambivalence derived from IBM's long-standing efforts to make its OS/2 operating system software successful against Microsoft Windows. *Business Week* reported in October 1994 that IBM had decided in September: "[N]o personal computers based on the PowerPC chip will be introduced this year. The reason? IBM has decided that such machines must have OS/2. . . . But the project to rewrite the OS/2 operating system—which now runs only on Intel chips—has bogged down."[18] In other words, IBM—still stuck in its old hardware-based vertical industry concept—was making the fate of the PowerPC dependent on that of OS/2. The market, however, did not want to wait. Demand for IBM's IA-based PCs continued unabated, thereby further reducing the chances of PowerPC-based systems to be successful when finally introduced. In fact, IBM did not bring out PowerPC-based PCs.

Intel's competitive response. In 1993 many observers perceived the PowerPC as a serious threat to Intel. On the day after the announcement of the PowerPC 601 processor, Intel stock fell $5.25 to $87.38 per share. In November 1993, in the MBA elective course that he was coteaching at Stanford Business School, Andy Grove said he asked himself "Where do I want IBM to invest their resources—in the Intel Architecture or in the PowerPC?" Grove seemed to be of two minds on this question, going back and forth, but on balance he seemed to prefer IBM to invest in PowerPC. Investing in PowerPC would make it difficult for IBM to launch another microprocessor attack on Intel in the future if the PowerPC didn't take off, which Grove thought it wouldn't.

Intel countered claims of superior RISC performance in general use by pointing out that the *i*486 and the Pentium processor incorporated many RISC features and offered competitive performance in important benchmarks. Vin Dham explained in 1993:

> The team goal has always been to minimize the performance difference between our architecture and the best RISC guys. If we're close, our customers won't switch. It isn't worth their while. Switching takes a lot of effort. Some of our largest OEMs recently told me not to worry about the RISC guys. I told them that if I don't do my job right, they'll be telling

me to worry a couple of years from now. In the early Pentium processor development we did extensive investigations and asked our customers, "What would it take to get you to switch?" They said it would take more than a 2 × difference in performance. Our biggest advantage is compatibility. As long as we can offer world-class performance, our customers will continue to choose our architecture to maintain compatibility with the huge software base written to the Intel Architecture."

Albert Yu added:

There is a lot of marketing hype from our competitors about RISC processors being superior to our architecture. RISC versus CISC is not a technical discussion. RISC means simplifying as much as possible. This is good in any setting. RISC is a set of techniques that can be applied to microprocessor design to increase overall throughput. We continue to apply these techniques to the Intel Architecture. The 486 and Pentium architectures incorporate many of these design concepts.

Apple Computer, which used Motorola's PowerPC, continued to be the primary competitor to Intel-based systems in the PC industry. According to Dennis Carter:

In 1994, Motorola and Apple ran ads about the PowerPC that showed RISC growing in performance over time, and CISC and Intel running into a brick wall in a few years. They essentially said that Intel has a clumsy architecture, and no future. Every press interview I did, the press said, "You guys are dead." . . . From a marketing perspective, it was a disaster for Apple. Apple had always previously focused their positioning on the ease of use of the whole system. Now suddenly they were playing our game and calling out the microprocessor as the most important part of the PC. And on top of that, they were way over promising which cost them their credibility.

The capacity of the Intel Architecture to maintain parity in performance with the RISC architecture, combined with its enormous economies of scale advantage, eventually formed the basis for Intel's assault on the workstation market segment. The combination of the Pentium Pro microprocessors and Windows NT, coupled with ongoing improvements in such areas as bus architecture (PCI), graphics capabilities, and networking, significantly narrowed (and in some cases eliminated) the performance advantages offered by proprietary RISC/UNIX workstations. For example, Compaq claimed that its products offered performance similar to that of RISC/UNIX workstations at 75 percent of the cost. This combination also offered Intel the opportunity to enter the workstation and low and mid-end server market segments. This marked a shift similar to that experienced in the late 1980s when PC servers encroached upon the low-end minicomputer market. In both cases a new price/performance paradigm shift occurred which caused corporate MIS departments to actively consider a technology shift. To spur the momentum of this shift, new software applications for the Wintel platform were actively pursued.

During the mid-1990s, Intel collaborated with Hewlett-Packard to develop the 64-bit (IA-64) Merced processor for high-end servers. Merced was expected to offer as much as fifteen times the performance of current processors while maintaining compatibility with existing code. According to Albert Yu, the Merced was an offensive attack upon the RISC/UNIX world. The IA-64 provided the horsepower to compete with RISC servers. However, according to Pat Gelsinger, vice president and general manager of Intel's Desktop Products Group, Intel had multiple generations of 32-bit processors in development to be exploited before unleashing its IA-64 speed demon upon the desktop.[19]

The Emergence of Network Computing

NC or NetPC? In 1997, a confluence of factors were creating the emergence of a new networking PC paradigm: client-server/networking technology, the Internet, and Sun Microsystem's Java language. Within companies, the center of computing power continued to migrate from the desktop to the network. MIS departments were regaining control and centralizing purchasing decisions. Thus, computer companies needed to adjust, and transition to enterprise-computing business models and marketing strategies. Though the Wintel stronghold on the PC industry was compelling, some major players such as Oracle CEO Larry Ellison postulated a different future—that of the Network Computer (NC). Proponents of this option contended that applications and processing power should reside on a central server, with less powerful computers (thin clients) accessing the applications through a network. They predicted that the new network computer would consist of an inexpensive, relatively low-powered processor, a minimum amount of memory and a browser, connected to a variety of servers that store applications and data.

This was clearly a turn of events that would not be advantageous to Intel, nor to Microsoft. The reaction of both companies was swift. While discounting the likelihood that the network-computing paradigm would materialize, Intel and Microsoft combined forces to develop and introduce the NetPC as an alternative to the NC. Pat Gelsinger, vice president and two-in-a-box with Mike Aymar as general manager of Intel's Desktop Products Group, estimated in 1997 that there were about 30 to 40 million dumb terminals in the corporate environment that were prime targets for NC replacement. Overall, Gelsinger estimated that approximately 5 percent of the corporate market was at risk for the NC platform. His estimate assumed that medium/large business applications were about one-third of the market, one-third of which were appropriate for NC applications, one-half of which were inertia-bound to their current system. Gelsinger stated that the NetPC is "the most aggressive amplification of PC management technology aimed at the focused application user and providing a catalyst for management deployment in the company overall."

Managing PC maintenance costs. As Gelsinger's comments suggest, the emergence of the NC and NetPC concepts were, in part, motivated by an increasing concern about managing the costs of maintaining corporate computer systems. PC maintenance costs involved hardware and software upkeep, lost productivity, and training costs. The Gartner Group estimated that the cost of maintaining a PC was $25,000 over a three-year period. Mike Aymar, vice president and co-general manager of Intel's Desktop Products Group, reportedly said that "[t]he cost to maintain Intel's internal computer system had been projected to grow from $70 million in 1995 to more than $160 million in 2000, if the company stuck exclusively with PCs." In response to the maintenance cost concern, Intel had developed its Wired for Management software suite that was specifically aimed at controlling such costs.

Thus, the selling proposition of the NC had evolved. It was first postulated as an alternative for lower-income households that could not afford the expense of a home PC. Now that proposition had changed to target the cost of maintenance in the corporate PC market. The main selling proposition was now to managers and MIS groups within companies, rather than to end users. This approach was contrary to the trend toward increased variety, choice, and functionality at the desktop level.

One approach to characterizing these various computer concepts was to view them along a continuum, from "flexible PCs" at one end and "full network computing" at the other, as shown below:

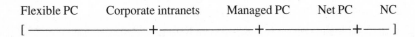

| Flexible PC | Corporate intranets | Managed PC | Net PC | NC |

The traditional computing environment resides more to the left of the continuum, with microprocessing power residing at the desktop (i.e., flexible PC) and corporate communications provided through an intranet. The Managed PC used hardware and software modifications to minimize the cost of PC ownership in an enterprise setting. The NetPC versus NC issue created some dissonance within Intel. Intel was developing both the managed PC (MPC) and the NetPC products that targeted the corporate market and the total cost of ownership (TCO) issue. In practice, the only difference between these products was a lack of a local disk drive for the NetPC. The price-points for the three products were: NC ($500–$700), NetPC ($900–$1,300), MPC ($1,000). Also, NetPC and MPC software was Intel's server software—potentially encroaching upon Microsoft's space.

In a SLRP session in September 1997, Andy Grove reviewed the strategic situation with respect to the network computer. He noted that the NetPC and NC were losing momentum and buzz, and viewed this as a perfect outcome for Intel. He said "We embraced it, but the illusion and intrigue with it is disappearing. People are buying Managed PCs." A greater strategic concern of Grove, however, had to do with the sudden growth of the low-end of the PC market segment—something that traditionally was called segment zero at Intel.

The Growth of the Below–$1,000 PC Market Segment

In 1997, the IA market segment encompassed high-end applications (e.g., Pentium Pro), midrange applications (e.g., x486 and Pentium), and low-end applications (Network PCs). Low-end consumer-electronics applications were also beginning to take root with popular appliances such as the Palm Pilot, a handheld organizer. For most of the 1990s, mainstream systems had typically been available for about $2,000. But the market share of the sub-$1,000 personal computer grew considerably in 1997.

In the September 1997 SLRP session, Andy Grove expressed concern about Intel's strategy with respect to the low-end market segment. He noted:

> We say we have a top-to-bottom strategy. But we don't act top-to-bottom, because Intel has low-end phobia. . . . But the low end is not going away. These are great machines! Thanks to us! The data about desktop sales out at the retail, reseller, and direct level all show a downward trend in price: $500 down in about a year! I have not seen that before. And the volumes at the low end are up.
>
> So, the good news about segment zero is that we have it on our road map. The bad news is that we don't have an engineered product.

Meeting the low-end challenge. Shortly thereafter, Grove was exposed to the idea of disruptive technologies. He was particularly alarmed by the story of how the mini steel mills had gradually worked their way up from successfully manufacturing and selling low-end rebar steel to the high-end steel market segments.[20] It is debatable that the growth of the low-end PC market segment represented an instance of the disruptive technology phenomenon. In fact, the emergence of the low-end PC was the result of a shift in customer demand, rather than precipitated by a change in technology, which was noticed and responded to by Compaq. Grove later explained that Compaq went to AMD to commission the development of a low-end microprocessor to capitalize on the demand shift. Be that as it may, Andy Grove did not want segment zero to become Intel's rebar equivalent. In late 1997, top management moved a large number of engineers to work on the new Celeron processor, which was optimized for the low end and was introduced in April 1998. The Celeron processor design was optimized to reduce manufacturing costs, whereas the Pentium processors were optimized for performance. Celeron processors were priced more aggressively than Pentium processors.

By 1998, low-cost PCs had captured a significant percentage of consumer sales within the highly visible retail channel. Many of these machines initially used low-cost microprocessors from AMD and Cyrix. As a result, AMD's market segment share of Intel-based microprocessors grew from 6.7 percent to 16.1 percent between the fourth-quarters of 1997 and 1998, while Cyrix's grew from 3.5 percent to 5.8 percent over the same period. Intel's overall market segment share dropped from 86.2 percent to 76.1 percent during this period. In early 1999, however, Paul Otellini, executive vice president and general manager of the Intel Architecture Business Group, was able to report success with the Celeron processor: "One year ago in the sub-$1,000 market segment, our share was about 38 percent. We then lost some ground, but we have regained our share so we are at about 38 percent again."

Stemming commoditization. In 1997, Grove was also concerned about what he called the waterfall effect: Lower prices on the low end of the PC market segment would trigger lower prices on the high end. To stem the commoditization tide, Intel systematically matched its microprocessor line with new products and brands in each of the major market segments. The Celeron processor was targeted at the low-cost, entry-level part of the market; the Pentium II and Pentium III processors were targeted at performance desktops and entry-level servers and workstations; and the Pentium II Xeon and Pentium III Xeon processors were targeted at midrange and high-end servers and workstations. All of these processors were derivatives of Intel's P6 Pentium Pro microarchitecture. This segmentation allowed Intel to maintain a huge pricing range, with Celeron processors selling for about $63 each and high-end Pentium Xeon processors selling for about $3,700 each. This segmentation strategy rested on the foundation laid by the Intel Inside investments. Dennis Carter pointed out that even on the low end, while some data seemed to indicate that customers were not willing to pay a premium for the Celeron brand, they still valued having an Intel processor in their PC. The strategy helped sustain Intel's historical average sales price for microprocessors. Intel's product breadth also made it more difficult for competitors to pursue niche strategies by exploiting holes in Intel's product line. Speaking to his MBA class at Stanford Business School in the fall of 1998, Grove said: "The laws of thermodynamics, applied to the computer industry, [mean] that everything gets commoditized eventually. Grove's law is that the last one to get commoditized wins."

Effect on distribution channels. Perhaps not surprisingly, it was Dell Computer—the OEM that had most readily recognized the commoditization of PCs—which was best able to cope with the maturation of the PC market segment. Dell's direct sales model, strongly enabled by the Internet, was extremely successful and enhanced the Dell brand name. Dell continued to focus on corporate accounts and high-end PC sales and was gaining market share at the expense of the retail channel and other OEMs. Compaq and other OEMs were trying to catch up in the late 1990s, but this was difficult given what Andy Grove called "their vicious embrace of traditional distribution channels."

The Evolving Relationship with Microsoft

Siamese twins in the PC market segment. IBM had brought Intel and Microsoft together in 1980 to provide the key components for the original IBM PC: the microprocessor and the operating system software. Since then, Intel and Microsoft's rise in the computer industry had been highly symbiotic, and the two had become the clear leaders in the worldwide PC industry. Microsoft's MS DOS, Windows 3.1, and Windows 95 operating systems ran on more than 85 percent of the world's PCs. These operating systems had a tremendous installed base of available applications running on them. And to Intel's benefit, these operating systems were written with the largest market in mind and therefore ran only on Intel Architecture microprocessors. The success of Windows 3.1 and Windows 95 were key factors in Intel's growth and profitability. These operating systems transformed the IBM PC from a character-based interface to a graphical environment, which required considerably greater processing power and stimulated the overall market for PCs and microprocessors. Andy Grove sometimes characterized the relationship between Intel and Microsoft in the PC market segment as "two companies joined at the hip."

Strong complementors in workstations and servers. Microsoft introduced Windows NT in 1993 and targeted the new operating system at high-end desktop PCs, workstations, and servers. Although Windows NT was designed to be easily ported to multiple microprocessor architectures and had been ported to several, the vast majority of systems that utilized NT did so on Intel microprocessors. From 1993 to 1999, Windows NT, combined with high-performance Intel processors, made steady and significant advances in the market segments for workstations and servers, increasingly displacing RISC/UNIX systems in the low and medium performance ranges.

Areas of (potential) rivalry between the giants. While Intel and Microsoft had a highly symbiotic relationship, some latent conflicts in their relationship sometimes became manifest. One area of potential conflict concerned differences in the logic of their strategy in the PC industry and in how they viewed the OEMs. Conflict could also flare up if one or the other company trespassed into the other's "home territory." Finally, as the computer industry evolved and converged with other industries, their interests were sometimes less strongly aligned than in the desktop PC market segment.

Strategic logic. Intel's strategic logic was to introduce a new microprocessor generation with double the performance for the same price every 18 months or so. Intel invested billions of dollars in manufacturing capacity in advance of demand and had an enormous stake in getting customers to buy the new processors. Intel's strategy was thus primarily oriented toward expanding the installed base for its products. Microsoft, in contrast, had a strong interest in selling upgrades for each generation of its operating system software. The economics of upgrades were exceedingly attractive. Microsoft's strategy was thus less strongly oriented toward expanding the installed base for its products, and perhaps more readily toward exploiting the existing installed base. Invariably, Microsoft had been delayed in bringing out the next generations of its operating system. Windows 94 had become Windows 95, Windows 97 had become Windows 98, and so on. In 1996, speaking to his Stanford MBA class, Andy Grove mentioned that he "would have been very worried if [he] had known that Chicago [the project name for Win 94] would become Win 95, because by that time Intel would have won or lost the shootout with the PowerPC."

Given the logic of their strategy, it was not surprising that Intel had spent a great deal of resources and effort on making sure that the OEMs would be able and willing to support the launch of a new generation processor. In doing so, Intel had effectively contributed to the reduced ability of the OEMs to differentiate their products. This, in turn, had contributed to reducing their ability to get high margins, making them even more dependent on Intel for innovation. Andy Grove, speaking to his MBA class at Stanford, said that he sometimes worried how this process looked from Microsoft's perspective, since the OEMs were its customers, too.

Trespassing into each other's territory. Intel and Microsoft were also very territorial with respect to their hardware/software home territory. On occasion, one company would trespass into the other's territory. For example, in the early 1990s, Intel Architecture Labs created Native Signal Processing (NSP). Through NSP, Intel would create multimedia capabilities through the microprocessor itself, creating a new platform standard, which would help the multimedia application software developers. NSP, however, would not only displace pieces of hardware (various add-in chips and add-in circuit boards), but software as well—thus threatening Microsoft. NSP invisibly enhanced Microsoft's Windows by controlling the manner in which the Pentium allocated its time, resulting in a better multimedia experience. Steven McGeady, vice president and general manager of the Communications Technology Lab in IAL, was quoted: "What we are doing is putting rabbits out there to run ahead of hounds like Microsoft to make them run faster. Sometimes, the hound might catch the rabbit—Microsoft could well provide its own alternative to our NSP software that ultimately wins. But to do that they must run faster, and that's what we really care about." [21]

Microsoft, however, was not pleased with this development and this initiative disappeared at Intel. Some time later, Andy Grove in a conversation with Bill Gates explained the decision to stop the NSP application: "We caved. Introducing a Windows-based software initiative that Microsoft doesn't support . . . well, life is too short for that." [22]

Diverging interests. By the late 1990s Intel's relationship with Microsoft had changed significantly, particularly on the low-end and the high-end. On the low-end, Microsoft had released Windows CE, which targeted handheld PCs and other information appliances. Unlike other versions of Windows, which were closely integrated with Intel processors, Microsoft initially ported Windows CE to several non-Intel processors. On the high end, Intel's Merced and future IA–64 processors were designed to work not only with Microsoft Windows NT but also with each of the major versions of Unix.

Nevertheless, the alliance remained strong. In September 1997, Andy Grove, speaking to Intel executives, summed up the state of the relationship with Microsoft. He said:

In the core PC business, Intel and Microsoft are equally dependent on each other. Away from it, neither company is dependent on the other; we are just two struggling companies.

If you zero in on any given activity, it is possible to say that the collaboration could be better. But that's not the right way to look at it. We have had a 17-year relationship—a unique, historic relationship. It is a tough one, but we are happy with it.

The Strategic Situation in 1998

A great success story. During 1994–98, the latter part of Epoch II, Intel continued to ride the enormous growth wave of the PC industry, effectively capitalizing on its favorable strategic position. In 1995, some observers predicted: "It is totally plausible . . . that Intel will become the world's most profitable company."[23]

While the company never quite reached that pinnacle, Intel did spectacularly well by the conventional standards of growth, profitability, and stock market performance. (So well, that in 1999 it became a bellwether stock included in the illustrious Dow Jones Industrial Average stock market indicator.) In 1997 *Time* selected Andy Grove as Man of the Year, which recognized the influence of Intel's success and impact on the world at large. Nevertheless, toward the end of Epoch II, Intel faced several strategic issues that derived directly from the company's extraordinary success in pacing the evolution of the PC market segment.

Is the pace sustainable? Andy Grove's worries in 1993 that Intel was not focusing strongly enough on executing the Pentium processor launch were not born out. Grove made sure that Intel did not drop the ball and provide an opening for its competitors. And he continued to focus the organization on the successful launch of several more generations of Pentium processors during the remainder of Epoch II. There were some signs, however, that the relentless drive and pace of change that Intel managers had experienced under Andy Grove's leadership was imposing some costs on the organization. Dennis Carter explained in 1999:

In the 1990s I remember being tired constantly. There was no respite. After every success, Andy would say "That's nice, but what are we going to do next?" For example, when the Intel stock reached $100 for the first time, we were in a meeting, and upon hearing the news, people were excited and started to cheer. But Andy looked very glum. He pounded the table with his fist and said, "The shareholders that bought our stock at

$100 expect us to bring it to $200." This created a sense of urgency, and I went from elation to almost a sense of panic. We have been successful largely due to efforts—extraordinary efforts. And we've been driven. But this is very tiring, even exhausting. So it is not sustainable.

Success breeds scrutiny. Intel's preeminence in the PC market segment attracted government scrutiny. While there were occasional concerns raised about Intel's alleged monopoly position in the microprocessor industry and its strong legal challenges to AMD, there was no action taken by any government agency during 1987–97. In 1998, however, the Federal Trade Commission (FTC) sued Intel for alleged anticompetitive practices. The FTC began to investigate Intel's business practices and included Intel's acquisition of Chips & Technologies, Inc., in the investigation. Intel collaborated fully with the investigation and seemed to be trying hard to accommodate any reasonable concerns the FTC might have. By the end of 1998, the FTC had not taken any action against Intel. But the investigation continued.

DISCUSSION AND IMPLICATIONS

Intel's strategy-making during the latter part of Epoch II shaped, and was shaped by, the evolution of the PC market segment. The Intel Architecture had achieved an extremely favorable strategic position in the PC market segment and Intel was able to capitalize on it. First, by becoming sole source and, second, by using its preeminence to decisively influence the evolution of the PC market segment. While Intel's success story during Epoch II is one of coevolution, it is also one of a company gaining and maintaining control over its destiny. Intel was able to influence its environment and shape its future like few other companies ever have.

As amply documented in this chapter, Intel's success during the latter part of Epoch II was by no means guaranteed. At least a significant part of it can be attributed to the company's strategic actions. Intel's strategy-making process during Epoch II closely resembled the rational actor model, with strategic decision-making increasingly concentrated in the position of the CEO and an organization finely tuned to simultaneous involvement of all operating groups in executing the corporate strategy. Intel's strategy-making during Epoch II moved from internal ecology to planned economy. But it was an extremely agile planned economy. Intel was a large organization that could literally "turn on a dime," as was illustrated by its swift reaction to the NC threat. This agility was significantly facilitated by the company's singular focus on its core microprocessor business.

Intel coevolved with its environment (the PC market segment) as the result of deliberate, mostly proactive adaptation. Tool I—the framework of dynamic forces driving a company's evolution—was helpful to examine the coevolution of the basis of competitive advantage in the PC industry and Intel's distinctive competencies. The dynamic matching of the basis of competition and distinctive competencies in combination with the strong alignment of its strategy and actions (chapter 6) allowed Intel to achieve superior economic performance during Epoch II. The coevolutionary process, however, also engendered unanticipated consequences for Intel's strategy-making process, some of which were becoming manifest in 1997. The analysis yields several insights that further contribute to theory about the role of strategy and strategic leadership in company evolution.

Understanding Strategic Position: The Evolving Basis of Competitive Advantage

Most industries contain a set of viable strategic positions that companies with different strategies can occupy. Each of these strategic positions is characterized by a somewhat different basis of competitive advantage: what it takes to win—the success factors. Traditional industry forces—customers, competitors, suppliers, entry barriers, and possible substitution—together with technological and regulatory forces, are important determinants of what it takes to win. Whereas most industries contain multiple viable positions, the PC market segment of the microprocessor industry experienced increasing returns to adoption. Increasing returns to adoption is associated with the fiercest and most definitive of competitive regimes: Winner takes (almost) all.

Increasing returns to adoption. Initially, increasing returns to adoption was a new economic force not well understood by the industry participants. Former Stanford professor Brian Arthur, a leading expert, points out that increasing returns to adoption can arise from several sources, five of which are particularly important.[24] The first source involves *learning by using:* The more a technology is used and the more is learned about it, the better the chances are to improve on it. A second source involves *network externalities:* If the technology serves to connect people, then the more people are using the technology, the higher its value for each additional user. A third source involves *scale economies in production:* If the technology can be produced in large volume, its average cost of production is likely to be lower and it can be priced more attractively. A fourth source involves *informational increasing returns:* The more the technology is used and the better it is known, the lower the perceived risk of adopting it. The fifth and final source involves *technological interrelatedness:* As a technology becomes more adopted, complementary technologies or products are likely to be made compatible with it and to become part of its infrastructure, which gives rise to the emergence of ecosystems. Ecosystems are potentially large sets of companies whose interests are mutual in that they provide complementary products or services and thereby increase the value of each other's products and services in the eyes of the customer.

The five sources of increasing returns to adoption, however, are only *potential* sources. To benefit from them, a company must somehow activate them and then continue to exploit them. Through its strategic actions, Intel benefited from all five sources of increasing returns to adoption throughout Epoch II.

Increasing returns to adoption keeps competitive architectures at bay. The mid-1990s saw a resurgence of RISC-based microprocessors; in particular, the PowerPC architecture developed by the IBM–Motorola–Apple Computer alliance. Increasing returns to adoption was one major reason that Intel was able to stave off the new competitive challenge. Intel had become the center of a fast-growing ecosystem involving ISVs. These complementors wrote applications programs for Intel-compatible PCs. Backward compatibility was a key link in the virtuous circle that had emerged between the installed base of Intel Architecture-based systems and the availability of applications that ran on these systems. Intel's brand premise of goodness assured complementors and end users that the many billions of dollars in software that were available for previous generations of Intel's microprocessors would also be easily usable with the next generation processors.

This was a meaningful promise, of course, only to the extent that the price-performance of Intel's microprocessors would not significantly fall behind that of rival architectures. One rule of thumb is that users are unlikely to switch to another technology as long as the difference in price/performance is less than 10X. Hence, Intel's microprocessor group's ability to maintain the price/performance progress of its CISC-based microprocessors in line with that of the newer RISC-based microprocessors was another major reason why the Intel Architecture continued to prevail. Intel made sure that PC customers had no incentive to switch and lose the advantage of the vast ecosystem supporting IA. As Andy Grove correctly anticipated in 1993, IBM continued to be stuck on its traditional vertical strategic logic and held the PowerPC hostage to its OS/2 operating system software. As a result, IBM did not bring out PowerPC-based systems. Only Apple Computer used PowerPC microprocessors, and its share of the PC market segment shrunk significantly during the mid-1990s.

Not only was Intel able to keep RISC-based rivals out of the PC market segment, the company had successfully entered the workstation market segment with Pentium Pro machines that ran Windows NT. In 1997, Intel was still gaining share in the lower and middle parts of that market segment, which promised to set in motion a virtuous circle in that market segment as well.

Scale and scope keep within-architecture competitors at bay. Besides threats from RISC, Intel had to face within-architecture competition from AMD, Cyrix, and NexGen. These competitors could benefit from the virtuous circle supporting the Intel Architecture, hence Intel's competitive strategy here involved more traditional forces associated with distinctive competencies (including the protection of intellectual property) and scale and scope advantages. While Intel's rivals tried to compete by bringing to market IA-compatible designs that would allow them to tap into the IA-based ecosystem, they were incapable of bringing next generation products to market in time to compete effectively with Intel. Delayed in part by Intel's forceful legal challenges, AMD was almost four years behind Intel with the 386 and 486 generations. Intel's scale and scope advantages made it possible to rapidly and drastically lower prices during the life cycle of each new microprocessor generation, putting enormous pressure on AMD's margins. Intel's ability to provide chipsets and motherboards to enable OEMs to quickly bring its technology to market also played a key role in limiting AMD's competitive effectiveness. AMD's K-5 was brought to market more rapidly after Intel's launch of the Pentium processor, but the company's inability to effectively manufacture the product in volume prevented it from taking significant market segment share away from Intel.

Increased influence with OEM customers and end users. With its sole-source strategy for the 386, Intel capitalized on the already established preeminence of the x86 architecture, and consolidated its position as the leading microprocessor vendor for the IBM-compatible PC market segment. (IBM was delayed by trying to come up with a better 286 processor in-house.) With Compaq becoming the first manufacturer to offer a 386-based PC and PC-clone manufacturers following suit, Intel (together with Microsoft) had begun to wrestle preeminence in the PC industry away from IBM. The spectacular success of the sole-source strategy for the 386 processor led the industry to refer to Intel-compatible rather than IBM-compatible PCs. The successful marketing campaigns for the 486 and Pentium processors targeted at the end users shifted the ability to influence the pace with which new technology was delivered to the market increasingly to Intel and away from the OEMs.

Intel's ability to capitalize on increasing returns to adoption, its scale and scope advantages, and its ability to influence the relationship with the OEMs to its advantage underscore the importance of top management understanding the key factors that make a company's strategic position favorable or unfavorable. A key element in Intel's success story during Epoch II was that early on top management very clearly understood the reasons why the company was lucky in the PC market segment of the microprocessor industry.

> **Insight 8.1.** The role of strategic leadership is to capitalize on the company's strategic position. This requires top management to clearly understand the evolving basis of competitive advantage in its product-market domain.

Capitalizing on Strategic Position: Coevolving Distinctive Competencies

Strategic position is an important determinant of success and is sometimes achieved because of luck or fortuitous circumstances, with little or no relationship to distinctive competencies; for example, in the case of a pure first mover or favorable physical location advantage. Strategic position, however, should not be taken for granted because it has a tendency to slip away over time if it is not linked in some ways to distinctive competencies. This raises the question to what extent Intel's ability to exploit its favorable strategic position during Epoch II was due to its distinctive competencies.

The data indicate that Intel's distinctive competencies coevolved with its evolving strategic position in the PC market segment. By 1998, Intel had developed a set of distinctive competencies in various functional areas as well as in integrating across functional areas that strongly supported its preeminent strategic position in the PC market segment. The development of these competencies involved huge investments in Property, Plant, and Equipment (PP&E), R&D, and marketing. These investments also constituted huge bets because they had to be made several years in advance of demand.

New distinctive competency: Integrating process technology and manufacturing. After the DRAM debacle, Intel realized that manufacturing was a weakness that needed to be turned into a competence, especially in light of the decision to become the sole-source for the 386 microprocessor. One cause of Intel's decline in DRAM was the company's lagging capital investments. The multibillion-dollar investments in PP&E during Epoch II indicate that Intel was not making the same mistake in its microprocessor business. Another major cause of poor manufacturing lay in the lack of standardized interface between process technology and manufacturing. A key decision therefore was to change the routine for transferring process technology to manufacturing. The introduction of the Copy Exact approach prevented the Intel U—the initial reduction in yields that accompanied the transfer of technology from one fab to the others—from recurring in microprocessors (see chapter 2), and enhanced speed as well as quality in manufacturing ramps. Throughout Epoch II, Intel's distinctive competence integrating process technology and manufacturing was very important in keeping AMD and other rivals at bay. This was also a critical distinctive competence in allowing Intel to sustain the torrid pace of new generation microprocessor introduction.

New distinctive competence: Outbound marketing. Throughout Epoch II, Intel remained a technology and manufacturing company. Dennis Carter pointed out that in 1999, 21 percent of Intel's employees were in R&D and 69 percent in manufacturing. During this period, however, Intel also developed very strong outbound marketing competencies. With the Red X campaign for the 386, the Intel Inside campaign for the 486, and the Pentium processor branding effort, Intel was increasingly able to influence the choices of the end users, thereby reducing the OEMs's influence. These marketing campaigns cost hundreds of millions of dollars, but the resulting marketing pull reduced dependency on the OEMs in bringing Intel's new technology to market.

New technological competencies: Chipsets and motherboards. As Intel's importance in the PC market segment grew, its resource commitments grew commensurately. Since Intel needed to make sure it would not be overly dependent on just a few major OEMs, it needed to be in a position to enable additional OEMs to bring its technology to market. To do so, Intel broadened its competencies to the systems level, becoming a leading chipset and motherboard designer and manufacturer. Intel's success in vertically integrating into the chipset and motherboard business was thus another key factor that increased its influence in the PC market segment. The decision of an OEM customer to design a particular microprocessor into its own products had far-ranging implications and was difficult and expensive to reverse. As Intel began to develop and sell chipsets and motherboards, the dependency of some OEM customers increased even more. It was this dependency of the OEMs that allowed—or required—Intel to become the driver of the PC industry.

Intel's success during Epoch II was made possible by top management's ability to capitalize on its understanding of what it would take to continue to win in the

PC market segment by investing very large amounts of resources in the requisite distinctive competencies in all the functional areas. Making these investments took courage, because they had to be made in advance of knowing whether the market demand that would make them worthwhile would materialize.

> **Insight 8.2.** The role of strategic leadership is to invest in the distinctive competencies necessary to capitalize on the company's strategic position. These investments can be large and must be made before top management can be sure that they will work.

Harmony among the Dynamic Forces Driving Company Evolution

Making *rational* bets requires courage and confidence. Intel's courage and confidence was rooted in having a clear strategy. Andy Grove's successful efforts to create a strongly focused induced-strategy process that aligned strategy and action were supported by the equally successful efforts to align the company's distinctive competencies with the requirements of its strategic position in the PC market segment. During Epoch II Intel was able to dynamically maintain tight links between strategy, action, position, and distinctive competencies.

The analysis of the coevolutionary process that gave Intel great control over its destiny during Epoch II highlights the importance of these linkages. Strategic action without position has limited effectiveness and without competencies is powerless. Position without strategy is unlikely to fully exploit advantage and without competencies is precarious and vanishing. Competencies without strategy are aimless and without position cannot be fully leveraged. Thus, strategy, action, position, and distinctive competencies mutually support each other. If one or more elements are missing, a company's prospects for maintaining control over its destiny are diminished.

> **Insight 8.3.** Strategic leadership involves creating links between position and distinctive competencies that are informed by strategy and support strategic action.

Intel's strategic diamond. During Epoch II, Intel's strategy-making tightly linked strategic action to strategy as well as strategic position and distinctive competencies. The result was tight and harmonious relations between the forces that drive a company's evolution. Metaphorically, the tight and harmonious linkages

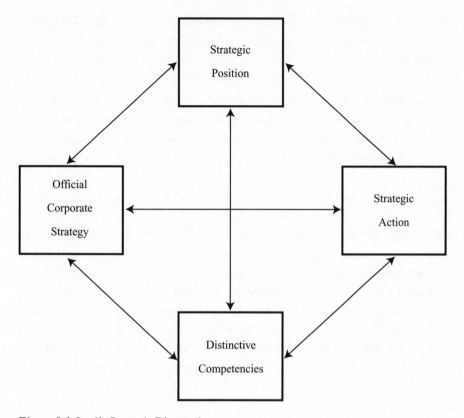

Figure 8.1. Intel's Strategic Diamond.

achieved in the forces identified in Tool I evoke the image of Intel's strategy-making during Epoch II as a diamond—perfectly clear and symmetrical, impossible to scratch, and extremely valuable. Figure 8.1 shows Intel's strategic diamond.

Strategic Consequences of Coevolution: Advantages and Potential Disadvantages

Creator *and* prisoner of the environment.   Being the driving force in the coevolution with the PC market segment had great advantages for Intel. The company was clearly in command of its own destiny during Epoch II. The coevolutionary process, however, created a positive feedback loop. With the relationship between Intel and its OEM customers becoming increasingly asymmetrical in terms of influence, the OEMs also became increasingly dependent on Intel for innovation. Conversely, Intel's leaders believed they had to make more and more investments to enable the industry to take advantage of its ever more powerful microprocessors. Intel's destiny and that of the PC market segment thus became more and more interdependent.

> **Insight 8.4.** Driving the coevolutionary process between itself and its product-market domain provides a company with the opportunity to exert great influence but also ties its destiny increasingly to that of its product-market domain.

Account control *and* limited inbound marketing. One of the most direct ways in which Intel could exert influence in the PC market segment was in the relationship with its OEM customers. A crucial tool in gaining that influence came from Intel's strong outbound marketing competencies developed during Epoch II. These competencies helped Intel establish a degree of influence that was not too dissimilar from the sort of account control that IBM had been able to exert in the halcyon days of the mainframe computer business. Such strong influence, however, tends to drive out the need for inbound marketing and runs the risk of losing touch with changes in the customer base, in particular the emergence of new categories of customers that may favor different types of products and services than the company provides.

> **Insight 8.5.** Driving the coevolutionary process tends to favor outbound marketing and account control over inbound marketing and new customer intelligence.

Top management intuition: Deep *and* narrow. As a result of Intel's singular focus, Andy Grove and the rest of Intel's top management developed deep understanding and intuition for the fundamentals of the PC market segment. This allowed them to make many strategic judgment calls correctly and quickly, before more complete information would be available. For instance, Grove developed strong intuition about the optimal timing of bringing new factories on line. Given the multibillion-dollar investments involved, investing too soon would unnecessarily cost the company tens of millions of dollars in financing costs. Investing too late, however, would provide competitors with an opening. By the same token, the depth of intuition that gave top management confidence to make strategic judgment calls in the PC market segment was lacking in new areas. As Intel focused more and more on the PC market segment, top management's intuition deepened but was also likely to become narrower.

Insight 8.6. Driving the coevolutionary process helps top management develop deep intuition for the key forces in its current product-market domain but tends to impede development of intuition in new areas.

Time-paced strategy: Exhilarating *and* exhausting. Some authors have suggested that time-paced strategy is a powerful alternative to event-paced strategy, and sometimes offer Intel as an example.[25] Event-paced strategy has a reactive connotation; time-paced strategy suggests that a company is really in control of its environment. Time-paced strategy therefore has a positive connotation for its proponents. Time-paced strategy, in principle, allows a company to dictate the pace of strategic change that other players—customers, competitors, and suppliers—must adhere to. As a major driving force of the PC market segment, Intel was able to influence the pace and the rate of change. It was clear in the mid-1990s that Intel's ability to do so had an exhilarating effect on many of its managers. People were aware of Intel's extraordinary momentum and the equally extraordinary riches and fame that came with it.

Nevertheless, Intel's time-paced strategy was not a simple-minded effort to try to unilaterally impose top management's strategic intent on the environment. As noted earlier, Andy Grove had learned from studying the data that the peak-to-peak production for past microprocessor generations had been three years. Hence, there was a natural adoption cycle in the PC market segment that Intel most likely would not have been able to change much. Based on this, Grove assumed that the next generation microprocessor—the Pentium processor—would follow the same adoption cycle, which informed the timing of his capital investment decisions. Using time effectively in strategy is essential, but to do so requires deep understanding, intuition, and respect for the realities of the dynamic environment.

Without such a thoughtful, data-based approach, time-paced strategy runs the risk of gaining its own momentum and exhausting the troops. Dennis Carter's observations, reported earlier, about the enormous pressures on the organization resulting from Andy Grove's relentless drive suggest that this was a potentially significant issue for at least some senior executives. In 1998, however, there was not yet systematic evidence of this becoming a major problem. This speaks well, perhaps, of Intel's executive development and human resource management capabilities, which seemed to continuously groom new generations of managers who could effectively take over and relieve their battle-fatigued colleagues.

Insight 8.7. Driving the coevolutionary process by deploying a time-paced strategy helps a company to strongly influence the rate of

change in its product-market domain. But it also runs the risk of
burnout and puts a premium on effective executive development.

Competitive intensity *and* specialization. In spite of its positional advantage and
its successful efforts to capitalize on it, Intel continued to face intense competition
in the PC market segment during the latter part of Epoch II. Some authors have
suggested that surviving competitors in intensely competitive industries may be
quite strong but also highly specialized in their competitive repertoire.[26] Hence,
when faced with new entrants using different competitive strategies, incumbents in
intensely competitive industries may be disadvantaged in coping with these new
competitive threats. Intel had been able to win the two defining battles—Intel
against other IA suppliers, and IA against RISC—that Andy Grove had identified
in late 1993 by developing competencies that were highly specialized for the PC
market segment. While Intel did not anticipate facing really different competitors
in the PC market segment toward the end of Epoch II, the question of how the company would compete with different types of competitors—say, consumer electronics companies selling Internet appliances—was not clear.

> **Insight 8.8.** Driving the coevolutionary process sharpens a com-
> pany's competitive strategy but also increasingly specializes it for its
> existing product-market segments.

Growth opportunities *and* limited new business development. Throughout
Epoch II, until 1998, Intel experienced very strong growth in the PC market segment. In 1989, Gordon Moore had predicted that Intel could continue along the
same high growth curve for another 12 years. Until 1998, Moore's prediction had
been accurate. And it was quite possible that the slowdown in 1998 simply signaled
a temporary lull, while a major transition from client to server products in the Internet computing industry took hold. In any case, throughout Epoch II, while Intel
could drive the coevolutionary process top management didn't need to worry about
growth. As a result, top management did not feel strong pressure to develop new
business opportunities.

> **Insight 8.9.** Driving the coevolutionary process allows a company to
> take advantage of the rapid growth of its product-market segments,
> but this also reduces its incentives to look for new avenues of growth.

CONCLUSION

CEO Andy Grove achieved the dream of all grand strategists: to use the company's induced-strategy process to shape the external environment to its advantage. Intel's evolution during Epoch II illustrates the rational actor model of strategy-making as few other corporate histories have. Grove clearly understood the forces that Intel could influence and the forces on which the company was critically dependent—in particular, increasing returns to adoption. Top management saw the strategic leadership task in terms of understanding and using the forces facing the company to its advantage. As a result, Intel's top management was able to set the company's course rather than have it set for them. They did not have to hope for the best. Position and competence were the levers of Intel's strategic action. And the rewards were great. During Epoch II, Intel became one of the fastest-growing and most-profitable established companies in the world.

The story of the coevolution of Intel's strategy and the PC market segment also suggests, however, that Intel was both creator and prisoner of its environment. Driving the coevolutionary process provided the company with the opportunity to exert great influence but also tied its destiny increasingly to that of its given product-market domain. This set in motion a powerful positive feedback loop associated with the core microprocessor business that tended to favor certain competencies over others, deepened but also kept narrow top management's intuition, and stimulated time-paced product introductions that could potentially exhaust the organization.

This positive feedback loop reinforced Intel's already strong induced strategy process, which became increasingly specialized for the PC market segment and dependent on it for additional growth. As long as the PC market segment remained munificent, Intel's new business development capability did not require a great deal of top management attention. When the growth prospects diminished, as appeared to be the case toward the end of Epoch II, it could be expected that Intel's new business development capability would be seriously tested.

9   COEVOLUTION AND

STRATEGIC INERTIA

The unintended consequence of the coevolution of Intel's corporate strategy and the PC market segment was *strategic inertia*. Strategic inertia manifested itself in two forms: First, strategic inertia made it difficult to pursue new business opportunities in ways that were different from the horizontal, frontal assault strategy that Intel had learned to deploy very effectively in the core microprocessor business. Second, strategic inertia also made it difficult to capitalize fully on new business opportunities that were not directly supportive of the core microprocessor business. This was exacerbated by Intel's deeply ingrained orientation toward enabling certain technological developments in the PC industry, such as PC interconnectivity, rather than to pursue these developments as new business opportunities in their own right.

THE EVOLUTION OF NEW BUSINESS DEVELOPMENT
DURING EPOCH II

Job 1 or Job 2

Throughout Epoch II, Intel supported a number of new business initiatives. Some were intended to help extend the core business strategy in new areas while others concerned growth opportunities outside the core business strategy. The latter were

250

called Job 2 efforts, but it was not always clear whether the purpose of a new business initiative was to support Job 1 or was really a Job 2 effort. The way in which the effort was treated, however, depended strongly on whether top management viewed it as Job 1 or Job 2.

Intel Products Group

During the early to mid-1990s, the new business development efforts were grouped together in the Intel Products Group (IPG). In 1993, IPG was headquartered near Portland, Oregon, and consisted of three divisions. One of these was the OEM Products and Services Division (OPSD). A second one, the Personal Computer Enhancement Division (PCED) encompassed PCED Mobile, PCED Networking, and PCED Business Communications. A third one was the Supercomputing Systems Division (SSD).

OPSD manufactured partial and complete PC systems to OEMs, which were then sold under these other vendors' names. PCED Networking had risen from obscurity in the late 1980s to become a leader in the market for Local Area Network (LAN) adapter cards, which allowed the PC to become part of a network connecting other PCs, peripheral devices such as printers, and large computers. Likewise PCED Business Communications had become a large manufacturer of fax modems and was leading Intel's entry into other communications applications. PCED Mobile focused on enhancement products for mobile computers, primarily through the relatively new PCMCIA (Personal Computer Memory Card Interface Association) standards (which Intel helped create) for credit-card size components, such as modems, and LAN cards. SSD, a venture founded in the mid-80s, manufactured massively parallel supercomputers. SSD was stopped in the mid-1990s because of a lack of demand for supercomputers.

The situation in 1993.   In 1993, the strategic role of IPG was perceived by its senior management to be to develop a second major business for Intel to balance the corporate portfolio. Frank Gill, a senior executive who headed Intel's Systems Group, was put in charge of the operation. Gill first took some strong measures to bring focus to the organization and improve its overall performance. He decided to shut down several operations and reduced the headcount by more than one thousand. In an interview in 1993, Gill, by then senior vice president and general manager of IPG, said: "My main challenge in coming to IPG was to find opportunities for Intel to develop a significant business without competing with our customers. Our goal is to help Intel become more than a one-product company; whether we'll be truly successful in this is yet to be seen."

Jim Johnson, a senior executive and veteran internal entrepreneur at Intel who reported to Frank Gill, also emphasized the importance of reaching critical mass for the new businesses outside the core microprocessor business: "We have received a great deal of support from the top of the corporation because we are viewed as strategically important to Intel. Andy [Grove] wants a second product line to balance microprocessors. Also, the [financial] markets perceive diversified products companies as being more stable. In order to fulfill this role in the company, we have to become a $1 billion business within the next three years. If we don't, we simply aren't significant."

OEM Products and Services Division (OPSD). OPSD evolved out of Intel's System Business Group, which made specialized systems used to automate PC hardware and software design in the 1970s and early '80s. This was a profitable business while it lasted, but the industry moved quickly to doing applications development directly on PCs, thereby making Intel's development systems obsolete. OPSD's mission then shifted to offering Intel-based PC products at every level of integration. This included designing, manufacturing, and selling both motherboards—circuit boards containing the microprocessor, system logic, memory, and connectors for the other components—and completely manufactured systems to be sold under other vendors' labels. With its systems business, Intel enabled many OEMs, that otherwise would have been unable to compete, to introduce their own PCs with leading-edge systems sourced from Intel.

Motherboards. The motherboards produced by OPSD played an important role in the introduction of Intel's Pentium processor. OPSD manufactured many of the first PCs to include Pentium processors. This allowed large customers to get product in the market while they perfected their internal designs and waited for production of Pentium chips to increase enough to allow large production runs. This was especially important in helping ramp up early shipments because the enhanced system design needed to take full advantage of a Pentium chip's power. In 1993, Frank Gill explained: "The first Pentium architecture system designs were difficult and involved working with higher clock speeds, thermal considerations, a new PCI (peripheral component interconnect) bus architecture, new graphics controllers, immature drivers, and a new BIOS (basic input-output system). By solving these problems, OPSD allowed many OEMs to enter the market faster than they could have by doing their own designs."

Initially, however, there had been a lot of resistance to Intel's strategic thrust into the motherboard business. This was so because the motherboard strategy was not always well-aligned with OEM manufacturers that were often content to extend the life of a processor generation, especially if they had invested significant R&D in the development of their own systems for that generation. Intel's largest OEM customers in particular saw the activity as competitive and complained to the senior management of the microprocessor business. In 1995, Gill recalled:

> In 1993, some people at Intel asked, "Why are we doing motherboards? Why compete with our customers?" We were the evil people in Oregon.
>
> But we also got very lucky because the 486 market segment softened and we put more capacity into Pentium. OPSD became significant in the Pentium ramp: we supplied 40 percent of all the Pentium motherboards.
>
> Today, we sell motherboards rather than chips. We will sell 10 million motherboards next year—$4 billion for 1995.

Dennis Carter confirmed the importance of the motherboard business for the introduction of the Pentium processor (see chapter 8). In the face of the reluctance of Compaq and IBM to design Pentium processor-based systems for the consumer segment, Intel was capable of enabling smaller companies to introduce Pentium processor-based systems that otherwise wouldn't have been able to. This was crucial for the success of the Pentium launch.

In 1999, Frank Gill recalled that Andy Grove had always understood the importance of the motherboard strategy for the microprocessor business, and supported it even though Intel's Executive Staff was generally against it. Andy Bryant, the controller for the systems group in the early 1990s confirmed this. Bryant recalled that when one major OEM customer told Intel that it was moving too fast from the 486 product line to the Pentium product line, Grove ordered the motherboard division to stop building boards for the 486 processors and to produce boards exclusively for the Pentium generation. He reaffirmed to the motherboard division that they were to aggressively sell the newer technology products; that their task was to move advanced technology products into the marketplace.

Personal Computing Enhancement Division (PCED). PCED grew out of an earlier venture—Personal Computer Enhancement Operation (PCEO)—that was founded in 1984 by two Intel employees who came up with the idea of selling add-on boards for PCs.

Developing a new channel for Intel. Jim Johnson, one of the founders, explained that PCEO's vision was to provide enhancements to the basic PC systems sold by Intel's OEM customers. PCEO's products, however, were to be sold through the end-user retail channel, which was new for Intel. PCEO helped develop that channel for Intel. Les Vadasz, who had been responsible for the Intel Development Organization (IDO), which supported Intel's internal corporate venturing efforts in the early 1980s, recalled in an interview in 1989: "Some middle-level managers had the idea to develop add-on boards for personal computers. The strategic planning process initially rejected the idea since channels of distribution were too different. The idea, however, was able to get support through Intel's internal corporate venturing program and became a separate business. After success of the business became evident, the venture was folded back into Intel's System Business."

In 1993, Jim Johnson recalled:

> Our vision was to provide enhancements to the basic PC systems being sold by Intel's PC OEM customers. This started with the math coprocessor, although this wasn't our idea initially. Our second product, called Above Board, was a memory expansion card. These two products gave us the money and volume to become significant. However, by 1989 both of those products had been absorbed into the basic system. So we've had to find other revenue opportunities.

He also said:

> We were an intrapreneurial operation from the start. We were told that we had to use Intel's lawyers, human resources, and finance practices, but otherwise were to act like an independent company. We moved into different office space and set up an independent entity. We weren't even allowed to hire from within Intel for the first year. We had a board of directors that reviewed our progress and were given money based on a series of milestones. Our business plan gave us four years to make the company work (i.e., go public), which we called "going Intel."

Going Intel meant that the participants in the venture would be able to cash in on the phantom stock options they had received, if they met their business objectives. At the end of that four-year time period, PCEO was integrated back into Intel and renamed PCED. However, reintegration proved tricky. In 1993, Jim Johnson noted: "We created a very entrepreneurial culture that prided itself on being different from the rest of Intel. Some of this was justified. We have a different business model, less complex technology, and we have to fight to gain market share against a bunch of smaller, tightly focused competitors. However, when we really looked at it, we often found that we were being different for difference's sake. We still don't talk much with other parts of Intel. My goal is to change that this year."

The reintegration of PCEO into PCED also created some friction because of the large financial rewards that the venture personnel obtained when they exercised their phantom stock options. Some people associated with the core business saw these financial rewards as out of proportion, given what the core business people had contributed to the venture's success. During the 1990s, no ventures were spun off and reintegrated using the PCEO model.

After gaining momentum with its initial products, PCED moved into, among other things, Ethernet adapter cards. These circuit boards, which can be installed into a standard PC expansion slot, allow a computer to connect with a LAN. PCED also introduced a successful LAN administration software package, LAN Desk Manager, as well as a line of specialized LAN servers. After beginning to ship Ethernet adapter cards in 1991, Intel finished 1992 with the fourth highest share in the segment. At the same time, PCED also began designing and manufacturing modems. Specializing in fax modems, Intel gained a strong market position largely on the strength of communications software bundled with the modem. Intel also ranked in the top five PC modem producers with an estimated share of 10 percent of the retail fax modem market.

Focused primarily on retail channels, PCED's products were sold by a specialized group within the sales organization, the Reseller Channel Operation (RCO). RCO field sales representatives sold both PCED products and the Microprocessor Products Group's OverDrive upgrade CPUs to the retail PC channels. Like most Intel organizations, RCO functioned as a matrix, reporting directly to the sales organization, with dotted line responsibility to IPG.

Conflict with Corporate Marketing Group. PCED products were marketed under the Intel brand name. In 1993, Jim Johnson said: "Our brand promise is consistent with Intel's overall goals, to provide the most advanced technology and safety. Advanced technology for us comes in many different forms. It can be in terms of ease of use or the fastest speed modem. In many cases software and hardware/software integration are the keys to a best-of-class product."

The Corporate Marketing Group (CMG) managed the massive Intel Inside advertising programs and general corporate communications. While PCED managers were quick to point out the benefit they gained from CMG's end-user advertising, they also acknowledged some friction in the relationship between the two groups. In 1993, Jim Johnson explained: "Sometimes our different situations lead us to different goals in our advertising messages. Dennis [Carter] can sell 'goodness.' He's selling an ingredient that's a market leader. That's a different task than battling for share in a very competitive market segment where we aren't number 1.

We sometimes have to compete on price, this is a different message than Intel's market leadership. I also see this conflict in other companies."

During the 1993 SLRP, the latent conflict between CMG's concern for clear and consistent communication about the Intel brand and IPG's concern to be able to run advertising that suited their specific business purposes had flared up (see chapter 6). CMG pointed out that there was a need for a consistent brand promise, and that the Product Line Business Plans (PLBP), which were owned by the product divisions, needed to be guided by the business plans made up by CMG—that CMG needed to define the rules. Andy Grove had intervened by forcing CMG to arrive at a modus vivendi with IPG before it could consider being discharged of its SLRP responsibility. The inherent tension, however, between CMG and new businesses outside the core business remained.

Internet Communications Group

In 1993 Frank Gill, Jim Johnson, and others in IPG thought that if they were able to reach $1 billion over the next few years that they would be relevant within Intel.

The situation in 1995. In 1995, however, Intel restructured IPG and created the Internet Communications Group (ICG), which was again headed by Frank Gill. This change signaled that top management had decided it was strategically important for Intel to turn the PC into a key communications device and that the new business development efforts should focus on supporting that core strategic thrust. In April 1995, Frank Gill commented: "There was a reorganization after the last SLRP. I am now the 'communications' guy, and my charter is closely related to Job 1: improving the PC as a communications device. Job 2 concerns finding applications that use more MIPS, but communications is no longer part of that." Another force that contributed to the change in top management's perspective on the role of the former IPG was that Intel had grown from about $8 billion to more than $16 billion in revenues between 1993 and 1995.

The situation in 1997. The role of ICG was changing again by 1997. Frank Gill explained: "In 1994–95, Andy [Grove] would tell me 'Frank, I make a billion dollars in profit per quarter and you make a billion dollars in revenue per year. This is all distraction, so focus on Job 1.' " Gill, however, added: "We have gone full circle. In the early 1990s, we were trying to build new businesses. Then we became a supporting player for Job 1. Since the most recent SLRP we are trying to get in new businesses again."

Top Management's Perspective during Epoch II

Is it strategic? In a Stanford MBA class discussion of the role of IPG in November 1993, Andy Grove's perspective was that IPG's businesses could be justified if they were strategic; that is, if they supported Intel's core microprocessor business. But he believed that they would have a very hard time as stand-alone businesses. The systems business, for instance, as we saw earlier with motherboards, had had great strategic value to Intel at some times. During those times, the profitability of the systems business was not an issue. Its value lay in supporting Intel's ability to introduce and accelerate the adoption of new processor generations. At other times, the strategic value of the systems business was less significant, and Intel managed the group differently in that circumstance. Andy Bryant, Intel's CFO, explained in 1999:

> At the point you are no longer getting a long-term strategic benefit from an activity, you have to make sure you are getting good short-term returns. . . . We manage businesses differently at different times. Systems and boards was a vehicle for bringing advanced technology to the market quickly. If the technology is already moving into the market fast enough, then the products that serve this purpose have less long-term value. When this happens, current profitability is more important, and we manage with a more short-term return focus.

Andy Bryant continued:

> We do our best to quantify the return of the strategic value. We say, "Let's define the long-term benefit and get a sense for what the cost is to accomplish this." Then we ask, "Does this make any sense?"

An example of how optimizing the strategy for the core microprocessor business could negatively impact the financial performance of a noncore business was provided in the chipset case, when Andy Grove ordered the motherboard business to use Intel's chipsets even though they were more expensive.

Do they have a strategy? Another aspect of the new business development efforts was that they lacked the clarity and crispness of the microprocessor strategy. This was to some extent due to the very nature of new business development efforts, which usually require some time to discover what the real opportunity is. But this did not sit particularly well with Andy Grove who, in a Stanford Business School class in late 1992, complained that: "In the systems business we put a dollar on every square of the roulette table. So, it's not a strategy at all!"

An MBA class discussion of IPG's activities in late 1993 shed light on Andy Grove's thinking about how to strategically manage the new business development activities. Referring to IPG, Grove asked, "Is this a focused strategy?" As the class observed the difficulties involved in installing IPG within Intel, given Intel's microprocessor-focused strategy and culture, he asked, "Would you rather do this inside or outside Intel?" The students pointed out that Intel's task orientation conflicted with a creative orientation, but also saw the benefits of having the Intel name associated with the activities. This led Grove to ask, "Is the use of the Intel name an advantage or a disadvantage?" which brought up the different perspectives of IPG and CMG that were alluded to earlier. After some students observed that IPG did not have a focused strategy but used more of a shotgun approach, Grove said:

> If it is a shotgun approach, many of the pellets will miss the mark—then I am worried using the Intel name. So, I must know whether it is a real growth strategy or a shotgun strategy before I know whether to do it inside or outside.

Continuing, Grove said:

> Look at the OEM products (OPSD). Is the Intel name on it? No! If you were in the PC building business, would you do it inside or outside? Outside! The constraints on the (core) business are stronger than on the PCED division. So, it goes back to the focused versus shotgun approach. If it is a shotgun approach, go outside, don't use the Intel name, and impose no constraints. If it is a focused approach, do it inside, use the Intel name, and impose constraints.

The Situation in 1999

By 1997, Intel was dominated by its microprocessor business, and the company's focus on this business was singular. Despite the emergence of many new opportunities across the computing industry, and the emergence of many new ideas within the company, Intel had had difficulty turning these opportunities into successful stand-alone businesses. Reflecting on Epoch II in 1999, Dennis Carter observed:

It was difficult for new ideas to evolve because of the internal infrastructure, not because of a lack of new opportunities. The business climate actually created many opportunities, but the question was how to pursue and exploit those opportunities. Andy tried to get Intel into other spaces, such as videoconferencing. But none ever quite jelled. None of the options that looked good four or five years ago have come to pass. . . . Les Vadasz through his CBD group knows every trend that's happening in the industry, but there is no mechanism for turning this knowledge into products. There is no serendipity.

Andy Grove's analysis. In summer 1999, during an executive education session with senior Intel executives, Grove enumerated some fifteen non-microprocessor initiatives pursued during Epoch II and observed that only chipsets, motherboards, networking, and Intel's external venture investments (through Corporate Business Development) had been clear successes. By success he meant that the new business had to be large (multibillion dollars in revenue) and had to have a proven business model and a sustainable large market segment share position. Thinking about factors that separated success from failure, he observed that the successes tended to be close to the microprocessor business. And that along a predictable-unpredictable continuum, the successes were close to the predictable end. This was definitely so for the chipset and motherboard businesses. However, it was not so for the Networking business, which was quite different from the microprocessor business.

Andy Grove's frustration. In late 1999, after an MBA class discussion of Intel's strategic situation in 1999, Andy Grove reflected on the slowing down of growth in the core microprocessor business and the importance of new business development. Reflecting on his efforts to develop new businesses during Epoch II, Grove said: "The old CEO knew that this was coming. He tried like hell to develop new business opportunities, but they almost all turned into shit."

Sources of Strategic Inertia during Epoch II

It is generally, but also somewhat trivially, true that new business development efforts that are closely related to the core business have a higher probability of success than those farther removed. To probe more deeply into the reasons for the success or failure of new business development at Intel during Epoch II, it is worthwhile to examine more closely how the organization, including top management, dealt with these efforts. Careful examination of the strategic management approach to new business development during Epoch II suggests that two forms of strategic inertia contributed to success and failure. These forms of strategic inertia derived from the single-minded pursuit of Intel's core microprocessor strategy. Strategic inertia made it difficult in some cases to bring a general management perspective to bear on new business development. In other cases, strategic inertia made it difficult to resolve potential conflicts between the strategy of a new business and the core business strategy.

If strategic, apply the core business strategy. Being viewed as strategic by top management caused a first form of strategic inertia. One manifestation of this was the potential for overspending in areas that appeared to have great promise in furthering the demand for evermore powerful microprocessors. This potentially undermined the strong financial discipline that was a key feature of Intel's structural context. Another manifestation was that it sometimes led to the presumption that the same logic that governed Intel's core microprocessor strategy should be applied in the new area. Consequently, top management left little room for the executives involved to *discover* what the appropriate strategy for the new business should be.

  Contrast with Epoch I: Declining role of the sales force. Dennis Carter explained that during the 1970s and early 1980s, Intel's business lines were relatively autonomous business groups that were run by general managers (chapter 5). Intel had a strong research and development group that generated many new ideas and product innovations. These products were brought to market by a talented technical sales force. The sales force was made up of field sales engineers and field applications engineers. The latter had to have experience as design engineers before they could join the sales force. They worked with the customers' engineers and understood where the technology had to go. They counseled the manufacturing people, who deferred to them because of their expert power. Carter observed that during Epoch II, the singular focus on microprocessors disempowered the sales force and made manufacturing too dominant. This happened because the customers' power increasingly declined.

  Contrast with Epoch I: Declining role of inbound marketing. Carter also explained how the core microprocessor business strategy during Epoch II had increasingly put great emphasis on outbound marketing, and that this had been at the expense of Intel's emphasis on inbound marketing during Epoch I:

> During the '70s, there was a very good process for inbound marketing. Our sales force was in excellent touch with our OEM customers. During the second epoch, our sales force stayed in tune with the OEMs, but our

marketing expanded to the much larger audience of PC consumers. We have limited marketplace feedback for things outside of processors and many of our internal processes withered. For the third epoch, it will be critical to redevelop these internal processes. . . . Product planning is often done too quickly by people too removed from the market. . . . Intel is very good at execution, and Intel management processes lead to the development of excellent intuition in familiar areas, but in new product areas we are bad at judging what will play in the market. . . . Today the link with the market is missing. . . . We need a closed loop into the product planning process.

If nonstrategic, pay as you go. Being viewed as nonstrategic by top management caused a second form of strategic inertia. One manifestation here was the ambivalence on the part of top management whether Intel should define its role as enabling the industry to develop the new business in general support of its core microprocessor business or as developing the new business as an opportunity for Intel in particular. Another manifestation was that it made it difficult to get resources beyond what the business could generate internally. But this pay-as-you-go approach was not conducive to establishing a strong strategic position in rapidly growing new business areas. Consequently, there was little room for the executives involved to get the appropriate strategy for the business *accepted* by top management.

    Lack of infrastructure to move from idea to business. Dennis Carter explained that during Epoch II Intel was still able to generate many ideas, but that the infrastructure to develop these into new businesses and to get top management to support them was lacking: "There are lots of ideas and new projects sprouting up everywhere within Intel, but the real question is how we can turn them into a business. We have the capacity to do so, but is the infrastructure there to support it? We have clever ideas coming from places like IAL and the Content Group, but little experience in making a business out of any of them. We need to develop the intuition for doing this. And we need to develop people with the entrepreneurial intuition."

Difficulty in developing general managers. Intel's extraordinary success in executing the core business strategy during Epoch II also had important consequences for the role and development of general managers. Over time, Intel's functional organization selected managers that were, on average, very bright, extremely reliable, and energetic implementers. The specialization inherent in a functional organization, however, did not provide these managers with much opportunity to learn to make the trade-offs among various functional considerations that are the hallmark of strong general managers and are important in new business development.

Lack of general managers. Looking back in 1999 on the role and development of general managers within Intel during Epoch II, Frank Gill said:

> Throughout most of the '90s, we did not grow GMs as we had a mostly functional organization for most of the company. . . . IA with Andy as the GM. Generally, we were good at growing people to get results within a budget. My group was an exception in that I was a true GM with multiple disciplines but had demonstrated difficulty in driving results with peers.
>
> In 1997, I wrote a long memo to Craig and Andy about problems with new business development within Intel. Craig in turn appointed a SLRP team to investigate and report out at the next SLRP. Generally, they reiterated my issues [years of frustration] of working within an organization that has optimized all the processes around a high-margin OEM processor business and functional organizations. Interestingly, the functional groups were all quite offended by this SLRP message. My memo had also pointed out that managers in Intel do not learn to make trade-offs between various functional requirements, so you don't develop general managers.

The remainder of this chapter examines three new business development efforts that illustrate the two forms of strategic inertia and their consequences during Epoch II. The PC-based videoconferencing venture (ProShare) and the effort to bring the PC into the living room (Hood River) are examples of the first form of strategic inertia. They also show the difficulty of developing a general management perspective in new business development efforts that were considered strategic. The efforts to develop Intel's Networking business illustrate the second form of strategic inertia. The fact that Networking was long viewed as nonstrategic left room for the development of a general management perspective, but this created important frictions with the core business.

STRATEGIC INERTIA I: IF STRATEGIC, APPLY THE CORE BUSINESS STRATEGY

Having a clear and focused concept of corporate strategy that is working well is likely to make a company conservative. That does not mean that the company does not want to take risks. Intel's willingness to bet billions of dollars by investing in plant and equipment in advance of demand, for instance, clearly illustrates this. It simply means that top management will want the company to do more of what it knows to do well. Such conservatism is a form of adaptation: A company only knows that it is good at something if the external environment selects it for that. And given that a company has survived external selection, it is quite rational to continue doing more of what it was selected for in the first place. A company's concept of strategy is thus loosely equivalent to genetic inheritance. And the induced strategy process is loosely equivalent to the company reproducing itself in its familiar environment. Andy Grove provided a great example with the story of the computer executive who had told him "we're good at bending sheet metal . . . I want to bend sheet metal" (see chapter 6). Ironically, Intel evolved its own genetic analogue during Epoch II.

During Epoch II, Intel's corporate strategy had a rare clarity and simplicity about it. Maintaining architectural leadership for Intel microprocessors and "making the PC it" were clearly understood throughout the organization as Job 1. Intel also became extremely good at executing Job 1. A related thrust of the corporate strategy was to enable the PC industry's receptivity to next generation Intel microprocessors by making sure that there would be enough demand for the rapidly increasing processing power and the elimination of technological bottlenecks to its use. PC-based videoconferencing and bringing the PC into the living room were two strategic initiatives that seemed to fit well with the corporate strategy.

Intel's PC-based Videoconferencing Business Strategy

Antecedents: NCCI and MOAD. One promising avenue for growing Intel's business in the early 1990s was perceived to be the New Computer and Communications Industry (NCCI). Since the late 1980s technologists had heralded the coming convergence between computing and communications. In the early 1990s, Intel believed that technology was approaching the ability to make the PC as a business communications tool a reality. In 1993, explaining how Intel's efforts in PC-based videoconferencing had started, Andy Grove said:

> This really came together bit by bit. It started in 1987 with our purchase of DVI, a division of RCA that produced special video-processing chips. We had this idea of applying video technology to the PC, but nothing ever seemed to come out of it. A couple of years later, in late '89, I saw a demo of an e-mail system that attached a picture of the author to a message. This impressed me so much that I went back to my office and wrote

an internal memo that said the future of the PC was in rich e-mail. Nobody really paid much attention to it though. A few months later, one of our managers associated with DVI, who was really excited about the potential of PC video, had me attend a demo of a videoconference between workstations utilizing DVI video boards connected across a LAN. Once again, I came back excited. There wasn't a clear vision, but it seemed like there was something interesting here. The next year [in November 1991], I was scheduled to give a keynote speech at Comdex about the future of computers. We decided that instead of me talking about it, we should demonstrate it. People ate it up! We made a video of the demonstration; over 20,000 copies of that tape have been requested.

Those involved in the NCCI initiative jokingly referred to the Comdex demo as MOAD (Mother Of All Demos). Drawn from several small research efforts within different parts of Intel, the demo took almost six months to prepare. It was enthusiastically received both inside and outside of Intel. This led quickly to an edict by the Executive Staff that Intel should investigate productizing the technologies involved. In 1993, Grove explained: "This looked like the future application for PCs. The only problem was that nobody was addressing the market. We decided that we couldn't wait for this nonexistent industry to develop."

PCED Business Communications. A small team was formed in IPG to structure the business opportunities involved. The product strategy was approved through Intel's annual strategic planning process and that small group began to grow rapidly. A new division was formed within IPG called PCED Business Communications. Expertise from several parts of the company was brought together and combined with PCED's fast-growing fax modem product line. Chosen to lead the group was Patrick Gelsinger, who at the time was in charge of the development of the P6 (Pentium Pro), a key next-generation microprocessor. On the subject of Gelsinger's transition, Grove noted in 1993: "Moving Pat off of P6, a product on which the future of our company truly depends, to run this new initiative was a very controversial step. But in many ways this is the test of it. We can't expect to succeed if we aren't willing to put our best people on the project. Because of the team that Pat has put together, we are a lot farther along than we might have been at this point."

Gelsinger, in 1993, explained:

My background had always been in microprocessor design. In fact, I've played most roles in microprocessor development. So, for me this is a big departure. Compared with microprocessor development, we are dealing with a much broader array of technologies. Both hardware and software are very important. The real key here is technology integration. Because these technologies come from the convergence of both the computer and communications industry, there is also less experience, inside and outside of Intel, than I was used to in MPG. When we were doing microprocessor design, we knew that no matter how hard a problem was to solve, we had the best minds and methods in the world. We were going to get to the answer. We are quickly building a similar base in communications technologies here and in IAL. However, because this is an emerging market and such a complex product set, nobody has expertise in everything. Everyone's trying to come up to speed on some part of the total solution.

Products in preparation for release in the fall of 1993 aimed to make the PC a communications tool. One product would enable a PC to interface with an office telephone or PBX system to make advanced PBX functions such as teleconferencing, call forwarding, and voicemail easier to use. Another would help make teleconferences more efficient by allowing PC users to "data conference" by sharing files and common work space among a group of PCs while they talked. These products could be installed easily on an existing PC and use standard modems and ordinary phone lines. Another set of products was being prepared to allow full videoconferencing between two or more advanced PCs. The PCs had to be outfitted with cameras, sound, and an enhancement card that contained both a digital modem and audio/video compression/decompression (CODEC) circuitry. Because of the amount of information being exchanged in a videoconference, specialized digital (ISDN) telephone lines would be used to connect the participants. Industry analysts and the trade press expected prices for PC or workstation based videoconferencing systems to trend downward—from tens of thousands of dollars to less than three thousand dollars in 1994.

Intel's competition in videoconferencing was expected to come from three tiers of competitors. First several companies specialized in outfitting conference rooms for videoconferencing. These systems usually cost $20,000 or more and were sold primarily by a small number of specialized firms, such as PictureTel, and groups within telecommunications equipment giants like AT&T and Northern Telecom. These players were now downsizing their videoconferencing systems to reach a broader, less specialized market. Second, several PC and workstation vendors such as Apple Computer, Silicon Graphics, Sun Microsystems, and IBM were also either shipping conferencing products or soon would be. Third, several successful PC networking vendors and peripheral suppliers were pursuing various conferencing and communications applications. Pat Gelsinger explained:

> Our industry has three problems to overcome to make this market happen. First we have to get people to make a cultural shift to accept and utilize the PC as a personal conferencing device. This means having affordable products [i.e., less than the price of a desktop PC] that enhance how we communicate, and are very easy to use. Second, the communications infrastructure has to continue to evolve. The RBOCs and Interexchange Carriers (IXCs) need to continue to upgrade their networks to make digital phone lines generally available. Third, we need to get product quality to acceptable levels. This is really important for video. People have very high expectations for video quality—especially if you're trying to read another person's body language during a videoconference.
>
> I think of the rationale for Intel's interest here in three parts. First, this is a potentially large market in which Intel can play a major role. Second, we are expanding the total PC market by helping make the PC a communications tool. Third, because communications, and especially video, demands a lot of CPU power, we are helping drive demand for our most advanced processors.

Andy Grove said: "If it works, getting into PC communications will be a revolutionary step for Intel. If it doesn't, it will be one more side attempt." [1]

Horizontal, frontal assault strategy. In January 1994, Intel introduced ProShare software, a desktop videoconferencing system that was designed to work with ISDN networks. ProShare utilized many of Intel's own technologies, including a video compression algorithm (Indeo, a contraction of Intel and video). Rather than participating in the market just as a component supplier, Intel would compete as a systems player. Andy Grove explained: "Twice before (with the PC and network cards) we sat by and played the component supplier as a system business grew haphazardly. These things aren't an Erector set that jumps together on its own. Somebody has to package our technologies and sell them. This time we're going to go out and help create the market, build the system as well as the components, and compete in the marketplace." [2] Asked whether market research had convinced Intel that there was a huge potential market for desktop videoconferencing systems, Andy Grove said, "Who the hell are you going to ask? This is a brand new market.

There's just something about live video on a computer screen. I can't walk away from it."[3]

With the launch of ProShare, Intel started to organize a consortium of PC makers named Personal Conference Work Group (PCWG). PCWG's primary purpose was to establish another industry standard around Indeo apart from the existing H.320 industry standard.[4] PCWG insisted that H.320 was not appropriate to integrate existing PC architecture. In other words, H.320 did not yet cover standards for the kinds of interactive software vital to PC-based videoconferencing, such as screen sharing and document transfer. Although H.320 provided better compression (or higher-quality pictures at a given bandwidth), Indeo was much more easily decoded on Intel microprocessors.

Intel leveraged its huge resources to influence the direction of the emerging industry. It was reported that total spending in 1994 was as high as $100 million, including R&D and promotional expenditures. Reportedly $8 million was allocated to advertising, making it the second biggest effort next to the long-running Intel Inside campaign. Advertisements were run in trade publications such as *InfoWorld, PC Week, Windows Magazine, PC World, PC Magazine, Information Week,* and *Communications Week.* A series of twenty-four sales seminars in thirteen cities around the country were planned during the first four months of the market launch. Intel also reached a distribution agreement for ProShare with Compression Labs, Inc., in exchange for a $2 million cash infusion.

Although established players in the PC industry such as Compaq, Lotus Development, Novell, and Hewlett-Packard joined PCWG, it eventually failed to win widespread support, primarily because H.320 had already established its installed base. PCWG was virtually disbanded in February 1995, shortly after Microsoft expressed support for H.320. Despite the fact that Intel failed to establish a new ecosystem around its own video compression algorithm, the company persevered and kept pursuing an aggressive price-cutting strategy.

The need for a vertical market segment strategy. In 1995, Pat Gelsinger had become convinced that the winning strategy for Intel with ProShare had to be different from that used in the microprocessor business. He had found that the PC market segment simply was not yet ready for a general purpose videoconferencing capability. On the other hand, he also discovered several vertical niche markets in which the technology could effectively meet customer needs. Gelsinger explained: "ProShare was viewed as a horizontal capability—that was Andy's wish. But customers wanted to integrate it for a more complete solution for customer support and for financial services." He also said:

Intel tried to sell horizontally to IT customers in the Fortune 1000. But within six months I realized that you cannot do market creation through advertising, and that it would be the vertical markets that were going to be successful—first, medical; and second, credit card application kiosks.

I used [Geoffrey Moore's] "Crossing the Chasm" to influence everybody.[5] I prioritized five vertical markets and put resources behind three of them.

While Gelsinger reported to Frank Gill, everybody at Intel knew that he had the total support of Andy Grove. According to Gelsinger:

That was a crucial advantage. There was no doubt on the part of anybody about Intel's commitment. We could sell our vision and build our team. Frank's action would not have been enough for this. There would have been no hope of success.

He also explained, however, that Andy Grove was not in favor of a strategy that would be built on approaching a series of relatively small vertical niche markets and that this had set his strategic efforts back:

The disadvantage was that we could have acted on the vertical markets six months sooner if Andy had not had such strong opinion. We had to do a skunk works. We had to get data on a smaller scale. We needed to add a sales force in Japan and Europe but had to wait four months.

Asked about the long-term success of ProShare in 1995, Gelsinger said:

From the perspective of Job 1, the PC is a communications tool. Period. We have moved this forward by at least one year, maybe two years. For instance, the Pentium processor is now used in real estate offices!

From the perspective of Job 2, as a large and profitable business in its own right, we are inching our way above competitors. We are the market segment share leader now. But margin pressures are strong. We are six quarters away from profits.

The horizontal deployment of ProShare needs more work. There is the issue of availability of ISDN. ProShare should be deployable over LANs and POTS [plain old telephone service]. There should be interoperability between all of these. This will take time.

The speed with which this will come about depends on the technological developments. But in spite of Andy's forcefulness it is difficult to move things through the organization. The business competencies are still lacking. We need mentors, tutors.

It is still Andy's baby. He is not detached; he continues to be involved. Frank doesn't make strategic decisions without Andy.

Escalation of commitment. ProShare became one of the largest commitments ever made by Intel in a non-microprocessor area and the effort eventually included 700 people. Intel also invested considerable marketing resources behind ProShare and priced the ProShare systems aggressively relative to competitive products. Yet, the market for the product did not materialize as expected. Intel had initially been crucially dependent on the local exchange telecommunications companies, which did not forcefully push the adoption of ISDN. But when the options to use LANs and POTS became available somewhat later, these did not lead to a major increase in the adoption rate of ProShare either.

Learning from ProShare. In 1996, Pat Gelsinger was promoted to the Executive Staff (ESM) and Frank Gill had begun to scale down the ProShare effort to about 60 people. Scott Darling took over as general manager at the end of 1996 and reported to Gill. Darling said: "[ProShare] was a classic case of marketing myopia. Rather than just define the market as videoconferencing, they should have looked at the market as the conference room workstation business, and combined the capabilities of audio and videoconferencing with the PC capabilities. The conference room is now viewed as a design center for the PC. For example, there are desktops, laptops, workstations, and now we see another market in conference rooms."

In his MBA class at Stanford, in the fall of 1998, Andy Grove confirmed that Intel had scaled back the ProShare effort significantly after five years of efforts and about $750 million in investments. Discussing what was learned from the experience, Grove said:

> We assumed that just because it could be done technically there would be high demand. I was an enthusiastic user and supporter, but I've stopped using it. The novelty wore off. It was difficult to set up and so forth, so the benefits were outweighed by the costs. Videoconferencing doesn't want to break out of its vertical orientation. . . . If the application had resonated in the market, we would have been heroes. We did all the things required for strategic leadership, it's just that we were wrong. If we were to do it over again, our approach would be not so much like the Normandy invasion, but more of a vertical market focus. . . . We brought a style and conceptual approach to an area in which it did not work.

Looking back in early 2000, Frank Gill, who had been the senior executive situated between Gelsinger and Grove, but who seemed to have been much out of the loop, commented: "It was not being out of the loop so much as not being sure . . . [I thought] maybe the throwing of massive resources at it would work. I didn't know for sure and Andy and Pat were quite confident. I am guilty of letting it go way too long before moving to get it under control, which I ultimately did but a couple of years too late."

Intel's Strategy to Bring the PC into the Family Room: The Hood River Project

Intel's Hood River project was a seed program that had been initiated in early 1996 with the objective of penetrating the family room with the personal computer.[6] Rob Siegel, a young Stanford MBA, who worked in Intel's Corporate Business Development Group (CBD) ran the project. CBD performed an important function within Intel by making outside equity investments in strategic companies, by making acquisitions, and by financing technology or business ideas that were generated initially within Intel. In 1996, Les Vadasz was in charge of CBD.

Antecedents: digital convergence and the war for eyeballs. Hood River was spawned by a number of events both internal and external to Intel. In early 1995, few people within Intel were focused on digital convergence, the increasing overlap between the computing, communications, and consumer electronics industries. Siegel recalled that during the SLRP of mid-1995, the question was raised about how to put the PC in the living room, and "sixty people started yelling at each other, each with a different opinion on the issue."

In late 1995, a debate was conducted as to whether the PC or the TV would become the dominant device of the future. Andy Grove had described this battle as the war for eyeballs. He clearly believed in the PC: "The PC is it. That sums up Intel's business plan and rallying cry. Some think the information superhighway will come through their TV. The information tool of the future is on your desk, not in your living room."[7]

A PC-based product concept. While other observers had different views, Intel's approach to the project was strongly driven by the Intel motto, "The PC is it." Consequently, Hood River was made to report into the Desktop Products Group (DPG), which was led by Mike Aymar. According to Les Vadasz: "I wanted Hood River to have a dotted line into DPG because I wanted a home for it by the time it would need real money."

DPG was right in the heartland of Intel's core business, and Siegel ran into significant difficulties in accessing technical, marketing, and sales resources in Intel's matrix structure. This was primarily because he was pursuing something that was not considered of the highest priority by the very busy functional groups supporting the core business. But it was exacerbated by the fact that Siegel was a fairly recent employee who hadn't yet developed the network of relationships necessary to be effective in Intel's matrix. According to Siegel:

There were a number of groups throughout Intel that were able to get working in this area, but nobody was really in charge. I could only influence others because I had passion for the product and Aymar's ear. Yet, coordinating all these groups and guiding them along the path of my vision was my task. OPSD (OEM Products and Services Division) had just been integrated into DPG, but it was still a loose federation. Some of the people in OPSD didn't want to be involved [with Hood River] and their marketing group was wondering why they needed me. OPSD thought that I was part of corporate marketing and that I was doing their job.

The Hood River product concept was positioned at the high-end of the family room PC market, selling for $2,500 or higher, without a monitor. The Hood River design called for the use of Intel's 233 MHz Pentium II processor, Intel's highest performance CPU at the time, and integrated a wide spectrum of applications, including communications, consumer electronics, and entertainment applications. The Hood River team had engaged a number of potential OEM customers in the consumer electronics market segment (including Sony, Matsushita, and Philips) as well as in the PC market segment (including Compaq and IBM).

PC industry or consumer electronics industry? In June 1996, Siegel had his first meeting with Sony, and then made a two-week trip to Japan that included visits with Sharp, Matsushita, JVC, NEC, and Fujitsu. According to Siegel:

During these meetings we discerned the six laws of the consumer electronics industry, which we compared to the five laws of the PC industry. The six laws of the consumer electronics industry are it's a hardware-driven market; de facto standards dominate; technology changes slowly; price points are in the range of $500 versus $2,000; boxes are not expandable; and ease of use drives sales.

By comparison, the five laws of the PC industry are the hardware/ software spiral and the virtuous circle; standards lead to volume; technology changes very rapidly; the high end drives the market; and price, place, promotion—the 3Ps—are essential. I realized that for the PC to succeed in the family room, our product would have to fit with the consumer electronics ecology, that we would have to make the product sexy.

In early 1997, none of the consumer electronics companies had committed to making volume shipments based on the Hood River design. In fact, these companies were still trying to get Intel to see that the Hood River design was not consistent with the needs of their customers. Compaq and Gateway 2000, on the other hand, were also developing PC entertainment systems for the family room, and had collaborated with Intel in this area (though neither used Hood River systems).

There were several weaknesses in the first generation product. Hood River had been dependent on Microsoft for several important features, including Instant On (for the system to boot instantly), which were delayed along with Memphis, Microsoft's successor to Windows 95. The system also had shortcomings in its user interface, which was much more like a PC than a TV in simplicity. Nevertheless, in early 1997, the Hood River team believed that they had made significant progress on the design.

External threat to the PC: The NC. During 1996, however, the network computer (NC) emerged as a potential threat to Intel's core business. Companies such as Sun Microsystems, Oracle, Netscape, and IBM were evangelizing a new computer paradigm, based on so-called thin clients and fat servers, that they claimed would dramatically reduce the cost of total ownership of desktop computers (TCO), especially maintenance and management costs. The NC was expected to include low-end processors running Sun's Java software; it would not include Intel's microprocessors or the Windows operating system (chapter 8).

Intel's response to this external threat was focused and swift. OPSD was given the charter to design a low-end PC, called the NetPC, which would include a Pentium processor and PC management software from Intel that would reduce the TCO of Intel PCs. OPSD quickly ramped up efforts for the NetPC, growing staff to approximately 70 engineers by October 1996. As a result, the NetPC competed for some of the same resources as Hood River. Todd Whitaker, a Hood River team member, noted, "We respond extremely well to threats, but perhaps not so well to opportunities." In 1999, Andy Grove agreed with this statement. He said: "Yes! See the title of my book!"

In the heat of the swift NetPC ramp up, the OPSD management decided to cut the funding for Hood River in late October 1996. This took Siegel by surprise, but he responded aggressively. He recalled: "I called Aymar right away, and also sent a strongly worded e-mail to ask about the decision. In essence I asked, 'How can we take risks in this company if it always ends up in the same place—defending the status quo?' " Aymar subsequently reinstated Hood River's funding.

Failing the market test. However, there was little customer interest in the Hood River design and Aymar began to question all the assumptions of the program. In December 1996, DPG was reorganized and Siegel was made to report to John Davies, who was responsible for consumer marketing and had recently been promoted to vice president. Davies was skeptical about the viability of the Hood River product concept. He said:

> It is interesting to see what we are trying to do with Hood River, which is to put the PC in the living room where it doesn't fit. You can think about interesting demos using the PC in the living room, like Star Trek games and so on. But there are some key challenges. First, nobody is using the PC in the family room. It's the last thing on my mind when I come home. In fact, I want to get away from it. Second, there is the chicken and egg problem. You need applications, but you can only get them if you have an installed base. With zero installed base, there is definitely a software problem.

Mike Aymar said:

> Originally we expected the [Hood River] project to go smoothly and to generate demand for another 1 million PCs per year. But market projections were for various vendors worldwide to ship only in the tens of thousands of units in '97 and '98. Suppliers could be counted on a single hand. Several OEMs seemed interested, but more in terms of keeping engaged with the experimentation. This was insufficient. So, thus far we had failed the market test.

Aymar wanted the Hood River team to bring Compaq on board as a committed OEM customer, but they failed to do so. As a result, Aymar decided to cut the funding for Hood River in early 1997.

Dispersed autonomous projects. With Hood River's demise, the challenges facing Intel in the family room market became more salient. Intel had a number of separate groups that were working on products or technologies relevant to the opportunity in the family room, but in mid-1997 these efforts were dispersed throughout Intel and not actively coordinated. According to Les Vadasz: "There are projects all over in nooks and crannies of Intel that deal with the PC in the home. These projects are looking for an overall strategy. Who will put this together is to be determined, but there is a recognition that there is a void here that needs to be filled. We don't yet have a unified project for the home, but our focus on the family room is broader than Hood River and continues. Aymar will put it all together and recommend what we should do."

Mike Aymar also commented on the lack of a unified strategic thrust for the family room: "I feel strongly about the opportunity for the PC in the family room because I feel that it is important, but there is no critical mass of activity [within Intel]. There are ten or twelve independent activities around the company that need to be put together, none of which is mainstream. . . . Intel may need to make more fundamental structural changes."

Learning from Hood River. Despite its cancellation, Hood River provided Intel with insight and information about the converging computer, communications, and consumer electronics industries. According to Ron Whittier, senior vice president and general manager of Intel's Content Group:

> With Hood River, we explicitly articulated for the first time that content would move into a different room. With this awareness, new issues came up and usability became very salient. We became more cognizant of the issues that might arise in different areas. This is consistent with the mass segmentation of the PC into every niche in the market. Intel is now looking at computers in cars, in each room in the house, and other places. Hood River was the leading-edge effort in this direction. From a monolithic market, with 100 million units of the same thing, we move to a segmented market. The content also segments, so now we need to make sure content plays in each segment and environment.

In the aftermath of Hood River, Intel continued to pursue the transition of the PC into new market segments and to refine its strategy for the family room. Mike Aymar moved on to other responsibilities and did not agglomerate the various dispersed projects related to the family room. In 1999, Claude Leglise headed the new Home Products Division, which was chartered with making appliances connected to televisions, phones, and cars, and reported into the Intel Architecture Business Group, headed by Paul Otellini. In 1999, Leglise said: "With Hood River, we learned that we were trying to take the technology up-river. We had the attitude that what we have is wonderful, so let's take it and sell it to consumers in the family room." While the technologies involved were difficult, Leglise said: "The technology is the easy part. We know how to get that. . . . The part that's frightening is What's the application?"

STRATEGIC INERTIA II: IF NONSTRATEGIC, PAY AS YOU GO!

The clarity and focus of Intel's corporate strategy during Epoch II helped top management decide which new business initiatives were strategically important for Job 1 and which were not. Having become a major driving force of the PC industry, top management had also learned that Intel could enable the industry to develop new business applications that required high-performance microprocessors, and that the company didn't necessarily have to do so itself. These two strategic orientations on the part of top management created problems for senior executives engaged in Job 2 efforts. These executives found that it was exceedingly difficult to determine the strategic context for the new businesses that they were trying to develop. Senior executives involved in the motherboards (Frank Gill) and chipset (Ron Smith) businesses were able to do so because they could fairly quickly and clearly establish the tie with the microprocessor strategy. The networking business, on the other hand, is the primary example of the difficulties encountered by a new business whose tie-in with the microprocessor strategy initially could not readily be established.

The Network Computing Group

Antecedents: PCEO. Intel's networking business grew out of the old PCEO venture. Jim Johnson recalled in early 1998: "PCEO helped establish the end-user channel. Now, today, if you ask what is PCEO, it has morphed into a half billion dollar networking business, and there's the math coprocessor/Overdrive business that is now a billion dollar business.[8] But PCEO didn't create either one. We just created the fundamental channel, and then some other people came along and really created these two opportunities."

In 1999, Mark Christensen, vice president and general manager of the Networking business, recalled:

> In 1988, I joined PCEO to start a graphics group. As we looked for something to do we found that the team had been working for two years but had no product. They were struggling. So we came up with the idea of enhancing printers to do graphical images better. We found a little com-

pany in Kansas that had some technology. We licensed it, and brought it to market. It was a big success in that we proved we could get a product to market in six months. But it was a failure in the marketplace. It didn't perform as well as we thought it would, both technically and financially.

But, in that process we went out and learned that people were hooking these print devices up to networks, and they were doing it through a dedicated PC. We learned about their usage model, and we discovered that what we ought to do is shrink the PC into a little tiny box—in essence a PC print server. So you could connect a printer anywhere you wanted it to be connected to a network. Out of the failure was born Netport. Netport was the first product introduced in 1990. It was the first networking product.

Now, we weren't a networking group at that time. We were playing around, trying to find out what would be the next big business. We then hired Mike Maerz. Mike viewed networking as a big growth opportunity for us. He built a team based on Netport. I was a business unit manager for Mike. In September 1991, we introduced something like fifteen new products. So, that was sort of the beginning of the networking division and how we kind of got there.

The networking business in the early 1990s. Intel's networking business got a jump in the early 1990s when an engineer in PCED had the idea to introduce a new LAN adapter card at a price performance point that was about half of what 3Com was selling adapter cards for. Intel had success with its early network adapter products, and quickly captured about 8 percent market segment share. 3Com, however, responded aggressively and held Intel at 8 percent share.

Intel's Networking group then took advantage of a market transition and developed a strategy that capitalized on its strengths in silicon technology and OEM channels. Most of its network adapters 3Com sold on fiberglass cards through reseller channels. Intel worked to integrate networking functionality into the PC platform, and then drove design wins and sales through OEM channels. Mark Christensen, who had become marketing manager for the networking business under Mike Maerz and had been instrumental in developing the OEM channel, explained:

In 1993 we were not winning the market segment share battle with 3Com, and we saw that we needed to change the ballgame to make significant progress. The best time to do it was during a market transition. The Fast Ethernet project started around this time and allowed dual

10MB/100MB performance. We were first to market in 1993, and were consistently six to nine months ahead of the competition. Our product went from fifteen chips to three chips to two chips to one chip, and in the process costs dropped rapidly. The pricing went from $300 in September 1993 to $179 a year later, then to $149 and then to $89. This rocked 3Com.

In spite of its successes, Intel's networking business was not considered strategic during this period and the business was forced to make trade-offs that favored short-term profitability over long-term strategic considerations to justify its continued survival. According to Mark Christensen: "For the first six years, from 1991 to 1997, it was basically pay your own way for growth. If you didn't grow, you had the threat of getting downsized. Much of the funding was being funneled into programs that would help microprocessor growth (Job 1)." In addition, the group was prevented from making acquisitions in large part because acquisitions would dilute Intel's price/earnings ratio. According to Mark Christensen: "We could have bought [a number of companies] in the early 1990s and turned them into multibillion dollar networking businesses had we had a bigger vision earlier. This shows that we were not thinking like a networking company at that time."

Looking back in 1998–99. Frank Gill, who had been in charge of the Networking business during most of the 1990s, gave his view on the evolution of the Networking business at Intel. Gill said:

> In the early 1990s, I had three major thrusts in the Systems Group: OEM motherboards and systems, Supercomputers, and Personal Computer Enhancement Operation (PCEO). PCEO was run by Jim Johnson, who reported to me. Within PCEO was the LAN enhancement run by Mike Maerz. This was the start of our networking effort.
>
> PCEO had historically been a potpourri of various PC add-on devices and math coprocessors. This organization had created our retail channel and had excellent working relationships with the commercial distributors and computer retailers. I was focusing PCEO on connectivity products: network adapters for business and modems for consumers. We had some good competencies in both, had our own Ethernet silicon, and at this time in history, the networking industry was very fragmented around product categories (e.g., 3Com did network interface cards, Cisco did routers, Synoptics did hubs, Hayes and USR did modems). I felt we could use our early client products [network cards and modems]

to build our channel, that the Intel brand would be welcome in this nascent marketplace, and that we could then expand our product line at the other end of the wire [hubs, switches, backup servers, access servers, etc.]. Ultimately, I did transition PCEO to become the Networking Division but never fulfilled my dream of broadening the product line through acquisitions and investment till the late '90s . . . we had lost five years.

With this strategy in mind, we introduced a family of products in September of 1991—primarily network cards for both PCs and printers. In both categories we added the notion of plug and play that greatly improved the install process and had two instant hits. Mike Maerz led this effort and within two years revenues hit $100 million. However, the business was not yet profitable and under attack on profitability and there was no support for increased investment or acquisitions. In the meantime, 3Com had started using acquisitions to broaden themselves from network cards to a full-line supplier.

Within Intel, we were unwilling to do anything but very small acquisitions. We could not use the pooling of interests basis since we routinely bought back our own stock. Our competitors were growing by acquisition and 3Com already had about $400 million in revenue the day we shipped our first product. So, after our initial burst to $100 million in sales, our growth rate slowed considerably to the low teens per year and we fell further and further behind.

I made Mark Christensen the division manager. Mark was an excellent marketing guy, good strategist, and had fresh energy. I wasn't ready to give up though many in the company were quick to point out our scale disadvantages.

In an interview in 1998, Mark Christensen elaborated on the transition from Mike Maerz to him as the general manager of the division:

Mike had a strategy, which I'll describe as a portfolio strategy. He would literally draw a grid and he would look at each grid. Each segment of the marketplace would be in one of those grids. . . . Then he would choose the ones that were the fastest growing and the biggest for us to go in. We were all over the map. . . .

So one of the first things we did was to focus. The new strategy had several parts. First, it was no longer going to be a portfolio strategy. We wanted to get scale and provide a total solution. . . . Second, we changed from a pure branded play to a branded plus OEM. We said, there's some real value that we can bring to the OEMs in that they play a key role in getting our drivers proliferated everywhere. So, we invested heavily in silicon and brought that silicon into our OEMs. Third, we brought together the [remote] management and the silicon messages. . . . We had two different sales teams: one selling [remote] management, and the other selling silicon. We wove them into one and we had one message. And that worked out great. That's why we were so successful with the OEMs.

Christensen also underscored the role of Frank Gill in protecting the networking business before others viewed it as strategic. In 1998, he said:

Frank was a real advocate for us. Frank is the reason why networking is still here, I think. I really do. I think he was our champion within the corporation to get exposure. This was before it was cool to be a start-up at Intel.

Frank said I know we're going to talk about all these wild ideas for growth, but pay attention here. We've got this $300 million business that's best in class in its product categories, that's in a market that's growing 50 to 100 percent per year. Maybe we should invest here some more and keep it going. Frank also argued that it was on a strategic path with the company. So, Frank has been a huge advocate for us. And Barrett has been a big advocate in the last year for us.

Frank Gill, on the other hand, pointed out that it was Christensen who had been able to better tie the networking business to the microprocessor strategy:

Mark clearly got Networking better connected within Intel. He came up with the fast Ethernet "big pipes for big processors" notion and building remote management hooks into the network cards. He also put more focus on OEM customers where Intel had channel power selling to PC companies. I was growing Mark as fast as I could to run networking after I left and made him the featured speaker of the Wired for Management symposium in New York and this gave Andy a chance to see him in action. After the success of the Wired for Management initiative, and newly accepted synergy with IA and networking, Mark was made a group vice president the following January [1998].

Determining the Strategic Context for Networking

Andy Grove's perspective. In late 1999, Andy Grove reflected on why it had taken him a long time to grasp the strategic importance of the networking business. Holding a pencil in his hand, making a metaphorical switch, Grove said: "There was a time when I could have flipped a switch between videoconferencing and networking. I was funding both opportunities. Much more funding was going to videoconferencing, but I didn't chicken-choke networking."

Grove returned several times to the point that he had devoted a great amount of resources to videoconferencing, "which the market didn't want," over networking, which proved to be a huge opportunity. He also reflected on Intel's reluctance to make acquisitions in networking:

> We considered—halfheartedly—buying Cisco. It was a $200 million company then. We looked at buying 3Com. We looked at buying Bay Networks, which was run by Dave House [a former Intel executive]. . . . We took to the board of directors an acquisition proposal [for another company]. I sat out the vote. They rejected it. It was the only time the board rejected management's recommendation. They were right about that particular acquisition.

Continuing, Grove said:

> We didn't have the distribution channel for a Cisco acquisition. But maybe we could have made it work. I have been rabid about four things in my career at Intel: motherboards, Intel Inside, chipsets, and videoconferencing. What if I had been equally rabid about networking? Intel could be a very different kind of company.

Lack of a crisp and firm strategy. Grove observed that the initial proposal to get deeper into networking was brought to him by Frank Gill, to whom the networking business reported during most of the 1990s. Grove said:

> Frank wanted it, but he wasn't sure. [Yet], I was the best chance he had [for a receptive audience at Intel].
> I sensed that he was petrified, turned into mush with respect to the networking business. I still don't understand why he would be intimidated by me. In the past, we had been very close on the sole source deci-

sion and I supported him in motherboards. . . . I thought highly of him; consider him the second best sales manager in Intel's history. He was tough—they called him Sluggo in his old territory in the Midwest—he rose through the ranks.

Further reflecting on the strategic discussions concerning networking, Grove said:

> I am not happy with statements that are somewhat right, but mostly wrong. Maybe I am too good for my own good. I weed out all the weeds, but also some of the potential seeds. . . . Barrett is more comfortable with leaving strategy a bit more murky, undefined.

Andy wondered what Gill's perspective on this was and agreed it would be good to ask him.

Frank Gill's perspective. Frank Gill had left Intel in June 1998, right at the time when Intel began to make some big bets—acquisitions—in networking. Frank had participated in one of Stanford Business School's executive programs in 1993 and had also participated in several interviews for case writing purposes over the years. Graciously and candidly, Frank was willing to share his views, parts of which have already been reported earlier in this chapter. Frank did not quite agree that he had been petrified or intimidated by the situation. Somewhat facetiously, he said that he had many problems but wimpiness was not one of them. Gill then gave his perspective on some of these problems. Talking about the early years, Gill said:

> In the mid-1990s, we reorganized every year or so. We had gone from the Systems Group to the Intel Products Group (IPG) to Internet Communications Group (ICG) to Small Business & Networking Group (SBNG). But one thing that I protected throughout was networking. I tried to minimize the impact of these reorganizations on networking division and buffer it from these and other corporate distractions.

Confirming Andy Grove's recall of the situation, he said that right before he left:

> We had gone to the board with a proposal to acquire a large system company for a couple billion dollars. But it was rejected. GEC, a British company, then bought them about a year later for about $3 billion plus. Barrett was supportive enough to go to the board with this. Shortly after

I left Intel, [they] bought Level One for $2.2 billion, so it was clear that the corporation was now in support of growing the business.

Asked what finally triggered top management's interest in networking as a major new business opportunity for Intel, Gill said:

This change was triggered by the realization that it was going to be hard to drive top line growth with the microprocessor business. Lower growth, together with price pressures on the low end translating in lower profitability, was going to affect the stock price. We all pretty much realized the next ten years going forward were not going to be as great as the last ten.

In view of the need to get in other businesses, I had made the point for a long time that Intel needed to address big markets, which networking certainly was. Also, we had some competencies in networking but in order to compete to win, it would require corporate support for acquisitions, network/connectivity branding, and dedicated sales support.

The ESM was preoccupied with the microprocessor business, even though they realized the need to diversify. The only real supporters were Vadasz and Barrett, who looked at it analytically.

Focus on Job 1. Asked to discuss the reasons for Intel top management coming to grips with the networking opportunity quite late in the game, Frank said that he wanted to give a balanced view and proceeded to list several factors. He said:

First, in the early 1990s, there was Andy Grove's ability to get everybody to focus on Job 1. Andy had great insight in the lucrative path that was available to Intel and put all our energy in microprocessors and in growing the market. Andy was able to align all the force fields, which meant there were only two strategic tasks at Intel: (1) develop, build, market, and sell microprocessors; and (2) make the market for microprocessors larger. Any other activity was viewed as a distraction.

There was a total preoccupation with Job 1. And this manifested itself in some insidious ways. In order to be able to turn on a dime, Andy organized the company around huge functional organizations reporting to him. My group was still organized as a business unit. While this functional organization worked great for our core microprocessor business, it was very difficult for my group who depended on the functional groups for support.

Frank added here: "It made me very well off, so it is hard to be too critical. I also think it was an excellent strategy for all shareholders and employees. Without this focus, we may not have done such a good job in processors."

Limitations of SLRP. Continuing his analysis, Gill said:

> A second factor was that our basic planning processes let us down. . . . We addressed lots of issues around our core business but never asked the questions like Should we diversify, and if so, in what market segments? until the Barrett-led SLRP in 1998.
>
> Another way our planning processes failed us was that since all the planning activity involving Andy was focused on Job 1, he did not have sufficient insight or knowledge to meaningfully contribute to our networking and connectivity businesses. Looking back, this was my biggest mistake, not finding a way to get Andy involved in the networking business as an opportunity that would both contribute to Job 1 and also held the potential to be another large business in the future.

Intel's role as industry enabler gets in the way of new business development.
Gill emphasized the importance of Intel's traditional view of its role as an enabler in the PC industry, and that this limited Intel's direct involvement in developing the business for itself:

> A key point: Our planning process clearly identified that bringing connectivity to the PC was critical to expanding the market. The controversy was that I felt this was a business opportunity for us and Andy felt we should enable and facilitate the industry to do it. A couple of examples: Andy gave many speeches about e-mail as a "killer app" to drive PC demand. E-mail clearly requires all PCs to be connected. Another example, [someone] came up with the idea of developing cable modems to bring both "always connected" and broadband connectivity to home users. Consequently, a group was chartered to build demo gear, work on standards, and evangelize this to the industry, and Andy gave several speeches evangelizing and demoing cable modems and chiding the telcos for their slow deployment of ISDN. However, he stopped short of charging anyone to go off and build the chips to bring cable modems into the affordable price range and ultimately we left this to Broadcom. Many of Intel's recent acquisitions, like DSP Group, are just now adding this kind of competency.

Lack of tie-in to the core business strategy. Asked what his views were on Andy Grove's favoring videoconferencing over networking, Gill said:

> Videoconferencing met the SLRP criteria in that it provided a potential MIPS sucking application to create demand for high performance Pentium processors and most competitors were using a DSP chip, not the Pentium processor for the encode/decode engine. Since the industry was not doing it, we should! The several hundred million invested in videoconferencing would have radically changed our position in the networking space.
>
> Networking was forced to live quarter by quarter. Any time we did not make the planned quarterly numbers we were put on notice [probation] and I got lots of questions about why we were wasting energy in this area.

Elaborating on the way the lack of strategic context affected his Plan of Record (POR) reviews, Frank said:

> When Barrett said to get networking profitable in the 1993 POR, it was clear that this was the only sure way to protect it. Therefore, we went into a mode of making sure near term financials were within acceptable range, and this precluded investment in new product categories and even made small acquisitions dubious given that we had to eat the goodwill write off. So, it is fair to say that it is truly pay as you go, but not fair to say that I had to defend it vigorously at each POR though it was a topic at many PORs.

He added:

> Once networking got critical mass, say, around 1993 or 1994, it was clear that it had value and many in Corporate Business Development and elsewhere suggested selling it. Often these rumors leaked to the field and customers. The danger became selling versus closure.

In describing the impediments deriving from the lack of strategic context for the networking business within Intel, Gill said:

> Consequently, within networking, we became a little creative about it. Internally, we positioned everything related to the networking business as supporting Job 1. We said big microprocessors need fat pipes (e.g.,

Fast Ethernet). So we began to get better support from Andy and the IA side. While the Fast Ethernet strategy was synergistic with Pentium processors, the reality of it, however, was that we were trying to drive the networking market to Fast Ethernet in order for us to grow fast. Market segment share in networking was of no interest to Intel, but we positioned it as providing fat pipes for the Pentium processor which made the activity better accepted within Intel.

Gill also said:

When we did start to get networking into a strategic context in 1995, we had compiled six or eight quarters of profitability, which made it difficult to [denigrate] the business.

Cross-group interference causes deteriorating personal dynamics. Frank added: "Besides Andy's focus on Job 1 and the right planning processes not being in place, there were also some personal dynamics contributing to [the impediments], dynamics between myself and Andy and the rest of ESM."

Tracing some of the factors that had contributed to the negative turn in personal dynamics between Andy Grove and the other ESM members and himself, Frank said he spent huge amounts of time fighting through cross-group issues. As a result:

I had become increasingly hostile in driving results and debating/defending my group's actions, creating my own force field. Clearly, I was doing a poor job of working effectively with my peer level colleagues. When my colleagues took these issues to Andy, it was always positioned as "Frank is putting his local P&L ahead of Job 1." After a couple of years of these continued internal battles, Andy came to view me as the problem. (Of course, I would argue that the lack of consensus on strategy and support was the root cause.)

The net-net of the situation was that Andy now thinks that I am putting the interest of my group ahead of Intel's interest. In fact, in one heated exchange with Andy, he told me point blank that he didn't trust me. At the same time, I was fighting very hard to make the struggling business a success, so by 1993 it created a personal crisis. Fortunately for me, the OEM motherboard strategy turned out to be profoundly correct and the Pentium processor ramp was helped immensely by offering it at the motherboard level.

So, by the end of '94 I had turned from an outcast into a hero with about 40 percent of all Pentium chips shipping on Intel designed and built motherboards. It was as if I had rejoined Intel and was once again an integral member to the ESM team but the damage to my relationship with Andy was done.

In 1996, I was made executive vice president (one of only three), which was a very nice recognition for the contributions of the motherboard effort.

And a breakdown in the strategic conversation. Continuing his analysis, Frank Gill said:

Back to my relationship with Andy. On the surface, there was a cordial relationship, but we no longer did openly brainstorm, talk, and communicate with a free-flowing discussion. I had come to believe Andy was so deeply vested in the "enable the industry" that he would never come around. Once he told me "that even if you get networking to $1 billion in revenue with normal 10 percent profits, then that would only equate to $25 million a quarter and I am making $1 billion a quarter profit on IA."

It was equally my own problem because I didn't reach out and gave up on convincing him. I decided that what counts at Intel is to get results. I believed the key to success and corporate support was revenue and profits. This is where I put my energy rather than in selling Andy and the rest of ESM on why this was important for Intel's long term.

Getting ready to leave. Asked when he started thinking about leaving Intel, Frank Gill said:

One more reorganization followed in 1997 creating the Small Business and Networking Group, and again I worked hard to buffer networking from all the reorganization distractions. By then, it was clear I would leave the next year and the networking division had clearly made a major move with the Fast Ethernet push. When I left in 1998, networking was at a billion dollar run rate in sales and clearly Barrett strongly supported this as witnessed by moving Mark Christensen [networking GM] to ESM.

If it could be played again. Asked what he would do differently if he could play the game over, Frank Gill said:

I would have tried to control my emotions, and find a way to communicate better that we could grow new businesses that don't hurt IA and could even be synergistic. I had developed a lot of anger because a few simple words from Andy to ESM could have made most of my cross group issues go away. Had I better managed the cross-group issues and thereby kept Andy's support, I think we would have moved faster on attacking this as a business rather than enabler.

I feel now that I should have used all my sales skills in convincing Intel to set up another company—to spin it out. That would have allowed us to solve the major barriers that the Job1 focus created; to create a network brand, to have a dedicated sales force, and to use pooling for acquisitions so that the goodwill wouldn't have to be written off against earnings. Intel could have remained the majority owner and repurchased all the shares at a later date if appropriate.

DISCUSSION AND IMPLICATIONS

Process Model Analysis of ProShare and Hood River

ProShare and Hood River were very different new business development efforts for Intel. ProShare was a huge effort and Hood River was mostly a small sideshow. Nevertheless, analysis with the help of Tool III of both efforts illustrates some key aspects of the strategic inertia that grew out of Intel's highly successful core business strategy during Epoch II.

Process model analysis of ProShare. In the case of ProShare, the strategic context for the venture was determined from day one. Andy Grove's forceful support made sure that the venture was viewed as strategically important to Intel's core business. His support also shielded the venture from the strong selection pressures of the structural context, in particular Intel's rigorous financial reviews, which would undoubtedly have stopped rather quickly other ventures with similar poor financial performance.

At first glance, top management's protection would seem to have created a large window of opportunity for ProShare to establish itself in the external environment. There were, however, important negative consequences associated with the corporate largesse. First, Andy Grove's insistence on applying a horizontal, frontal assault strategy for ProShare reduced the degrees of freedom of the executives in charge of the new business development effort. Instead of being able to find out what the real customer needs were, where these needs were emerging first, and how they were likely to evolve over time—a crucial discovery process—right away venture leader Pat Gelsinger was thrown in an execution mode. Second, the task facing the venture leader was one of delivering a technology to the market in the same vein that Intel delivered next generation microprocessors to the market. The effort was focused on outbound marketing rather than inbound marketing. Hence, the difficult, intuition building, technical, and need linking efforts were not adequately performed. Discipline-instilling product championing efforts were not required to secure resources internally. Strategic forcing efforts were not carried out with a product about which the team was deeply confident because it reflected their best efforts to link technology and customer needs. Rather, the venture team had to work somewhat surreptitiously to get around the preconceived notions of top management about what type of product should be delivered to the market.

Third, Frank Gill, the senior executive positioned between Andy Grove and Pat Gelsinger was mostly left—or rather, as he put it, able to stay—out of the loop. As a result, this senior executive was not able—not required—to add much strategic value. For instance, it is not clear that strategic building efforts on the part of Gill might have led to acquiring complementary products that might have reduced the pressure on reaching critical mass with ProShare alone. Also, with Andy Grove usurping the role of Gill in the strategy development process, the discipline-instilling organizational championing efforts—requiring Frank Gill to convince peers, as well as top management, that the continuation of the videoconferencing venture was in the long-term interest of the corporation—were not performed. Finally, as a consequence of too much and too early support from the CEO, the opportunity costs associated with ProShare were not seriously considered until 1996. As Frank Gill pointed out, Andy Grove's confidence in ProShare did not force Gill to get involved as much as he should have and led him to intervene later than he normally would have.

Process model analysis of Hood River. In the case of Hood River, like ProShare, the strategic context was determined early on. Rob Siegel, the project leader, took to heart Intel's "The PC is it" rallying cry, and let the Hood River product definition be completely determined by the company's desire to base the PC in the living room on Intel's state-of-the-art microprocessor (the Pentium II). On the other hand, quite different from ProShare, there was no direct and forceful support from the CEO for this project. Consequently, the selective effects of Intel's structural context were very strong in the Hood River case. This was most clearly illustrated when funding was cut off without warning as a result of OPSD's efforts to harness resources to face the threat of the NC to Intel's core business.

Because the corporate-level strategy strongly influenced the business-level strategy and product development process, the technical and need linking activities were not performed adequately. This also made it impossible for the Hood River project team to work effectively with the consumer electronics OEMs. This, in turn, prevented the project team from developing a product concept with a chance of winning in the living room market segment. Product championing activities were vigorously but somewhat ineffectively pursued by Siegel, who was most of the time on the defensive and could not exert influence in the network of resource controlling relationships of Intel's matrix. Strategic forcing never even started, as no OEM customers—neither consumer electronics nor PC OEMs—were willing to adopt the Hood River product concept. As a result, Mike Aymar, the senior executive in charge, had no foundation to stand on and could not continue to ask top management for support. Also, several other initiatives related to the family room that had sprung up in different parts of the company remained disparate and were not integrated with a new strategic thrust. Strategic building was completely lacking. This was in part due to a lack of general management perspective at the middle level of management. Mike Aymar was strongly preoccupied by his demanding responsibilities as general manager of the Desktop Products Group, which put him right in the heartland of executing on Intel's PC-oriented corporate strategy. It was not possible for him to develop a general management perspective for Intel's efforts in the family room, and to engage in strategic building and organizational championing to set the stage for determining a strategic context commensurate with the consumer electronics nature of the opportunity.

Summary. While the ProShare venture and the Hood River project were very different, they both involved market creation. In both cases, the corporate-level forces associated with the core microprocessor business strategy reached deeply into the business-level development efforts. This is shown in figure 9.1, a simplified version of the process model of new business development.

Figure 9.1 shows the strong influence exerted by the corporate management level on the business strategy level, affecting the definition part of the new business development process. This influence was particularly strong in the ProShare case, in which Andy Grove monitored closely Gelsinger's efforts from the very start of the venture. The corporate influence was also strong in Hood River, if not as strong as in ProShare, simply because Hood River was made to report into the Desktop Products Group. Hood River, however, also ran into the very strong selection effects of Intel's structural context, which dealt with it erratically in financial support. The strong corporate influence early on in the development prevented the managers involved in the new business from engaging in the technical and need

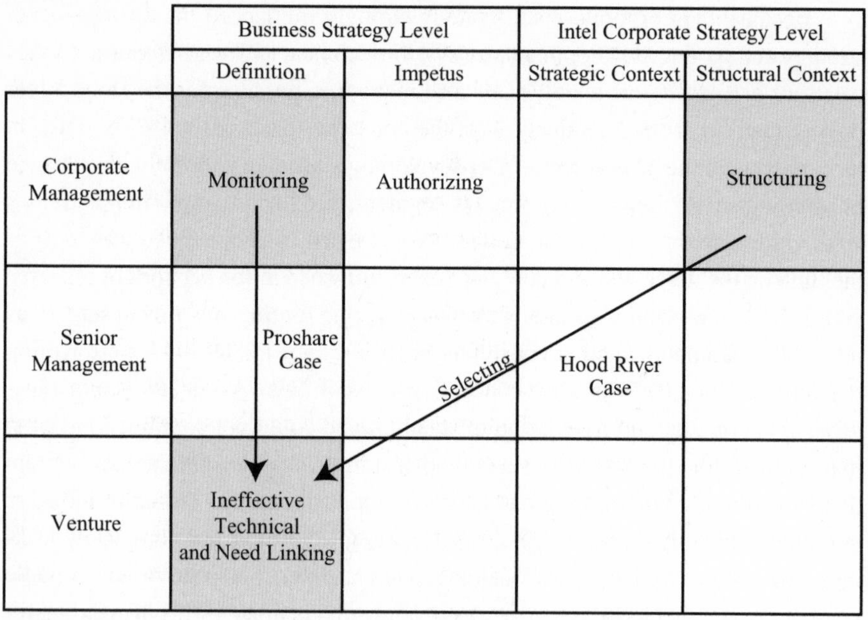

	Business Strategy Level		Intel Corporate Strategy Level	
	Definition	Impetus	Strategic Context	Structural Context
Corporate Management	Monitoring	Authorizing		Structuring
Senior Management	Proshare Case	*Selecting*	Hood River Case	
Venture	Ineffective Technical and Need Linking			

Figure 9.1. A Simplified Process Model of ProShare and Hood River.

linking activities necessary to find out what the new business opportunity really was and how it could be most effectively pursued. In both cases, the logic of the extremely successful core business strategy was misapplied.

Process Model Analysis of the Networking Business

Andy Grove and Frank Gill's reflections indicate that personal dynamics played a role in the evolution of the networking business within Intel. Yet, these personal dynamics had little if anything to do with the personalities involved. Rather, the personal dynamics reflected the strategic forces at play inside and outside Intel, which made various senior executives perceive the interests of the company differently.

In terms of the process model of new business development, the second form of strategic inertia—be strategic or pay-as-you-go—highlights the extreme difficulty experienced by senior executives of networking to define the strategic context for a new business that was outside the core microprocessor business. In contrast to ProShare and Hood River, where the strategic context was probably determined prematurely, in networking the strategic context became determined only late in the game.

The case data suggest that there were at least two reasons for this: First, top management looked at networking in terms of the logic of Intel as industry enabler, rather than as a new business for Intel. But, second, as Frank Gill candidly admits, he basically gave up on organizational championing efforts in the face of peer resistance and top management's recalcitrance, and focused on short-term financial performance to protect the business. This created a vicious circle. Unsuccessful organizational championing led to unsuccessful negotiating of the structural context, which limited the amount of corporate resources made available for the networking business. This, in turn, limited the scope of the strategic building activities that Gill could engage in; large acquisitions were simply not permitted. And this, in turn, limited the growth of the business to what could be achieved with the strategic forcing activities based on the internally developed products. Fortunately, these products were based on effective technical and need linking activities and experienced strong market acceptance. The effectiveness of these activities was at least in part the result of Gill's successful shielding of the networking business at the ESM level. However, in contrast to the chipset business, where the opportunity was sufficiently large that strategic building was not necessary, this was not the case in networking. As a result, while the networking business continued to grow, Intel's strategic position relative to companies like Cisco and 3Com remained disadvantageous because of the high-growth rate of the industry relative to what could be achieved with strategic forcing alone. Hence, while Gill's efforts most of the time were able to shelter the networking business from changes in resource allocation driven by concerns about the core business, it also isolated networking from the rest of the corporation.

Gill, however, groomed his successor—Mark Christensen—who would be able to do what Gill himself had not been able to do; that is, clearly determine the strategic context for networking within Intel. Similar to Ron Smith forging a link between the fate of the Pentium processor and the PCI chipsets, Christensen's idea that fat processors needed fat pipes forged a link in top management's mind between the destiny of the microprocessor business and the destiny of the networking business. Christensen, of course, was benefiting, as he pointed out himself, from the successful strategic forcing efforts under Gill's direction. In addition, as Christensen pointed out in 1998, he was able to capitalize on Andy Grove's strategic recognition that Intel's networking products could be part of the solution to the Total Cost of Ownership problem that had given rise to the so-called NC (network computer) in 1997. These newly conceptualized strategic links also mobilized support on the part of senior executives associated with the microprocessor business for the networking business. The rest followed.

	Business Strategy Level		Corporate Strategy Level	
	Definition	Impetus	Strategic Context	Structural Context
A. Grove Corporate Management C. Barrett	Monitoring	Authorizing	No Retroactive Rationalization No Strategic Recognition	Structuring
F. Gill Senior Management J. Johnson	Coaching	Limited Strategic Building	Unsuccessful Organizational Championing No Clear Delineation	Unsuccessful Negotiating
Venture Team M. Maerz M. Christensen	Technical and Need Linking	Strategic Forcing	"Flying Under Radar"	Questioning

Strong Selecting Force · *Product Championing*

Figure 9.2a. A Process Model of the Networking Business until 1997.

Summary. The networking business at Intel went through two stages. These are conceptualized using the process model of new business development and represented in figures 9.2a and 9.2b. Figure 9.2a depicts the first stage. During the first stage, roughly until 1997, the strategic context of the networking business remained indeterminate. There was no strategic recognition of its importance and no retroactive rationalization to make it part of the corporate strategy. Frank Gill was able to insulate the business from changes in the structural context but was not effective as an organizational champion. As a result, he was left to support the growth of the business with its own funds, with no additional corporate resources allocated to it. This limited the opportunity for strategic building activities. Relying solely on strategic-forcing activities got the business up to more than a half billion dollars in sales revenues but nevertheless kept it in the position of a second tier player in the fast-growing industry.

Figure 9.2b depicts the second stage. During the second stage, started in early 1998, the strategic context determination process was activated under the leadership of Mark Christensen, who was able to engage in successful organizational championing activities and successfully negotiated the structural context. This provided corporate resources necessary to engage in strategic building (acquiring

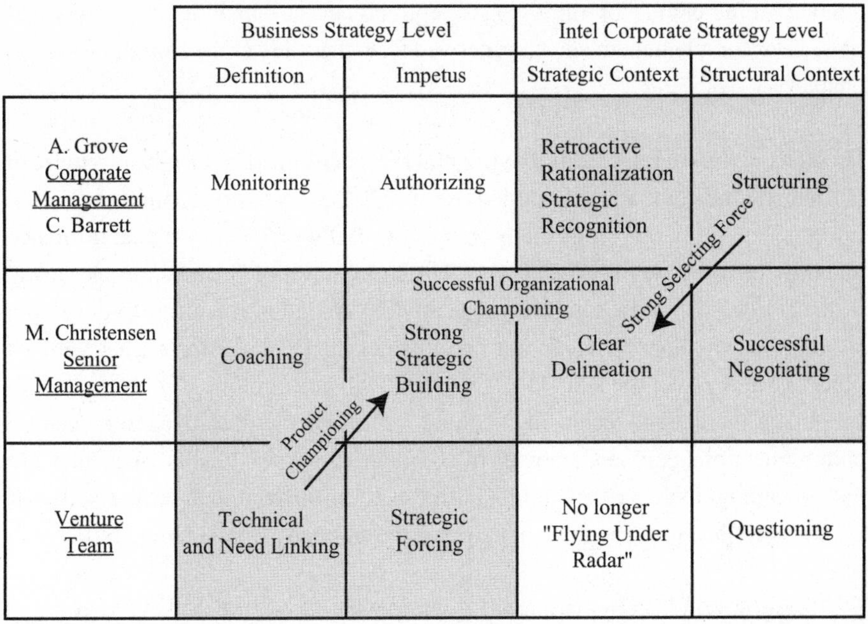
Business Strategy Level
Intel Corporate Strategy Level
Definition
Impetus
Strategic Context
Structural Context
A. Grove
Corporate Management
C. Barrett
Monitoring
Authorizing
Retroactive Rationalization
Strategic Recognition
Structuring
Strong Selecting Force
M. Christensen
Senior Management
Coaching
Successful Organizational Championing
Strong Strategic Building
Clear Delineation
Successful Negotiating
Product Championing
Venture Team
Technical and Need Linking
Strategic Forcing
No longer "Flying Under Radar"
Questioning

Figure 9.2b. A Process Model of the Networking Business since 1997.

companies with complementary and supplementary products). Through strategic recognition and retroactive rationalization on the part of top management, networking became integrated into the corporate strategy. Leveraging off the foundation built by Frank Gill, Christensen seemed poised in 1999 to move Intel into a leadership position in some networking market segments and to more broadly delineate Intel's strategic position in the industry.

Implications for Strategic Leadership

The process model analysis of ProShare, Hood River, and networking highlights the strategic leadership difficulties associated with the forms of strategic inertia identified in this chapter. This analysis produces insights in the strategic forces that impeded new business development at Intel during Epoch II. Some of these insights pertain primarily to the first form of strategic inertia, which complicated the development of strategic new businesses. Others pertain more to the second form of strategic inertia, which impeded the development of new businesses that were initially categorized as nonstrategic. These insights not only have implications for theory about new business development in established companies but they also contain useful lessons for improving the entrepreneurial capability of such companies. They complement the insights derived from the study of the chipset venture in chapter 7.

Hazards of top management driving market creation. The ProShare venture in particular indicates that it is hazardous for the CEO to try to drive a market creation effort, even—or perhaps especially so—for a CEO with the intellectual brilliance and drive of someone like Andy Grove. The sheer power of Grove's presence made it difficult for the relatively junior executive in charge of the effort to develop a strategy that was appropriate for the new business and to act in accordance with his objective analysis of the situation. Also, the involvement of the CEO early on, before major market and technical uncertainties had been reduced, led to premature commitment of significant amounts of corporate resources. Finally, once the CEO had committed to the new, fledgling business it was difficult to avoid escalation of commitment and to scale down or extricate the company from a failing business.

> **Insight 9.1.** Top management driving market creation is likely to impede the discovery of an appropriate strategy for the new business, to precipitate premature commitment of significant amounts of corporate resources, and to lead to escalation of commitment and the inability to timely scale down or exit.

Logic of core business impedes a general management perspective. In the ProShare and Hood River ventures, the close link with the corporate strategy made it virtually impossible for the executives in charge of the new business to develop a general management perspective. Pat Gelsinger (ProShare) and Mike Aymar (Hood River) found themselves applying the logic of the core business strategy rather than discovering the appropriate strategy for the new business. In the networking venture, the fact that the business was not viewed as strategic provided more room for Frank Gill to develop a general management perspective. The price of this, however, was less support from corporate management for the venture.

> **Insight 9.2.** If strategic new business development is driven by the logic of the core business strategy, it is difficult for the new business managers to develop a general management perspective.

Lack of general management perspective impedes integration of related but dispersed initiatives. The lack of opportunity to develop a general management perspective for a new business also increases the chances that different initiatives related to the new opportunity, but springing up in different parts of the company, will remain disparate. Strategic building was lacking in all three ventures, if for different reasons. Yet, strategic building is necessary for the integration of such dispersed initiatives and to create a strong strategic thrust that serves as the foundation for organizational championing and strategic context determination.

> **Insight 9.3.** The lack of opportunity for middle managers to develop a general management perspective for a new business impedes the strategic building activities necessary for integrating related initiatives that are dispersed throughout the company. This, in turn, impedes the organizational championing activities necessary to set the stage for the strategic context determination process for the new business.

Core business infrastructure incapable of supporting new business development. Strategy and structure in Intel's core business were extremely tightly aligned during Epoch II. While Intel's matrix structure facilitated the successful execution of the core business strategy, it was not supportive of new business development. Strategic (ProShare, Hood River) as well as nonstrategic (Networking) new businesses found it difficult to get the organization to execute on new business strategies. Getting and keeping the support of the centralized sales force, for instance, could be extremely difficult, especially for nonstrategic new businesses. In addition, since the needs of the core business always dominated those of the new businesses, the latter were constantly in danger of experiencing random shocks when critical resources were taken away to cope with a perceived threat to the core business. Hence, the organizational infrastructure that was almost perfectly attuned to executing the core business strategy could not readily support the development of new businesses.

> **Insight 9.4.** A strong organizational capability to execute the core business strategy tends to be less capable of supporting new business strategy development and execution.

Gravity associated with the size of the core business. Internally developed new businesses are inherently relatively small when they start. If they are initially viewed as nonstrategic, they are likely to be considered distractions from the perspective of allocating scarce top management time. During Epoch II, Intel's massive and rapidly growing core microprocessor business developed extremely strong gravity; it was very difficult for new businesses to attract top management attention. Andy Grove sometimes referred to new businesses with the potential to reach several hundred million dollars in revenues as chicken feed.

> **Insight 9.5.** If a company's core business grows to be very large, it becomes increasingly difficult for nonstrategic new business development efforts to attract and sustain top management attention.

Gravity associated with the profitability of the core business. A second type of gravity derived from the profitability of the core business. During Epoch II, nonstrategic new business initiatives at Intel competed for scarce resources in Intel's fiercely competitive resource allocation process. Invariably, they ran into competition with microprocessor-related initiatives that supported the very high gross-margin core business. Only new initiatives that were strategically important did not have to meet the same profitability standards as nonstrategic business initiatives. Sometimes, a business (e.g., motherboards) would move back and forth between being considered strategically important and not strategically important.

> **Insight 9.6.** If the profitability of a company's core business is very high, it is difficult for nonstrategic business development efforts to attract corporate resources.

Gravity associated with the core business brand image. A third source of gravity associated with the core business came from the success of the Intel Inside marketing campaign. Nonstrategic new business initiatives sometimes required a business strategy that was not fully consistent with Intel's technology and product leadership image in the microprocessor business. The new businesses sometimes had to fight for market segment share and compete on price, which was not consistent with the messages associated with Intel Inside. They were therefore bound to run into conflicts with Intel's Corporate Marketing Group, which did not want the Intel brand to be associated with the new business.

> **Insight 9.7.** If the brand image of a company's core business is very strong, it is likely that conflicts with nonstrategic new business development efforts will arise.

Gravity associated with enabling the industry. A fourth, and final, form of gravity associated with the core business came from Intel's very success in becoming a major driving force in the development of the PC industry. Although much of Intel's R&D investments went into technologies that complemented the microprocessor and thereby offered opportunities to launch other new businesses, the company rarely attempted to do so. An important reason for this was that any technology advance that enriched the PC environment was likely to create more demand for microprocessors. Thus, it was generally more valuable for Intel to give away technology and quickly disseminate it in the market, rather than try to build a business around it. The chipset venture discussed in chapter 7 had to overcome this form of gravity. The Networking business experienced this problem more strongly because its importance for the core business could not be as easily demonstrated early on.

> **Insight 9.8.** If a company's capacity to enable the industry for the purpose of advancing its core business is very strong, nonstrategic new business development efforts find it difficult to receive corporate support.

Little room for strategic context determination. Initially, as in the case of networking, there is great ambiguity about the importance of a nonstrategic new business. Resolving this ambiguity requires the activation of the process of strategic context determination. Strategic context determination is inherently somewhat exploratory and iterative, with the new business strategy taking shape through experimentation and selection. Andy Grove's extremely strong focus on the PC-oriented core business and his determination not to allow himself to be distracted, together with his pronounced preference for clear and crisp strategies, made strategic context determination a very difficult process at Intel during Epoch II.

> **Insight 9.9.** It is difficult to activate the strategic context determination process for nonstrategic new businesses if top management has little tolerance for ambiguity.

Conflicts with the core business slow the impetus of a new business. While determining the strategic context of new businesses is inherently difficult, especially in a strongly focused company like Intel, the problems are exacerbated if the new business's strategy is perceived by top management to potentially interfere with the core business strategy. This was the case with networking, and it limited the ability of Frank Gill to engage in strategic building and organizational championing activities. In contrast to the chipset business, strategic building through the acquisition of companies in various segments of the networking industry was necessary for networking to augment its size and scope and reach critical mass. Limits on the ability to engage in strategic building slowed down the impetus of networking within Intel. The limited effectiveness and eventual fading of Gill's organizational championing—giving up on trying to convince his peers of the strategic importance of the networking business—also impeded further the determination of the strategic context of networking within Intel.

> **Insight 9.10.** Conflicts between the strategy of a nonstrategic new business and the core business strategy slow down the new business's impetus and exacerbate the difficulty of determining its strategic context.

Optimal cycle time of strategic change. The preceding analysis confirms that strategic change can be too fast or too slow. For ProShare it was arguably too fast; for networking it was arguably too slow. Strategic context determination is the critical process through which the cycle time of strategic change is regulated. Activating the strategic context determination process for ProShare would have tempered the influence of the CEO in driving the strategy of the videoconferencing venture. This would have given senior management and venture management more time to develop a strategy that was commensurate with the nature of the business (sum of vertical niches rather than one horizontal market segment). Activating the strategic context determination process for networking would have made it possible to recognize its strategic importance for Intel sooner. This would have given senior and venture management the opportunity to capitalize faster on the opportunity. While Monday morning quarterbacking is always easy, it is reasonable to use the quality of the strategic context determination process as a measure to evaluate, ex post facto, the performance of senior and top management in relation to the cycle time of strategic change.

> **Insight 9.11.** Strategic context determination is the process through which top management can affect the cycle time of strategic change. Effectiveness of using this process is a measure of senior and top management performance with respect to new business development.

CONCLUSION AND RECAPITULATION

Conclusion

During Epoch II, the season of enormous growth in the PC market segment of the microprocessor industry anticipated by Gordon Moore in 1989 did indeed arrive. And CEO Andy Grove was the perfect leader for that season. Grove's strategic leadership made it possible for Intel to drive the evolution of the PC market segment. The resulting coevolution between its microprocessor strategy and the PC market segment made Intel one of the most successful companies in history. Many thousands of employees and shareholders reaped great riches from Intel's success during Epoch II.

As Gordon Moore had also anticipated in 1989, however, Andy Grove's relentless focus on the PC market segment of the microprocessor industry significantly narrowed Intel's internal ecology of strategy-making. The balance that more or less existed during Epoch I between induced and autonomous strategy tilted almost completely toward induced strategy during Epoch II. To be sure, the clear and crisp content of the microprocessor strategy disciplined Intel's strategy-making process. But it left little room for strategic content that was not microprocessor related. Toward the end of Epoch II, Intel was facing a paradox. Andy Grove's extraordinary strategic leadership, which resulted in spectacular success during Epoch II had also become a source of significant strategic inertia.

The process model analysis of the ProShare and Hood River ventures showed the extent to which the logic of Intel's core microprocessor strategy pervaded all initiatives that were deemed strategic during Epoch II. ProShare and Hood River both required market creation. But the misapplication of the core business strategy—which worked exceedingly well in delivering new technology to an *existing* market—hampered the technical and need linking efforts necessary to understand the *new* customer needs. This form of strategic inertia not only reduced the success chances of new businesses requiring a different logic but also made it difficult to develop general managers who could devise new strategies for new markets. In the case of Hood River it impeded strategic building activities required to integrate dispersed initiatives into a new strategic thrust.

The process model analysis of the Networking venture, on the other hand, highlighted the difficulties that a nonstrategic new business encountered in determining its strategic context within Intel. The comparison of the process model analysis of the networking business and of the chipset venture was instructive in this respect. In contrast to ProShare and Hood River, the chipsets and networking ventures addressed existing markets, but ones in which Intel did not yet have a major business presence. The potential revenues associated with the networking venture's initial products, however, were far smaller than those of the chipset venture. Consequently, the general manager of networking needed to engage in strategic building efforts through acquisitions to reach critical mass internally as well as externally. But strategic building required obtaining corporate resources over and above those that the venture could internally generate. Obtaining corporate resources, however, depended on effective organizational championing, on convincing peers as well as top management that the success of the Networking business was in the company's strategic interest. This was virtually impossible, given the strong focus of top management on the microprocessor business. (In addition, the general manager ran into resistance from his peers for the microprocessor business because of some of his other business activities that were perceived as threats to the core business.) Hence, for several years the networking venture was caught in a vicious circle. It was not until a new general manager was able to come up with the fat pipes for fat processors idea that the strategic context for networking within Intel became unambiguously determined. The fact is, however, that the strategic context for Networking *did* become determined, and by 1998 the networking business was fully part of the corporate strategy.

Recapitulation: Intel's Internal Ecology of Strategy-Making at the End of Epoch II

Using Tool III, chapter 7 identified conditions under which some autonomous strategic action could still be successful during the early part of Epoch II. Using Tool I, chapter 8 showed that the coevolutionary process of Intel's strategy and the PC market segment during the latter part of Epoch II further reinforced Intel's induced-strategy process. Using Tool III again, the present chapter identified two forms of strategic inertia that grew out of the successful strengthening of Intel's induced-strategy process throughout Epoch II. Strategic inertia of the first type involved a sort of self-induced resistance (impedance) to exploring on its own terms the real opportunity associated with new businesses that were viewed as strategic for the core microprocessor business. Strategic inertia of the second type involved a sort of organizational insulation against new businesses that seemed nonstrategic, that is, outside of the core microprocessor business.

Tool II serves to conceptualize the state of Intel's internal ecology of strategy-making at the end of Epoch II. This is illustrated in figure 9.3, which suggests that at the end of Epoch II, the autonomous strategy process faced significant challenges in Intel's much-tightened structural context. Yet, while it was subject to the strategic inertia that afflicts all large, established companies, Intel remained a

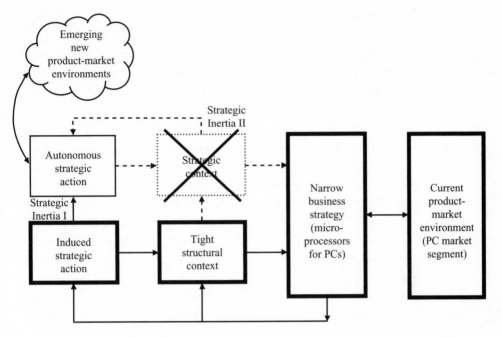

Figure 9.3. Two Forms of Strategic Inertia.

highly vibrant and resilient company. In spite of Andy Grove's successful efforts to vectorize Intel's strategy-making, top management did not actively try to weed out all autonomous strategic action. Top management was simply strongly focused on the core business. While it was not a good idea for anyone to get in the way of Andy Grove's determination to fully capitalize on the core business opportunity, there was still room on the sidelines and lots of new ideas still were being generated.

The strategic leadership infrastructure to turn new ideas into businesses, however, had been largely dismantled as a consequence of the intense focus on executing the core business strategy. The balance between induced and autonomous strategy processes was no longer adequate. Restoring the balance would be critical in maintaining the adaptive capability of Intel's strategy-making process. This was a major strategic leadership challenge that Craig Barrett, Intel's new CEO in 1998, would have to address at the start of Epoch III.

Epoch III:

Intel the Internet Building Block Company

> I try to challenge the new ventures to grow their businesses so that they're relevant, and I challenge the people in the microprocessor business to be successful enough so that the new ventures won't matter.
>
> Intel CEO CRAIG BARRETT, 1999

10 MAINTAINING AND EXTENDING THE STRATEGY VECTOR

The industry that we're in has changed. We made a transition from the '70s to the '80s from being an integrated circuit company to being a microprocessor company. Now we're transitioning to an Internet building block company. If you look at our mission statements, you'll see that they reflect this transition from being a microprocessor company to being an Internet building block company. Every third word makes a reference to the Internet.

CRAIG BARRETT, CEO, April 1999

Epoch III Has Arrived

In early 1998, Andy Grove passed the CEO mantle on to Craig Barrett and remained chairman of the board. While some at Intel were not yet sure that Epoch III had really started, Barrett and Grove were convinced it had. According to Andy Grove in early 1999:

Intel is undergoing an adaptation today that is a different version of the adaptation that occurred in the mid-'80s. And it's almost as dramatic. The adaptation today is to the connected computer universe. . . . It remains to be seen how well our senior management is tuned to that. I have some concerns. We have a number of people that were very competent in

305

the second epoch of Intel. Right now the [company's] actions are not convincingly in tune with the new epoch.

An exchange with Sean Maloney, senior vice president and general manager of sales and marketing showed that Grove still had doubts about Intel's understanding of the new world of a billion connected computers:

> GROVE: [to Maloney] What percentage of ESM [Executive Staff Management] would you say gets it?
> MALONEY: I would say a majority of ESM now gets it.
> GROVE [shaking his head in disagreement]: If by a majority you mean 51 percent then I agree with you.

Grove himself had felt compelled to become more educated in the Internet area and he had begun meeting with a wide range of successful Internet companies to better understand their businesses and financial models. Speaking to Intel's top management team in mid-1999, Grove encouraged them to expand their expertise as well, telling them: "There is lots of expertise and knowledge here. Most of us are engineers by training and one thing we know is how to learn. You need to go out in your own space and learn everything you can about this new environment."

New Strategic Vision: The Internet Building Block Company

By early 1999, Craig Barrett had articulated his strategic vision for Epoch III. At a meeting of Intel's top management, he described Intel's strategy to become the "building block supplier to the Internet economy" by focusing on four areas: client platforms, server platforms, networking infrastructure, and solutions and services. Barrett said: "The world changes and the center of gravity shifts. We need to shift with it. We want to be the center of gravity in each of these four areas."

Barrett realized that Intel faced the challenge of maintaining the strategy vector created by Andy Grove during Epoch II: Intel needed to continue exploiting growth opportunities in its core microprocessor and related products business, servers in particular. Intel also needed to extend the strategy vector by further developing its networking business, and capitalizing on the role of its Flash memory business in the fast-growing wireless communications industry. Solutions and services were a further extension of Intel's strategy vector into new businesses. For Barrett this strategy was closely tied to the vision of a billion connected computers.

Strategic Challenges in Epoch III

Slowing growth in the client market segment. At the time of the CEO transition, there were some signs of a slow down in the steep revenue and profit growth trajectories of Intel's core business. At the end of 1998, Intel's revenue had grown only 5 percent to $26.3 billion, after 20 percent growth in 1997. Intel's net profit growth rate had declined over the last few years: from 56 percent in 1995 and 45 percent in 1996 to 35 percent in 1997. In 1998, net profit actually declined 13 percent to $6.1 billion. Intel's gross margin percentage fell in '98 to 54 percent, from 60 percent in '97 and 56 percent in '96. On the positive side, Intel generated $9.2 billion in cash during 1998, and its market capitalization exceeded $200 billion for the first time.

Some analysts were predicting annual PC sales to peak at around 100 million units, only slightly higher than 1999 levels.[1] This posed a serious challenge for Intel's future profitable growth. Intel's profitable growth depended on three factors: (1) the number of PCs sold, (2) the share of Intel products in the total value of a PC, and (3) market segment share. In 1999, Intel could not expect to grow market share much in the PC market segment. As the share of low-end PCs grew, it was also difficult for Intel to grow the absolute number of dollars it could expect to gain from every PC sold. Finally, slowing of overall PC market segment growth would limit the incremental number of units that Intel could expect to sell above current volumes.

Good news and bad news. In early 2000, Intel surprised analysts with unexpectedly strong fourth-quarter earnings.[2] Demand was reportedly strong across all product lines and all geographies. For 1999, Intel reported revenue of $29.4 billion, up 12 percent from $26.3 billion a year earlier. Net profit was $7.3 billion, up 21 percent from $6.1 billion a year earlier. The company's optimistic outlook was reflected in its plans to spend $5 billion on capital investment during 2000, compared to $3.5 billion in 1999; and $3.8 billion on R&D, compared to $3.1 billion in 1999. It was also reflected in the company's stock price, which had again passed the $100 mark after a two-for-one stock split during 1999. Yet another stock split was planned for mid-2000. September 2000, however, brought bad news for Intel's core business.[3] Intel's warning that third-quarter revenues would be lower than expected sent the company's stock down precipitously. This surprise revived fears that growth in the PC market segment might be slowing down and raised questions about Intel's ability to drive, and therefore predict, demand for new PCs. Within a period of five weeks, Intel's stock was down by more than 45 percent, ceding thereby its second place in market capitalization to Cisco Systems. At the same time, AMD continued to do much better beating analysts' expectation for the third quarter of 2000. AMD reportedly did better because the company focuses on the consumer market segment, which remained strong. Intel, on the other hand, suffered from sluggish demand in the corporate market segment.[4]

MAINTAINING THE STRATEGY VECTOR

Several developments in the PC market segment had the potential of changing the harmonious relationships among the dynamic forces that had made it possible for Intel to drive the evolution of the PC market segment during Epoch II.

Evolving Basis of Competitive Advantage in the PC Market Segment

Increased competition in the client market segment. In February 1999, AMD introduced its K6–III processor—the Athlon—a rival to the Pentium III processor. AMD had dramatically reduced its time-to-market disadvantage—in earlier years it had taken AMD as long as four years to match Intel's new product releases. The Athlon processor, for the first time, attacked Intel at the high-end and competed for the bragging rights of the fastest processor. AMD beat Intel to market with the first 1-gigahertz (1GHz) chip. AMD's Athlon processor affected Intel's pricing of high-end microprocessors. Industry observers noted that Intel's most expensive chips used to be introduced at around $1,000 to $1,900, but that in January 2000 Intel brought out its 800-Megahertz Pentium III Xeon processor at $901. Average microprocessor prices in the fourth quarter of 1999 were $191, down from $220 a year earlier.[5] In spring 2001, AMD also challenged Intel in the mobile market segment with its Athlon 4 processor, which it planned to sell for $425 against Intel's comparable Pentium III. Some observers believed that this move would extend the price war going on in the desktop segment into the mobile one.[6]

Ongoing sideshows. In June 1999, National Semiconductor announced that Cyrix would be acquired by Via Technologies, a Taiwanese developer of chipsets that already had a clone of Intel's Celeron processor in development. It was unclear what the future competitive consequences of this acquisition would be for Intel. On the RISC side, Apple Computer had regained some market segment share with its PowerPC-based iMac product line, but in 1999 it remained to be seen how much more unit market segment share it would be able to regain. By September 2000 it seemed that Apple's resurgence had stalled.[7]

Emergence of new competitors. In early 2000, another renewed RISC threat was emerging from Transmeta, a well-funded start-up company that announced a radically new microprocessor design that consumed substantially less power, was less costly to manufacture, and was compatible with Intel's chips. Transmeta's chips promised to be especially competitive in the mobile Internet computing market. The company reportedly had received IBM's commitment to manufacture the new chips.[8]

Relationship with OEM customers. At the start of Epoch III, the dependence of the OEMs on Intel was still very high, yet perceived by Intel as less antagonistic. In summer 1997, Albert Yu had already observed that the relationships with the OEMs had improved over the past several years. He said:

> Dell has perfected the no inventory model. Other vendors such as Compaq have moved toward that model to compete more effectively. Previously, OEMs such as Compaq were overwhelmed by Intel's propensity to continually force new product introductions—which is a problem for vendors carrying considerable inventory.
>
> So their reluctance to bring out new processors is less. Everybody now wants to be the first mover! Our new product ramp is much faster now. Most recently, it took less than 12 months to convert everything; that compares to two-and-a-half years for the conversion from the 486 to the Pentium processor.

Relationship with complementors. Though the so-called Wintel alliance remained strong, Intel's relationship with Microsoft was changing too. On the low-end, Microsoft had released Windows CE, which targeted handheld PCs and other information appliances. Unlike other versions of Windows, Microsoft initially ported Windows CE to several non-Intel processors. On the high end, Intel's future IA-64 processors were designed to work not only with Microsoft Windows NT but also with each of the major versions of Unix and the emerging Linux operating system. Underscoring the continued importance of Microsoft for Intel's microprocessor strategy in the PC market segment, however, it was expected that the introduction of Windows 2000 in early 2000 would boost demand for Intel's products.

Besides working closely with Microsoft, Intel continued to develop its own ecosystem. The company worked actively with numerous development partners, providing them early access to new technologies, so that Intel's new microprocessors would have strong applications that supported them at launch. Intel also used venture capital investments made by its Corporate Business Development Group to help develop the PC industry in new directions consistent with the objectives of its corporate strategy (see below).

The Internet. The Internet was causing revolutionary changes in the computing industry, and these changes presented both threats and opportunities to Intel's core business. In 1999, the primary driver of PC sales was the demand for Internet connectivity. It was widely held that microprocessor power was not important to a user's Internet experience, and this trend threatened to devalue desktop processing power. But there was a potential opportunity for Intel as well. The Internet caused more processing power to be needed in high-end servers that distributed content and processed online transactions, and this was a potential growth market for high-end Intel processors.

Intense competition in the server market segment. The potentially lower growth potential in the client market segment raised the strategic importance of the server market segment for Intel's future growth. However, in the high end of the server market segment, Intel faced stiff competition from the established RISC/UNIX systems from Sun, IBM, HP, SGI, and others. Despite gains by Windows NT and Intel systems in the low end of the workstation and server markets, these RISC/UNIX systems continued to hold market share on the high end. Sun Microsystems was perceived by many as the leader in the Internet server segment. During the late-1990s Sun had transformed itself from a workstation OEM to a leading Internet server company. Sun had adopted a vertical strategy, selling only servers that were integrated with its Solaris operating system. In an MBA class discussion at Stanford in fall 1999, Andy Grove said that Sun had replaced AMD as Intel's most dangerous competitor. Grove was respectful of Sun's highly focused strategy. In early 2000, Sun was still gaining market share against less focused IBM and Hewlett-Packard.

Digital appliances: The real disruptive technology? The market for digital appliances, such as cell phones, handheld computers, cable TV set top boxes, automobile PCs, and game consoles such as Sony's Playstation II, was rapidly taking shape in 1999. These products were relatively inexpensive, and generally required processors that cost around $20 or $30. To the extent that these devices would begin to support functions that had hitherto been performed on PCs, they might substitute for PCs for a significant number of end users.

Corporate Strategy: Increased Complexity

In response to greater market segmentation in the computing industry, Intel revamped its product-market strategy with new products and brands in each of the major market segments. The Intel Celeron processor was targeted at the low-cost, entry-level part of the PC market segment. The Pentium II and Pentium III processors were targeted at high-performance PCs and entry-level servers and workstations. And the Pentium II Xeon and Pentium III Xeon processors were targeted at mid-range and high-end servers and workstations. All of these processors were derivatives of Intel's P6 (Pentium Pro) architecture. This segmentation strategy allowed Intel to maintain a huge pricing range, with Celeron processors selling for about $63 each and high-end Pentium Xeon processors selling for about $3,700 each.[9] The strategy had also helped sustain Intel's historical average sales price for microprocessors slightly below $200. Finally, the strategy made it more difficult for competitors to pursue niche strategies by exploiting holes in Intel's product line.

Client platform strategy. Intel's Pentium II and Pentium III microprocessors remained the core of Intel's business. The Pentium II was Intel's largest volume microprocessor in 1998. In February 1999, Intel launched the Pentium III microprocessor, which the company positioned as ideal for Internet users. The Celeron microprocessor, introduced in April 1998, was optimized to reduce manufacturing costs. Celeron was priced more aggressively than the Pentium processors, and it had helped Intel recoup market segment share losses on the low end. According to Paul Otellini, in early 1999: "We've made a lot of progress on the low end. One year ago in the sub-$1,000 market segment, our share was about 38 percent. We then lost some ground, but we have regained share so we're at about 38 percent again."

Intel also developed specialized versions of its microprocessors that were targeted at the mobile computing market segment. These processors were modified versions of the Celeron, Pentium II, and Pentium III processors, but had lower power consumption and size requirements compared to the standard processors.

Server platform strategy. On the high end, Intel was increasingly targeting the computers that ran corporate data centers and the World Wide Web. The company believed it could establish a standard processor design in this segment, much like it had years earlier in the market for PCs, and more recently in the market for workstations and entry-level servers. The Pentium II Xeon microprocessors targeted at this market segment offered improvements in performance, reliability, and security, and were designed for use in multiprocessor systems. In 1999, 50 percent of Intel's development dollars were being spent on servers and workstations, despite the revenues in these segments being much less than 50 percent.

Intel faced challenges in penetrating the high-end market segment. Intel had worked with Hewlett-Packard on defining the architecture for a new family of 64-bit microprocessors. Intel owned the chip and was planning on making it available to all OEMs at the high end. The first member of the family, Merced, had been delayed several times, however. As a result of the delays with Merced, Hewlett-Packard and SGI had both decided to extend the lives of their own chip architectures. According to Paul Otellini. "Overreach is our biggest challenge. We were working on the IA–64, the Xeon processor, and 8-way systems [a single system that uses eight microprocessors] but were running behind schedule. We're moving this forward, but we've encountered technical challenges. This is truly rocket science, and there are very few companies who do this well."

Internet strategy. In early 1999, Paul Otellini said that in spite of the gloom and doom scenario of end users not needing anything more than a 500 MHz Celeron processor to browse the Internet, he was optimistic about future needs for microprocessor performance. He said that the Pentium processor had represented a step function relative to previous generations because of Windows 95, and he thought that another step function was now ahead. Situating Intel's broad strategy for the Intel Architecture in relation to the Internet, Otellini said: "In the Internet hardware space there are three activities: viewing things, creating content, and sharing content. To create content you use workstations, and we're developing a class of machines for creating highly analytical and visual content. To share content, you use servers. To view things, we're coordinating the activities of Leglise (appliances), Gelsinger (desktop) and mobile."

Otellini further pointed out that "There is an architectural advantage to homogeneity across these three areas of activity." He also emphasized that the client-server dichotomy was not the right one, and that Intel did not want to be locked into the client terminology. To communicate and implement his strategy for the Intel Architecture, Otellini said, "I'm doing a major speech a week. If I say it enough times, the message will get through."

From a slightly different strategic angle, however, Intel was concerned that it was not perceived as a central force in the Internet world. According to Renee James, former technical assistant to Andy Grove, in 1999: "We have struggled for the last two years with how to make an impact on the Internet. . . . This is one of Intel's biggest long-term strategic challenges. There has been a view that the Internet is happening without us." Having missed the opportunity to exert first generation leadership in the Internet world, Intel was looking for ways to catch up fast and to be perceived as a key player.

Digital appliances strategy. Intel competed in digital appliances with Pentium and Celeron processors, as well as with StrongArm processors. The Pentium processors targeted at these segments were generally several generations old. StrongArm, acquired as part of a legal settlement with Digital Equipment Corporation, was noted for its high performance, its low power consumption, and—with a price between $21 and $33 in volume—its low price. These characteristics made StrongArm well suited for many applications within this market segment. Some analysts were skeptical about Intel's resolve to compete in the new appliances market. Craig Barrett observed: "Over the next three to five years our main focus will be on traditional computing devices, including more powerful workstations and servers. There may be some overlap, but we still think the main processor market will be for a computer that has the ability to do a wide variety of tasks."[10]

Speaking of the appliance market, Les Vadasz said, "We'll compete, but this is not a major growth area for Intel. There's not that much silicon value and no segment will match the PC in volume. The appliances market will consist of many smaller categories rather than singular winners."

Home Products Group. As noted earlier, Paul Otellini did not want to be locked into the client terminology; but rather wanted the Intel Architecture group to think of devices for viewing content on the Internet. Speaking in this context about Intel's efforts in appliances, Otellini referred to the newly created Home Products Group, which was chartered with making appliances connected to televisions, phones, and cars and was led by Claude Leglise. Otellini said: "There is a quote from Bob Noyce in our lobby that says "Don't be encumbered by the past." I have told Claude that his only constraint is to use the IA, not StrongArm. Our customers prefer IA inside appliances to ensure full web compatibility."

Claude Leglise pointed out that his challenge was to leverage Intel's valuable assets while protecting his staff from some of the liabilities. The assets such as Intel's silicon and software expertise are very valuable, he said, and some of the liabilities are obvious whereas others are subtle. Because everybody at Intel is thinking PC, Leglise observed, some of the marketing processes and the PC OEM orientation of the sales force can make things difficult. For example, he said, he was expected to talk to the PC OEMs, which have little that is useful to the Home Products Group. Instead he wanted his people to call on telecom companies. Leglise felt that "the gravity of the organization is strong." On balance, however, he believed that with Barrett as CEO, things were getting easier for new business development that was not strictly PC related. In January 2000, the Home Products

Group announced its first products, a line of Intel-branded web devices. Leglise said: "We are targeting the whole half of the [U.S.] population that doesn't have a personal computer as well as the gadget lovers." [11]

Intel's web devices emphasized ease of use, low cost, and quick access to the Internet. They came with a screen, a browser, and the Linux operating system and used Intel's Celeron processor. They attached to a phone and were phonelike in appearance and use. They were expected to ship by the middle of 2000.

Impact on OEM relationships. Intel's appliance strategy had potentially important implications for several key factors associated with the core microprocessor strategy. First, Andy Grove believed that Pentium rather than Intel was the relevant brand name in the microprocessor business (personal communication). With the appliance strategy, however, it seemed that Intel was the brand name. According to Leglise: "We think the Intel brand will mean a lot to consumers worldwide in this space, since consumers see Intel as representing good technology and safe, reliable products." [12]

Also, selling complete products under its own brand name represented a shift away from Intel's Epoch II strategy of enabling the industry. Frank Gill, former executive vice president, underscored the importance of this shift: "We [Andy Grove and corporate PR] even convinced the press that we weren't in business for the sake of anything except to enable more Pentium processors."

Impact on Microsoft relationship. Claude Leglise reportedly said that Intel was using the Linux operating system, a free variant of Unix, because customers requested it. [13] This further distanced Intel from Microsoft and its efforts to establish Windows CE as the dominant operating system in the emerging appliance market segment (using non-Intel Architecture processors).

Intel Architecture or Strong Arm? Consistent with Paul Otellini's guidelines, Leglise's line of web devices used the Celeron processor. Intel anticipated that for other devices, in particular portable ones needing low-power consumption, the StrongArm processor might be the appropriate choice. StrongArm had been absorbed in Ron Smith's Computer Enhancement Group, which also contained other RISC processors and embedded IA processors. Craig Barrett saw no reason for internal rivalry between the two microprocessor architectures:

> People try to raise this as a religious argument. It's IA on the desktop and StrongArm in low power, handheld, or other areas with interesting I/O characteristics. . . . We basically let the customers decide. To a large extent, this is for the OEMs to decide.
>
> One thing I want to do is to knock down the walls of religious wars.

The thought of pushing another architecture, for anything, has met with some resistance.

Strategic Action: Execution Issues

Managing increased complexity. The new product-market strategy entailed far greater organizational complexity. Paul Otellini, executive vice president and general manager of the Intel Architecture Business Group, who, except for a stint as director of the sales and marketing organization during 1994–98, spent most of his 25 years at Intel with the microprocessor business, explained:

> When I left for Sales, we didn't have vertical product groups. We then created the server, mobile, and desktop groups. . . . The vertical groups had no development. Their job is product definition, design wins, industry enabling, and customer relations. They all reported to the Executive Staff. Without the verticals, we wouldn't have had the segmentation strategy. So, that was a good outcome. [But] running the Field [sales force] this drove me bananas. The different verticals would all say different things to the same customer. They would each independently go to Albert [Yu, general manager of the Microprocessor Group] and ask him to incorporate the features that benefited their vertical.

Otellini also pointed out, however, that the market segmentation was part of a natural evolution and simply raised a new management challenge: "It's analogous to comparing (Ford's) Model T to automobiles today, when we have sport utility vehicles, compact cars, luxury cars, etc. It's a natural progression for PCs. Eventually you'll buy exactly what you need."

To develop a product-market strategy that meets the end users' desire to buy exactly what they need, Otellini believed, required a supply capability where you can build to order (like Dell), a knowledgeable end-user base and knowledge about the end users, and critical volume in each market segment. Elaborating on the process that he had put in place to manage the increased complexity of the interface with the microprocessor group and the chipset group, Paul Otellini said in 1999: "During the last nine months we've put in place the processes to better support the verticals. We want to keep the energy of the verticals. But there is a structured process in place for the overall product road map and for resource utilization. We all agreed it was time to bring things together to provide a common voice to customers and a common prioritization process to the development agencies."

Execution glitches. During the third quarter of 2000, Intel had to recall some chips because of design flaws and chipset problems. More bad news came when Intel announced that it had canceled plans for a new low-end chip code-named Timna, which could again give AMD the opportunity to gain market segment share at the low end with its new Duron processor. The bad news was further compounded by the announcement that the introduction of the next-generation processor, the Pentium 4, would be delayed. Several of Intel's problems were reportedly related to its efforts to get the PC market segment to adopt a new memory technology developed by Rambus, a small innovative memory design company. This memory technology turned out to be too expensive and was falling behind in performance relative to other types of memory products.[14] Intel also delayed introduction of the Itanium processor, jointly developed with Hewlett Packard, which hampered its ability to meet the competitive challenges at the high-end of the server market segment.

Evolving Distinctive Competencies

Design and product development. According to Andy Grove, "Intel has pursued a technology-driven strategy, which we've executed relentlessly." In 1998, Intel spent $2.7 billion for R&D, up from $2.3 billion in '97 and $1.8 billion in '96. Intel's R&D spending allowed it to design multiple generations of new microprocessors concurrently. In 1998 and 1999, Intel continued its tremendous pace of product development. In 1999, revisiting the perspective he had shared ten years earlier, Gordon Moore spoke again about the future applicability of Moore's Law and the industry's ability to continue making technology advancements and linewidth reductions:

> We can still see 12 years down the road. I can generally see three to four generations ahead. Beyond that, it always looks like we will hit a wall, but we've been fortunate so far. As we move along, because of the physics of semiconductors, we will eventually hit one. Matter is made of atoms, and eventually we'll reach the limit of what the technology can do. It's amazing that the technology has been able to go this far . . . I think we'll move on more or less the same curve until about 2010 or 2020. Then we'll be approaching the limits of the atomic nature of matter. It will take a tremendous investment in technology to continue the advance.

Staying ahead of the industry. One of Intel's distinctive competencies in the product and technology area was its ability to learn fast about the needs of the end users. Albert Yu said Intel talked to end users all the time, as well as to the OEMs and people in the software industry. He also explained why Intel could stay ahead relative to the rest of the industry:

> Dell, Compaq, and other OEMs have a huge amount of data about end users. But it is historical data. We focus on the future needs. So you must listen to data, yet make up your own mind. For instance, you cannot get information about visual computing from Dell's customers. You must find that out yourself. You must consider what is possible; you must smell it. Andy (Grove) does this. He goes out; he makes observations. We do the same thing. This makes our job interesting. For instance, what does it mean for Intel that bandwidth is expanding?

Albert Yu explained that his components marketing people (in MPG) worked closely with the platform marketing people (in Otellini's vertical product groups). Referring to the conflicts that could arise between the three vertical product groups and the interface issues this created, he said:

> The components marketing people try to figure out the microprocessor needs for the three business groups; we don't want to have three different ones. The platform marketing people, on the other hand, look at the whole system. They often seek features that fit the needs of their product and customers. Each group has slightly different wants and needs. The component marketers often act as the arbitrators. An example of the trade-offs involved is performance versus power consumption. Note-books (mobile) need to conserve power, whereas desktops are concerned primarily with speed. Minor engineering tweaks and features can often help tailor solutions to such issues; however, trade-offs must be continu-ally made. There are zillions of issues like these. This is very compli-cated. It requires good teamwork. And it is becoming more important as the market continues to segment.

32-bit and 64-bit Intel architectures. While several times delayed, the 64-bit Merced was expected to be available in sample volumes in late 1999 and initial production volumes in mid-2000. Albert Yu pointed out that Merced would be backward compatible with IA-32 applications. He viewed IA-64 having major ad-vantages over RISC in the server market segment. Yu felt that Intel had won the RISC versus CISC battle at the desktop and that the IA-64 would win the server platform. Yu also felt that the 32-bit and 64-bit Intel Architectures would continue to be developed in parallel for years to come, because "The desktop will stay 32 bit until it has more than 32 gigabytes of RAM."

Technology and manufacturing. Intel's distinctive competency in integrating advanced microprocessor designs (done by MPG) and manufacturing (done by TMG) continued to be an important source of competitive advantage. Intel continued to invest heavily in state-of-the-art manufacturing facilities, spending $4 billion on capital additions in 1998, compared to $4.5 billion in '97 and $3.0 billion in '96. Intel was renowned for its ability to manufacture its chip designs, and continued the practice of optimizing the manufacturing process for a given chip, and then rolling out that process to Intel's other fabs with the Copy Exact process. Andy Bryant, Intel's CFO, underscored that Intel's ability to reduce costs continued to be a function of its distinctive competencies in process technology (linewidth reduction) and the transfer of new process technology into manufacturing: "The company managed to bring its costs down during the quarter as it shifted production to factories that can create circuitry at finer dimensions, resulting in smaller chips, higher manufacturing yields, and lower material costs. That also allowed Intel to build chips at higher speeds, resulting in a small increase in average microprocessor prices." [15]

AMD had often come up with microprocessor designs that theoretically matched Intel's performance, only to fall short in the transition from the lab to the factory floor.

Sales and marketing. International markets had relatively low PC penetration and were viewed by Intel as an area of major potential growth. In 1998, more than 50 percent of Intel sales were outside the United States. Craig Barrett had focused significant effort on growing international sales, opening new sales offices in a number of countries. Some senior executives, however, felt that Intel would have to redefine the mostly tactical role of its geographical organizations. One senior executive characterized this as the "just do it" mentality, which he felt was pervasive in the U.S.-based product organizations.

During Epoch II, Intel's outbound marketing efforts had become a key driver of its microprocessor business. Since launching the Intel Inside campaign in 1991, Intel had invested heavily in marketing, advertising, and promotions. For the Pentium III processor launch in early 1999, Intel spent about $300 million in advertising, more than double its investment on any previous chip launch. [16] Intel's technology leadership and time-to-market advantage allowed the company to recoup its R&D investments. Intel's practice was to aggressively reduce prices over time, especially as competitive products were introduced, which allowed the company to maintain market segment share and stimulate market growth. This pricing strategy continued to put enormous pressure on Intel competitors.

Developing a corporate venture capital competency: The role of CBD. Throughout the 1990s, Intel developed a strong competency in corporate venture capital, which resided in its Corporate Business Development Group (CBD) led by Les Vadasz. CBD's main role was to support the development of Intel's ecosystem by acquiring or making equity investments in strategic companies. Initially, CBD invested in companies that developed technologies that were important to Intel, such as makers of certain types of chips, equipment manufacturers, and certain types of software to support chip design. During the mid- and late-1990s, CBD invested more in companies that produced applications that helped fuel demand for high-end PCs, such as three-dimensional graphics chips. CBD also invested in broadband communications and Internet companies. Since 1996, Intel had invested about $2.5 billion in some 200 companies, making it one of the largest venture capital firms in the United States. Discussing Intel's objectives, Les Vadasz said: "You judge your success on how you met your strategic goals, and count the money later." [17]

During 1998 and 1999, CBD made some serious money for Intel. The *Wall Street Journal* reported that Intel's portfolio at the end of 1999 was worth $8.2 billion and comprised 350 companies, compared to only $500 million and 50 companies at the end of 1997. Major successes in the software space included VA Linux and Red Hat Software. Some notable success stories in the Internet space included Inktomi, Broadcom, eToys, and Broadcast.com. [18] Les Vadasz, senior vice president and director of CBD commented in 1999: "CBD seeks to accelerate the creation of new market ecosystems, in part by using our financial resources. . . . [For example], we've made a number of investments in hardware and software companies to accelerate their plans to adapt their products to the new Intel platforms."

By 1999, CBD was also making significant investments in Asia, Europe, and Latin America to support Intel's international growth objectives. In May 1999, Intel established a $250 million venture fund targeted at hardware and software companies that supported its next generation 64-bit architecture.

EXTENDING THE STRATEGY VECTOR

Strategy and Action in the Networking Business

By 1999, despite its slow start, networking had become a sizable and strategic business for Intel, with sales of approximately $1.2 billion. Since 1991, Intel's networking business had grown 58 percent per year and was expected to grow another 75 percent in 1999. Building on Frank Gill's successful strategic-forcing efforts during the early to mid-1990s, Mark Christensen, vice president and general manager of the Network Communications Group (NCG), was finally able to determine the strategic context for networking within Intel in 1997. This had put the full support of the corporation behind the networking business and had made it possible to engage in strategic building efforts, involving major acquisitions, to rapidly grow the business. Christensen said: "Craig came up with the creosote bush image to illustrate to the company the challenge of trying to grow new businesses in one of the most highly successful companies of all time.[19] He encouraged people to develop new businesses rather than just supporting Job 1. The creosote bush was deep here . . . [but] we've gotten lots of support from Craig and have now made significant progress in growing several new areas."

Growth through acquisitions. Acquisitions had become a central aspect of Intel's growth strategy in the networking business. This was a major departure from tradition for Intel. According to Mark Christensen:

> Around 1996, we said that we needed to do acquisitions, but this was very painful since the internal view was that any acquisition would fail due to the strong culture of Intel. But, we convinced the board of directors, Andy, and Craig that we could do them successfully. Since then, we have continued to get a lot of support from Craig and Andy and we have now done seven or eight acquisitions with very good results thus far. It remains a critical element of our growth strategy.

After the Level One acquisition, CNET quoted Craig Barrett: "We're continuing to look for other acquisition candidates. We are deadly serious about our networking communications group."[20] Other acquisitions in 1999 included Softcom Microsystems for $149 million, NetBoost for $215 million, and the telecom chips group of Stanford Telecommunications (price not disclosed).

In typical Intel style, a large capability was created as part of CBD to focus on the preacquisition and postacquisition integration issues and processes. The support infrastructure had been very helpful. Christensen was pleased that he had been able to keep the CEOs and the management teams of the various acquired companies and integrate them into Intel. This was a nontrivial achievement because Intel's track record in retaining senior executives from the outside had been quite poor. This had been a by-product of Intel's strong culture in which influence power with peers was earned over a long period of time. Ron Smith, who had just been instrumental in acquiring DSP Communications (see below), said that networking's example had helped "set the table for us" and that Intel now realized it had to "learn to adapt to new faces." Christensen said he wanted the teams of the acquired companies to continue running their business and saw his own role as "strategist, recruiter, acquirer, the 'grease' internally; and the visionary communicator externally."

Delineating Intel's strategic position in the networking business. Intel had identified four market segments in which it could grow the networking business, each of which needed a targeted approach: home networking, network adapters, small to medium-size systems for business, and communications silicon. According to Mark Christensen: "Looking forward, every segment that we play in is different. We have different competitors, different channels, different customers, etc. We're taking a targeted, segment-by-segment approach, and we've developed a unique strategy for each of these segments."

Network processors: A new horizontal vision. In early 1999, Craig Barrett had discussed the charter of NCG:

> The charter of Christensen is to be the silicon building block supplier, not just to the LAN, but also to the WAN, and to also be a network building block supplier to the home and small business. This ties into the vision of a billion connected computers. We want to have the hearts and brains of the clients, servers, and some of the networking components. We're not into competing with the Ciscos and Nortels. . . . We want to supply the Nortels, Ciscos, Lucents, etc. with building blocks.

Nevertheless, Intel's advances in the communications silicon market segment had in some ways complicated the company's relationship with Cisco. Intel's approach was to leverage its own strengths in silicon, OEM channels, and consumer brand awareness, and to avoid competing directly in the enterprise market where Cisco's strengths in direct sales to large accounts and servicing of end users were advantages. Mark Christensen said: "Intel's networking business draws on Intel's core competencies as a hardware company. . . . Cisco is basically a software company with some hardware wrapped around to protect them. Cisco doesn't want to be on the client side. They sold us the Granite chip when they acquired Granite. We became partners with them for the gigabit chip and added proprietary Cisco features to it."

Barrett's and Christensen's vision for the horizontalization of the networking industry, however, had the potential for a clash of the titans. Barrett said:

> Look at the big picture of what's happening in that market. . . . Networking will experience the same transition that the computer industry experienced, from a vertical orientation to a horizontal orientation, and to standard interfaces and building blocks. We're already seeing the first inklings of this as voice and data collide. Today everyone has a proprietary solution. I think this will transition to a horizontal structure, and I want to be the building block supplier. Rather than everyone having their own architecture, there will be a standard architecture, standard interfaces, and standard silicon building blocks. There's a huge possibility that we can be the leading building block supplier.

He added:

> The voice communication people are taking a serious look at how they're competing looking forward. I believe that this is a case of the irresistible force meeting the movable object.

Intel thus anticipated the convergence of networking equipment and servers and the horizontalization of the industry into distinct component layers, similar to what happened in the PC industry. Being the only major player present in both networking and servers, Intel saw itself as uniquely well positioned to become a supplier of network processors to all major OEMs in the new horizontal industry. But this would not be an easy task. Networking companies understood well the history of the PC industry. In addition, the Intel brand was associated with the computer products, not networking products per se. Ultimately, the irresistible force would have to come from the power of general-purpose network microprocessor technology to produce greater than 10X improvements in price/performance and the ability of Intel to provide complete products based on a new class of network processors. It remained to be seen whether the story of Intel in the computer industry could be repeated in the networking industry.

Strategy and Action in Flash Memory and Wireless Communications

While the strategic context of Flash had been determined in the late 1980s, its position as a quasi-commodity memory product within Intel had always been somewhat precarious. Craig Barrett, who had been a supporter of Flash within Intel's top management, said that there was some synergy between Flash and the microprocessor technology, but that there were a lot of differences as well. He thought Flash could be an important component of PC cellular phones. "But, in the end," he said, "they each have to stand on their own merits."

The Computer Enhancement Group. In 1999, Flash was part of the Computer Enhancement Group lead by Ron Smith. This group had been reorganized right before Christmas 1999. Smith was made general manager of the new Wireless Computing and Communications Group. Wireless communication was really a hybrid of Intel's core business and a new business. It used, among other building blocks, Flash memory, the StrongArm microprocessor, chips from recently acquired DSP Communications, as well as new software. In early 2000, Smith reflected on the prospects of Flash:

> Even last year, there were questions about why we are in this. Craig had the foresight to stay in it. Previous managers—who had been former CFOs—wanted to use it to generate cash. When I came in (a few years ago), I wanted to make it a growth deal. We didn't have competitive technology nor competitive manufacturing at the time. So, I said we must become state-of-the art. We must invest. And we did! But then the market cratered and the finance people wanted us to exit.

Continuing, Smith said:

> But we stuck to the knitting. Because of favorable supply-demand conditions we could raise prices. So within one year, we went from being zero to one. We grew faster than the rest of Intel. Now, the CFO says what a great business! We still compete for capacity within Intel. People still raise questions, but they have to do with the growth and not with the viability.

Smith explained that Flash had become a "strategic capability" for wireless communication devices, for instance to store protocols. He said: "Flash has become a major ingredient in cellular phones and palm devices. It is a beachhead (for developing new businesses). Smith saw Flash as a vehicle for strategic-forcing and strategic-building efforts to develop a new business for Intel in wireless communications. Smith said:

> Most cellular activities now report to me. As wireless moves from voice to data and the wireless Internet, we have the opportunity to be a major building block supplier, even though we don't want to do cellular phones. In October 1999, we acquired DSP Communications [a communications chip company] for $1.6 billion. The opportunity is huge. Last year 265 million wireless phones were sold. And the market is growing 40 percent per year. Intel wants to become big in this space.

INTEL'S NEW TRANSFORMATION

Sharpening the New Vision

By mid-2000, Andy Grove had gained several insights that were guiding Intel's strategy as the Internet building block company. He noted that "the Internet runs on silicon," and that Intel must "follow the bits." This means that: "Intel must have tentacles in every nook and cranny of the Internet . . . and put as [many] silicon chips as possible along the bit path . . . but without competing in the PC space with our traditional OEM customers."

Grove noted that this expansion of Intel's product scope required different microprocessor design principles and that it was now necessary for Intel to acquire some of the associated new competencies from the outside. He also observed that Intel had to deal with many new customers—various types of systems integrators, network and communication OEMs, e-business solutions providers, Internet service providers (ISPs), webhosting companies, and application service providers (ASPs). This expansion of product-market scope required the creation of new support programs for the new types of customers. And this, in turn, required changes in the organization because Intel needed the support infrastructure to support the new products.

Not the post-PC era! In a presentation to Stanford MBA students in May 2000, Andy Grove was keen to emphasize that "The Internet era is not the post-PC-era!" Grove pointed out that in contrast to Intel's transformation from memory company into microprocessor company, the old core business was not going away this time.

In fact, the growth of the PC business during 1999 had been the largest since 1995, and PC demand for 2000 looked strong at the time. He explained why he believed that Intel with its strong competencies in silicon had a good chance to continue to be the major driving force in the computer industry: "Silicon cycles are faster than software cycles. Hence, as long as performance matters, silicon will stay ahead."

Grove also thought that wireless data appliances were complementary to the PC and therefore good for Intel. Grove noted, however, that managing the Internet-based transformation would be more difficult for Intel than the transformation from memory company to microprocessor company. He pointed out that the current transformation added workload on top of a robust core business, and that it was not possible this time to redeploy resources from the core business to the new initiatives.

DISCUSSION AND IMPLICATIONS

In early 2001, Intel's core microprocessor strategy remained strong. With the Celeron processor family, the company had successfully responded to the threat of the low-end PC. The Celeron effectively helped protect the margins of Intel's core Pentium brand. It had helped avoid what Andy Grove called the waterfall effect: prices across the entire price structure tumbling as a result of price declines on the low end. Nevertheless, the old tension between specialty products and commodity products had reappeared. As Paul Otellini put it: "There is a tension between the high end and commoditization." On the high end, Intel counted on its new IA-64 architecture to take a major share of the fast-growing and very large server market. Hence, Andy Grove's second law—the last one to get commoditized wins—did still apply. In the server market segment, however, Intel's strategic position was far less strong than in the PC market segment. Intel had also begun to be a player in appliances. Appliances were to some extent a threat because they could become the disruptive technology for PCs. But they were also an opportunity because they gave Intel the opportunity to sell systems products under its own label, thereby leveraging the Intel brand in a potentially major new way. The networking, Flash, and communications businesses were also offering new profitable growth opportunities.

How Can Intel Maintain its Strategy Vector in the PC Market Segment?

Intel's role as driver of the development of the PC market segment during Epoch II came about as the result of several complementary strategic thrusts. These thrusts were not the implementation of a comprehensive *ex ante* formulated strategic plan to take control of the PC market segment. But they did reflect top management's capacity for strategic recognition of the requirements for maintaining the strategy vector and the capacity of Intel's internal selection environment to dynamically maintain alignment between the evolving basis of competition and the company's distinctive competencies and between strategy and action during Epoch II. Analysis using the framework of dynamic forces driving company evolution—Tool I— revealed that Intel faced a more complicated strategic situation at the start of Epoch III than during Epoch II.

Reduced ability to pace the race. Intel was still highly adept at delivering new microprocessor generations to the entire PC market segment, but it was no longer uniquely pacing the race. AMD had been able to regain viability as a competitor when the demand for PCs costing less than $1,000 grew dramatically during 1997 and 1998, which had caught Intel somewhat by surprise. Intel came back strongly with its low-end Celeron processor, but for the first time AMD was able to challenge Intel at the high end of the desktop segment as well as in the mobile segment. At the start of Epoch III Intel had ceased to be a sole-source provider. Intel's product introduction strategy was no longer simply time-paced; it was now also paced by the competitive interactions with AMD.

> **Insight 10.1a.** In dynamic, unregulated environments a sole-source strategy is unlikely to last forever.

> **Insight 10.1b.** Competitive dynamics reduce the possibility to pursue a time-paced product introduction strategy.

Sustained pricing power. On the other hand, Intel still maintained enormous economies of scale and learning against AMD, which gave it the opportunity to continue to use experience curve-based pricing as a competitive weapon. Intel's strategic long-term interests were clearly served by preventing AMD from expanding its market segment share.

Reduced branding power. Intel continued to expend large amounts of resources on sustaining its brand image with end users, but it remained to be seen whether the differentiation from AMD's microprocessors could be sustained in a maturing, increasingly segmenting PC market segment. For instance, while end users might still prefer an Intel processor to an AMD processor, they might not necessarily be willing to pay a significant premium. Also, in a maturing market the branding power of OEMs such as Dell, Compaq, and Hewlett-Packard might gain in relative strength to the Intel brand, thereby potentially decreasing the relative importance of the processor brand in their systems. This would reduce Intel's bargaining power with the OEMs.

> **Insight 10.2.** In maturing consumer market segments, effectively maintaining the differentiation of a component brand is increasingly difficult.

Reduced ability to enable the industry. Intel's successful sole-source strategy during Epoch II gave it the ability to appropriate a large part of the available profits in the PC market segment. PC OEMs had become increasingly dependent on Intel for technological innovation. It was unclear to what extent technologies developed by Intel Architecture Labs (IAL) would continue to establish industry standards for enabling the adoption of new generations of processors by the OEMs. Also, with increasing competition from AMD, microprocessor margins were likely to come down further, potentially leaving more resources with the OEMs and enabling them to innovate at the system level. To gain more control over their own destiny it was clearly in the strategic interests of the OEMs to try to help AMD be a viable competitor against Intel.

> **Insight 10.3a.** In maturing market segments, there is less room for a dominant component supplier to enable the industry with new technological industry standards.

> **Insight 10.3b.** Given the opportunity, OEM customers will try to reduce their dependency on a single-source supplier.

Sustained advantage of vertical integration. Intel's vertical integration into chipsets and motherboards had also played a major role during Epoch II. This provided the company with the opportunity to enable OEM customers who did not have the resources to develop these system-level products to introduce PCs with Intel's latest microprocessors. This in turn was helpful in reducing its dependency on the stronger OEMs in case the latter were reluctant to stay with Intel's road map for developing next-generation microprocessors. Some industry observers believed that Intel's leading chipset business still provided it with a major competitive advantage in launching new processor generations, because it reduced problems of compatibility between various board level components and thus made faster introduction and ramp up possible.[21] It was unlikely that the OEMs would be able to regain control over chipsets, which they had ceded to Intel with the introduction of PCI-based chipsets (see chapter 7). But it was paramount for Intel to avoid further execution glitches with chipsets to maintain this advantage.

Reduced effectiveness of ecosystem investments. During Epoch II, Intel developed internal support groups to help other independent software vendors develop applications requiring high processor power to stimulate demand for its next generation processors. Intel also provided its partners with advance information about its next microprocessor designs and support products. In addition, Intel's CBD made many equity investments in external start-up companies developing promising technologies for growing the demand for microprocessor power-hungry PCs. While developing the ecosystem for the Intel Architecture advanced the strategic position Intel held against other architectures, it also potentially benefited AMD's processors.

> **Insight 10.4.** In a competitive industry, investments in ecosystem development may also benefit competitors.

Implications. At the start of Epoch III, changes in the external selection environment had significantly changed the basis of competitive advantage in the PC market segment. Some of these changes were mostly outside of Intel's control. Most important for future growth was the continued demand for PCs. From a global perspective, there seemed to be still enormous room for growth. The rate at which that growth would come, however, remained unclear. Most important for future profitability was the continued demand for more powerful microprocessors. This too was unclear even though so far consumers and corporations had continued to buy increasingly higher powered PCs. It was also unclear to what extent digital appliances would be complements or substitutes for PCs, and this too would affect Intel's profitable growth prospects.

By mid-2000, Andy Grove's view that Epoch III was not the post-PC era suggested that the strategy vector of Epoch II would continue to be a strong driver of Intel's strategy-making during Epoch III. Intel would continue to try to develop significant growth opportunities within and adjacent to the PC market segment. Intel, however, was to some extent back to where it was before the sole-source decision for the 386 microprocessor fifteen years earlier. One viable competitor had been able to reassert itself and the PC OEM customers were regaining bargaining power, thereby possibly reducing Intel's potential margins and the resources it could deploy to maintain its strategic dominance. Intel's strategic imperatives in the core business seemed clear. Intel must maintain its technological lead in design and continue to incorporate greater amounts of functionality into its microprocessors to add more value and capture a high percentage of the available industry rents. It must continue to exploit its economies of scale in manufacturing to keep a cost advantage. It needs to use its vertical integration to consistently maintain the lead in product introductions and reap first mover advantages. It must use its pricing power to keep its competitor's market segment share from growing, while restraining itself from actions that could be interpreted as attempts at trying to kill its only viable competitor. If anything, the relentless pace of product introductions was likely to continue. As noted earlier, already in 1997 Craig Barrett realized that Intel was going down the road "at 150 miles per hour and might run into a brick wall." But he also realized that "the worst thing we can do is stop too soon and let somebody else pass us." [22] Even more than during Epoch II, Intel must make sure to execute flawlessly in the PC market segment.

Can Intel Create a Strategy Vector in the Server Market Segment?

In 1999, Intel's internal selection environment was signaling the importance of servers for Intel's future profitable growth by allocating 50 percent of development resources to server development, which far exceeded their share in revenues. Intel had effectively extended its strategy vector in the workstation and entry-level server market segments where it was competing with its Xeon processor family. At the high end of the server market, however, the strategic situation was very different. Here a battle royal loomed between Intel's new IA-64 architecture and those of Sun Microsystems and IBM. Intel needed badly to be able to start that battle and had been hampered by multiple delays. It was unclear whether Intel would be able to decisively beat the alternative architectures in the high-end Unix market segment, which was expected to remain about 30 percent of the server market segment and the source of the highest available margins in the foreseeable future. Clearly dominating this market segment had to be one of Intel's top strategic priorities for the next three to five years.

Can Intel Extend its Strategy Vector in the Networking Business?

Not surprisingly, Intel's strategy in the networking business, as in the computer industry, was predicated on industry horizontalization. Intel was counting on the possibility to develop a network processor architecture with price/performance advances that would inexorably lead to the breakup of proprietary vertical systems offered by players such as Cisco, Lucent, Nortel, and others. While this strategic approach was highly aligned with Intel's distinctive competencies, it also provided further evidence of the powerful inertial forces associated with strategic success.

> **Insight 10.5.** Top management is likely to cast new business opportunities in terms of the strategy that they have deployed successfully in the company's core business.

Even if inexorable technological forces will engender the development of a new class of network processors as envisioned by Craig Barrett, it will be important to manage the relationship with prospective customers. These customers might not want to develop the same level of dependency on Intel as the OEMs in the PC market segment. The cable industry, for instance, having observed the situation in the PC market segment, did not allow Microsoft to become the sole-source provider for software for TV set top boxes during the mid-1990s. Intel is likely to face significant challenges in its efforts to extend its strategy vector equally forcefully in the networking business as it has been able to do in the PC market segment.

> **Insight 10.6.** Once a new strategic force such as increasing returns to adoption is widely understood, its potential beneficiaries face increasing resistance from customers to exploiting it.

CONCLUSION

In 2001, the several hundred billion dollar question is, Can Intel continue the Golden Age that Epoch II created? At the start of Epoch III, the alignment between the evolving basis of competition in the PC market segment and Intel's evolving distinctive competencies, and between its official strategy and strategic action, remained strong but no longer as strong as during Epoch II. In the server market segment, the basis of competitive advantage was significantly different from that of the PC market segment, but Intel's IA–64 Itanium processor promised to be a powerful weapon for conquering a large share of that market segment. In the networking and communication businesses, Intel faced customers that would be reluctant to let it become a sole source. While Intel's corporate strategy still seemed directionally right, it could afford even less than before any lapses in execution. In late September 2000, preparing for a discussion of the Intel DRAM case of the mid-1980s with Stanford MBA students, Andy Grove worried about potential parallels with the current strategic situation, noting the various product delays that had hampered Intel's ability to compete effectively in the DRAM business. Intel's success during Epoch II had depended greatly on the discipline that Andy Grove had instilled in the organization. Lifting the organization to the next level of excellence in the discipline of executing a more complicated corporate strategy—maintaining and extending the strategy vector—had to be one of Barrett's main concerns.

11

DESIGNING THE INTERNAL ECOLOGY OF STRATEGY-MAKING

Intel's singular focus on the microprocessor had been a critical factor in the company's extraordinary success during Epoch II. By 1997 then COO Craig Barrett, however, did not believe that Intel could sustain its historical growth rates and profitability solely with microprocessors. According to Barrett: "Microprocessors by themselves will not be the growth engine that they've been in the past."

The Creosote Bush

In spite of Intel's strongly focused induced-strategy process during Epoch II, a surprisingly large number of autonomous strategic initiatives had sprung up throughout the company.[1] Barrett worried, however, that Intel was not able to effectively develop new businesses. As noted earlier (chapter 10), in 1997 he compared Intel's microprocessor business to the creosote bush, a desert plant that poisons the ground around it, preventing other plants from growing nearby. There had been problems even in related new businesses, such as the ProShare videoconferencing venture, because Intel tried to impose the successful core business strategy in a new area where it did not apply. Also, even though much of Intel's R&D investments went into technologies that complemented the microprocessor and thereby offered opportunities to launch other new business units, the company rarely attempted to do so. The reason for this was simple. Any technology advance that enriched the PC environment was likely to enable more demand for microprocessors.

332

Thus, it was generally more profitable for Intel to give away technology and quickly disseminate it in the market, than to try to build a business around it.

In 1998, an internal study had shown that out of fifteen new ventures, the chipset venture had continued to show steady increases in sales and profits. The networking venture had continued to show steady increases in sales but somewhat erratic profit performance. Motherboards had achieved large size (over $2 billion in sales in 1996) but had struggled during the last few years. Flash (about $1 billion in sales in 1996) had also struggled but had good prospects because of the link with the new wireless communications business. The other ventures had remained small and unprofitable, and many seemed ready for triage.[2] In 1999, Andy Grove observed that the successes were in new businesses that were highly predictable from Intel's perspective given its strengths in the core microprocessor business.

Growing the Business Course

Under Barrett's impulse, Intel began to focus on augmenting its new business development capability. In 1997, he commissioned a course on "Growing the Business." During 1997–98, each of the top 400 managers in the company attended a week of classes focused on the process of developing new businesses in established companies. Intel's top management was also exposed to a condensed version of ideas on how to manage new ventures, how to capitalize on disruptive technologies, and how to identify potential beachheads for developing new businesses.[3] The course helped develop a common vocabulary to discuss the issues associated with the company's entrepreneurial capability. As a result of this course, Intel managers began to refer to the core microprocessor business as the "blue" business (managed through the induced strategy process), and to new business ventures as "green" businesses (managed through the autonomous strategy process).

THE NEW BUSINESS GROUP

In response to suggestions by senior executives who had taken the Growing the Business course, Barrett organized many of Intel's green businesses into a single organization, called the New Business Group (NBG). In early 1999, he asked Gerry Parker, one of two executive vice presidents at Intel, to lead the group. Parker recruited senior Intel people throughout the organization. Enthusiasm to join the new effort was very high, especially from managers who had completed the Growing the Business training. According to one of Parker's direct reports,

"Gerry is very process oriented, he's very senior, and he's one of the few people that can effectively manage Craig and Andy. He's working on a process to develop a portfolio of new businesses. He's combining a formula of getting great people, training them, practicing, etc., and he ends up being a lot like the coach on the sidelines."

Describing his approach in general terms, Gerry Parker said: "One of our challenges is to grow revenues. The microprocessor side can take care of itself. To grow in other areas, one extreme is to buy something completely unrelated to our current business. This is not what we want to do. This has forced us to think about where we have competencies and about where there are opportunities. We're focusing on two areas, the Internet and appliances." Parker was highly conscious of the need to maintain good lateral relations with the core business. He kept Paul Otellini informed, for instance, on the use of Linux versus NT in the new ventures. He also said he worked with Sean Maloney, senior vice president and director of sales and marketing, to develop his sales infrastructure.

Big Green: Intel Data Service

In early 1999, Intel announced plans to develop a major Internet hosting service. As part of the plan, Intel would host Web applications and data in huge bit factories—data centers—around the world with thousands of servers. A network of 12 data centers was planned. Mike Aymar, a 25-year Intel veteran, was chosen to lead Intel Data Service (IDS), reporting to Gerry Parker. According to Parker: "Our ideal dream is to host a significant percentage of the world's digital content on our servers, and to be number one or number two in this market."

Renee James, the group's marketing manager, had been instrumental in developing the unit's business plan. As a former technical assistant to Andy Grove, she had been asked to research new business opportunities around the Internet. She had defined the business opportunities, and presented her findings to the top executive team at Intel's strategic long-range planning (SLRP) meeting. James discussed three different opportunities; Internet hosting was one of them, and it got the go-ahead. Explained James, "We knew we were never going to be a portal, a content company, or a phone company. But we wanted [the opportunity] to be big enough to capture interest. Some people in IT [at Intel] had similar ideas, and we've retained some of what they had been thinking. They were looking at out-sourced IT, but were not necessarily Internet focused."

The Internet data services industry was expected to experience phenomenal growth. Some expected a tenfold increase by 2003 of the $1.8 billion of sales revenue for United States-based providers in 1999. Intel reportedly planned to invest more than $1 billion in IDS.[4] Intel believed that its competencies in streamlining complex processes, running tight operations, and managing large investments would give it an advantage in this business. Intel planned to refine one data center, and then replicate the data center following Intel's Copy Exact process for building chip factories. Intel was used to selling microprocessors and related products to OEMs like Dell and HewlettPackard. But IDS would be selling services to ISPs and businesses providing content (broadly defined) on the Internet. Some viewed this as a major challenge for Intel. Sean Maloney, however, responded: "People are surprised we're moving into services. . . . Well, the microprocessor is the most complicated thing in the world to manufacture. It's been hammered into us to do it with reliability, and that skill does transfer."[5]

On the other hand, Ellen Hancock, CEO of potential rival Exodus Communications, observed: "I think it's a stretch for them to say they have some expertise here. We've taken years to set up our operations. I'm befuddled that they think this is like building chip factories."[6]

Medium and Small Green Opportunities

Besides the major initiative in Internet Data Services, numerous small green initiatives had sprung up within Intel during Epoch II, testifying to the resilience and vibrancy of its autonomous strategy process. These various initiatives were all brought together under one roof in the NBG. Gerry Parker pointed out that that gave top management the opportunity to better assess the merits and business potential of these initiatives. He said: "NBG is fighting two things: First, we're inside a big blue company. Second is finding something worth doing. Many of the previous green businesses were bad businesses; it's not just big bad blue. . . . The idea is to aim your shotgun where the geese are flying."

All of these green initiatives required effective product championing and strategic forcing to be able to continue to gain impetus for their development within Intel. Some people associated with these green initiatives feared that this could quickly lead to triage, and Parker did indeed shut down a number of businesses that he thought had little hope to succeed.

New Business Investments

New Business Investments (NBI) was established in late 1998 with the charter of creating new businesses within Intel. NBI played a role similar to that of a venture capitalist, and focused on capitalizing on ideas that were emerging within Intel. NBI worked closely with Corporate Business Development (CBD), but had different goals and objectives. While CBD emphasized external investments and acquisitions, NBI was more internally focused. NBI invested relatively small amounts of money in a venture's early stages of development (as in a seed or first round), whereas CBD invested relatively larger amounts in later stages of development. This also implied that NBI would take a relatively active management and advisory role with its investments compared to CBD.

It was not quite clear yet how NBI would be different from the Intel Development Organization (IDO), which was operative during the 1980s and led by Les Vadasz, who together with Bob Reed (CFO at the time) and Gordon Moore (CEO at the time) had overseen internal start-up activities and spin-offs during Epoch I. Nor was it clear whether and how NBI would use the lessons that were learned from the experience with IDO. One venture had been PCEO, led by veteran corporate entrepreneur Jim Johnson (chapter 9). People associated with PCEO, such as Kirby Dyess, vice-president and director of Intel Capital strategic acquisitions in 2001, had raved about it. They had been strongly motivated by the intense start-up atmosphere, the long working hours and camaraderie, the tight alignment between strategy and action fostered by the strong financial incentives associated with phantom stock options tied to clear milestone objectives, and so on. However, when the time for Going Intel (their equivalent of going public) arrived, there had been some difficult personnel problems in reintegrating people into Intel. Also, PCEO's uncapped financial bonus plan had stirred resentment among some in the mainstream who felt they had contributed to the venture's success but were not rewarded commensurately. Clearly, these were important lessons to heed.

Intel Architecture Lab

For most of the 1990s, Intel Architecture Lab (IAL) had a primary role of supporting Intel's microprocessor business. Many important developments came out of the lab, including chipsets, motherboards, software, and many of the company's networking products. In 1998, the charter of the group expanded to include the goal of generating new businesses for Intel. For example, IAL engineers contributed to the development of the electronic toys made in partnership with Mattel. It could be anticipated, however, that new ventures would force some important trade-offs in the future in light of Intel's "enable the industry" strategy during Epoch II. Top management would have to decide between giving a technology away to the industry to facilitate adoption of new microprocessor generations, or keeping it proprietary as part of the competitive advantage of a new Intel business. One senior executive observed: "There still is the attitude that Intel can do anything around the IA and get a return. So, we are willing to throw money at it in order to sell more

PCs. In the case of IAL, we give the technology away. We will have to watch that, because IAL might be giving away the new business."

Remaining Skepticism

In spite of Intel's recent efforts to create new businesses, Chairman Andy Grove was not satisfied. Asked about the new businesses at Intel, Grove said in early 1999: "We've been very consistent and uniform. All of the new efforts, like all of the other efforts before them, have all been failures. . . . Nobody can fault us for not trying. We've learned a lot, but we've not yet put those learnings into the creation of a third business." Grove then brought Sean Maloney, senior-vice president of sales and marketing, into the discussion:

> GROVE [to Maloney]: How have the new businesses gone?
> MALONEY: We've succeeded at changing the attitudes in the company from unrealistic expectations and an unsupportive management structure to more realistic expectations and a more supportive management structure. But at this point we have no results.
> GROVE: I rest my case.

Intel's new ventures were driving the company into uncertain terrain with respect to the requisite distinctive competencies. During Epoch II, Grove had been able to crisply state how Intel's distinctive competencies had changed from silicon-based competencies in memory products to competencies in implementing computer architectures in silicon chips between Epoch I and II. When asked, in late 1999, how Intel's distinctive competencies were changing going from Epoch II to Epoch III, Grove said: "It is easier when looking back. What is common among microprocessors, networking and IDS? Microprocessors and networking are close—for instance, network protocols are embedded in chips. Product versus service, however, is a bifurcation. . . . The strains are already showing."

Strategic Leadership Discipline for New Business Development

To realize Craig Barrett's intent to augment Intel's entrepreneurial capability, the appropriate strategic leadership discipline for the autonomous strategy process would have to be defined and adopted by the senior management ranks. Discipline—understood as intellectual and behavioral rigor—was one of Intel's traditional core values. No manager could get ahead very far at Intel, or get the company to move in a particular direction, without closely adhering to that value.

It was paramount that the approach would be viewed as equally disciplined, if different from, the discipline that continued to be applied in the induced strategy process. Claude Leglise observed: "The core business is 95 percent of what Intel's doing, and it's not broken, so let's not fix it. The chaos that I'm fostering (in my new business focus) would be disastrous in the PC business. We need to adapt the management approach to the demands on the organization."

SIDE EFFECTS OF THE STRATEGY VECTOR

Andy Grove's strategy vector during Epoch II effectively aligned strategy and action in the core microprocessor business, leading to extraordinary success in growth and profitability. At the start of Epoch III, however, it was becoming clear that the very success of the strategy vector was having some unanticipated negative side effects on new business development. While developing a new discipline for managing new business development, top management would also have to alleviate some of these negative systemic side effects.

Impediments of the Structural Context

Gravitational force of the core business. Being inside a $26 billion company that made more than $6 billion in profits caused even the most promising new ventures to struggle to become relevant. Reflecting the view of many Intel managers, Jim Johnson said: "Building new businesses within Intel can be very hard. The microprocessor business is so large that it wipes out anything that gets close to it." Claude Leglise (Home Products Group) observed: "Everyone's thinking PC around here. . . . The gravity of the organization is strong."

There also seemed to be a common perception that Intel lacked patience with new ventures. According to Dennis Carter: "A key challenge that we face in new businesses is patience—the popular conception is that we don't have any. Craig says that these green businesses will be successful within two years. People respond, 'But the networking business took eight to ten years to build up.' Craig correctly counters, 'Yes, but if it was managed better, we could have grown it more quickly.' " Referring to the objectives of IDS, Renee James observed: "The edict from Craig [Barrett] is to make this a $1 billion business in three years." Scott Darling (Business Communication Products Division) observed: "We tend to want to go from zero to a multibillion dollar business very rapidly. . . . We've been too mechanistic. We are an engineering company, and we've approached new businesses like you'd solve an engineering problem. But there is serendipity in new ventures. We're often wrong about new markets. . . . And we have tended to micromanage, although Gerry [Parker] has avoided this."

Ron Smith compared the situation he is facing with the Wireless Computing and Communications Group to the one he faced with the chipset venture:

> In the wireless/cellular business we face even bigger external challenges due to the more formidable competitors and customers and I believe the internal barriers are even bigger. The latter is due in part to the fact that since we did an acquisition ($1.6 billion) this venture is on the executive radar screen with an expectation of instant success. Yet the vision is to capture this market when it moves from voice to data. This is starting now, but the market will not emerge until 2003. . . . The key issues I face are how to keep the executive office from expecting instant returns and how to keep corporate resources supporting this venture.

Craig Barrett addressed the patience issue head-on:

> For the people involved with the new ventures, I'm sure they see us as being impatient. What I tell them is, show me how you're going to be number 1 or number 2, and how you're going to build a viable business. If they can't do this, then we're not going to be patient. There are examples, such as chipsets and networking, in which we've been very patient. My philosophy is to deal out patience in small doses. But I believe we've demonstrated to the company that we have a degree of patience. The damn environment changes so fast, that we have to adjust priorities and resource requirements as the environment dictates.

Nevertheless, in early 2001 it looked like Intel's growth objectives for IDS (renamed IOS—Intel Online Services) had been too ambitious. Revenue growth was behind schedule. Intel was able to keep losses as planned because of disciplined cost cutting.

Top management attention: Too little or too much. Frank Gill had observed that it was difficult for businesses that were not viewed as strategic for the core business to get top management attention at the SLRP meetings. On the other hand, given the centralization of strategic decision-making at the top during Epoch II, managing activist top managers could be one of the most difficult strategic leadership challenges for the senior executives in charge of new businesses. Gerry Parker pointed out that it was sometimes difficult to maintain the initiative in dealing with Intel's aggressive top management. Giving IDS as an example, he said: "Andy wants to jump in and announce the data center. But I want to be more cautious. I want to able to position it first and be able to modify it. [Intel has announced things before that didn't work] and we had to go back to the analysts and explain ourselves. I prefer to take a different approach. I'm getting good support from Andy and Craig." Parker thought, however, that he could manage the upward relationship effectively: "I keep Craig and Andy informed. I set a strategic direction that they are comfortable with."

In early 2001, it looked like the tension between top-down and bottoms-up opportunity identification was still strong. One senior executive observed that branded products was a new business that was going well, even though it had come about serendipitously and did initially fail to get top management support. This executive also noted, on the other hand, that Andy Grove and other top managers had driven Intel's recent foray into optical components. It was not yet clear how well this new business would succeed.

Top management sponsorship: Reduced financial discipline. A somewhat related view on the part of some other executives was that having top management sponsorship for an opportunity was important for getting funded. A view held by some within the organization, however, was that Intel's top executives did not always apply the same level of financial discipline to their own projects. Representing a common theme, one senior manager said: "One weakness within Intel is that new business activities get decided by executive prerogative." According to another manager: "When they broke up the ProShare division (which had been strongly endorsed by Andy Grove) and moved it to the Create and Share division, they had to establish a culture of fiscal discipline because they had had an entitlement mentality. They had to do a similar thing with the silicon people because this had been Craig Barrett's pet project."

Les Vadasz (CBD) summarized part of the challenge that top management faced in this area: "One of the biggest dangers for big companies is not being able to manage small amounts of money. For some top managers, these new ventures are trivial stuff. But these ventures are necessary to stay on the bleeding edge. On the other hand, you can easily overspend too early. I have done this various times in my life!"

Impeding influence of the finance group. Intel's hard-nosed culture and financial discipline continued to serve it well in the core business but could be a liability to the new businesses. Gerry Parker, one of Intel's most senior executives, ran into resistance from the finance organization as he tried to implement the new strategy in IDS. While building the first data center, which would cost approximately $250 million, the finance group stopped the purchase orders for the equipment. According to Parker:

> Three levels down finance stopped the PO (purchase order). They said "you don't have Andy [Grove]'s approval." I said, who gives a [damn]. We need to be able to balance moving fast with the discipline of the company. The real issue in an internal bureaucracy is that if it thinks upper management doesn't like it, they will stop it at every level just to ask more questions and look at more alternatives, whereas if Grove says "Do it," no one in the bureaucracy dares slow it down. In my case Craig (Barrett) acted hesitant at the wrong moment and it was a license for every level of finance to slow it down for more justification. We are working our way through this but I'm constantly amazed at how difficult it is to do something different in an area in which none of us have a good experiential base or good intuition.

Parker pointed out that he had not yet shown a P&L for NBG. He felt he could get away with that for a while because he keeps Craig and Andy informed and has an exit strategy. He said: "I've been given a fair amount of rope on this thing. . . . I'm trying to be fiscally responsible. But with the data center, for example, I try to avoid pitching a real detailed plan that locks you in. [I say], don't get too enamored with any part of the plan."

Short-term orientation of the plan of record (POR). Speaking about being locked-in by the plan and the funding challenge that new ventures faced at Intel, Tom Lacey (Sales and Marketing) explained:

> We apply the POR process to establish budgets for all of our projects. . . . Virtually every single quarter, the requests outweigh the willingness to spend. We would end up ZBB-ing [zero-based budgeting] the lower ROI projects. The larger ROI projects were almost always related to the mainstream CPU business. Therefore, if you were not part of the mainstream business, you needed to be very spirited and very persevering to drive your projects through that POR process every quarter. In many cases they were great businesses by any other metric, just not compared to the microprocessor business. Three or four years ago I asked Craig [Barrett], shouldn't we be diversifying more? His answer was "Absolutely not. It takes every bit of our energy to execute on the microprocessor business." If you were in a non-CPU business, it was tough.

Another senior executive said:

> My controller runs my business. He spends very little time on it, and he
> doesn't understand my strategy, my customers, etc. Yet, he controls my
> purse strings and gives me very little flexibility. With the POR process,
> you go in with your request by department. He says which department
> gets funded and which one does not. This happens every quarter. We
> spend the last 30 days of the quarter preparing for the budget review,
> then the first 30 days of the next quarter appealing the budget cuts. So we
> end up spending 60 out of 90 days negotiating our budget.

Inflexible measurement and reward system. At Intel, the evaluation system
worked as follows: Goals and objectives for the coming year were established in
December. Performance was evaluated the following December based on the
achievement of these objectives. Employee bonuses (EB), which were typically a
very significant portion of overall compensation, were based on these evaluations.
According to Dennis Carter: "Unfortunately, [objectives] are often hopelessly outdated after 12 months. Things just change too much. In the case of a start-up effort,
it's even more difficult. . . . The system penalizes you for the downside, but does
not reward you for the upside associated with these changes. A mechanism for relief might be useful." Gerry Parker was already experiencing some of these difficulties in the NBG: "The EB payouts were bad for my groups. . . . Right now, it's
all downside. This makes things not terribly easy."

One of Intel's core cultural values was risk taking. The philosophy was that
with a leading-edge technology strategy, Intel would always compete in an environment of constant change. Intel viewed attempts to maintain the status quo in an
environment of change as a recipe for failure. Therefore, risk taking was encouraged. However, as Epoch III began to unfold, a common view was developing in
the organization that Intel did not particularly support risk taking any more. According to Dennis Carter: "It is a commonly held belief among middle managers at
Intel that it is difficult to take risks, that Intel doesn't reward risk takers who fail,
only those who have succeeded. This is certainly the perception, and possibly also
the reality."

This was not always the case because as noted earlier, the PCEO team had received high financial rewards when Intel bought back their phantom stock in the
venture in the late 1980s. In fact, the high financial awards had created some resentment in the rest of the organization and Intel had not done a similar transaction
since. Clearly there was room to refine the approach.

Another aspect of the compensation issue for entrepreneurs, however, was that they were not always willing to make a choice between the upside that was possible if the venture was successful and the regular Intel compensation package, which had been a very rich one for thousands of Intel employees during the 1990s. Addressing the issue, CFO Andy Bryant said:

> [The new businesses] say, we want the benefit that a start-up would have. Fine, then I'm going to take away the Intel stock options. I see it as a risk-reward issue. If you want to be rewarded like a start-up then you need to have the same motivation as another start-up. . . . The problems that we're having are often related to the expectations of the people who do it. They say we want to go off and be independent and have the upside of a start-up. OK, so we take away your Intel stock options. The translation when they go back to their groups is that "they're not working with us. I had a great idea, but they wouldn't fund it." But [venture capitalists] only fund 20 percent of the plans. So if we do the same, the 80 percent that don't get funded complain and say we're not being supportive. Meanwhile we've funded the other-20 percent and they're busy getting implemented.

Marketing and brand strategy constraints. The consensus view was that the Intel brand created many advantages for new ventures, but that there were significant challenges to using it effectively. The Intel name inspired trust and confidence, and helped open doors with potential customers, partners, and suppliers, giving Intel new ventures a significant advantage relative to typical start-ups. But there were also major challenges related to marketing and branding. For example, Mark Christensen (NCG) noted: "Intel's brand stands for a lot of things . . . [but] we're probably not known as a networking company. It's probably easier for us to extend the brand to 'The Internet building block company' than it is to extend it to 'The networking company.' "

Dennis Carter discussed how the role of marketing had evolved across the three epochs:

> During the first epoch, marketing allowed us to differentiate our products from others. We made a number of innovations in sales and marketing techniques that allowed us to sell high value semiconductors. We were virtually unknown outside of the engineering community, but were innovators in business-to-business marketing. During the second epoch, we were again able to differentiate our product from a marketing perspective, but this time via Intel Inside. We successfully took our brand to

the end user. Marketing was a key element in the success of our microprocessor business. During the third epoch marketing must again play a key role, we will need to move our brand to include a broader set of products, and we need to make the Intel brand relevant in the Internet space.

Gaining sales and marketing channel mind share. For the most part, the new ventures relied on Intel's existing sales forces to sell and market their products in the field. This created challenges in mind share, and conflicts in funding occasionally arose. According to Jim Yasso, a veteran of Intel's sales force before his tenure as general manager of the Reseller Product Division:

> The sales force is part of the blue process. For anything that's green, it's very hard to get resources, unless they are explicitly included as part of the original plan and budget allocations. You also need to have marketing people in place in the geographies. . . . We have quarterly POR processes where we get funding approved or adjusted. Within a division or geography, we can be subject to headcount or spending cuts, and in some cases these budget decisions can conflict [with funding for the new ventures]. This can be a real killer for green businesses. . . . With NBG, we've kept the [green] businesses separate and shielded them from the ongoing [blue] business."

The new emphasis at Intel on non-core businesses created challenges for the sales force. According to Tom Lacey (Sales and Marketing):

> A lot of the sales reps at Intel have been here for a long time. Most of them grew up on the IA bandwagon. We're now trying to sell more Intel products through the same channels. This is requiring people to learn more about some of our other products. . . . This has been a bit of a transformation for the sales force. . . . We're in the process right now of reorganizing the sales force. We're creating a separate sales force that is focused on non-CPU businesses.

Gaining manufacturing support. Ron Smith, in charge of the Wireless Computing and Communications Group in 1999 and formerly the leader of the chipset venture, believed that dealing with the sales force was actually easier than dealing with the factories, because the salespeople are the first to notice strategic dissonance. He said he had told Craig Barrett, "The field is the easy part; we must deal with the factories. You need factory support if you want to diversify." Smith, of course, had had first-hand experience with the difficulties new businesses had in competing for scarce manufacturing capacity with the microprocessor business. Also, as Dennis Carter pointed out, Intel remained truly a manufacturing company with almost 70 percent of its employees associated with manufacturing.

Lacking Intuition and General Managers

Developing new intuition requires experimentation. During Epoch I, Intel's technical sales and field engineering teams played an essential role in applying the company's products and finding new applications for them. During Epoch II, the application—the PC—was clear, relatively homogeneous, and changing in a predictable way. This reduced the importance of inbound marketing, as well as Intel's capabilities in this area.

> In 1999, Dennis Carter expressed concern that Intel had lost most of its inbound marketing competencies, which had been very strong during Epoch I (chapter 9). While Intel's sales force continued to be in touch with OEM customers during Epoch II, Intel's marketing had focused on the much larger PC end-user audience. Carter worried that there was little market feedback for anything other than microprocessors during Epoch II. He believed that new product planning was being done too quickly and by people too removed from new markets. Also, Intel's excellence in execution and excellent intuition in the core microprocessor business did not necessarily transfer readily into new product areas. As a consequence, Carter believed that Intel had become bad at judging what new products were likely to be successful in new markets, and that it would be critical during Eopch III to redevelop Intel's inbound marketing processes necessary to establish a link with the market and to support the new product planning process.

Gerry Parker said: "At Intel, we have a propensity to focus on one thing: build it big, and then say, "Here it is!" We have the mentality of Build it and they will come. . . . We're now making some real progress on being more customer responsive and my green teams are spending time at every staff meeting on customer status and finding customers." In 1999, it seemed Andy Grove had also come to realize the need to develop new intuition. In a discussion with Intel's top management he said: "There's a lack of a merchant mentality inside Intel. We're not good at it. We need to get experience, and then build on that experience."

Developing new intuition for different markets and customer needs, however, would require experimentation, even somewhat of a trial-and-error approach. This was quite orthogonal to Intel's culture, which valued reducing uncertainty and identifying home-run opportunities up front. Kirby Dyess reflected on her experience with the Intel Development Organization (IDO) in the 1980s:

> [M]y perspective was that in order to be successful or get a home run, we would need to go to bat multiple times. This doesn't assume you do it arbitrarily; you have to do your homework each time you go to bat but you have to get there and get there multiple times. It does mean that having fingers in a number of pots is probably not a bad idea. This way of thinking was not shared by everyone at Intel. Often it was assumed that you could do enough research up front to understand exactly what your home runs would be without failing or just playing the game. You learn and adjust by being in the game.

Kirby Dyess identified another structural impediment to developing new intuition. New intuition usually is embodied in new people—people with deep experience in areas that are unfamiliar to the persons in the mainstream of the corporation. Such people must be recruited from the outside. However, Intel lacked experience in recruiting people in unfamiliar areas and was not confident that it could select the best ones. The company valued its ability to select the right people highly and had put in place routines and a network of contacts that gave it confidence it could do so very well in its traditional areas of hardware engineering competence. The very confidence it had in its ability to recruit effectively in familiar areas impeded the recruitment of different new people. According to Dyess:

> One concern I had was that we really hadn't hired a lot of software engineers in the past. So it put us in a position in which we had to go out and look for people that we were not sure were good . . .
>
> We weren't sure what to look for in some cases. While we could describe what we wanted them to do, we weren't as well connected in the software engineering field to be able to check through our internal sources to find out who were the top candidates in the field. I contrast that to the hardware field where, if we wanted to hire a hardware engineer, we had such an incredible informal network that it was very easy to hire someone. It was a challenge bringing in critical software resources initially.

Intel, of course, had learned to hire software engineers rather well during Epoch II. But the same hesitancy with respect to new categories of talent existed at the start of Epoch III.

Developing general managers for new businesses. A related challenge facing Intel was developing general managers—corporate entrepreneurs—who could turn good ideas into good businesses. According to Craig Barrett: "[During the second epoch] we became much more vertical behind IA and related businesses. Now we're much broader, with networking, Parker's businesses, and so forth. This requires less top-down management and more P&L and line management." This went beyond coming up with new ideas. According to Claude Leglise: "We have labs in Oregon that are concocting ideas all day long. We have a resource pool for ideas. We've made equity investments in a couple hundred small companies. It's a matter of sifting through and seeing what makes sense, and taking the products to customers."

Dennis Carter added:

> There are lots of ideas and new projects sprouting up everywhere within Intel, but the real question is how we can turn them into a business. We have the capacity to do so, but is the infrastructure there to support it? . . . We have clever ideas coming from places like IAL and the Content Group, but little experience in making a business out of any of them. We need to develop the intuition for doing this. And we need to develop people with the entrepreneurial intuition.

In early 2000, Gerry Parker said his experience with NBG taught him that: "It is a lot harder to get going on a new business than it looks at first blush. The distance between a great idea and a successful profitable business is long."

Lacking Strategic Context Determination Processes

Organizational champions. Besides developing new intuition and business-level general managers who could take a new idea and turn it into a viable business, Intel also needed to develop senior general managers. These senior general managers champion the new business within the larger organization and get top management to embrace it as part of the corporate strategy. Discussions with senior executives, who had experience in trying to determine the strategic context for a new business, indicated that it was still a difficult process at Intel. Here are some of their views:

- Fighting the blue space gets tiresome. It would be easier with dedicated resources. Instead of being judged on a quarterly P&L, we should be given a five-year runway. We should be worrying about growing revenue, not profit.

But quarterly earnings-per-share dominates everything. Finance is very strong at Intel.

- There is progress, but at a high personal price. It requires internal wrangling. You face a dilemma; emotionally, you ask yourself, why do I have to do this? Intellectually, you know it is a necessary evil. Also, you may get typecast as not being a team player.

- It is my job to convince top management. But then I am focused on that rather than the business. And you cannot hire staff people to do the fighting for you. People don't want to be diplomats; they want to be entrepreneurs.

- It takes top management help. Craig will do it to some extent. But I am more concerned about Andy because of his singular focus. Andy says that PCs are becoming a commodity. So, we must focus on servers, and not let Sun (Microsystems) capture this. It is like going back to the old days.

Senior executives, however, also pointed out that there was great opportunity for new businesses to leverage off Intel's capabilities to have a real impact on the world. For instance, Ron Smith, who had played a big role in the chipset venture, observed: "If I had taken the same group of people and developed chipsets as an independent venture, it would not have been so successful. We could perhaps have become the largest chipset company, but we would still have been one of many. With Intel, we were able to become *the* chipset manufacturer."

Resolving inherent conflicts in strategic context determination. Senior executives engaging in organizational championing were also necessary to resolve various types of strategic conflicts that unavoidably are generated and encountered by new business development in relation to the core business. In early 2000, Gerry Parker observed: "Even though we get quite a bit of latitude on the green businesses, we do inevitably conflict with blue, in the sense that either I wind up competing with other Intel customers, or Intel blue sells to, helps, or invests in my green competitors."

These issues were not new to Intel. The chipset and motherboard ventures, for instance, had to cope with concerns of the core business regarding OEM customer relations during Epoch II. But the greater diversity of initiatives engendered by the NBG will unavoidably produce many more of these.

Looking Ahead

In 1999. In leading Intel into the new millennium, CEO Craig Barrett seemed to relish the challenge of balancing the simultaneous exploitation of core business and new business opportunities:

I've tried to spread a couple of messages around here. First is that there's a different vision. We have more business opportunities than just the microprocessor. Microprocessors by themselves will not be the growth engine that it's been in the past. . . . I try to challenge the new ventures to grow their businesses so that they're relevant, and I challenge the people in the microprocessor business to be successful enough so that the new ventures won't matter. . . . The creosote bush is still here. It hasn't gone away, and I hope it doesn't! We need to grow some other bases, but it would be inappropriate to say we have changed 100 percent.

Asked how he was spending his own time in relation to the challenge of balancing core and new business development, Barrett said:

One organization change that I made was to put Otellini in charge to a large extent of the core business. This gives Paul full-time responsibility to do that. That's allowed me to spend more of my time on other new businesses than I had imagined I would. I spend approximately 60 percent of my time with IA-related businesses, and 40 percent with the other businesses, such as Networking and new businesses. I'm spending enough time and energy in these areas to be noticed.

Chairman Emeritus Gordon Moore had his own views of the challenges facing Barrett:

Craig is a strong hands-on guy, like Andy, but even more so. He keeps himself in the loop a lot more. It's pretty amazing that he can do this, and it's because he has so damn much energy. . . . Eventually Craig will need to find someone to complement himself. . . . He has done a tremendous job, moving our focus from the microprocessor to the Internet building blocks. The key issue here is getting critical mass in an area. . . . Jack Welch at GE says that you have to be number one or number two in an industry, and this is especially true in technology. Hangers-on tend to not be very good. At the same time, we can't neglect the microprocessor business.

In 2001. In early 2001, top management was beginning to review what had been learned from Intel's new business development efforts. This review was not independent of the execution setbacks in the core business (chapter 10). There was also some unease that a fair number of employees seemed to be somewhat keener on joining the green businesses than the blue ones. In April, Gerry Parker announced his upcoming retirement. John Miner, a vice president and member of Intel's top management team, was to become the new general manager of the NBG. Intel also seemed to be gravitating back to a stronger focus on the PC market segment. Top management seemed to have concluded that it was difficult to develop businesses that were not related to the core business. The "Extended PC" or "PC Plus" was a new strategy that had emerged from the period of experimentation with new businesses. Intel wanted to find various new product-market areas adjacent to the PC product market that could leverage its strong position in the PC product market. This was consistent with Andy Grove's strategic vision that Epoch III was not the Post-PC-era (chapter 10). NBG's vision was likely to be brought in line with the PC Plus strategy. It remained of course to be seen whether the growth opportunities available with the PC Plus strategy would be sufficient.

IMPLICATIONS: BALANCING CORE BUSINESS AND NEW BUSINESS DEVELOPMENT

Barrett's Challenge: Going Beyond the Golden Age

The challenges facing Barrett during Epoch III were in some ways a combination of the ones faced by his predecessors in Epochs I and II. As a start-up company and throughout Epoch I, Intel's strategy-making process resembled the internal ecology model, with a prominent role played by the autonomous strategy process. During Epoch I, Intel was not particularly effective in defending its strategic position in its core semiconductor memory businesses, but it was able to replace these as they became commoditized with a new core microprocessor business that was consistent with its differentiation-based generic strategy. At the start of Epoch II, Intel was blessed with an enormously rich growth and profit opportunity in its new core microprocessor business. Under the strategic leadership of Andy Grove, Intel's induced strategy process became extremely focused on exploiting that opportunity, making the PC market segment adapt to its strategic moves. With strategic decision-making concentrated at the top and the ability to get the various parts of the organization to execute forcefully and coherently, Intel's strategy-making in the core business closely resembled the rational-actor model during Epoch II. The extreme emphasis on the induced strategy process during Epoch II, however, had reduced the effectiveness of the company's autonomous-strategy process.

At the start of Epoch III it was clear that Intel's future as a growth company and its concomitant market valuation would depend at least in part on Intel's ability to develop new businesses. Building on the achievements of Epochs I and II, Barrett's challenge was to design a new robustly adaptive internal ecology of strategy-making for Epoch III; one that would be able to simultaneously exploit existing and new business opportunities. Such an adaptive organizational capability would have to balance the induced and autonomous strategy processes—Intel's blue and green processes—in a more deliberate fashion than during Epoch I, but would no longer be completely dominated by the induced process as during Epoch II.

Internal Ecology of Strategy-Making Revisited

The study of Epoch I yielded several insights about the role of the induced and autonomous-strategy processes in a company's evolution (chapter 5).[7] During Epoch II, the validity of these insights was unclear in light of the enormous success Intel enjoyed with its narrowly focused and tightly run induced-strategy process. The start of Epoch III, however, saw the reemergence of the importance of the autonomous-strategy process and the need to better balance the two processes in Intel's future strategy-making.

Process and content. A key insight suggested by the study of Epoch I was that companies that are relatively successful over long periods of time, say, ten years or more, are likely to have a top management that is concerned with building the induced- and autonomous-strategy processes as well as with the content of the strategy. During Epoch II, Andy Grove articulated the content of Intel's strategy and relentlessly drove the company to execute it. Grove, however, was less concerned with the details of the strategy process than with its content.[8] At the outset of Epoch III, Barrett seemed more inclined to let general managers define the content of the strategy of their businesses. Barrett was also trying to reinvigorate the autonomous strategy process and needed to develop a new discipline for managing this process. A delicate balance was needed, because applying the discipline of the induced strategy process to the autonomous strategy process was likely to fail. The temptation to do so, often unwittingly, is great in established companies. Gerry Parker seemed to be aware of this and was trying to shield managers in the NBG from too much top management intervention too soon to give them a chance to discover what the right opportunities were and what the right strategy was to pursue them. Ultimately, of course, top management will have to stay on top of Intel's strategic direction. One senior executive observed that "Barrett at some point will be expected to set the corporate strategy; and if he doesn't, Andy will." Hence, future strategy-making will require a careful balancing act between top-driven direction setting and bottoms-up strategic initiative.

Top down and bottom up. A second insight suggested by the study of Epoch I was that companies that are relatively successful over long periods of time are likely to simultaneously maintain top-driven strategic intent and bottoms-up driven strategic renewal. Most companies, however, find it very difficult to systematically manage the induced and autonomous strategy processes simultaneously. In part this is so because top management often views new business development as a form of insurance against the core business going bad. This leads to a "now we do it; now we don't" pattern in new business development over time that makes it very difficult to build the company's entrepreneurial management capability. In early-2001, it remained to be seen whether Intel's top management would continue to focus on the autonomous (green) strategy process as an integral part of corporate strategy-making, independent of recent fluctuations in the fortunes of the core (blue) business.

Evolutionary antecedents to strategic transformation. A third insight suggested by the study of Epoch I was that successful strategic transformations are likely to have been preceded by internal variation and selection processes. During Epoch I, Intel's transformation into a microprocessor company was clearly preceded by internal variation and selection processes. During Epoch II, Intel did not transform itself to the same extent as it did during Epoch I. Nevertheless, successful new businesses—motherboards, chipsets, and networking—contributed to Intel's expansion beyond the core microprocessor business narrowly defined. Even though in retrospect they seem like obvious extensions of the corporate strategy, these new businesses also constituted internal variations and survived internal selection processes before they were embraced as part of the official corporate strategy. During Epoch III, new business development paradoxically faced the potential problem of premature exposure to top management. Having recognized that new business development was important to sustain Intel's prospects as a growth company, top management was now pushing new business development with traditional Intel drive and determination. The challenge facing new businesses at Intel during Epoch III was to remain sufficiently long protected from top management's very high-growth expectations to be able to find out where a sustainable beachhead could be developed. This protection needed to be provided by senior executives, who could shield the new businesses from too much top-management scrutiny too soon.

Evolutionary Path of the Strategy-Making Process

The study of Epochs I and II suggests that there is no fixed optimal combination of the induced- and autonomous-strategy processes throughout a company's evolution. But it is critical to keep both processes in play at all times. The weights on each of these processes in the share of corporate resources and top management attention will vary over time, but the weights on either process should never be zero. In other words, for any given level of corporate resources, both the induced and the autonomous process must always receive some resources and attention.

> **Insight 11.1.** Throughout a company's evolution, strategy-making as adaptive organizational capability needs to combine the induced- and autonomous-strategy processes, with shifting weights on these two processes reflecting the key strategic leadership challenges faced by the company during different epochs in its evolution.

Matching CEO and Strategic Challenges

The study of Epochs I and II also suggests the need to match the CEO's strategic leadership approach with the relative importance of the induced and autonomous strategy process during different periods of a company's history. Gordon Moore seemed very well suited for Epoch I. Andy Grove was the right CEO for Epoch II. And Craig Barrett seems to be an excellent fit for Epoch III. To some extent this series of felicitous matches may simply have been a stroke of good luck. However, it seems reasonable to believe that there was also strong intuition on the part of top management (and the board of directors) involved in grooming the right person for the strategic leadership challenges of Epochs II and III. The framework of strategic leadership challenges associated with the induced and autonomous strategy processes may be useful in future top management and board deliberations concerning CEO succession.

> **Insight 11.2.** The anticipated relative importance of the induced- and autonomous-strategy processes in a five-to-ten-year time horizon should inform CEO succession planning.

DESIGNING THE INTERNAL ECOLOGY OF STRATEGY-MAKING

At the start of Epoch III, Craig Barrett was trying to bring Intel to the next level of excellence by balancing the exploitation of core business and new business opportunities simultaneously. Such balance could not simply be a pragmatic compromise. Giving up large and highly predictable opportunities in the core business simply to pursue some uncertain opportunities in new businesses would be viewed as foolish and heavily resisted within Intel's results-oriented and highly disciplined culture. It had to be an integrated effort: pursuing to the fullest the core business opportunities and finding resources to pursue truly promising new business opportunities simultaneously. While autonomous strategic initiatives continued to spring up, Intel's infrastructure for capitalizing on them had withered. At the start of Epoch III, Barrett faced the problem of making more room for strategic context determination processes in Intel's strategy-making. Determining the strategic context for a new business puts senior and top executives outside their comfort zone, requiring them to make decisions on substantive strategy issues for which they do not have deep intuition. Effectively facilitating strategic context determination processes required modifications of the structural context. Barrett's solution was to create the NBG.

Organization Designs for Corporate Entrepreneurship

Creating the NBG was a good first step. But one of the traps of corporate new business development is to treat all ventures in the same way; for instance, putting all of them together in the NBG and keeping them there isolated from the rest of the company. Intel needed a framework to help senior executives determine the degree of interdependence between a new business and the core business at a particular moment.[9] The assessment framework presented during the Growing the Business course comprised two important dimensions: *operational relatedness* and *strategic importance*. Operational relatedness regards the degree to which the new business opportunity needs to draw on the company's existing distinctive competencies (including resources and capabilities), which are located in various parts of the core business. This part of the assessment raises concerns about efficient use of the company's distinctive competencies. Operational relatedness therefore points to operational linkages (e.g., establishing technical and/or marketing liaisons) that are sustained by networking between the new business leaders and leaders in the core business as a design parameter for structuring the relationship between the new business and the core business.

Strategic importance regards the degree to which the new business is important for the company's future strategic position. Sometimes the new business opportunity promises to complement or supplement the company's core business, opening up a new area of opportunity to help sustain the company's future profitable growth. Sometimes, on the other hand, a new business opportunity threatens to become a substitute for the company's current core business (e.g., it involves a disruptive technology), which raises the issue of how it will impact the future strategic position of the company's core business. Strategic importance speaks directly to concerns about future control over the company's destiny. Strategic importance, therefore, points to administrative mechanisms (e.g., integration of strategic plans of the new business into the corporate strategic plan) that are sustained through authority as a design parameter for structuring the relationship between the new business and the core business. The framework based on these two dimensions is presented in figure 11.1. Analytical questions concerning the two dimensions are listed in Appendix III. Appendix III also presents a corresponding framework of organization design alternatives.

The assessment framework helps management to decide on an organization design commensurate with the interdependence between the new business and the core business at a given time. In addition, each organization design needs to be matched with a commensurate measurement and reward system, which will be different in some major ways from the one used in the core business. An important benefit of systematically using the assessment framework is that reaching conclusions regarding operational relatedness and strategic importance requires the serious involvement of senior management of both the core business and the new businesses. Applying the assessment framework, however, requires careful analy-

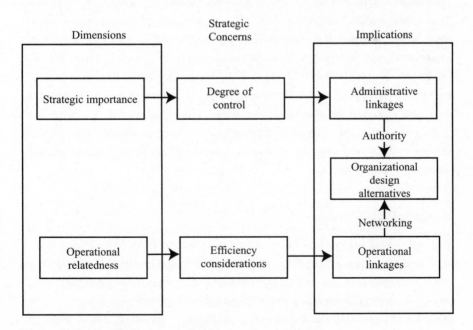

Figure 11.1. Assessment Framework for Autonomous Initiatives.

sis, which is time-consuming. In 2001, it was not yet clear to what extent Intel was using the framework effectively.

Strategic Planning, POR, and Resource Allocation

Intel's POR system of management by objectives and results, tightly linked to employees' rating and ranking and compensation, creates tremendous discipline in the induced-strategy process. An equally disciplined yet different management system needs to be developed for the autonomous strategy process. It will have to allow objectives to change during specified periods of time—sometimes longer and sometimes shorter periods. But it will also have to insist on measurable results on some dimensions, such as lessons learned and problems solved as well as relevant quantitative outputs. Intel also needs to separate the application of the zero-based-budgeting system in the new businesses from its application in the core business. To be sure, senior management of the new businesses needs to make sure that resource allocation is as disciplined in the new businesses as it is in the core business. This will require halting new ventures that do not deliver on promises at key milestones.

Measurement and Reward System

Performance appraisal of new business development will have to be somewhat more qualitative and subjective. This will require the development of new assessment skills on the part of middle and senior managers. Intel has had useful previous experiences with creating a different measurement and reward system for new businesses, in particular PCEO. But it is not clear whether the lessons from these experiences have been captured and whether top management is ready to deal with the taxing requirements of differentiated measurement and reward systems tailored to the specific situations faced by different new ventures at various stages in their evolution. This reinforces the need for a framework for deciding on organization designs for new ventures.

Executive Development

Intel needs to develop a new cadre of general managers to lead new businesses as well as work closely with colleagues in the core business for the sharing and sometimes transferring of key resources. One part of this involves augmenting the capacity for strategic thinking at levels below top management. In early 1997, Craig Barrett's initiative to create the Growing the Business course for Intel's senior executives served that purpose. Another part of executive development is training or learning by doing. New business development efforts often fail because a company's most talented executives have no incentive to get involved in it. This is likely to happen if the new business efforts are viewed as potential career killers. It is, therefore, crucial to create a structural context that motivates talented executives who have the ambition and drive to become top managers to view new business development as an integral part of career development. The NBG can provide an umbrella for developing new general managers as business leaders, even though the ventures themselves are likely to have a high failure rate. The development of general management talent that can be promoted and deployed everywhere in the company will have to become viewed as a metric of success of NBG. This will, again, require great discipline in stopping losing ventures, so that learning can be maximized but potential damage to careers carefully controlled.

Emerging Tension during Epoch III: Diversification *and* Integration

Each of Intel's Epochs was characterized by a fundamental tension. During Epoch I, the tension was between specialty products and commodity products. During Epoch II, the tension was between core business and new business development. While these two fundamental tensions continued to exist during Epoch III, a third one is looming. This new tension is between corporate diversification and integration. This will raise the issue of how to optimally reorganize the company. Intel is still the vectorized organization par excellence and able to achieve strong collaboration among its different businesses to maximally exploit the opportunities associated with its core microprocessor business. Intel needs to create room for new strategic initiatives in product-market areas in which it may not immediately be able to achieve the same extreme degree of preeminence. Farther down in the future, Intel may very well comprise several large businesses glued together by a common culture and a strong discipline-instilling corporate management.

New Role of the CEO

The tension between being diversified and integrated at the same time has implications for the role of the CEO. Craig Barrett will have to strike a careful balance between setting the overall corporate strategy for the company and allowing the new business leaders to set the strategy for their businesses. As the new businesses grow and become more complex, this will become a more important issue. Eventually, Barrett's role (or that of his successor in the longer run) will become more one of driving the competitive spirit in the organization by getting the different businesses to pace each other in striving for leadership in their product-market environments, while also encouraging pursuit of cross-business opportunities through strategic integration.[10] Internal competition must be about winning in the external environment, not winning internal political battles. The business-level executives will have to determine the winning strategies. A key top management role will be to pick the right business-level strategists.

CONCLUSION

In previous chapters we had the luxury of learning from history. This chapter, in contrast, addressed the question of how Intel's strategy-making can help the company to continue achieving extraordinary performance in the future. During most of Epoch II it seemed that Intel could continue to do just fine with its strongly focused induced-strategy process. Toward the end of Epoch II, however, the need to capitalize on new initiatives outside the core business again became highly salient. The analysis of the early part of Epoch III corroborated previously derived insights about the importance of keeping both the induced- and autonomous-strategy processes in play at all times, even though the weights on the two processes may have to be different at different times. It also suggested that CEO succession should be informed by the particular mix of strategic leadership challenges that a company is likely to face in the next five or so years at the time of CEO transition.

At the start of Epoch III, Craig Barrett recognized the need to increase Intel's capability for developing new businesses. By early 2001, however, the emergence of the PC Plus strategy suggested that Barrett was keen on refocusing new business development efforts in areas more or less adjacent to its core business. It is crucial, of course, to exploit all the available opportunities closely related to the core business. It is usually also easier to do so effectively. Nevertheless, this would have to be managed carefully to prevent the gravitational force of the induced-strategy process from overwhelming again the autonomous one. Intel needed to continue to develop the process through which major new opportunities are likely to arise to support future growth.

Craig Barrett's fundamental strategic leadership challenge for the remainder of Epoch III is, therefore, to balance the outstanding management discipline that Intel has already developed in its core business with a novel discipline for new business development. This will require adjusting the structural context that worked well for over a decade in the core business. Balancing existing and new business development simultaneously is extremely difficult and a true frontier of strategic leadership in established companies. Intel has the opportunity to be in the vanguard of learning to develop the requisite approach.

Conclusion:

Implications for Strategic Leadership

> [T]he test of a first-rate intelligence is the ability to hold two opposed ideas in the mind at the same time, and still retain the ability to function.
>
> F. Scott Fitzgerald, *The Crack-up*

12 FOUR STRATEGIC

LEADERSHIP

IMPERATIVES

At the end of this book, Magritte's warning still stands: This is not Intel. Yet, its thesis—strategy is destiny—concisely captures the role of strategy in Intel's evolution. During Epoch I, Intel lost control over its destiny as initially envisioned when its strategy in the core DRAM business faltered. The company's internal ecology of strategy-making, however, generated new business opportunities that enabled Intel to pursue a new destiny. Strategy thus shaped destiny. During Epoch II, Intel's rational actor strategy-making process secured control of its destiny in the core business as few other companies have. But the strategic focus on the PC also tied its destiny increasingly to that product-market segment and made it difficult to capitalize on new business opportunities. Destiny thus also shaped strategy. At the start of Epoch III, Intel was seeking to maintain control of its destiny as a growth company by developing a strategy-making process that could explore new business opportunities while simultaneously continuing to exploit its advantageous position in the core business.

Four Strategic Leadership Imperatives

Evolutionary organization theory guided the research for this book. The three conceptual frameworks of the evolutionary research lens helped bridge the general, abstract, and nonexperiential processes of evolutionary organization theory and the particular, concrete, and experiential reality of Intel's strategy-making. They

361

produced many general insights in the role of strategy-making in company evolution. These are synthesized in this final chapter as four imperatives:

- Embrace strategy to control destiny.
- Capitalize on strategic dissonance.
- Exercise two strategic disciplines simultaneously.
- Manage the cycle time of strategic change.

The notes for this chapter offer brief references to the Intel data that inspired these four imperatives, as well as to examples from other companies that they illuminate.

EMBRACE STRATEGY TO CONTROL DESTINY

Strategy Is About Forces

Company leaders need vision to identify the destiny they seek. But to help a company gain and maintain control over its destiny they must define the games in which that company can win consistently. Strategy is the means toward this end. Great visionaries are not necessarily great strategists.[1] In the end, winning depends on strategy. Strategy helps leaders not only to understand which forces affect a company's chances to win at any given time but also to decide how these forces can be used to the company's advantage. If strategy is about forces, leaders want to make sure that their company is a force!

Strategy is concerned with the forces on which the company depends and the forces that it can influence. Low influence and low dependency characterize situations of strategic indifference. Here, strategy is largely irrelevant.[2] High influence and low dependency characterize situations of strategic dominance.[3] Low influence and high dependency characterize situations of strategic subordination.[4] High influence combined with high dependency produces situations of strategic interdependence. Companies in high-technology industries, in particular the computer and telecommunications industries that have moved from a vertical to a horizontal structure, experience such a situation. They face what one observer has aptly called mutual assured dependence.[5] They can control their destiny, but the strategies involved are multifaceted.[6]

Strategy Is About Alertness

Strategy raises alertness. It helps company leaders identify forces that fall outside the categories considered in traditional industry structure analysis, such as increasing returns to adoption, complementors, ecosystems, and disruptive technologies. It also helps them perceive the confluence of forces that signal impending radical industry changes and helps them decide the right time to take action. Strategic alertness is particularly important in dynamic industries where it is virtually impossible to have clear foresight.[7] In such industries, there is a premium for intuition-based strategic recognition, the capacity to correctly understand the links between rapidly evolving forces, consequential actions, and their outcomes.[8] Leaders engage, then see: A strategy's effectiveness becomes clear when consequential action is taken that leverages position and competence simultaneously in seeking sustainable competitive advantage.[9] Strategically alert leaders oblige luck by examining its sources and are ready to recognize when their good luck is replicable.

Strategy Is About Tempered Boldness

Ideally, strategy provides the means to radically change the game. Audacity and boldness are the hallmarks of great strategists. Using speed, mobility, and surprise they find ways to circumvent and neutralize some or all of the traditional forces and put in play new ones that were not part of the set contemplated by rivals. In business, this ideal corresponds to the Schumpeterian entrepreneur who leaves creative destruction in his path.[10] Most of the time, however, company leaders cannot change the game in dramatic ways. But their strategic actions can always be directed at shaping the forces in the situation so competitors see that it is to their advantage not to challenge the company in its domain and allies know that it is to their advantage to stay involved with the company.

Strategy Is About Interdependence

Strategy is in first instance a state of mind and a way of approaching the world. Company leaders who are clearheaded strategists are aware that others also desire to gain and maintain control over their destiny, and they respect this. Company leaders increasingly operate in a world of strategic interdependence. The more powerful their companies are, the more they need to be aware of the potential repercussions of strategic dominance. This leads them to forbear where possible and rational, and to compete vigorously where necessary. In that sense, clearheaded strategy may be a sound foundation for an ethics of competition.

Strategy Is About Reasonable Competitiveness

Strategy helps company leaders avoid several psychological traps associated with extreme competitiveness. Getting completely caught up in the dynamics of competition is one of the perils that energetic and motivated company leaders face. Sometimes company leaders lose the sureness of their footing as they contemplate possible moves of potential competitors and abandon their carefully-thought-out strategy. At other times, company leaders become obsessed by their urge to win and lose sight of why winning a particular competitive battle is strategically important.[11] At still other times, company leaders' urge to compete is simply driven by envy of others' success.[12] Strategy helps avoid these psychological traps. It helps resist temptation and gives company leaders confidence to stay the course.

Strategy Is an Antidote to Hubris

Finally, while strategy gives company leaders who must make risky decisions confidence, it also helps avoid hubris, that excessive self-confidence often associated with the archaic meaning of destiny as fate. A healthy degree of modesty as well as confidence is maintained by being able to separate luck from proficiency and by recognizing the fortuitous factors in a strategic situation that can be used to sustain success over time.

CAPITALIZE ON STRATEGIC DISSONANCE

The Rubber Band Theory of Strategic Alignment

If strategy is about forces, what are they and how can they be examined? The framework of dynamic forces driving company evolution (Tool I) yields insight in company-level and industry-level strategic forces. It serves as a diagnostic tool at the industry-company interface level of analysis to examine the extent to which the forces that affect destiny are changing and to determine what it will take for the company to be able to stay in control of its destiny. Think of the connections between the basis of competitive advantage in the industry, distinctive competence, official strategy, and strategic action in Tool I as rubber bands.[13] During periods of strategic alignment, the rubber bands are evenly stretched because the dynamic forces are in harmony. Over time, however, the dynamic forces tend to diverge. The rubber bands get stretched unevenly and harmony turns into disharmony.

Diagnosis 1: Sources of Strategic Dissonance

Divergence of the dynamic forces creates strategic dissonance in the organization. Strategic dissonance, in first instance, appears to have a negative connotation. But, signaling a strategic inflection point (SIP) is an important function of strategic dissonance. If top management does nothing when faced with a SIP, the company may die or, at the least, its prospects may be severely diminished. If top management is able to come up with a new strategy that takes advantage of the new industry conditions, it can enter a new era of profitable growth. Andy Grove observed that a first indication of an impending SIP is that people in the organization are confused: "Do people seem to be losing it around you? If people don't get it or you don't get it, maybe it is because the it has changed." [14]

Basis of competition and distinctive competence. One source of strategic dissonance derives from a divergence between the changing basis of competition in the industry and the firm's distinctive competencies. Sometimes the latter become less relevant for competitive advantage. Sometimes unanticipated new developments in the company's competencies open up new business opportunities. The first signals of a divergence between the basis of competition and distinctive competence are usually weak. The sooner such signals are picked up, the better are top management's chances to respond effectively. This is particularly important given the strong inertia associated with distinctive competence. It takes time to make significant changes in the company's competencies or to deploy them toward new opportunities. [15] Top management must closely watch the evolution of industry forces. For instance, Andy Grove uses the silver bullet target test to identify Intel's most dangerous competitor(s) at a particular moment in time. If it is no longer clear which company is the target, the basis of competition may be changing.

Official strategy and strategic action. Another source of strategic dissonance originates in the divergence between corporate strategy and strategic action. Sometimes strategic action leads strategy. [16] Preferably strategy should lead strategic action. But top managers sometimes change the corporate strategy too dramatically or too fast, stretching beyond what the company is capable of doing and/or the market is ready to accept. [17] The divergence of corporate strategy and strategic action is sometimes driven by actions taken by middle-level managers. Such actions often explore new business opportunities outside the corporate strategy. [18] Strategic actions taken by middle-level managers that diverge from the corporate strategy, however, also carry potential danger. [19] The first signals of divergence between official strategy and strategic action are also likely to be weak. Being alert to such divergences gives top management the opportunity to recognize their strategic implications sooner.

Diagnosis 2: Adaptive Capability of the Internal Selection Environment

Top management cannot prevent the rubber bands connecting a company's dynamic forces from stretching unevenly. Being unhappy about it has no effect. It is like being unhappy about gravity when dropping something—gravity is here to stay. Top management, however, can create an internal selection environment—a culture—that will help prevent the rubber bands from snapping. Such an internal selection environment has the following four attributes:

Resource allocation. In the first attribute, the role of the internal selection environment is to regulate the allocation of the company's scarce resources—cash, competencies and capabilities, and top management attention—to strategic action. Top management must ensure that the company's resource allocation process continues to reflect the competitive pressures in the external environment, rather than inertia or politics. But this implies that top management understands competitive reality, which is not always the case. A necessary condition is that the company has accounting and management information systems that reflect how its businesses are really doing in the competitive environment.[20] Top management needs to ask sharp questions, on a regular basis, about why the company's businesses are performing the way they are—who is winning and who is losing in their competitive environments—and what are the real costs and returns of various activities.

Internal debate. Internal debate is the second attribute. The company's internal selection environment must value dissent and controversy surrounding tough issues and strategic arguments. This is difficult because organizations are uncomfortable with internal dissent. Debating tough issues, such as the prospect of exiting a current business, is possible only where people can speak their minds without fear of punishment. A key role of top management is to provide an umbrella against such fears. Top management may not be competent to personally judge the issues but it must create a fear-free internal selection environment. Strategic arguments are often about resource allocation decisions that involve executives leading businesses that make money today and executives that are championing new businesses that promise to make money tomorrow. Allocating resources to only existing businesses is shortsighted. The company must also be able to develop new businesses. It is important that top management create a forum to allow champions of new businesses to present their cases. These should be tough sessions for would-be champions. But if top management disagreed with the champions who turn out to be right, top management should congratulate them.[21]

Strategic recognition. A third attribute concerns the company's capacity for strategic recognition: This is the capacity of senior and top managers to appreciate the strategic importance of new internal and/or external developments *after* they have come about but *before* unequivocal environmental feedback about their strategic importance is available. In dynamic environments the opportunities for strategic recognition are often first available to middle- and senior-level leaders because they are closer to the frontiers of technologies, customers, and markets. Hence, the capacity for strategic recognition at middle and senior levels of management is vital. Generally strategic recognition is easier in relation to threats to the core business than in relation to new opportunities because the costs of unrecognized threats to the core business are usually heavier than those associated with missed opportunities. Swift strategic recognition can determine whether a new development is perceived as a threat or an opportunity. This can help prevent grave potential consequences.[22]

Strategic leadership. Strategic leadership is the fourth attribute. Top management must try to surmise how the new equilibrium of forces in the industry will look and what the new winning strategy will be, knowing that they cannot get it completely right. Top management must use the information that is generated by strategic dissonance when trying to discern the true new shape of the company. It must be a realistic picture grounded in the company's distinctive competencies—existing ones or new ones that are already being developed. Coming out of a difficult period, top management is more likely to have a sense of what they *don't* want the company to become before they know what they *do* want it to become. This hardly seems visionary. But in these situations leadership implies changing with the environment and the organization. Reality must lead top management rather than the other way around. This is difficult because top management is expected to have a vision to guide the company.[23] Once the new direction is clear, the ferment needs to stop, and all hands need to be committed to this new direction.

There is an inverted-U type of relationship between the intensity and duration of constructive intellectual debate in a company and its long-term ability to manage through SIPs. At one extreme, too little debating means that middle and senior managers do not challenge one another as long as the favor is reciprocated. The result is a lack of strategic dissonance and a hard fall off the curve. At the other extreme, too much debating paralyzes the company because most energy is used up in winning the debate rather than helping the company to win. Strategic action is delayed indefinitely. A hard fall off the curve is again the likely result. So, during strategic dissonance, top management must let go some while it is not sure. This too is not easy because top management is paid for being sure! But then managers must pull strategy and strategic action, and the basis of competition and distinctive competence, back in alignment—reestablishing the symmetry of the rubber bands. Strategic leadership means encouraging debate *and* bringing debate to a conclusion. This, in turn, requires two defining conditions for exerting leadership: first, developing deep insight in what the company's real capabilities are; and second, mustering the courage to follow through on a conviction that may not yet be widely shared.[24]

A Culture of Constructive Confrontation and Commitment

Strong bottoms-up and top-down forces characterize a strategic leadership culture that has the four key attributes discussed above. If the top-down force dominates, chances are that the company will efficiently march in lockstep toward an important strategic intent, but the strategic intent had better continue to be the right one. If the bottom-up force dominates, chances are that the company will drift aimlessly from one limited strategic intent to another and dissipate its resources. If both the top-down and bottom-up forces are weak, the company will experience something like Brownian motion.

But how can these forces both be strong at the same time? They can, if the company has the rugged, confrontational/collegial culture that is desirable in high-technology industries. Such a culture tolerates—even encourages—debates of the sort discussed above. At Intel, the name for it is "constructive confrontation." These debates are vigorous, devoted to exploring issues, and indifferent of rank. They are focused on finding in first instance what is the strategic truth and what is best for the company (as opposed to what is best for the individual or group). Such a culture is also capable of making clear decisions, with the entire organization supporting the decision, including those who still are not convinced that the decision is the right one. At Intel the name for it is "disagree and commit." In the end top management determines whether the bottoms-up force remains strong. Top management by definition has the power to impose its will, so the dynamic tension between bottoms-up and top-down forces is a precarious one. Top management must work hard to keep the bottoms-up force strong.

EXERCISE TWO STRATEGIC DISCIPLINES SIMULTANEOUSLY

The study of Intel's evolution suggested that strategy-making serves to exploit opportunities associated with the core business, to develop and exploit new business opportunities outside the core business, and to balance the exploitation of existing and new opportunities as the company evolves. It was reassuring that these three strategy-making challenges are consistent with previous research that focused on industrial giants of an earlier age.[25] They seem to apply generally and to impose themselves across the ages. Meeting them allows companies to continue to control their destinies. The induced and autonomous strategy processes of Tool II, which are in play simultaneously in established companies, offered insight into these challenges. During Epoch III, they were called the blue and green processes respectively at Intel and managers invariably were able to locate themselves in relation to them. Each strategy process requires its own discipline, and exercising both disciplines simultaneously requires unusual strategic leadership competence.

Discipline 1: Exploiting Opportunities in the Core Business

The first discipline, associated with the induced strategy process, is familiar to all surviving companies. To understand how companies develop discipline 1, it is useful to track the path that leads from start-up company to established one. Start-up companies usually face severe external selection pressures—fierce competitors, difficult customers, powerful suppliers, etc.—and must overcome liabilities of newness, such as lack of a track record and name recognition, and customer and supplier uncertainty about their staying power.[26] If a start-up survives external selection, it can leverage what it has learned about the reasons for its survival by creating an induced strategy process. The induced strategy process is inherently oriented toward reducing variation. This makes sense, because the company survived external selection by satisfying its customers in certain ways and wants to continue to do so. To that end, it puts in place a strategy and a structural context to make it reliable, predictable, and accountable, which is what strategic leadership discipline 1 is about.

Benefits of a narrow business strategy. What some scholars have called a narrow business strategy facilitates the development of strategic discipline 1.[27] A narrow business strategy presumably facilitates the CEO's ability to be clear about strategy and to communicate it effectively to the organization as well as to external parties such as market analysts.[28] It facilitates concentration of strategy-making in the CEO and has strong advantages in terms of his or her ability to structure incentives to tightly align the firm's strategy and the actions of its managers. Andy Grove's efforts to strengthen Intel's induced strategy process during Epoch II were helped by focusing the corporate strategy narrowly on the microprocessor business and creating a structural context, including strategic planning, organization design, resource allocation, and measurement and reward systems that strongly aligned strategy and action. He was able to clearly observe the commitment of middle and senior executives to the new strategy and move managerial personnel in and out of leadership positions accordingly.

Discipline 2: Exploiting New Opportunities Outside the Core Business

Benefits of broadening the business strategy. Recently these same scholars have formalized parts of the evolutionary framework encompassing induced- and autonomous-strategy processes.[29] In their mathematical model, the firm employs a visionary CEO who is consistently biased in favor of certain projects and against others, but who leaves the door open for pursuing sufficiently good opportunities outside the existing vision. They show that this may offer greater profit-maximizing possibilities than committing to a narrow business strategy. They show the important role that objective middle managers play when they are willing to support promising projects outside the CEO's vision. Importantly, they also show that the biased CEO must not interfere with the autonomy of these middle managers in allocating resources to such projects.[30] Their model thus supports the potential value of the autonomous-strategy process in a company's success.

Strategic leadership discipline 2, which is associated with the autonomous-strategy process, is concerned with turning new ideas outside the scope of the existing strategy into new businesses. Autonomous initiatives explore the boundaries of the company's competencies and product-market opportunities.[31] They can be complements to the core business or potential substitutes, and it is not always immediately clear whether they are one or the other.[32] Given their potential strategic importance, top management must take autonomous initiatives and discipline 2 seriously. Many companies operate on the assumption that they already know discipline 2. Yet, their autonomous-strategy process often breaks down because they fail to appreciate the difference between exploration (generating new ideas) and exploitation (turning them into new businesses).[33]

Role of strategic context determination process. The process of strategic context determination is key for turning autonomous initiatives into new businesses for the company. Strategic context determination depends on middle and senior executives looking for ways to take advantage of unanticipated innovations generated by the autonomous-strategy process, and to engage top management in their efforts to support those that they believe can be winners for the company. Top management must be clear about how strategically important a particular autonomous initiative is and how it relates to the company's core competencies and capabilities. This involves conceptually difficult and time-consuming work for persons who are already highly taxed by the demands of the core business.[34]

To see the importance of the strategic context determination process, one need simply ask, Where can autonomous strategic initiatives go if strategic context determination processes cannot be activated? One option is that in the face of a lack of corporate interest, such initiatives eventually wither away as their originator gets tired or moves on. A second option is for the originators of the initiative to leave the company and to seek venture capital in support of pursuing the business. This may very well be the best option for certain types of initiatives. But to make such determination in an informed way still requires the activation of the strategic context determination process. A third option is for autonomous initiatives to be evaluated within the structural context created in support of the core business strategy. In this case, the autonomous initiative is likely to lose out against proposals associated with the core business. Finally, internal entrepreneurs are sometimes able to go directly to top management for support. While occasional success stories along these lines can probably be told, this is potentially quite hazardous because top management is usually not in the best position to assess the technological and market uncertainties and risks involved early on in the process (they are too far removed).

Since each of these alternative avenues for pursuing autonomous strategic initiatives is potentially flawed, the importance of paying serious attention to the difficult process of strategic context determination should not be underestimated. Working through this process provides both those proposing the autonomous initiatives and top management with the best available information and assessment concerning the merits of the opportunity and how it can best be pursued within the corporation.

Tolerance for ambiguity. Low tolerance of ambiguity on the part of top management impedes the activation of strategic context determination processes for new businesses.[35] It is simply the case that new business opportunities are seldom fully specifiable at the outset. Strategy formulation in a new business area initially will often be less crisp than in the core business. While discipline 2 is different, however, it does not have to be less rigorous than discipline 1. The strategic context determination process provides a testing ground for the rigor of discipline 2. But top management needs to recognize that discipline 2 involves a certain degree of ambiguity in the early stages and should allow for well-reasoned and well-supported changes in strategic plans as the strategic situation unfolds. More frequent top management strategic reviews might be in order in new business development to maintain discipline while also allowing for more ambiguity. Top managers, however, need to moderate their own direct influence by consciously leaving room for new business leaders to formulate the appropriate strategy for the new business.[36]

Extended corporate entrepreneurship. Autonomous strategic initiatives are the seeds of the internal Schumpeterian process of creative destruction. In dynamic environments, however, external variations are likely to exceed internal variation and some external variations may potentially materially affect the company's future. To control the company's destiny it is better to bring these variations inside than to let them overtake the company from the outside. This implies that a company must be able to not only hold on to its own internal entrepreneurial initiatives but must also learn to bring relevant external entrepreneurial initiatives into its fold. This extends the challenge of discipline 2. Internal entrepreneurial initiatives must be complemented with external entrepreneurial initiatives: identifying, funding, and integrating relevant external ventures. Corporate venture capital is an important tool for the first step of the process: identifying and funding relevant external ventures.[37] The second step involves integrating these into a broader corporate strategic thrust. This again involves strategic context determination processes to optimally structure the relationships between internal and external ventures and those existing parts of the corporation that can optimally leverage their contributions.

Maintaining linkage. Motivated by consequential logic, leaders see the autonomous-strategy process as an alternative structure for achieving career progress. They may have experienced bad luck with previous outcomes in the induced process, or they may realize that other strategists have already preempted access to the best opportunities. Probably more often, leaders engage in autonomous strategic action because of an obligatory logic.[38] They feel it is the right thing to do given who they are. The latter motivation, however, implies a certain distance between leaders and the rest of the organization. Strategy-making also involves people and their emotions. Given enough time, strategy-making almost unavoidably will involve key players in some conflicts between the induced- and autonomous-strategy processes. Even when constructively resolved, the emotional fallout may linger and continue to color the relationships between senior managers as they move on.[39]

Motivational and emotional tensions exacerbate the inherently strong but wrongheaded inclination of people operating in the autonomous-strategy process to declare themselves different from the rest of the company, and to develop an us-versus-them mentality, which almost always comes to grief. Senior and top management should shield autonomous initiatives but should not let them isolate themselves from the rest of the company. If alignment is the driver of discipline 1, linkage should direct discipline 2. Linkage, however, may come at a price that some are not willing to pay. As one leading organization theorist puts it, "You can have autonomy or power, but not both. Power depends on linkages, and linkages destroy autonomy.[40] Not all managers operating in the autonomous-strategy process will be able or willing to continue to participate once the linkages are established. This creates important human resource management and executive development challenges.

Terminating clear failures. Strategic leadership discipline 2 also requires that top management has the will to terminate autonomous initiatives that after careful examination fail to achieve important milestones or do not fit the company. The willingness to terminate experiments has to be viewed as an integral part of the process of creating such experiments. Otherwise, the weight of accumulated and undisposed of experimentation will eventually dissipate the company's resources and inhibit the start of new experiments.[41] Careful efforts to determine the strategic context reduce the probability that those involved in autonomous initiatives will perceive such unfavorable decisions as arbitrary or frivolous. Top management, however, also needs to be concerned with redeploying people who are freed up when an autonomous initiative is halted.[42] This requires that the persons involved were perceived as excellent employees to begin with. Staffing new ventures with castoffs from the core business who are not welcome back in the core business is one of the surest ways to make it very difficult to stop new ventures.

Simultaneity Is Key

Mastering strategic leadership disciplines 1 and 2 puts high demands on senior and top management. Yet, the demands do not stop there. Top management must also help the company exercise both disciplines simultaneously. Companies find it extremely difficult to do so. They are more likely to focus on one and neglect the other during different periods in their evolution.[43] To master both simultaneously, top management must learn to balance opposing forces and to recognize the gravitational force associated with the induced strategy process. Managing these forces helps top management temper the fluctuations in corporate support of the autonomous strategy process that otherwise naturally happens. In the end, successfully balancing the two disciplines poses the ultimate test for top management's ability to use strategy-making as adaptive organizational capability.

Forces affecting simultaneity. Two forces that make it difficult to exercise both disciplines simultaneously are (1) the prospects of the core business and (2) the availability of uncommitted financial resources. Sometimes the company has un-committed financial resources that accumulate in good times to support au-tonomous initiatives. If the prospects of the core business continue to be sufficient to achieve profit and growth objectives, however, it is difficult for top management to give attention and support to new business development because everybody is very busy exploiting the existing opportunities. Under such circumstances, top management is likely to pay lip service to supporting autonomous initiatives; it is easy to delay action to tomorrow. A number of orphan initiatives are likely to linger on. If, on the other hand, the prospects of the core business are insufficient to meet objectives, top management's efforts to actively develop new business opportuni-ties are likely to be stronger. If it looks like the core business can be fixed, however, new business initiatives may again end up as orphans or suffer cutbacks as the con-sequence of a renewed focus on the core business.

Sometimes there are no uncommitted financial resources available—for in-stance when the company has recently experienced a severe downturn of its core business as a result of the industry cycle. If the cycle turns upward and the prospects of the core business are sufficient to meet corporate objectives, however, the drive to develop new business opportunities is likely to be weak. If, on the other hand, the core business prospects are insufficient, top management may be tempted to desperately latch on to the first available new opportunity. This has a high probability of failure.

Internal competition and cooperation. Inevitably, induced and autonomous strategic initiatives are somewhat at odds as they compete for the company's lim-ited resources. Balancing the two disciplines may involve encouraging friendly in-ternal competition that paces the development of both the core business and new business opportunities.[44] In the end, the winners in the internal competition should be those that win in their external environment. New businesses, however, may take some time to establish themselves as winners in their relevant product-market environment and to grow to a size that is meaningful from the perspective of the corporation. Senior and top management must give them some time to get their feet on the ground before comparing their results and size with those of the established businesses. At the same time, the pacing process must be complemented with a process that exploits the potential for synergy between the core business and the new opportunities. The internal competition should never get in the way of one part of the company helping the other for the benefit of the whole, let alone lead to destructive action that diminishes the prospects of one or the other. This refers back to the attributes of the internal selection environment discussed earlier.

MANAGE THE CYCLE TIME OF STRATEGIC CHANGE

The study of Intel's evolution suggests that gaining and maintaining control over the company's destiny requires the replacement of old product-market strategies by new ones and the displacement of old distinctive competencies by new ones. Strategic business exit and entry thus play a key role in the strategy-making process. Cycle time of strategic change—the calendar time between defining a new business exit or entry and concluding the process—is a key parameter of strategy-making as adaptive organizational capability.[45] Strategic change can be too fast, leading to potential disaster; for instance, changing to a new technology too soon in the mistaken belief that the current one is on its way out and thereby providing an opening for competitors.[46] Strategic change that is too slow, however, is the greater and more frequent danger in dynamic environments. Managing the cycle time of developing new businesses is a key concern of top management.

Understand the Pattern of Strategic Leadership Activities

The cycle time of strategic change depends on the patterns of interlocking, sequential, and simultaneous value-added activities of leaders situated at different levels in the company. Process models (Tool III) depict these complex patterns of strategic leadership activities and organizational forces in a parsimonious way. They help explain the paradoxes, vicious circles, dilemmas, and tensions that derive from the activities of leaders who are differentially situated in the organization and respond to different external and internal pressures. They show the underlying order and sources of rationality in strategy-making processes that, on the surface, look chaotic.

Providing a picture of the complete processes—showing simultaneous as well as sequential strategic leadership activities and contextual forces—also helps understand better the difficulties in establishing when exactly a strategic exit or entry decision was made and when strategic business exit or entry has actually occurred. Such strategic changes may take place before they are recognized or acknowledged by top management. As a diagnostic tool the process model draws top management's attention to business-level strategic activities that are already clearing the road to exit or entry but whose corporate-level strategic implications have not yet been fully realized, and vice versa.

Internal Corporate Venturing

The success of a new venture depends on whether enough real customers are willing to pay for the new products or services to turn it into a profitable business for the company. The process model of internal corporate venturing indicates that this requires difficult technical and need linking activities performed at the operational level. Often the managers involved must circumvent regular internal channels to obtain resources and need to spend enormous efforts to establish a beachhead in the market that provides a basis for senior managers to convince the company to continue to support the venture. Without these key entrepreneurial activities at the operational level, there simply is no new business.

The process model analysis indicates, however, that the pattern of leadership activities involved in new ventures often breaks down at the middle/senior level. Activities at this level, such as strategic building and organizational championing, require difficult cognitive and political skills. High-level cognitive skills are necessary to be able to articulate a compelling strategy for a new business over and beyond the one generated by the operational level venture manager. Such a strategy is critical for middle/senior leaders to keep the initiative and aggressively ask for continued top management support. High-level political skills are necessary to muster support from peers—for instance to negotiate the transfer of projects from different parts of the company to the new venture. As noted earlier, obtaining such support may sometimes be difficult because leaders operate in a network of relationships with peers, with time interdependence between their current initiative and past experiences.

The New Business Group: A Transit Station, Not a Destination

Internal ventures are different from the ones that venture capitalists typically invest in because they have an umbilical cord with the company. Their chances of success are strongly determined by their ability to leverage the company's resources, competencies and capabilities and/or strategic position. Often companies, like Intel, form a New Business Group (NBG). Forming such a separate group, however, is only the first step. The second step is to determine the appropriate organization design and measurement and incentive system to maximize their chances of success. This requires sophisticated understanding of the interdependencies involved in the new business development process, which can be established and tracked using the assessment framework discussed in chapter 11.[47] For instance, if a new venture needs to share resources or competencies with some part of the core business, it will be important to give the core business people involved a stake in the success of the venture as well.[48] The important point is that the NBG should be used as a transit station for new ventures and not as a destination.

Complex Strategic Integration

As companies add new businesses, fully exploiting growth opportunities requires also pursuing those that span more than one business. Most of these will be within the scope of the given corporate strategy, but some will reach beyond. Pursuing cross-business opportunities requires a strategic integration capability that so far eludes most multibusiness companies.[49] This capability depends again on general managers at the senior level possessing complex skills. One part of the skill set involves alliance building aimed at integrating the strategic actions of multiple business units within the existing strategic context. Another part involves high-level strategic thinking aimed at renewing the strategic context and amending the corporate strategy.

Developing and Deploying General Management Talent

The key actors in new business development are middle- and senior-level leaders with strong general management capabilities. That is, leaders who can bring together the necessary resources to turn a new business concept into a real business and who can envision how the new business enhances the profitable growth prospects of the company. Such general management talent is relatively rare and needs to be spotted and recruited, nurtured and developed. Executive mobility between core and new businesses may help promote the development of these general management skills. As noted earlier, such mobility is often hindered by the tendency of people involved in new business development to isolate their venture from the mainstream. This is understandable, because unenlightened colleagues in the core business sometimes try to impress on them that what they are doing has no chance of success, is wrong, is a waste of time and corporate money, and so on. As also noted earlier, real strategic conflict between new business development and the core business does sometimes emerge. New business leaders occasionally feel the need to circumvent some of the regular corporate ways and means that are viewed as roadblocks to change. These sorts of frictions make it difficult for employees that joined a new business initiative to go back to the mainstream. While some strongly prefer the more certain work environment of the core business and others equally strongly prefer the more chaotic environment of new business development, most employees are usually somewhere in the middle and could successfully operate in either environment. Nevertheless, often the extremists on both sides define the atmosphere for the working relationships between the core business and new business people. Isolation and noncollaborative working relations between core and new business people are bound to increase the cycle time of strategic change.

CONCLUSION: PAST AND PROLOGUE

The good fortune of meeting Andy Grove in summer 1988 and getting the opportunity to study Intel's evolution made it possible to see the fundamental challenges that strategy-making must confront over time in one of the most important and well-run high-technology companies in the world.

Studying Intel's strategic evolution offered the opportunity to observe two different models of strategy-making. During Epoch I, strategy-making under Gordon Moore's direction resembled the internal ecology model, which helped Intel transform itself and rise from the ashes of its original core business. During Epoch II, strategy-making under Andy Grove resembled the rational actor model, which is often viewed as the ideal one. Like other great leaders, Grove was able to recognize the unique opportunities facing Intel and to mobilize his organization to exploit them. Grove created a strategy vector that drove the PC industry. There is little doubt that companies that find themselves in the fortuitous circumstances that Intel faced after its defeat in the DRAM business can greatly benefit from leaders with exceptional strategic recognition capacity and determination to capitalize on them. But even in such cases, the benefits of the rational actor model must be tempered by the realization that eventually the relative force of the strategy vector will decline and that the company's future prospects will depend on how well it has continued to develop its strategic renewal capability. A key lesson of this book is that over the very long run, spanning multiple generations of CEOs, the genius of individual leadership is no substitute for maintaining a company's internal ecology of strategy-making as adaptive organizational capability.

Intel's strategic evolution continues. Looking forward in spring 2001, Intel's core business is under more severe competitive attack than it has been in fifteen years. This raises questions of how Epoch III is likely to deal with the strategy-making challenges. Will Craig Barrett be able to reassert Intel's competitive strength in the core business and execute forcefully in both the client and server markets while simultaneously continuing to pursue new business opportunities?

Or will he revert back to a singular focus on defending the core business and push all distractions to the side? The unfolding of Epoch III will provide further insight in how Intel's top management learns to meet these challenges simultaneously—or fails at it as most other companies have before. Designing the internal ecology of strategy-making to simultaneously exploit existing and new business opportunities is Barrett's key strategic leadership challenge.

A Final Thought

This chapter offers four strategic leadership imperatives to help top management design the internal ecology of strategy-making: Embrace strategy to control destiny, capitalize on strategic dissonance, exercise two strategic disciplines simultaneously, and manage the cycle time of strategic change. The latter three are further augmentations of Alfred D. Chandler's integrative hierarchy, the managerial capability to supervise and coordinate complex activities and processes that helped make the modern industrial enterprise possible.[50] They are key parts of the strategic leadership capability of the corporation of the future.

The first one—embrace strategy to control destiny—is important at the individual as well as the company level. This book has depicted a world in which the cliches about change being the only constant are true. It is a world in which one stays ahead or falls behind—there is no safe haven to wait out the storm. It is a world of great ambiguity with high interdependence between players who collaborate and compete with each other in a continually evolving network of relationships and resources. Leaders who want to be effective must learn to work in this network and accept its interdependencies and ambiguities. This book proposes that strategy understood as the intelligent appreciation and manipulation of the forces that affect destiny helps leaders gain and maintain control of their own destiny while contributing to that of their company. As leaders face the perpetual tension between order and chaos, *Strategy Is Destiny* may help them resolve it at a high level of integration rather than as choice or compromise—if only each time for some time.

A P P E N D I X   I
Research Method

LONGITUDINAL FIELD-BASED RESEARCH

The study was based on a longitudinal, multistage, nested case study design within one corporate setting.[1] The research was carried on almost continuously over a period of twelve years between 1988 and 2000, but involved several stages—periods of intense data collection. The research used the methodology of grounded theorizing. Grounded theorizing is a qualitative method for inductively gaining theoretical insights grounded in data through comparative analysis.[2] At the company-environment interface level of analysis, the framework of dynamic forces driving company evolution—Tool I in figure 1.3—served to compare the coevolutionary process between Intel's strategy and its product-market environments during Epochs I–III. At the company level of analysis, the evolutionary process framework of the strategy-making process—Tool II in figure 1.3—was used to compare modes of strategy-making across the three Epochs. At the intracompany level of analysis, the process model of internal corporate venturing—Tool III in figure 1.3—was used to compare the relative success of different new businesses in Intel's internal selection environment. This research design was well suited for the purpose of generating new theoretical insight in the role of strategy-making in company evolution.

STAGES IN THE LONGITUDINAL FIELD-BASED RESEARCH

Each of the stages in the research was carried out with the help of research associates and yielded research cases that were also turned into teaching cases. Teaching these cases with Andy Grove in Stanford Business School's MBA program every year since 1989 provided additional real-time data as Andy reflected on Intel's evolving strategic situation. The cases were also taught in various executive training programs within Intel. More than one thousand of Intel's middle and senior executives attended these sessions between 1994 and 2000, offering each time the opportunity to confirm or refine some of the data and to collect additional views.

Stage One (Fall 1988–Spring 1991)

After initial interviews in October 1988 with CEO Andrew S. Grove and Dennis Carter, Grove's technical assistant, it was decided to focus the first stage of the research on Intel's decision to exit from the dynamic random access memory (DRAM) business. At the time, this decision was situated in October 1985, but later it was found that it had actually started almost one year earlier in November 1984.[3] The first part of this stage involved retrospective research of Intel's exit from the DRAM business and the company's transformation into a microprocessor company in the mid-1980s. The second part focused on events since 1985, covering several key strategic areas. The most important of these included the development of Intel's major Complex Instruction Set Computing (CISC) microprocessors (the x86 product family), the emergence of Reduced Instruction Set Computing (RISC) processors (the i860), the development of a new semiconductor memory called Flash, and the evolution of the strategic importance of the Erasable Programmable Read Only Memory (EPROM) business. Other important developments included Intel's experience with Application Specific Integrated Circuits (ASIC), the emergence and spinoff of the Electrically Erasable Programmable Read Only Memory (E^2PROM) venture, and the growing importance of the Systems business. While most of the data collection was retrospective, this stage of the research was long enough to observe some strategic decisions in real time, especially the decision to adopt RISC as part of Intel's corporate strategy and the uncertainty about Flash memories.

The final part of this stage, from fall 1990 through spring 1991, focused on the implementation of the DRAM exit decision. This retrospective research sought to document the difficulties that Intel encountered in getting the organization to stop all activity in DRAM in the mid-1980s. During this period, Intel's top management also made important decisions regarding the exit from EPROM and from further development of the RISC-based i860 microprocessor. The latter decisions were tracked in real time. The first stage of the research is captured in the Intel (A), (B), and (C) case studies.[4]

Stage Two (Throughout 1993)

The second stage of the research took place during most of 1993. This stage involved retrospective research of the development of the Pentium processor, and real-time research of its launch. It focused on the competition Intel experienced from Intel Architecture rivals such as AMD and Cyrix, as well as from rivals associated with the RISC architecture, such as IBM and Motorola. The research also focused on several new businesses that Intel pursued in its Intel Product Group (IPG) during the late 1980s and early 1990s, including ProShare, the early networking business, and Flash. This research is captured in the Intel (D) and (E) case studies.[5]

Stage Three (Mid-1990s–1999)

The third major stage began in 1996 and continued through 1999. One part of this stage focused on Intel's enormous success with successive generations of the Pentium processor during the mid-1990s and the emergence of several strategic threats, including the much-hyped Network Computer (NC) and the fast growth of the low end of the PC market segment. This research is captured in the Intel (F) case study.[6] Another part focused on Intel's efforts to develop PC-based videoconferencing as a new business and the company's efforts to bring the PC into the family room. This research is captured in four case studies: "The PC-Based Desktop Videoconferencing Systems Industry in 1998," "Intel Corporation: The Hood River Project (A) and (B)," and "Intel's Strategic Position in the Family Room, 1998."[7] Still another part of the third stage drew on data collected by Intel staff in collaboration with a consulting firm concerning several new ventures, including chipsets and networking, that Intel pursued during the 1990s. This research is reported in chapters 7 and 9 of this book. The final part of the third stage involved a large-scale case study of Intel's evolution, documenting three Epochs in Intel's history: Intel the memory company, Intel the microprocessor company, and Intel the Internet building block company. This research is captured in the case study "Intel Corporation: The Evolution of an Adaptive Organization."[8]

Stage Four (Beyond 1999)

The fourth stage of the research is ongoing, tracking Intel's evolution during Epoch III.

DATA COLLECTION

Interview Data

During the twelve years of research, close to one hundred senior and top Intel executives were formally interviewed, many several times. Some former senior and top Intel executives were also interviewed. The interviews yielded several hundred pages of transcripts. Managers from different levels, different functional groups, and different businesses were involved. Throughout the research period, informal, usually brief, discussions with many current and former Intel employees were used to corroborate data obtained from the formal interviews. Between 1994 and 1999, more than one thousand Intel executives took part in various executive training sessions in which the case studies and conceptual tools were used to stimulate discussion.

Most interviews lasted between one and two hours and were open-ended. Follow-up interviews were semi-structured, for clarification about key events, people, and issues that had been identified.[9] Key events centered, for instance, around the introduction of successive generations of products in each of the businesses, because these introductions drove and were driven by the competitive dynamics in the industry. Key people were individuals or groups from different functional areas or different hierarchical levels that made critical decisions, or made proposals that, while not necessarily implemented, triggered high-level reconsideration of strategic issues. Key issues included, among many others, the importance of DRAM as a technology driver at Intel, the allocation of scarce manufacturing capacity, the allocation of R&D resources to different businesses, the integration of process technology development and manufacturing, the deployment of key talent, Intel's ability to compete in commodity businesses and Intel's ability to develop new businesses. No tape recorders are used, but the interviewers made extensive notes. I conducted many of the interviews with a research associate. Transcripts of the research associates' notes, when compared with mine always showed agreement on the substantive content of the interview. This provided some confidence that the data were valid and reliable, and that the data collected by the different research associates on their own over the years were likely to be of high quality. Quotations were constructed based on the interview transcripts. These quotations were submitted to the interviewees, who reviewed them for accuracy and appropriateness.

Archival Data

Archival data, such as documents describing the company's history, annual reports, and reports to financial analysts, were obtained from Intel. Additional archival data were obtained from outside sources, such as industry publications, and financial analysts' reports and business press articles about Intel and the semi-conductor and computer industries. These archival data made it possible, for instance, to construct a quantitative picture of the evolution of the semiconductor memory industry and Intel's evolving strategic position in major segments. The archival data could be juxtaposed to the interview data to check for potential systematic biases in retrospective accounts of past strategy.[10] Discrepancies between interview data and archival data discovered in the course of the research raised a number of questions that guided further data collection and analysis. A few other studies of Intel provided useful sources of additional data as well as a validity check for the new data collected in this study. As prescribed by the methodology of grounded theorizing, data collection was concluded when a level of saturation was reached: patterns became clear and the incremental value of additional data became small.[11]

AN EVOLUTIONARY THEORETICAL LENS

The field data served to test, to some extent, the validity of Tools I–III of the evolutionary research lens. Experts in methodology have discussed several conditions for making a single case study useful as a probe for theory, two of which could be addressed in relation to the Intel study. These are (1) keeping track of confirming and disconfirming observations, (2) choosing the theory without knowledge of the confirmatory value of the case study.[12] Regarding the first condition, while initially not intended to serve as a test of an evolutionary theory of strategy-making, the first two stages of the study did offer confirmatory support for the relevance of the strategic processes proposed in the conceptual tools. Disconfirming observations were not systematically sought out, but some unexpected findings suggested some amendments.

Regarding the second condition, the availability of Intel as a research site was a fortuitous event and it was not at all clear in advance whether the research would produce support for the evolutionary framework or not. In fact, since the research was started with the purpose of developing research-based teaching material that would allow Andy Grove to participate in teaching at Stanford Business School, there was no initial intent to use the research for that purpose. In addition, neither my first research associate nor I were familiar with the strategic management approaches of Intel. The initial expectations were that Intel would probably not be an interesting site for studying strategy-making from an evolutionary perspective. I assumed, wrongly of course as it turned out, that there would be little room for autonomous strategic action at Intel. Furthermore, my research associate, who was not involved in developing the conceptual framework, did several of the very first, open-ended interviews. This limited the potential for confirmatory bias in the data collection.

LIMITATIONS OF THE RESEARCH

The research combined longitudinal company-level comparative analysis with longitudinal intracompany comparative analysis of different businesses. As a result the study could examine in depth how the company dealt with partial failure—and the threat of complete failure—at a critical point in its history. Nevertheless, the research has several limitations. It concerns a single high-tech company still run by some of its founders. The company grew up in a cyclical but very expansive industry. It was able to transform itself and become a driving force of its new industry, and achieved extreme success. Clearly it would be useful to study a larger sample including failing organizations. Also, the study kept track of Intel's competitors throughout its history, but it would have been fruitful to study these organizations more systematically if time and access had permitted it. On the other hand, by concentrating on one organization with thirty years of continuity in leadership, the research could access sources with intimate knowledge of the details of the company's evolution. Having excellent access made it possible for the researchers to put themselves into "the manager's temporal and contextual frame of reference."[13] Excellent access also made it possible to reconstruct the strategy-making process with input from people at the different levels of management involved in the process. This provided a basis for triangulation and may alleviate some of the concerns associated with retrospective data. The longitudinal dimension of the research provided the opportunity to examine how the company achieved great success by following in real time its extraordinary expansion path. It could also in real time examine some of the consequences of success—the inertial aftermath of success—for its strategy-making process.

APPENDIX II
Financial Highlights of Intel's Evolution

Net Sales ($Millions)

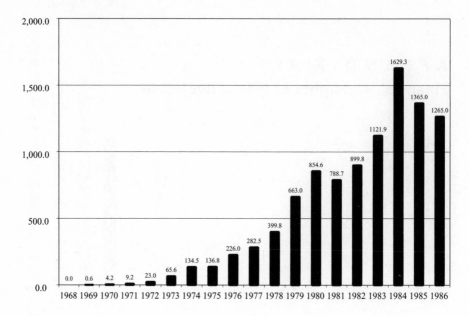

Net Profit ($Millions)

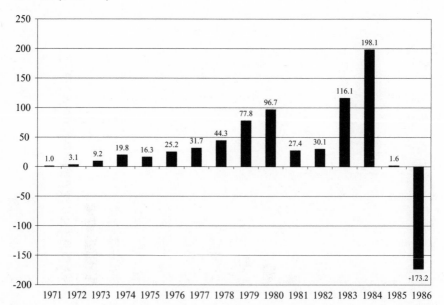

Figure AII.1. Intel Financial Highlights: Epoch I (1968–1986). (SOURCE: Intel documents.)

R&D Expenditures ($Millions), 1971–1986

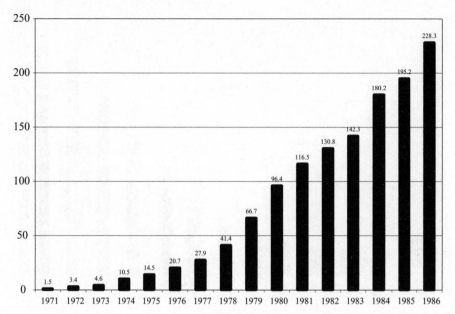

Property, Plant and Equipment Expenditures ($Millions), 1971–1986

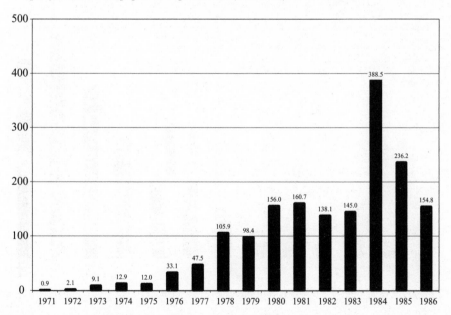

Figure AII.2. Intel Financial Highlights: Epoch I (1971–1986). (SOURCE: Intel documents.)

Net Sales ($Billions)

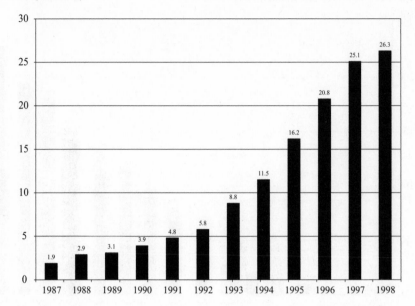

Net Profit ($Billions)

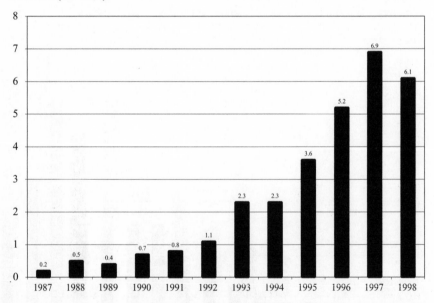

Figure AII.3. Intel Financial Highlights: Epoch II (1987–1998). (SOURCE: Intel documents.)

R&D Expenditures ($Billions), 1987–1998

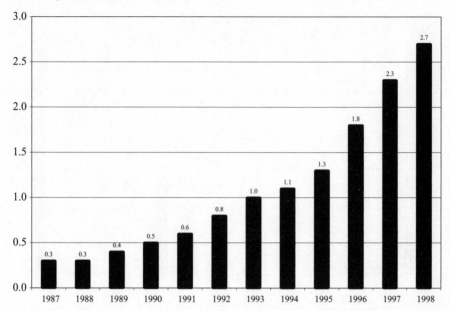

Property, Plant and Equipment Expenditures ($Billions), 1987–1998

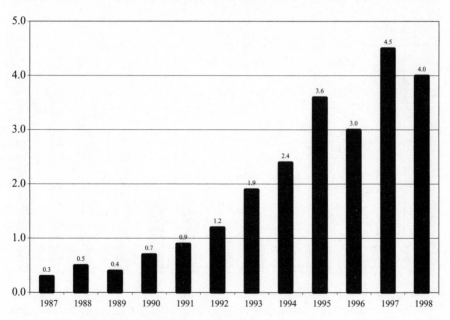

Figure AII.4. Intel Financial Highlights: Epoch II (1987–1998).
(SOURCE: Intel documents.)

($ Millions, 1973–1987)

($ Billions, 1987–1999)

Figure AII.5. Intel Market Capitalization (1968–1999). (SOURCE: Intel documents.)

Processor	Date of Release	Clock Speed (MHz)	Number of Transistors (millions)	Typical Uses
4004	Nov 1971	0.108	0.002300	Busicom calculator
8008	Apr 1972	0.200	0.003500	Dumb terminals, bottling machines
8080	Apr 1974	2.0	0.006000	Traffic light controller, Altair PC
8085	Mar 1976	5.0	0.006500	Toledo scale
8086	Jun 1978	5.0–10.0	0.029000	Portable computing
8088	Jun 1979	5.0–8.0	0.029000	IBM PCs and clones
80286	Feb 1982	6.0–12.0	0.134000	PCs
386 DX	Oct 1985	16–33	0.275000	Desktop computing
386 SX	Jun 1988	16–33	0.275000	Entry level desktop and portable PCs
386 SL	Oct 1990	20–25	0.855000	Portable PCs
486 DX	Apr 1989	25–50	1.2	Desktop computing and servers
486 SX	Apr 1991	16–33	1.185	Entry level desktops
486 SL	Nov 1992	20–33	1.4	Notebook PCs
Pentium processor	Mar 1993 to Jun 1996	60–200	3.1–3.3	Desktops, notebooks, and servers
Pentium Pro processor	Nov 1995	150–200	5.5	High-end desktops, workstations, and servers
Pentium processor with MMX tech.	Jan 1997	166–233	4.5	High-performance desktops and servers
Mobile Pentium proc. with MMX tech.	Sep 1997	200–300	4.5	Mobile PCs and mini-notebooks
Pentium II processor	May 1997	233–450	7.5	High-end desktops, workstations, and servers
Mobile Pentium II processor	Apr 1998	233–400	7.5–27.4	Mobile PCs
Celeron processor	Apr 1998	266–466	7.5–19.0	Low-cost PCs
Mobile Celeron processor	Jan 1999	266–400	18.9	Low-cost mobile PCs
Pentium II Xeon processor	Jun 1998	400–450	7.5	Midrange and higher workstations and servers
Pentium III processor	Feb 1999	450–550	9.5	High-end desktops, workstations, and servers
Pentium III Xeon processor	Mar 1999	500–550	9.5	Business PCs, 2-, 4-, and 8-way servers, and workstations

Figure AII.6. The Evolution of Intel's Microprocessors. (SOURCE: Intel documents.)

APPENDIX III
New Business Development in Established Companies[1]

ASSESSMENT QUESTIONS FOR INTERNAL CORPORATE (GREEN) VENTURES

Figure AIII.1 lists some questions to help assess the strategic importance and operational relatedness of internal corporate ventures.

ORGANIZATIONAL DESIGN ALTERNATIVES FOR INTERNAL CORPORATE VENTURES

Figure AIII.2 presents a framework of organization design alternatives for structuring the relationship between new ventures and the corporation. The framework can be used in a dynamic way by moving ventures to different organization design alternatives as more information about strategic importance and operational relatedness becomes available.

Strategic Importance	Operational Relatedness
•How does this initiative maintain our capacity to move into areas where major current or potential competitors might move?	•What are the key capabilities required to make this project successful?
•How does this help us find out where not to go?	•Where, how, and when are we going to get them if we don't have them yet, and at what cost?
•How does it help to create new and defensible niches?	•Who else might be able to do this, perhaps better?
•How does it help mobilize the organization?	•How will these new capabilities affect the capabilities currently employed in our mainstream business?
•To what extent could it put the firm at risk?	•What other areas may possibly require innovative efforts if we move forward with this project?
•When should we get out of it if it does not seem to be working?	•What additional new things may we be able to do if we can learn to handle this project?
•What is missing in our analysis?	•What is missing in our analysis?

Figure AIII.1. Assessment Questions for Strategic Importance and Operational Relatedness. (SOURCE: R. A. Burgelman, "Designs for Corporate Entrepreneurship in Established Firms," *California Management Review,* Spring 1984, p. 159.)

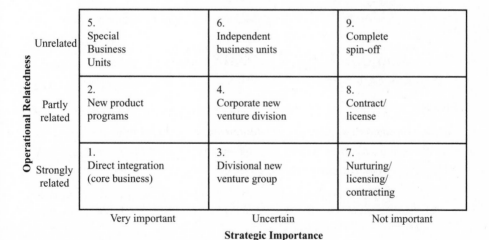

Figure AIII.2. Organizational Design Alternatives for New Ventures. (SOURCE: R. A. Burgelman, "Designs for Corporate Entrepreneurship in Established Firms," *California Management Review,* Spring 1984, p. 161.)

NOTES

All quotations that are not specifically documented in these notes were drawn from personal interviews the author and his research associates conducted with Intel staff members from 1988 through early 2001.

Acknowledgments

1. See J. J. Rotemberg and G. Saloner, "Visionaries, Managers, and Strategic Direction," *Rand Journal of Economics*, 2000, 31:693–716.
2. See W. P. Barnett, "The Dynamics of Competitive Intensity," *Administrative Science Quarterly*, 1997, 42: 128–180.

Preface

1. See "The 21st Century Corporation," *Business Week*, August 28, 2000: 278.

Chapter 1. Strategy Is Destiny

1. Apparently, there is an extensive body of literature discussing this painting. In particular, see Michel Foucault's whimsical essays in *This Is Not a Pipe* (Berkeley and Los Angeles: University of California Press, 1982).
2. Strategy, in contrast to destiny, implies degrees of freedom and the possibility, to some extent, to choose one's future. The difference between a strategic approach to life and a belief in destiny or fate helps explain why the Ancient Greeks failed to develop a quantitative approach to probability even though they had the necessary mathematical knowl-

edge. See P. Bernstein, *Against the Gods: The Remarkable Story of Risk* (New York: Wiley, 1996):17. Bernstein points out that it was not until the Renaissance that Europeans began to explore the possibility that the future might be predictable and controllable to some degree and great advances in probability theory were made. (*Against the Gods:* 20) The economists Frank Knight and John Maynard Keynes went further. They showed the limitations of the use of probability theory in a world of true uncertainty, a world according to Keynes for which there exists no scientific basis on which to form any calculable probability. Bernstein notes that if uncertainty rules out an inevitable future with outcomes governed by a given probability distribution it also makes us free. (*Against the Gods:* 229). For an early effort to reconcile both choice and determinism in the explanation of organizational behavior see L. G. Hrebiniak, and W. F. Joyce, "Organizational Adaptation: Strategic Choice and Determinism," *Administrative Science Quarterly* 30 (1985): 336–47. Also, D. C. Hambrick, and S. Finkelstein, "Managerial Discretion: A Bridge Between Polar Views of Organizational Outcomes." In L. L. Cummings and B. Staw, eds., *Research in Organizational Behavior* 4 (Greenwich, Conn.: JAI Press, 1987):369–406.

3. Jack Welch admonished his executives to control their own destiny. I learned of Jack Welch's admonition from a videotape of a presentation he made in 1990 to The Southern Company, a large GE customer. During that presentation, Welch points out that achieving high productivity sets managers free and gives them control over their own destiny. This resonated strongly with me since I had offered the view that strategy is the means for gaining and maintaining control of one's destiny in my courses at Stanford Business School since the early 1980s. Also see N. M. Tichy and S. Stratford, *Control Your Destiny or Someone Else Will: Lessons in Mastering Change from the Principles Jack Welch Is Using to Revolutionalize GE* (New York: HarperBusiness, 1999).

4. Alfred D. Chandler's *Strategy and Structure* (1962) offered *strategy* as the unifying theoretical concept for studying the managerial actions that guide a company's development: "Strategy can be defined as the determination of the basic long-term goals and objectives of an enterprise, and the adoption of courses of action and the allocation of resources necessary for carrying out these goals" (pp: 15–16).

Chandler offered insight in the process through which companies develop internal competencies and capabilities in response to exogenously arising external growth opportunities. He argued that companies then seek to deliberately exploit these competencies further through diversification in response to new market opportunities and that they develop new structural and administrative arrangements to support their growth strategy. Edith Penrose's *The Theory of the Growth of the Firm* (1959) elucidated the internal dynamics of a company's growth. Penrose offered novel insights in the managerial actions that constitute a company's internal impulse to grow. H. Igor Ansoff drew on these and other important positive studies in organization theory and finance, in particular Selznick's *Leadership in Administration* (1958), Cyert and March's *Behavioral Theory of the Firm* (1963), and Markowitz's *Portfolio Analysis* (1959). In *Corporate Strategy* (1965), Ansoff provided the first comprehensive analytical apparatus with normative implications for strategically managing an enterprise faced with strategic competitors. In the forty years since *Strategy and Structure,* the field of strategic management has blossomed into many different theoretical views. Henry Mintzberg and his colleagues in *Strategy Sa-*

fari (1998), a recent synthesis of the field of strategic management, identify five meanings of strategy, and ten schools of thought. This shows the fertility of the strategy field for academics but can be mind-boggling for practitioners.

5. Waiting to act is also part of strategy. Nonaction may have value if useful additional information becomes available while waiting. Nonaction, however, may also offer an opponent the opportunity to make preemptive moves. Hence, strategy must consider the expected benefits and costs of nonaction. The basic criterion remains the same: As long as there is no risk of irreversible consequences associated with nonaction, nonaction is not strategic.

6. Peter Paret in the introduction to the 1986 sequel to *Makers of Modern Strategy* (1943), a classic of the military strategy literature, points out that once the broader historical context is considered, it might be better to title the book *The Making of Modern Strategy*. Even in the case of Napoleon, Paret observes: "Napoleonic strategy was not created by the emperor alone. It was made possible because he had the genius and the compulsion to combine and exploit the ideas and policies of others" (p. 7). In the field of strategic management, Henry Mintzberg was among the first to pay systematic attention to strategy as an organizational process. See "Patterns in Strategy Formation," *Management Science* 24 (1978): 934–48. See also J. L. Bower, and Y. L. Doz, "Strategy Formulation: A Social and Political Process," in D. E. Schendel and C. W. Hofer, eds., *Strategic Management: A New View of Business and Planning* (Boston: Little Brown, 1979).

7. Graham Allison proposed the rational actor model as Model I in his analysis of the Cuban missile crisis. See G. Allison, and P. Zelikow, *Essence of Decision: Explaining the Cuban Missile Crisis,* 2nd. ed. (New York: Addison Wesley Longman, 1999). There exists a significant literature refining Allison's work. See, for instance, J. Bendor, and T. H. Hammond, "Rethinking Allison's Models," *American Political Science Review* 86 (1992): 301–322.

8. The bureaucratic model is similar to Allison's Model II: organizational process.

9. The internal ecology model is perhaps closest to Allison's Model III: governmental politics. For an early discussion of the internal ecology model, see R. A. Burgelman, "Intraorganizational Ecology of Strategy Making and Organizational Adaptation: Theory and Field Research," *Organization Science* 2 (1991): 239–62.

10. For a discussion of the "garbage can" model, see J. G. March, and J. P. Olsen, *Ambiguity and Choice in Organizations* (Bergen, Universitetsforlaget, 1976).

11. For a discussion of the use of game theory in strategic management, see C. F. Camerer, "Does Strategy Research Need Game Theory?" *Strategic Management Journal* (winter 1991): 137–52; G. Saloner, "Modeling, Game Theory, and Strategic Management," *Strategic Management Journal* (winter 1991): 119–36.

12. Richard Rumelt, Dan Schendel, and David Teece point out that to motivate research, a fundamental question must offer at least one clear path to follow in seeking answers. See *Fundamental Issues in Strategy* (Boston: Harvard Business School Press, 1994):40. Evolutionary organization theory offers such a path for the fundamental questions raised in this book. Evolutionary organization theory emerged as an offshoot of cultural evolutionary theory more than thirty years ago. See D. T. Campbell, "Variation and Selective Retention in Sociocultural Evolution," *General Systems* 14 (1969):69–85. And K. E. Weick,

The Social Psychology of Organizing, 2nd ed. (Reading, Mass: Addison-Wesley, 1979). Another branch rooted in the study of population dynamics in biology emerged independently in organizational sociology. See M. T. Hannan, and J. H. Freeman, *Organizational Ecology* (Cambridge: Harvard University Press, 1989). A third branch rooted in the behavioral theory of the firm provided an evolutionary perspective on economic change and organizational learning. See R. R. Nelson and S. G. Winter, *An Evolutionary Theory of Economic Change* (Cambridge: Harvard University Press, 1982). All three branches of evolutionary organization theory inform the perspective on strategy-making adopted in this book.

13. Howard Aldrich offers a thorough discussion of these evolutionary processes and provides a synthesis of research that has adopted an evolutionary perspective in organization theory. See *Organizations Evolving* (Thousand Oaks, Calif.: Sage, 1999). Also *Organizations and Environments* (Englewood Cliffs, N.J.: Prentice-Hall, 1979). These are generic processes, which are not necessarily biological in nature and can be equally fruitfully applied to social and cultural processes. Several seminal contributions have helped clarify the dual inheritance mechanism in social and cultural evolution. Social and cultural entities evolve not only because of the transmission of a genetic heritage but also because of learning processes. See R. Boyd, and P. J. Richerson, *Culture and the Evolutionary Process* (Chicago: University of Chicago Press, 1985). This extension is important because it avoids the fallacy of unwarranted analogy and the pitfalls of crude biology-based evolutionary metaphors. Gould, for instance, explains that biological evolution is a bad analogue for cultural change for at least three reasons: "First, cultural evolution can be faster by orders of magnitude than biological change at its maximal Darwinian rate.... Second, cultural evolution is direct and Lamarckian in form: The achievements of one generation are passed by education and publications directly to descendants.... Biological evolution is indirect . . . they arise as products of genetic change. Third, . . . biological evolution is a system of constant divergence without subsequent joining of branches. Lineages, once distinct, are separate forever." See S. J. Gould, *Bully for Brontosaurus: Reflections in Natural History* (New York: W.W. Norton & Co., 1991), 64–65. Gould nevertheless uses evolutionary analogy effectively to further elucidate some interesting findings in the adoption of particular technologies. Other distinguished evolutionary scientists have pursued the implications of evolutionary theory for understanding the behavior of social systems. See, for instance, R. Dawkins, *The Selfish Gene* (Oxford: Oxford University Press, 1976) and *The Blind Watchmaker* (New York: Norton, 1986). For a more radical statement that social science will ultimately have to be built on the foundations provided by biology, see O. E. Wilson, *Consilience: The Unity of Knowledge* (New York: A. E. Knopf, 1998).

14. The first systematic linking of the strategy-making process and the key processes of evolutionary organization theory can be found in R. A. Burgelman, "A Model of the Interaction of Strategic Behavior, Corporate Context and the Concept of Strategy," *Academy of Management Review* 8 (1983): 61–70. For a more recent sampling of evolutionary studies in strategy, see W. P. Barnett, and R. A. Burgelman, "Evolutionary Perspectives on Strategy," *Strategic Management Journal,* summer 1996.

15. See R. A. Burgelman, "Intraorganizational Ecology of Strategy Making." For a recent

overview of research adopting an intraorganizational ecological perspective, see C. Galunic and J. Weeks, "Intraorganizational Ecology." In J. A. C. Baum, ed., *Companion to Organizations* (forthcoming).

16. Sid Winter offers a clear statement of the importance of bridging this gap:

> Within each microcosm of expertise or skill, there is of course a specialized language in which *that* subject—or at least articulable parts of it—can be discussed. At the opposite extreme, there is terminology of very broad scope. There are words like *information, innovation, skill, technology transfer, diffusion, learning,* and (of course) *knowledge* and *competence.* These name parts of the realm of discourse but do not do much to point the way toward advancing the discourse. The problems of managing technological and organizational change surely lie between these two extremes of low and high generality, and in that range there seems to be a serious dearth of appropriate terminology and conceptual schemes.

See S. Winter, "Knowledge and Competence as Strategic Assets." In D. J. Teece, ed., *The Competitive Challenge: Strategies for Industrial Innovation and Renewal* (Cambridge, Mass.: Ballinger, 1987), 180. I am grateful to my former doctoral student Alva Taylor for bringing this quote to my attention. A. H. Taylor, "A Process Study of the Influence of Competition between New Product Initiatives on Innovation and Organizational Learning" (Ph.D. diss., Stanford University, 2000)

17. Coevolution refers to the process whereby particular units of analysis evolve in a reciprocal influence relationship, affecting each other's evolutionary success. See, for instance J. A. C. Baum and Singh, J. V. (eds.), *Evolutionary Dynamics of Organizations* (New York: Oxford University Press, 1994). For a discussion of Tool I see R. A. Burgelman, "Fading Memories: A Process Theory of Strategic Business Exit," *Administrative Science Quarterly* 39 (1994): 24–56.

18. The so-called resource-based view of the firm and the more traditional industrial organization economics view in the strategic management field emphasize competencies and position as bases of competitive advantage somewhat differently. The former emphasizes competencies; the latter, position. For an excellent analysis and conceptual integration see M. E. Porter, "What Is Strategy?" *Harvard Business Review,* 1996: 61–78.

19. For similar ideas about the concept of corporate strategy, see J. Freeman, and W. Boeker, "The Ecological Analysis of Business Strategy," *California Management Review* 26 (winter 1984): 73–86; and Karl E. Weick, "Substitutes for Corporate Strategy." In David J. Teece, ed., *The Competitive Challenge,*

20. Disruptive technologies focus on a different subset of performance dimensions in a product's multidimensional performance space. These technologies are typically rejected by a company's existing customers and therefore are not further supported within the company's resource allocation process. Often the internal entrepreneurs associated with such initiatives leave the company to start a new one. After finding new customers interested in the different performance characteristics of the technology, performance on the other dimensions also improves over time. As a result, the customers that were earlier not interested are likely to eventually find the new technology good enough and may switch. This leaves the incumbent companies still working with the old technology in a difficult

strategic situation. See C. Christensen, *The Innovator's Dilemma* (Boston: Harvard Business School Press, 1997).

21. See H. Mintzberg, "Patterns in Strategy Formation," *Management Science* 24 (1978): 934–48.

22. See J. G. March, "Exploration and Exploitation in Organizational Learning," *Organization Science* 2 (1991): 71–87.

23. See M. L. Tushman, and C. A. O'Reilly, III, *Winning Through Innovation* (Boston: Harvard Business School Press, 1997).

24. See R. A. Thietart, and B. Forgues, "Chaos Theory and Organization," *Organization Science* 6 (1995): 19–31. Ilya Prigogine, Nobel laureate in Chemistry, uses the Lotka-Volterra equations of prey-predator competition, which are part of the conceptual foundation of organizational ecology, in a discussion of self-organization to examine structural stability. Structural stability, according to Prigogine, "seems to express in the most compact way the *idea of innovation,* the appearance of a new mechanism and a new species, which were initially absent in the system." See I. Prigogine, *From Being to Becoming: Time and Complexity in the Physical Sciences* (San Francisco: W. H. Freeman and Company, 1980): 109. Keeping in mind the pitfalls of the fallacy of unwarranted analogy (see note 13), there seems nevertheless to exist a potentially interesting isomorphism between Prigogine's analysis and the analysis of the role of the induced and autonomous processes in strategy-making. Autonomous initiatives generate innovations (new ideas) in the organization, but they are viable only if they can be integrated into the corporate strategy and eventually become part of the induced strategy process. Strategic context determination is the part of the process through which this integration is attempted. How strategic context determination works and what the determinants are of its success may be the central issues in a theory of corporate entrepreneurship. See R. A. Burgelman, "Corporate Entrepreneurship and Strategic Management: Insights from a Process Study," *Management Science* 29 (1983): 1349–64. Also: R. A. Burgelman, "Strategy Making and Evolutionary Theory: Toward a Capabilities-Based Perspective," Research Paper No. 755, Stanford Business School, June 1984.

25. For various viewpoints on applying the punctuated equilibrium model, adopted from biology, in organization theory, see M. L. Tushman, and E. Romanelli, "Organizational Evolution: A Metamorphosis Model of Convergence and Reorientation," in B. Staw and L. L. Cummings, *Research in Organizational Behavior* 7 (Greenwich, Conn.: JAI Press, 1985: 439–65; M. L. Tushman, and P. Anderson, "Technological Discontinuities and Organizational Environments," *Administrative Science Quarterly* 31 (1986): 439–65; C. J. G. Gersick, "Revolutionary Change Theories: A Multilevel Exploration of the Punctuated Equilibrium Paradigm," *Academy of Management Review* 16 (1991): 10–36; and S. L. Brown, and K. M. Eisenhardt, "The Art of Continuous Change: Linking Complexity Theory and Time-Paced Evolution in Relentlessly Shifting Organizations," *Administrative Science Quarterly* 42 (1997): 1–34.

26. The first generation of the process model resulted from Harvard Business School professor Joseph Bower's efforts to conceptualize the strategic resource allocation process in large corporations. See J. L. Bower, *Managing the Resource Allocation Process* (Boston: Harvard Business School, 1970). Several of Bower's doctoral students further refined the resource allocation process model. See Bower and Doz, "Strategy Formulation." The sec-

ond generation of the process model resulted from Burgelman's efforts to extend the model to conceptualize the complete strategy-making process involved in internal corporate venturing in large corporations. See R. A. Burgelman, "A Process Model of Internal Corporate Venturing in the Diversified Major Firm," *Administrative Science Quarterly* 28:223–44. More recently, the extended process model was also found to be useful to conceptualize the strategic business exit process. See R. A. Burgelman, "A Process Model of Strategic Business Exit: Implications for an Evolutionary Perspective on Strategy," *Strategic Management Journal* 17 (September 1996):193–214.

27. See M. T. Hannan and J. Freeman, "The Population Ecology of Organizations," *American Journal of Sociology* 82 (1977): 929–64.

28. See M. T. Hannan and J. Freeman, "Structural Inertia and Organizational Change," *American Sociological Review* 49 (1984): 149–64.

29. See W. P. Barnett, H. R. Greve, and D. Y. Park, "An Evolutionary Model of Organizational Performance," *Strategic Management Journal* 15 (1994): 139–57.

30. See W. P. Barnett, "The Dynamics of Competitive Intensity," *Administrative Science Quarterly* 42 (1997): 128–80.

31. Ibid. An alternative to corporate venture capital is outright acquisition of winning variations. This is the strategy that Cisco Systems successfully pursued throughout the 1990s. Cisco was able to quickly observe which technology-based variations in the external selection environment were successful and to use its highly valued shares to acquire these emergent winners.

32. H. Aldrich, *Organizations Evolving* (London's Sage Publications, 1999): 35.

33. R. A. Burgelman, "Strategy Making as a Social Learning Process: The Case of Internal Corporate Venturing," *Interfaces* 18 (1988): 74–85; K. Kuwada, "Strategic Learning: The Continuous Side of Discontinuous Strategic Change," *Organizational Science,* 9 (1998): 719–736.

34. J. J. Rotemberg and G. Saloner, "Benefits of Narrow Business Strategies," *American Economic Review* 84 (1994): 1330–49.

35. J. J. Rotemberg and G. Saloner, "Visionaries, Managers, and Strategic Direction," *RAND Journal of Economics* 31 (2000): 693–716.

36. Discussing key aspects of his strategic approach to major battles, Napoleon supposedly said, "*On s'engage, et puis on voit*" (We engage, and then we see).

37. Henry Kissinger points out that top political leaders are "strategies-in-action" who are unlikely to change their fundamental strategic premises in office. See H. A. Kissinger, *The White House Years* (Boston: Little Brown, 1979).

38. R. A. Burgelman and A. S. Grove, "Strategic Dissonance," *California Management Review* (Winter 1996): 8–28.

Chapter 2. Genesis and Transformation

1. See R. A. Burgelman, D. L. Carter, and R. S. Bamford, "Intel Corporation: The Evolution of an Adaptive Organization," Stanford Business School Case SM–65, 1999. The research for this book did not cover in depth the period when Robert Noyce was Intel's CEO. For an in-depth historical analysis of Robert Noyce and his career, see L. Berlin,

"Robert Noyce and the Rise of Silicon Valley 1956–1990" (Ph.D. diss., Stanford University, 2001).

2. Integrated circuits are configurations of transistors that can execute logic functions. First invented at Bell Labs in 1948, the transistor is a solid-state device that can be thought of as an electrical switch. The first transistors replaced vacuum tubes and were fabricated one at a time. Robert Noyce and Jack Kilby shared credit for inventing the planar transistor in the late 1950s, which allowed fabrication and interconnection of many transistors on one substrate—forming an integrated circuit. In 1965, Gordon Moore predicted that the number of transistors on semiconductor chips would double approximately every 18 to 24 months. This became known as "Moore's Law."

3. Metal oxide semiconductor (MOS) refers to a generic type of transistor and to a family of processes used to make it. The MOS process typically requires fewer processing steps than the bipolar process.

4. Bipolar refers to a generic type of transistor and to the family of processes used to make it. The bipolar transistor consumes more power than the MOS transistor, but can be made to switch faster. Excessive power consumption limits the density of bipolar products. The bipolar process is a relatively complex semiconductor process.

5. George Gilder reports an interview with Andy Grove that testifies to Grove's deep understanding of organizational dynamics early in his career:

> Grove explains: "A company is really its middle management. If middle management is gone, nothing will put that company back together. At first, Fairchild's middle echelons were very good, and the fact that top management left would not have mattered if the new leaders were backfilled in right away." But in this case, "the middle management left also. And after that I don't care who was going to buy the company or how much money they were going to pour into it, it wouldn't work."

See G. Gilder, *Microcosm: The Quantum Revolution in Economics and Technology,* (New York: Simon & Schuster, 1989): 90.

6. Static Random Access Memory (SRAM) is a RAM device that does not require "refreshing" (see note 9) as long as power is constantly applied. Random Access Memory (RAM) refers to a family of information storage devices in which specific memory locations can be accessed (to retrieve or store information) in any sequence. RAM is usually "volatile" memory. Thus a constant power supply is required to retain stored information.

7. Magnetic core memory was a form of random access computer memory utilizing ferrite cores to store information.

8. See A. S. Grove, *Only the Paranoid Survive* (New York: Doubleday, 1996): chapter 2. In *Microcosm* Gilder points out that it is sometimes also called the Peter Drucker test; see pages 55 and 110.

9. Dynamic Random Access Memory (DRAM) is a variety of RAM that maximizes utilization of silicon "real estate" and minimizes power consumption per storage bit. Each "bit" is stored as an electrical charge. Since the charge dissipates rapidly even when power is constantly supplied to the device, the information within each memory location must be refreshed (rewritten) hundreds of times per second.

10. One kilobit (1K) equals 2^{10} or 1024 bits. Each DRAM generation has four times as much capacity as its predecessor. Because computers operate in binary code, the actual memory contents are multiples of 2. Thus, the 1K generation has 2^{10} bits, the 4K generation has 2^{12} bits, the 16K generation has 2^{14} bits, and so on. The One Megabit (1Meg) generation has 2^{20} or 1,048,576 bits.

11. A wafer is a circular slice of silicon that serves as the substrate for integrated circuits. Each wafer contains a number of "chips." The first silicon wafers used in production were 2 inches in diameter.

12. Electrically Programmable Read Only memory (EPROM) is a variety of Read Only Memory (ROM) that can be erased and programmed at the user's factory. Read Only Memory (ROM) normally contains a fixed set of information that cannot be altered. Within a typical computer system, ROM contains a sequence of data that has been embedded in the chip at the factory. Thus, ROM chips are custom-made for each application. The classical EPROM comes with a quartz window in its package so that ultraviolet light can be used to erase its contents. Then each memory location can be programmed to permanently contain desired information. EPROM is used in applications in which low volume or time constraints prevent the fabrication of a custom ROM, or in which the user may intend to make future modifications to the nonvolatile memory.

13. Microprocessors are logic devices, sometimes called computers on a chip. Intel's first microprocessor, the 4004 was introduced in 1971. It contained 2,300 MOS transistors and could execute 60,000 instructions per second. It was a general-purpose microprocessor. While its performance was not as good as custom-designed logic, Intel believed there was a significant market for it.

14. Gilder, *Microcosm:* 97. In 1975, Noyce had passed the CEO mantle on to Gordon Moore and Andy Grove had become executive vice president. This gave Grove the opportunity to replace Noyce's more entrepreneurial and freewheeling style with a greater emphasis on managerial control and discipline. See Berlin, "Robert Noyce and the Rise of Silicon Valley."

15. Gordon Moore called the 1103 "the most difficult to use semiconductor product ever invented." Ironically, that may have helped in its market success. According to Moore:

> There was a lot of resistance to semiconductor technology on the part of the core memory engineers. Core was a very difficult technology and required a great deal of engineering support. The engineers didn't embrace the 1103 until they realized that it too was a difficult technology and wouldn't make their skills irrelevant.

16. Smaller chip size leads to higher processing yields; that is, a higher number of good chips per wafer. Higher processing yields translate into lower manufacturing costs.

17. Dielectrics are insulating materials. They are used in several areas of integrated circuits.

18. Metal Oxide Semiconductor (MOS) transistors came in two polarities: n-channel (NMOS) and p-channel (PMOS). Several generations of logic were built on NMOS circuitry. A cell of 6 NMOS transistors replaced Intel's traditional PMOS logic family. NMOS transistors were faster than PMOS devices due to fundamental physical properties. NMOS, in turn, was replaced by CMOS.

19. Industry observers noted that Japan's MITI had targeted semiconductors as a strategic in-

dustry and were investing for the long term. In the years between 1980 and 1984, U.S. firms invested a total of 22 percent of sales in new plant and equipment, while Japanese firms invested 40 percent. The result was that by 1983, Japanese total investment in semiconductors exceeded the U.S. investment. Some observers estimated that production yields of Japanese semiconductor companies exceeded those of U.S. producers by as much as 40 percent. "While the best U.S. companies obtained yields of 50–60 percent the best Japanese were getting 80–90 percent." See C. Prestowitz, *Trading Places* (New York: Basic Books, 1988): 46.

20. Semiconductor fabrication plants are perhaps the cleanest areas ever created. One particle of dust that settles on a silicon wafer is enough to ruin an entire chip. The "class" of a facility refers to the amount of particulate in the air. Class X means that one cubic foot of air will contain, on average, X or fewer particles. To give a sense of the cleanliness, a typical hospital operating room is between class 1,000 and 10,000.

21. US Memories, Inc., was a joint DRAM venture formed by a group of semiconductor and computer companies in June of 1989 in response to concerns about U.S. dependence on foreign suppliers. The group included Hewlett-Packard, Intel, IBM, DEC, LSI Logic, National Semiconductor, and Advanced Micro Devices.

22. NMB Corporation was a traditional supplier of ball bearings that entered the DRAM industry. In 1989, NMB had an annual sales run rate of $350 million, having reached sales of $200 million in 1988 on an estimated investment of $200 million in plant and equipment. The president of NMB reportedly viewed the DRAM as the ultimate commodity: "A chip . . . is merely a miniature ball bearing—flattened out, with a picture on it." See Gilder, *Microcosm:* 154.

23. Other researchers have documented the longevity of corporate strategies. See, for instance, H. Mintzberg, and J. A. Waters, "Tracking Strategy in an Entrepreneurial Firm," *Academy of Management Journal* 25 (1982): 465–99.

24. For a discussion of "historical efficiency" see W. P. Barnett, and R. A. Burgelman, "Evolutionary Perspectives on Strategy," *Strategic Management Journal* 17 (Summer 1996): 5–19.

Chapter 3. Dynamic Forces Driving Company Evolution

1. Not much systematic research has focused on strategic business exit. Research in industrial organization economics has discussed exit primarily in the context of declining industries and has focused on capacity divestment decisions, using stylized models of competitive interaction. See P. Ghemawat, and B. Nalebuff, "Exit," *Rand Journal of Economics* 16 (1985): 184–94; and "The Devolution of Declining Industries," *Quarterly Journal of Economics* 79 (1990): 167–86. Other research in economics has been cross-sectional. See for instance C. F. W. Baden-Fuller, "Exit from Declining Industries and the Case of Steel Castings," *Economic Journal* 99 (1989): 949–61. In organization theory, rich literatures exist on disbandings, organizational decline, permanently failing organizations, and escalation and deescalation processes. See Hannan and Freeman, *Organization Ecology,* R. I. Sutton, "Organizational Decline Processes: A Social Psychological Perspective," in B. M. Staw and L. L. Cummings, eds., *Research in Organizational Behavior* 12 (1990): 205–53; M. W. Meyer, and L. Zucker, *Permanently Failing Organiza-*

tions (Newbury Park, CA: Sage, 1989), J. Ross, and B. M. Staw, "Organizational Escalation and Exit: Lessons from the Shoreham Nuclear Plant," *Academy of Management Journal* 36 (1993): 701–32; I. Simonson, and B. M. Staw, "Deescalation Strategies: A Comparison of Techniques for Reducing Commitment to Losing Courses of Action," *Journal of Applied Psychology* 77 (1992): 419–26. Research specifically focusing on organizational exit, however, is relatively rare. Ross and Staw, for instance, in their study of escalation and exit concerning the Shoreham nuclear power plant note that "prior research provided few leads about the exit of organizations from losing causes of action." "Organizational Escalation": 724. In strategic management, the most extensive literature related to exit concerns portfolio planning, corporate restructuring, and divestiture. See, for instance, R. E. Hoskisson, R. A. Johnson, and D. D. Moesel, "Corporate Divestiture Intensity in Restructuring Firms: Effects of Governance, Strategy, and Performance," *Academy of Management Journal* 37 (1994): 1207–51; K. R. Harrigan, "Deterrents to Divestiture," *Academy of Management Journal* 24 (1981): 306–23.

2. The concept of distinctive competency was first introduced by Philip Selznick. See P. Selznick, *Leadership in Administration* (New York: Harper & Row, 1957). Distinctive competency is similar to core competence. For a discussion of core competence, see C. K. Prahalad, and G. Hamel, "The Core Competence of the Corporation," *Harvard Business Review* 68 (May–June 1990): 79–91. Distinctive competency emphasizes the relative uniqueness of the competencies that the company initially assembles and the evolutionary processes through which they evolve. As a result of these evolutionary processes, distinctive competencies have inertia and may become "competence traps" or "core rigidities." For competence trap, see Barbara Levitt and James March, "Organizational Learning," in W. Richard Scott, ed., *Annual Review of Sociology* 14 (Palo Alto, Calif.: Annual Reviews, 1988: 319–40. For core rigidity, see D. Leonard-Barton, "Core Capabilities and Core Rigidities: A Paradox in Managing New Product Development," *Strategic Management Journal* 13 (summer 1992): 111–26. For some important empirical contributions, see Tushman and Anderson, "Technological Discontinuities;" R. M. Henderson, and K. B. Clark, "Architectural Innovation: The Reconfiguration of Existing Product Technologies and the Failure of Established Firms," *Administrative Science Quarterly* 35 (1990): 9–30.

3. For normative statements, see K. R. Andrews, *The Concept of Corporate Strategy* (Homewood, Ill. Richard D. Irwin, 1980); C. K. Prahalad, and G. Hamel, "The Core Competence of the Corporation."

4. For an excellent discussion of Intel's technical OEM marketing competencies, see W. H. Davidow, *Marketing High Technology* (New York: Free Press, 1986).

5. In many industries, a dominant design emerges after considerable variation and experimentation. See W. J. Abernathy, and J. M. Utterback, "Patterns of Industrial Innovation," *Technology Review* 80 (1978): 40–47. David Teece points out that such a design must be able to meet a whole set of user needs in a relatively complete fashion. See D. J. Teece, "Profiting from Technological Innovation: Implications for Integration, Collaboration, Licensing, and Public Policy," *Research Policy* 15 (1986): 285–305. Once a dominant design arrives, all competitors adopt it and offer products that try to optimize on its key dimensions. Also, the basis of competition tends to shift from product innovation to process (manufacturing) innovation. DRAM was an excellent example, as the following quote from Les Vadasz referring to MOSTEK's entry indicates:

Even though you have invented the product, sometimes it is easier for new entrants to seize an opportunity and beat you to the punch. They are not encumbered by the same things you are.... The real problem in technological innovation is in anticipating the relevant issues. Once a technological box has been defined, it is easy for a team of great engineers to optimize everything in that box. Choosing the box is the hard part.

6. Personal communication, interview in early 1990s.
7. For more on Intel's tweaking habit in manufacturing engineering, see M. Jelinek, and C. B. Schoonhoven, *The Innovation Marathon* (Cambridge, Mass.: Basil Blackwell, 1990).
8. G. Moore, "The Tough Choices," *Electronics,* August 1990: 95.
9. For various empirical studies of firms' inertial tendencies related to technology strategy and innovation, see A. C. Cooper, and D. E. Schendel, "Strategic Responses to Technological Threats," *Business Horizons* 19 (1976): 61–73; R. M. Henderson, and K. B. Clark, "Architectural Innovation: The Reconfiguration of Existing Product Technologies and the Failure of Established Firms." *Administrative Science Quarterly* 35 (1990): 9–30; M. E. Tushman, and P. Anderson, "Technological Discontinuities and Organizational Environments," *Administrative Science Quarterly* 31 (1986): 439–65; C. Christensen, *The Innovator's Dilemma* (Boston: Harvard Business School Press, 1997).
10. For sources of inertia related to distinctive competencies, see B. Levitt, and J. G. March, "Organizational Learning," *Annual Review of Sociology* 14 (1988): 319–40; D. Leonard-Barton, "Core Capabilities and Core Rigidities: A Paradox in Managing New Product Development," *Strategic Management Journal* 13 (summer 1992): 111–26.
11. This phenomenon is documented in the following large sample empirical study: K. L. R. Pavitt, M. J. Robson, and J. F. Townsend, "Technological Accumulation, Diversification, and Organization of U.K. Companies, 1945–83." *Management Science* 35 (1989): 81–99.
12. The early theoretical formulations concerning the resource-based view of the firm can be found in E. T. Penrose, *The Theory of the Growth of the Firm* (Oxford: Basil Blackwell, 1968); B. Wernerfelt, "A Resource-Based View of the Firm," *Strategic Management Journal* 5 (1984): 171–80.
13. For a discussion of technology push and its implications for innovation, see R. A. Burgelman, and L. R. Sayles, *Inside Corporate Innovation: Strategy, Structure, and Managerial Skills* (New York: Free Press, 1986): chapter 3.
14. See C. Argyris, and D. A. Schon, *Organizational Learning: A Theory of Action Perspective* (Reading, Mass.: Addison-Wesley, 1978); H. Mintzberg, "Patterns in Strategy Formation," *Management Science* 24 (1978): 934–48.
15. See J. L. Bower, *Managing the Resource Allocation Process* (Boston: Harvard Business School, 1970).
16. For the first major study drawing attention to threat-rigidity in organizations, see B. Staw, L. E. Sandelands, and J. E. Dutton, "Threat-Rigidity Effects in Organizational Behavior: A Multilevel Analysis," *Administrative Science Quarterly* 26 (1981): 147–60.
17. According to Schelling, focal points facilitate coordination without communication. More generally, they are ideas, values, criteria, and so forth around which the organization's members naturally coalesce or toward which they naturally converge. In the case of Intel the maximize margin-per-wafer-start resource allocation rule can be viewed as a

focal point. Focal points are useful for operationalizing corporate culture as a rational concept. See T. C. Schelling, *The Strategy of Conflict* (Cambridge: Harvard University Press, 1963); C. Camerer and A. Vepsalainen, "The Economic Efficiency of Corporate Culture," *Strategic Management Journal* 9 (1988): 115–26; D. M. Kreps, "Corporate Culture and Economic Theory," in J. Alte and K. Shepsle, eds., *Rational Perspectives on Positive Political Economy* (Cambridge: Cambridge University Press, 1990): 90–143.

18. For a theoretical discussion of how social arrangements constrain individual behavior, see J. S. Coleman, "Social Theory, Social Research, and a Theory of Action." *American Journal of Sociology* 9 (1986): 1309–35.

19. See J. L. Bower, *When Markets Quake* (Boston: Harvard Business School Press, 1986); C. F. W. Baden-Fuller, "Exit from Declining Industries and the Case of Steel Castings," *Economic Journal* 99 (1989): 949–61.

20. One study documents how a firm's acquisition of another created new resource demands that made top management sharply aware of the relatively low profitability of the existing business and thereby activated the divestment process. See C. S. Gilmour, "The Divestment Decision Process," Ph.D. diss. Harvard Business School, 1973.

21. Baden-Fuller, "Exit from Declining Industries" 956.

22. Acquisition-based strategies carry their own hazards. See, for instance: M. E. Porter, "From Corporate Strategy to Competitive Advantage," *Harvard Business Review* 65 (1987): 43–59.

23. For theoretical arguments concerning change that is too fast, see Levitt and March, "Organizational Learning," for empirical research, see D. C. Hambrick, and R. A. D'Aveni, "Large Corporate Failures as Downward Spirals," *Administrative Science Quarterly* 33 (1988): 1–23.

24. Prahalad and Hamel, "The Core Competence of the Corporation."

Chapter 4. Coevolution of Generic and Substantive Strategies

1. Intel also exited from magnetic bubble memory, which was a nonvolatile, non-semiconductor memory technology in which Intel played a leadership role. Viewed as a promising technology during the 1970s, it was complicated to manufacture and was not able to replace magnetic disk drive technology in mainstream applications.

2. For a discussion of generic strategy, see M. E. Porter, *Competitive Strategy* (New York: Free Press, 1980).

3. D. Manners, "Intel 20th Birthday," *Electronic Weekly,* July 20, 1988: 15.

4. *Stepper alignment* refers to a new generation of equipment for photolithography processing that became available in 1981. The accuracy of the photolithography process determined the minimum linewidth of wires in a circuit, and therefore the transistor density on a chip. Steppers were an order of magnitude more expensive than the previous generation equipment but allowed smaller feature definition (linewidth) and smaller die size which, in turn, led to higher yields and lower manufacturing costs.

5. Once top management had structured the internal selection environment consistent with the generic corporate strategy, it was not easy to change it. For instance, the maximize margin-per-wafer-start rule had the unanticipated consequence of leading Intel out of the DRAM business. Yet, top management did not interfere with the rule. Top management

could have done so, but probably knew intuitively that changing the rule would radically change the culture and identity of the company with even greater unforeseeable consequences.

Chapter 5. Internal Ecology of Strategy-Making

1. See chapter 1 for a discussion of evolutionary organization theory.
2. Comparing the Fortune 100 lists between 1960 and 2000, for instance, illustrates the process of replacement and selection among the giant companies.
3. See chapter 1 for a brief discussion of the internal ecology model of strategy-making.
4. See A. S. Grove, "Breaking the Chain of Command," *Newsweek,* October 3, 1983.
5. See Gilder, *Microcosm,* 108.
6. See W. H. Davidow, *Marketing High Technology* (New York: Free Press, 1986).
7. Ibid, 4.
8. See L. McCartney, "Teaching the Elephant to Tap Dance," *Electronic Engineering Times,* November 17, 1997: 97.
9. Ibid, 100.
10. Ibid, 100.
11. See Gordon Moore, Intel Corporation, Presentation to New York Society of Analysts, February 13, 1986.
12. See Andy Grove, Intel Corporation, Presentation to New York Society of Security Analysts, January 24, 1980.
13. See A. S. Grove, *Only the Paranoid Survive* (New York: Doubleday, 1996): 143.
14. See M. T. Hannan, and J. Freeman, "Structural Inertia and Organizational Change," *American Sociological Review* 49 (1984): 149–64.
15. C. C. Snow, and D. C. Hambrick, "Measuring Organizational Strategies: Some Theoretical and Methodological Problems," *Academy of Management Review* 5 (1980): 527–38.
16. W. P. Barnett and G. R. Carroll, "Modeling Internal Organizational Change," *Annual Review of Sociology* 21 (1995): 217–36.
17. For references to the literature on "punctuated equilibrium," see various literature references in note 25, chapter 1.
18. See Staw, Sandelands, and Dutton, "Threat Rigidity Effects."
19. See Cooper and Schendel, "Strategic Responses."
20. See Christensen, *The Innovator's Dilemma.*
21. See D. C. Hambrick, and R. A. D'Aveni, "Large Corporate Failures as Downward Spirals," *Administrative Science Quarterly* 33 (1988): 1–23.
22. See J. G. March, "Footnotes to Organizational Change," *Administrative Science Quarterly* 26 (1981): 567.
23. Grove, *Only the Paranoid Survive:* 22.
24. Also see D. Levinthal, "Organizational Adaptation and Environmental Selection—Interrelated Processes of Change," *Organization Science* 2 (1991): 140–45.
25. See Chandler, *Strategy and Structure.*
26. As the strategies and valuations of many start-ups, especially dot-coms, suggest this may not be right for start-up companies. For instance, building brand and attracting an audience, even while not being quite clear about what the business strategy actually is, may be

more highly valued than securing profits early on. Amazon.com is perhaps the best example. Recently, however, the question of profitability has begun to become much more salient even for dot-com start-ups.

27. See Hambrick and D'Aveni, "Large Corporate Failures."
28. See N. Rosenberg and L. E. Birdzell, Jr., *How the West Grew Rich* (New York: Basic Books, 1986).
29. See O. E. Williamson, *The Economic Institutions of Capitalism* (New York: Free Press, 1985). During the 1990s, a rich literature has emerged on incomplete contracts and the economics of Human Resource Management.

Chapter 6. Creating a Strategy Vector: Induced Strategic Action

1. Source: Silicon Valley.com, February 21, 1999.
2. D. Kawamoto and S. Galante, "The Legacy of Andy Grove," *CNET News.com,* March 26, 1998.
3. For a brief discussion of disruptive technologies, see chapter 1, note 36. See also C. Christensen, *The Innovation's Dilemma* (Boston: Harvard Business School Press, 1997).
4. For a systematic analysis from the perspective of economic theory, see J. Farrell, H. Monroe, and G. Saloner, "The Vertical Organization of Industry: Systems Competition Versus Component Competition," *Journal of Economics and Management Strategy,* 7 (Summer 1998): 143–82.
5. For a discussion of "increasing returns to adoption," see W. B. Arthur, "Competing Technologies: An Overview" in G. Dosi, et al., eds., *Technical Change and Economic Theory* (New York: Columbia University Press, 1987): 590–607.
6. In other industries, only Dolby, Nutrasweet, and Goretex readily come to mind.
7. RISC technology was actually first invented by IBM, which reportedly already had developed a RISC processor in its labs by 1975. See Mips Computer Systems (A), Harvard Business School Case 9-792-055, revised December 1992.
8. At this first meeting, Andy Grove discussed three potentially interesting strategic issues for writing a case: Intel's experience with application-specific integrated circuits (ASIC), Intel's strategy relative to reduced instruction set instruction (RISC), and Intel's relatively recent experience with exiting from its core DRAM business. Eventually the DRAM exit was chosen, which produced the Intel Corporation (A): The DRAM Decision case.
9. Grove suggested it might be interesting to interview the engineer, trace the story, and incorporate it in a new case study. The research is presented in the Intel Corporation (C): Strategies for the 1990s case. Grove led the case discussion in Stanford MBA classes in 1990, 1991, and 1992.
10. See B. R. Schlender, "Intel Produces a Chip Packing Huge Power and Wide Ambitions," *Wall Street Journal,* February 28, 1989.
11. For a discussion of ecosystems, see J. F. Moore, "Predators and Prey: A New Ecology of Competition," *Harvard Business Review,* May–June 1993.
12. B. R. Schlender, "Fast, Costly Chip from Intel Signals Firm's Endorsement of RISC Design," *Wall Street Journal,* February 28, 1989.
13. N. Tredennick, "1991: The Year of the RISC," *Microprocessor Report,* February 6, 1991: p. 16.

14. See A. Pollack, "An 'Awesome' Intel Corners Its Market," *New York Times,* April 3, 1988.
15. See B. R. Schlender, "Intel Produces a Chip Packing Huge Power and Wide Ambitions," *Wall Street Journal,* February 28, 1989.
16. See Intel Corporation, First Quarterly Report, March 30, 1985; and Annual Shareholder Meeting Report, March 26, 1985 (no numbered pages).
17. See "Why Andy Grove Can't Stop," *Fortune,* July 10, 1995.
18. See Dave House, quoted in "Can Andy Grove Practice What He Preaches?" *Business Week,* March 16, 1987.
19. Ibid.
20. In *High Output Management,* Grove describes the one-on-one method used to provide feedback on employee performance. See A. S. Grove, *High Output Management* (New York: Random House, 1983).
21. See R. Wrubel, "Man of the Year: Intel's Andrew Grove," *Financial World,* December 11, 1990.
22. See *Time,* December 29, 1997.
23. See S. K. Yoder, "Intel Faces Challenge to Its Dominance in Microprocessors," *Wall Street Journal,* April 8, 1991.
24. Ibid.
25. R. Wrubel, "Man of the Year," p. 43.
26. Source: *New York Times,* January 14, 1993.
27. Source: Intel and Dataquest.

Chapter 7. Facing a Strategy Vector: Autonomous Strategic Action

1. The interviews with the venture's key managers were carried out by Cambria Consulting with the help of Intel personnel as part of a research project mandated by Craig Barrett during 1997–98, which focused on Intel's new business development capability. These data were made available to me for the purpose of analyzing them with the help of Tool III and to help me prepare seminars on Growing the Business for senior Intel executives. I collected additional data from senior and top executives.
2. The two-in-a-box management structure is an administrative innovation. Two-in-a-box is Intel's solution to jobs that are extremely complex and require complementary skills for example, technical versus business; strategic versus tactical; internal operations versus external relations. As pointed out in the internal Intel publication, *Making 2-In-A-Box Managers More Effective:* "Our first goal should be *not* to have 2-in-a-box! Our second goal should be to create the *right* 2-in-a-box." Albert Yu points out that this structure works well if the two managers involved have complementary skills and each has a clear area of responsibility. It does not work if the two managers have too much overlap in skills and responsibilities and bump into each other all the time. They then end up competing with each other rather than cooperating as a team. Yu also points out that it is critical that the two managers have great respect for each other and are in constant communication. See: Albert Yu, *Creating the Digital Future* (New York: The Free Press, 1997): 159–60.
3. For a complete description of the internal corporate venturing process, see R. A. Burgelman, and L. R. Sayles, *Inside Corporate Innovation: Strategy, Structure, and Managerial*

Skills (New York: The Free Press, 1988). The chipset venture provided a particularly interesting opportunity to test the usefulness of the ICV process model as a diagnostic tool, because persons who were not familiar with the details of this model collected most of the data.

4. *Bus* refers to the electronic connection between the CPU ands other systems components (memory or other peripherals). By 1990, the use of popular graphics programs (including Windows) had increased the level of graphics performance needed for a desktop PC. For example, 486 CPUs had enough power to run graphics applications but the bus was operating at the same speed as 10 years earlier. It was becoming tied up with graphics and slowed down everything else.

5. According to Albert Yu. See *Creating the Digital Future:* 56.

6. Ibid: 56.

7. IHV is an acronym for Independent Hardware Vendor.

8. Alpha, Beta, Gamma, and Delta are code names used here to refer to PC OEM companies.

9. See Burgelman and Sayles, *Inside Corporate Innovation.*

10. In an interview in 1999, Ron Smith said that Andy Grove's note had meant a lot to him. He said "this incident is evidence that no CEO (or VP for that matter) has all the answers when it comes to seeing the future. . . . It is critical for all of us to let our people test their wings a bit."

Chapter 8. Coevolution of Strategy and Environment

1. Other sources of revenue included Flash memory products (estimated to be less than 5 percent by 1996), embedded controllers (less than 3 percent) and networking products (around 5 percent).

2. "Coevolution" is defined in chapter 1, note 17. See also J. A. C. Baum and J. V. Singh (eds.), *Evolutionary Dynamics of Organizations* (New York: Oxford University Press, 1994).

3. See R. Wrubel, "Man of the Year: Intel's Andy Grove," *Financial World,* December 11, 1990: 48.

4. See S. K. Yoder, "Intel Faces Challenge to Its Dominance in Microprocessors," *Wall Street Journal,* April 8, 1991.

5. See J. Markoff, "Intel is No Longer Having It All," *Wall Street Journal,* February 20, 1994.

6. One determinant of performance of a microprocessor is clock frequency. The higher the clock frequency, all else equal, the faster the processor. For the *i*486, for instance, Intel offered 25 MHz, 33 MHz and 50 MHz clock speeds.

7. "Packaging" refers to the plastic or ceramic and metal case that encapsulates a microchip and connects it to leads on a circuit board.

8. Intel's 486 processors carried two basic designations, SX and DX. These referred to the feature set included on the processor. DX indicates that a math-coprocessor (or floating point unit) is included on-chip. Because of the additional computational support, DX processors were more powerful (i.e., executed software more quickly) than SX processors under normal circumstances.

9. See *Business Week,* December 22, 1997.

10. Ibid.

11. March 29, 1993.

12. Source: SiliconValley.com, February 21, 1999.

13. Ibid.

14. For instance see: "In Court Filing, Intergraph Blames Intel for Layoff, Collapse of Computer Unit," *Wall Street Journal,* August 26, 1999. The court filing alleged, among other things, that "Intel came up short on information about a microprocessor support product, and canceled a plan to supply a computer board to Intergraph in July and failed to supply graphics information and data on flaws in Intel products." The court dismissed most of the allegations in the fall of 1999.

15. Some OEMs were reluctant to adopt PCI and other Intel system enhancements because it decreased their ability to differentiate their systems through proprietary graphics designs. The analysis of the development of the PCI chipset venture in chapter 7 revealed that it took significant entrepreneurial effort on the part of the venture team to overcome the initial reluctance of the OEMs. Traditional Intel-based PC OEMs weren't the only ones interested in PCI. In July 1993, Apple Computer announced that it would adopt PCI for its second generation PowerPC based Macintoshes. In addition, DEC announced plans to offer a version of its Alpha RISC microprocessor with PCI functionality built into the microprocessor. Adopting PCI would allow both Apple and DEC computers to use any peripheral cards built to the PCI specification.

16. The *i*486 and Pentium maintained strict software compatibility with all previous Intel Architecture microprocessors. However, new features were introduced which improved performance over the previous generations. Therefore, code written for the 286 worked perfectly well on an *i*486 but was slower than it could be. Part of the problem was caused by compilers, which hadn't been updated to take advantage of the new features. Beginning in 1990, Richard Wirt, leader of the compiler project in IAL, assembled an elite team of specialized software engineers to address this issue. Wirt felt that by 1993, Intel had one of the best compiler technology centers in the world. Intel worked with all of the leading PC compiler companies to incorporate IAL's compilers into their products. Wirt pointed out that the royalty charged for the license was nominal because the technology is key to Intel's most advanced processors. In 1993, he said they were already well underway with compiler development for the P6.

17. Besides providing enabling technologies that facilitated the PC's use of the rapidly increasing performance of Intel's microprocessors, Intel also focused on stimulating the supply of and demand for high-performance content and applications. In 1993, Claude Leglise, marketing manager for Intel's Indeo video technology, explained that in the early 1980s the PC replaced two things—the Selectric electric typewriter and the HP35 electronic calculator. He said that the two replacing applications—word processing and spreadsheets—still overwhelmingly dwarfed other uses of PCs. Leglise's group was helping evangelize video as the next addition to PC functionality. Digital video required a large amount of computing power. Traditionally for a PC to run video, expensive add-in boards were needed with specialized hardware to decompress and display video. Intel's Indeo video software enabled PCs based on *i*486 or Pentium processors to decompress and display video without additional hardware. After being developed within IAL, Indeo video was incorporated into Microsoft's Video for Windows application and was offered

to independent software vendors (ISVs) for incorporation into software for Intel based PCs. Intel actively evangelized Indeo video to the industry. It charged no licensing fee for the basic technology, to get new functions into the PC, and to encourage new software to take advantage of it.

18. See "Are IBM and Apple a Day Late?" *Business Week,* October 24, 1994.

19. Albert Yu agreed, stating that over 2GB of RAM were necessary to take advantage of 64-bit processing power, whereas a typical $2,000 personal computer at that time had about 32 to 64 MB of RAM.

20. See C. Christensen, *The Innovator's Dilemma* (Boston: Harvard Business School Press, 1997).

21. See B. Schlender, "Why Andy Grove Can't Stop," *Fortune,* July 10, 1995: 94.

22. See B. Schlender, "A Conversation with the Lords of Wintel," *Fortune,* July 8, 1996: 56.

23. See *Wall Street Journal,* June 7, 1995.

24. See W. B. Arthur, "Competing Technologies: An Overview," in G. Dosi et al., eds., *Technical Change and Economic Theory* (New York: Columbia University Press, 1987): 590–607.

25. See: K. M. Eisenhardt, and S. L. Brown, "Time Pacing: Competing in Markets That Won't Stand Still," *Harvard Business Review,* March-April 1998. Renowned military strategists, such as Napoleon, successfully pursued a time-paced strategy—for a while. Invariably, successful time-paced strategies become the victim of their own success, exhausting the troops and leading alarmed opponents to put their differences aside and form coalitions against the menace. See, for instance, A. Horne, *How Far From Austerlitz: Napoleon 1805–1815* (New York: St. Martin's Press, 1996).

26. See W. P. Barnett, "The Dynamics of Competitive Intensity," *Administrative Science Quarterly* 42 (1997): 128–80.

Chapter 9. Coevolution and Strategic Inertia

1. See *Bloomberg Business News,* October 7, 1993.

2. See *Forbes,* December 6, 1993.

3. Ibid.

4. H.320 was the first videoconferencing systems standard. It was an umbrella standard that contained some sub-standards. H.320 as a whole mainly defined video signal (including sound) exchanges between different videoconferencing equipment over ISDN or T1 telecommunication lines. By 1998, most manufacturers' products complied with H.320.

5. See G. A. Moore, *Crossing the Chasm* (New York: Harper Business, 1992).

6. For a more complete narrative of the Hood River project, see R. S. Bamford, and R. A. Burgelman, "Intel Corporation: The Hood River Project (A)," Stanford Business School case SM–49A, 1998; "Intel Corporation: The Hood River Project (B)," Stanford Business School case SM–49B, 1998; and "Intel's Strategic Position in the Family Room, 1998," Stanford Business School case SM–50, 1998.

7. See "The Square Off Between the TV and Computer," *Los Angeles Times,* 29 October 1995.

8. In the late 1980s, Intel built a significant business of selling math coprocessors, which provided floating point math capabilities for the 286 and 386 processors. In 1991, this

product was part of the End-User Component Division, whose manager saw that the functionality of the math coprocessor would be integrated into the core processor beginning with the 486 generation. The division therefore adapted its product strategy, and it proposed the creation of a business around the sale of microprocessor upgrades. The proposal went through Intel's traditional POR process successfully, and the business came to be known as OverDrive.

Chapter 10. Maintaining and Extending the Strategy Vector

1. Source: Silicon Valley.com, February 21, 1999.
2. See D. Takahashi, "Intel Posts Profits, Beats Expectation." *Wall Street Journal,* January 14, 2000.
3. See M. Williams, "Intel Chip Setbacks Heighten Strategy Concerns," *Wall Street Journal,* October 2, 2000.
4. Ibid. See also M. Williams, "AMD Beats Estimates for Third Quarter," *Wall Street Journal,* October 12, 2000.
5. Ibid.
6. C. Gaither, "A New Chip for Laptops from AMD Takes on Intel," *New York Times,* May 15, 2000.
7. See M. Richtel, "Signs of Market Saturation in PC World," *New York Times,* October 9, 2000.
8. See J. Markoff, "New Design for Processor to Test Intel," *New York Times,* January 20, 2000.
9. Source: Silicon Valley.com, February 21, 1999.
10. Ibid.
11. See D. Takahashi, "Intel Moves from Windows with Line of Web Devices," *Wall Street Journal,* January 5, 2000.
12. Ibid.
13. Ibid.
14. Williams, "Intel Chip Setbacks."
15. Takahashi, "Intel Posts Profits."
16. *Wall Street Journal,* February 17, 1999.
17. See D. Takahashi, "Intel Rolls Dice on Tech Upstarts—and Hits Jackpot," *Wall Street Journal,* February 8, 2000.
18. Ibid.
19. The creosote bush is a desert plant that poisons the ground around it, preventing other plants from growing nearby.
20. Source: "Intel Inks $2.2 Chip Deal." *CNET,* March 4, 1999.
21. D. Kent, "Windows of Opportunity Closing on AMD," *Real World Technologies,* September 1999.
22. "Intel," *Business Week,* December 22, 1997.

Chapter 11. Designing the Internal Ecology of Strategy-Making

1. See R. A. Burgelman, D. L. Carter, and R. S. Bamford, "Intel Corporation: The Evolution of an Adaptive Organization," Stanford Business School case SM–65, 1999.
2. D. L. Preston, and J. Hendrickson, "The Luna Solution: An Intel Green Business Case," Internal Document, Intel Corporation, 1998.
3. Besides this author the other instructors were HBS Professor Clayton M. Christensen and Dr. James F. Moore, founder and chairman of GeoPartners Research, Inc.
4. See "Internet Ho! Intel Launches into Cyberspace," *Wall Street Journal,* May 18, 1999.
5. See Dan Fost, "Intel Launches into Cyberspace," *San Francisco Chronicle,* November 15, 1999.
6. *Wall Street Journal,* "Internet Ho!"
7. See chapter 5. These insights were first published in R. A. Burgelman, "Intraorganizational Ecology of Strategy Making and Organizational Adaptation: Theory and Field Research, *Organization Science* 2 (1991): 239–62.
8. Source: A. S. Grove, Presentation on the history of Intel's approach to strategy at the Strategic Management Society Conference in San Francisco, October 1989.
9. See R. A. Burgelman, "Designs for Corporate Entrepreneurship in Established Firms," *California Management Review* (spring 1984).
10. See R. A. Burgelman, and Y. L. Doz, "The Power of Strategic Integration," *Sloan Management Review* 42, (2001): 28–38.

Chapter 12. Four Strategic Leadership Imperatives

1. Comparing Steve Jobs and Bill Gates in the PC industry illustrates the distinction between visionaries and strategists. In 2001, most people still mention Steve Jobs as the great visionary of the PC industry, but they view Bill Gates as the great strategist. If strategy is about understanding the forces that shape a company's destiny, then this makes sense. Gates was among the first to understand the importance of a new economic force that would later be called increasing returns to adoption and of what it takes to break the virtuous circle associated with it. This helps explain why Gates, in 1985, was willing to explain to John Sculley the ways in which Apple Computer could make the Macintosh operating system the standard in the PC industry. Gates must have realized that the Macintosh was at that time at least ten times better than MS-DOS and therefore had the opportunity to replace MS-DOS in spite of its large installed base. In that scenario, Gates probably understood that Microsoft could continue to do well by remaining the largest applications software vendor for the Macintosh. With Microsoft Word and Excel, Microsoft was already the largest application software vendor for the Mac at that time. In the IBM-compatible PC market segment, on the other hand, Microsoft was lagging far behind Lotus and WordPerfect as an applications software vendor. Sculley and Jobs, however, apparently did not understand these forces to the same extent as Gates did and ignored his advice. The rest is history.
2. Utopian visions often correspond to this situation.
3. During Epoch II, Intel's ability to impose a sole-source strategy in the PC market segment is an example.

4. For instance, small independent software vendors in the PC market segment that depend on access to Microsoft's operating system code or Intel's microcode to write their applications could potentially face strategic subordination. If their application is sufficiently important, however, they can move into a situation of strategic interdependence.

5. One astute observer has facetiously called this "mutually assured dependency." See H. W. Jenkins, Jr., "High Tech Bites the Hand," *Wall Street Journal,* November 18, 1998, Section A: 23.

6. The relationship between Intel and Microsoft in the PC market segment is a good example.

7. For a general discussion of the difficulty of foreseeing the implications of new technologies, see N. Rosenberg, "Uncertainty and Technological Change," paper prepared for the Conference on Growth and Development: The Economics of the 21st Century, organized by the Center for Economic Policy Research of Stanford University, June 3–4, 1994.

8. For a penetrating discussion of the role of intuition in strategic decision-making, see G. Klein, *Sources of Power: How People Make Decisions* (Cambridge, Mass.: MIT Press, 1998).

9. Napoleon famously said in relation to his approach to strategy "On s'engage, et puis on voit" (we engage, and then we see).

10. See for instance, G. Hamel, and C. K. Prahalad, *Competing for the Future* (Boston: Harvard Business School Press, 1994).

11. The competitive interactions between Microsoft and Novell in the early 1990s seemed to be driven by competitive obsession. Novell's efforts to take on Microsoft in desktop applications software (e.g., the acquisition of WordPerfect) attacked Microsoft in its core business, made it take its eyes off the ball in its own core network operating system business, and gave Microsoft a greater chance to catch up in that market segment. Intel's competitive battles with AMD during the early 1990s occasionally also seemed to border on competitive obsession.

12. For instance, in a strategic planning session in fall 1997, discussing one of the businesses in which some at Intel wanted to compete more vigorously, Andy Grove asked one of his senior executives "What do we bring to the party other than coveting someone else's business?" He wanted Intel to be able to provide some unique value rather than simply compete for the same business with entrenched competitors.

13. I am indebted to Andy Grove for suggesting the rubber band metaphor for Tool I.

14. See Grove, *Only the Paranoid Survive;* R. A. Burgelman, and A. S. Grove, "Strategic Dissonance," *California Management Review* 38 (winter 1996): 8–28.

15. Inertial deployment of process technology competencies contributed to Intel's demise in the DRAM industry when the basis of competitive advantage changed and large-scale precision manufacturing competencies were necessary to meet it. The inertia of distinctive competence at the personal level can be vividly illustrated with the poignant story of basketball great Michael Jordan's efforts in the early 1990s to become a baseball player. Jordan was strongly motivated to succeed in these efforts because his father, who died under tragic circumstances, had wanted him to be a baseball star. Jordan made the attempt but did not reach a level of success consistent with his aspirations. He soon returned to basketball.

16. This was the case at Intel in the DRAM business, when middle managers allocated scarce manufacturing capacity away from DRAM to EPROM and microprocessors.

17. This was the case at Apple Computer in the early 1990s, when John Sculley, Apple Computer's CEO, tried to get Apple to become a dominant player in the emerging Personal Digital Assistant (PDA) market segment. Apple developed a new operating system—called Newton—for that purpose. The Newton technology, however, was still too unreliable and the market was not yet ready. Apple's efforts failed and Sculley resigned shortly thereafter in the face of major problems in its core personal computer business. See, for instance, J. M. Hurstak, and D. B. Yoffie, "Reshaping Apple Computer's Destiny," Harvard Business School case 9-393-011, 1992.

18. The invention of the microprocessor at Intel is an example. Initially, top management was disinclined to pursue the microprocessor business because it was viewed as outside the scope of the core semiconductor memory business.

19. The actions taken by the initiator of the development of the i860 RISC microprocessor is an example at Intel.

20. Intel's maximize margin-per-wafer-start rule, which guided manufacturing resource allocation, reflected the competitive reality faced by its different businesses.

21. Andy Grove's note to Ron Smith, the general manager of the chipset venture, after the chipset venture became successful in spite of Grove's doubts is an example.

22. Microsoft's response to the Internet is a good example. During 1991–92, a junior program manager in Microsoft's network operating business unit (a unit that was probably considered a loser at the time inside Microsoft) tried to convince top management to integrate a browser into Windows 94 (which became Windows 95) because he believed strongly that the Internet would become extremely important. It is crucially important to realize that this junior manager viewed the browser and the operating system as *complementary* products. Top management did not react to his prodding, which is quite understandable given the number of suggestions top management probably receives in a company like Microsoft. Nevertheless, by 1995, in light of newly founded Netscape's success, Microsoft began to realize that the browser could become a new platform for software development that might threaten the desktop operating system's relative importance. Note that senior managers at Microsoft were now defining the browser as a potential *substitute* for the desktop operating system. Microsoft's aggressive competitive strategy to deal with the Netscape threat reflected this important distinction and may as yet have enormous ramifications for the company's future.

23. The dismay created by Louis Gerstner saying upon becoming the new CEO of IBM, "The last thing IBM needs right now is a vision," is an example. See M. W. Miller, and L. Hays, "Gerstner's Nonvision for IBM Raises a Management Issue," *Wall Street Journal*, July 29, 1993.

24. Strategic leadership must meet the tests for statesmanship put forth by Henry A. Kissinger. Kissinger writes: "The ultimate test of statesmanship . . . is a combination of *insight and courage* (emphasis provided). Insight leads to assessments that define a society's freedom of action, while courage enables the statesman to act on his convictions before they are generally understood. Great statesmen operate on the outer margin of their society's capabilities; weak statesmen tend to be overwhelmed by events." See Henry A. Kissinger, Review of *Churchill: The Unruly Giant* by Norman Rose. *New York Times Book Review*, July 16, 1995: 7.

25. The earlier research concluded:

> The challenge for established firms, we believe, is not either to be well orga-
> nized and act in unison or to be creative and entrepreneurial. The real challenge,
> it would seem, is to be able to live with the tensions generated by both modes of
> action. This will require top management's exploitation of existing opportuni-
> ties to the fullest (because only relatively few will be available), the generation
> of entirely new opportunities (because today's success is no guarantee for to-
> morrow), and the balancing of exploitation and generation over time (because
> resources are limited). Strategic management approaches will have to accom-
> plish all three concerns simultaneously and virtually continuously.

See R. A. Burgelman, and L. R. Sayles, *Inside Corporate Innovation: Strategy, Structure, and
Managerial Skills* (New York: The Free Press, 1986): 191. For related ideas, see J. G.
March, "Exploration and Exploitation in Organizational Learning," *Organization Science*
2 (1991): 71–87; M. L. Tushman and C. A. O'Reilly, III, *Winning through Innovation*
(Boston: Harvard Business School Press, 1997). These are briefly discussed in chapter 1.

26. For a discussion of the "liability of newness," see M. T. Hannan, and J. Freeman, *Organizational Ecology* (Cambridge: Harvard University Press, 1989).

27. See J. J. Rotemberg, and G. Saloner, "The Benefits of Narrow Business Strategies," *American Economic Review* 84 (1994): 1330–49.

28. See E. W. Zuckerman, "Focusing the Corporate Product: Securities Analysts and De-Di-
versification," *Administrative Science Quarterly* 45 (2000): 591–619.

29. See J. J. Rotemberg, and G. Saloner, "Visionaries, Managers, and Strategic Direction,"
Rand Journal of Economics 31 (2000): 693–716.

30. Rotemberg and Saloner refer to the role played by the company's culture, which may contain norms of providing autonomy for middle and senior managers that the CEO cannot
easily ignore. The board of directors can play a direct role in discouraging the CEO from
intervening.

31. Recently, some evidence has been presented that successful growth strategies involve exploiting the full potential of the core business, expanding into logical adjacencies to the
core business, and preemptively redefining the core business in response to market turbulence. See C. Zook, and J. Allen, *Profit from the Core: Growth Strategy in an Era of
Turbulence* (Boston: Harvard University Press, 2001). The problem with these recommendations is that logical adjacencies and/or a redefinition of the core business are often
logical only after the fact. Intel, for instance, did not consider the microprocessor an adja-
cency at the time of its invention and did not preemptively redefine itself as a microprocessor company. It probably could not have. The autonomous-strategy process serves
to *discover* new opportunities that can become defined as logical adjacencies as a result of
the process of strategic context determination.

32. This was the case with Intel's *i*860 microprocessor, which initially was used for workstations but then threatened to bring the RISC architecture into the PC market segment where
it would compete with Intel's x86 architecture.

33. Perhaps the most poignant example is the Xerox Corporation, which is facing great difficulties in 2001. Xerox created the fabled Palo Alto Research Center (PARC) in 1970.

Some of PARC's most significant inventions include the first personal computer, the graphical user interface, the mouse, the flat-panel display, the Ethernet standard for local area networks, and the laser printer. Yet, Xerox was not able to capitalize on these major inventions, leaving it to other companies to do so. See: "The Fading Copier King: Xerox Has Failed to Capitalize on Its Own Innovations," *New York Times,* October 19, 2000.

34. This was Xerox's major problem. PARC was far removed from corporate headquarters in Stamford, Connecticut. Xerox was also a massive functionally organized organization, with very strong sales and product development groups intensely focused on reprographics, but lacking true general management skills throughout the company.

35. Andy Grove's limited tolerance for ambiguity in matters of strategy may have affected the prospects of the networking business at Intel during the mid-1990s. Grove believed that Craig Barrett had greater tolerance for strategic ambiguity.

36. Andy Grove's strong involvement with the ProShare venture is an example at Intel.

37. Corporate venture capital activities should therefore be viewed as different from the activities of regular venture capital firms. Regular venture capital firms invest in independent start-ups within some portfolio strategy logic. The role of corporate venture capital as viewed here is to invest in start-ups that have potential strategic linkages to the company's businesses. There is little reason to believe that corporate venture capital can effectively compete with regular venture capital firms in the latter's domain. Differences in recruitment of key personnel and incentives, for instance, favor regular venture capital firms. Unusually strong results of corporate venture capital investments during 1999 and 2000 are currently being corrected by the downturn in the stock markets. See Williams, M., "Little Gain, Less Venturing: Company Investments Slow," *Wall Street Journal,* July 5, 2001.

38. See J. G. March, "Wild Ideas: The Catechism of Heresy," *Stanford Magazine,* Spring 1988.

39. Frank Gill believed that his earlier involvement with developing the motherboard business, which had created strong frictions with Intel's core business organization, made it difficult to get peer support for his strategic efforts in the networking business.

40. Professor Emeritus James G. March, personal communication, March 2001.

41. Part of Gerry Parker's mandate as general manager of Intel's newly formed New Business Group was to sort out which green ventures should be discontinued.

42. After Intel discontinued development of the *i*860 microprocessor, Claude Leglise was able to redeploy the vast majority of the employees that had been involved with the venture.

43. For instance, in the mid-1970s many U.S.-based companies were interested in pursuing internal corporate ventures. During the late 1970s and early 1980s, many of these companies had become disenchanted with new ventures and became interested in Japanese-style approaches that emphasized integrative cultures and manufacturing excellence in the core business. During the mid-1980s, intrapreneurship again became the rage for a few years. The early to mid-1990s saw the emergence of reengineering and a renewed focus on the core business and operational excellence. The late 1990s and early 2000s, again, seem to be calling for more emphasis on new business development. Looking back over the last twenty-five years, the dominant pattern in many companies' support for the autonomous-strategy process seems to have fluctuated in terms of "now we do it, and now we don't." Besides signaling the danger to managerial careers of getting involved in new ventures,

such discontinuities also imply that the company starts from scratch each time it wants to develop its entrepreneurial capability.

44. For instance, at the start of Epoch III, Craig Barrett said, "I try to challenge the new ventures to grow their businesses so that they're relevant, and I challenge the people in the microprocessor business to be successful enough so that the new ventures won't matter."

45. A discussion with Intel's Steve McGeady in 1995 was helpful in developing the idea of "cycle time of strategic change."

46. The *i*860 microprocessor story is again an example.

47. Intel's New Business Group is an example. It helped bring all the green ventures together and gave senior and top management a better opportunity to assess their prospects. In 2001 it was not clear, however, whether Intel was already capable of using the assessment framework for more refined analysis of the interdependencies between different ventures and the core business.

48. Intel's experience with the PCEO (the PC Enhancement Organization) venture is an example (chapter 9). The reintegration of PCEO created some friction because of the large financial rewards that the venture personnel obtained when they exercised their phantom stock options. Some people associated with the core business saw these financial rewards as out of proportion, given what the core-business people had contributed to the venture's success.

49. See R. A. Burgelman, and Y. L. Doz, "The Power of Strategic Integration," *Sloan Management Review* 42 (Spring 2001):28–38

50. See A. D. Chandler, Jr., *Scale and Scope: The Dynamics of Industrial Capitalism* (Cambridge: Harvard University Press, 1990): 31.

Appendix I: Research Method

1. See R. K. Yin, *Case Study Research,* Applied Social Research Methods Series, 5. (Beverly Hills, CA: Sage, 1984); and K. M. Eisenhardt, "Building Theories from Case Study Research," *Academy of Management Review* 14 (1989): 532–50.

2. See B. G. Glaser, and A. L. Strauss, *The Discovery of Grounded Theory* (Chicago: Aldine, 1967).

3. Initially, Andy Grove was not convinced that the first step in the decision to exit DRAM had really been made in November of 1984, rather than in October 1985. He agreed, however, after gathering further evidence himself that corroborated the finding.

4. See G. W. Cogan, and R. A. Burgelman, "Intel Corporation (A): The DRAM Decision," Stanford Business School case PS-BP-256, 1989; B. K. Graham, and R. A. Burgelman, "Intel Corporation (B): Implementing the DRAM Decision," Stanford Business School case PS-BP-256B, 1991; and G. W. Cogan, and R. A. Burgelman, "Intel Corporation (C): Strategies for the 1990s," Stanford Business School case PS-BP-256C, 1991.

5. See D. Steere, and R. A. Burgelman, "Intel Corporation (D): Microprocessors at the Crossroads," Stanford Business School case S-BP-256D, 1993; and D. Steere, and R. A. Burgelman, "Intel Corporation (E): New Directions for the 1990s," Stanford Business School case S-BP-256E, 1993.

6. See K. Fine, and R. A. Burgelman, "Intel Corporation (F): Going Beyond Success in 1997," Stanford Business School case S-BP-256F, 1997.

7. See O. Suzuki, and R. A. Burgelman, "The PC-Based Desktop Videoconferencing Systems Industry in 1998," Stanford Business School case SM-51, 1998; R. S. Bamford, and R. A. Burgelman, "Intel Corporation: The Hood River Project (A)," Stanford Business School case SM-49A, 1997; R. S. Bamford, and R. A. Burgelman, "Intel Corporation: The Hood River Project (B)" Stanford Business School case SM-49B, 1997; R. S. Bamford, and R. A. Burgelman, "Intel's Strategic Position in the Family Room, 1998," Stanford Business School case SM-50, 1998.

8. Burgelman, Carter, and Bamford, "Intel Corporation: The Evolution of an Adaptive Organization."

9. See A. H. Van de Ven, "Suggestions for Studying Strategy Process: A Research Note," *Strategic Management Journal* 13 (Summer 1992): 169–88.

10. See, for instance, B. R. Golden, "The Past Is the Past—Or Is It? The Use of Retrospective Accounts as Indicators of Past Strategy," *Academy of Management Journal* 35 (1992): 848–60.

11. Glaser and Strauss, *The Discovery of Grounded Theory.*

12. See D. T. Campbell, "Degrees of Freedom and the Case Study," *Comparative Political Studies* 8 (1975): 178–93.

13. Van de Ven, "Suggestions for Studying Strategy": 181.

Appendix III: New Business Development in Established Companies

1. For a research-based discussion of the complete internal corporate venturing process, see Burgelman and Sayles, *Inside Corporate Innovation.*

INDEX

ABOUT THE AUTHOR

Robert A. Burgelman is the Edmund W. Littlefield Professor of Management and Director of the Stanford Executive Program of the Stanford University Graduate School of Business. He has taught at Stanford since 1981. During 1991–92 he was a Marvin Bower Fellow at Harvard Business School. He studied applied economics at Antwerp University (Belgium), and sociology and management of organizations at Columbia University, where he was a European Doctoral Fellow supported by the Ford Foundation and Belgium's Interuniversity College of Management. His areas of expertise include the role of strategy in company evolution, corporate entrepreneurship, and the strategic management of technology and innovation. He is co-author of *Strategic Management of Technology and Innovation,* 3rd ed. (New York: McGraw-Hill-Irwin, 2001), the leading textbook in the field. He is also co-author of *Inside Corporate Innovation* (New York: Free Press, 1986), which describes the complete management process involved in internal corporate venturing. Dr. Burgelman has published numerous articles in leading academic and practitioner journals. He has taught executive programs and led senior and top management seminars for major companies worldwide. He serves on several boards of directors and advisory boards.